国家の法的関与と自由
―アジア・オセアニア法制の比較研究―

STATE LEGAL INTERVENTION AND FREEDOM
Comparative Studies on Asian Oceanic Legal Systems
ISBN4-7972-3031-2 C3332
Published by
THE INSTITUTE OF COMPARATIVE LAW WASEDA UNIVERSITY
1-6-1, Nishi-waseda, Shinjyuku-ku, Tokyo, ZIP 169-8050
©2001 by Authers & editor All rights reserved. Printed in Japan.
Produce & Sales by
SHINZAN-SHA Publishing Co., LTD.
6-2-9-102, Hongo, Bunkyo-ku, Tokyo, ZIP 113-0033

国家の法的関与と自由

――アジア・オセアニア法制の比較研究――

大須賀 明 編

State Legal Intervention and Freedom
Comparative Studies on Asian-Oceanic Legal Systems
edited by Akira Osuka

早稲田大学比較法研究所叢書
28
WASEDA UNIVERSITY Comparative Law Study Series 28

信 山 社

──────〔執筆者紹介〕(掲載順)──────

大須賀 明　(Osuga Akira) 早稲田大学法学部教授
藤倉皓一郎　(Fujikura Koichiro) 元東京大学法学部教授
　　　　　　　　　　　　　　　帝塚山大学法政策学部教授
シェリル・ソンダーズ　(Cheryl Saunders) メルボルン大学法学部教授
棚村 政行　(Tanamura Masayuki) 早稲田大学法学部教授
土田 和博　(Tsuchida Kazuhiro) 早稲田大学法学部教授
マイケル・クロムリン　(Michael Crommelin) メルボルン大学法学部長
　　　　　　　　　　　　　　　　　　　　同法学部教授
大野 理彩　(Ono Lisa) 弁護士（ニューヨーク州）
劉 海年　(Lui Hainian) 中国社会科学院学術委員会　委員
渠 涛　(Qu Tao) 中国社会科学院法学研究所民法室
　　　　　　　　副研究員
梁 承斗　(Yang Seung Doo) 延世大学校法科大学教授
上村 達男　(Uemura Tatsuo) 早稲田大学法学部教授
マイケル・ティルベリー　(Michael Tilbury) メルボルン大学法学部教授
佐野 隆　(Sano Yutaka) 東洋大学法学部非常勤講師
ウォーレン・ブルックバンクス　(Warren Brookbanks)
　　　　　　　　　　　　　　　　オークランド大学法学部助教授
洲見 光男　(Shumi Mitsuo) 朝日大学法学部教授
田口 守一　(Taguchi Morikazu) 早稲田大学法学部教授
マルコム・スミス　(Malcolm Smith) メルボルン大学法学部教授
村山 史世　(Murayama Fumiyo) 麻布大学環境保健学部環境政策学科専任
　　　　　　　　　　　　　　　　講師
宮川 成雄　(Miyagawa Shigeo) 早稲田大学法学部教授

〔Authers〕

Akira Osuka, Professor of Law, Waseda University
  Emeritus Professor of Northwest University, China
Koichiro Fujikura, Former Professor of Law, University of Tokyo; Tezukayama University
Cheryl Saunders, Professor and Director, Institute for Comparative and International Law, The University of Melbourne.
Masayuki Tanamura, Professor of Law, Waseda University
Kazuhiro Tsuchida, Professor of Law, Waseda University
Michael Crommelin, Zelman Cowen Professor of Law, Dean of the Faculty of Law, The University of Melbourne.
Lisa Ono, Attorney-at-law, Debevoise&Plimpton (New York)
Lui Hainian, Member of Academic Committee of Chinese Academy of Social Sciences
Qu Tao, Associate Professor of Civil Law Research Division, Law Institute, Chinese Academy of Social Sciences
Yang Seung Doo, Professor of Law, Dean, College of Law, Yonsei University
Tatsuo Uemura, Professor of Law, Waseda University
Michael Tilbury, Rowland Professor of Commercial Law and Director, Commercial Law Institute, University of Zimbabwe, Edward Jenks Professor of Law, The University of Melbourne
Yutaka Sano, Lecturer of Law, Toyo University
Warren Brookbanks, Associate Professor of Law, The University of Auckland
Mitsuo Shumi, Professor of Law, Asahi University
Morikazu Taguchi, Professor of Law, Waseda University
Malcolm Smith, Professor and Director, Asian Law Centre, The University of Melbourne
Fumiyo Murayama, Lecturer of Law, Department of Environmental Policy, College of Environmental Health, Azabu University
Shigeo Miyagawa, Professor of Law, Waseda University

はしがき

大須賀　明

　われわれが活発に学術交流を行なっているアジア・太平洋地域は、実に広大で活力にみちた地域である。その特徴といえば、まず第1に、先進国や発展途上国など様々な発展段階の国々を包含しており、その意味で発展への大きな潜在的可能性をもっている。さらに東洋と西洋が、文化的な多様性をもちながら共存している。それ故、国家間のコミュニケーションは必ずしも容易ではないが、もし成功すれば、文化的な多様性を相互に交換しながら、発展する可能性は無限である。そのうえ国際的交流が活発に行なわれているこの地域の平和と福祉は、直接に世界の平和と福祉に結びついている。したがってアジア・太平洋地域は、世界の平和と福祉の鍵を握るものであるといえよう。

　東西冷戦の終結とともに、世界にはグローバル化という新しい時代が到来してきた。世界の多くの国や地域が、民主主義と市場経済の確立と発展を軸にしながら、大きく関連し合う状況が形成されており、アジア・太平洋地域もその例外ではありえない。法はそうした状況を確固たるものにし、その発展を促進する力をもっているので、法制を確立し法文化を交流することは、必須の事柄になった。

　だがアジアは、様々な民族、言語、宗教、文化からなり、法文化も多様である。植民地時代に線引きされた国境線は、必ずしも民族などの分布を考慮していなかったので、文化的、歴史的に共通する集団が国境線により分断されていることも珍しくない。したがって一国内においても多元的な法制度が併存しており、多岐に分化している。またアジアは、歴史的にも起伏に富んだ、多難な状況を推移している。第2次世界大戦前の長きにわたる植民地支配は、経済的な収奪を行ない、法制度の立憲主義的な発展を阻害した。さらに戦後は、政治的に独立したものの、国内的には、極度の貧困からの脱出が緊急の課題となって、政治権力が強化され、国際的には、東西の冷戦下反共体制の確立が優先され、権威主義的な統治体制や開発独裁が形成された。また社会主義諸国も国民の権利と自由の確立を妨げ、経済ののびやかで持続的な発展をすることができなかった。そして1980年代になって漸やく、アジアの経済的発展が急速に進み、それとともに形成された中間市民層が中軸となって、

民主化の要求が台頭し、東西冷戦の終結さらには社会主義諸国の市場経済の導入ともあいまって、本格的な立憲主義の展開の可能性が生みだされてきた。

そこで立憲主義の普及が課題となるのだが、アジア諸国の法制度も、その大半がすでに、西欧立憲主義法制との緊張関係のもとで形成され運用されてきている。まず独立のさいには、宗主国たる欧米諸国の憲法に影響されることを強く宿命づけられていたし、さらに社会主義体制の崩壊、グローバリゼーションの進行のなかで、市場経済システムのもと、国際場裡での競争を行なうために、自国の法制を西欧諸国の法制に見合ったかたちで整備することを迫まられてきた。したがってそのさい理論的に直面するのは、西欧とは歴史的、社会的、文化的基盤の異なるアジアに、西欧立憲主義法制が、果して全面的に適応するのであろうかという問題である。かかる法制のうち、そのまま直接アジアに適用できるものもあるし、適用するさいに一定の修正ないしは発展的な応用の必要なものもあろう。それらが何であり、どこの国・地域でそれらが必要とされるかを理論的に検討する必要があるのである。そして最後には、アジア的価値とは何であり、それが法的価値たりうるのかどうかという根本的な問題にも、理論的なメスを入れる必要があるといえよう。

そうした問題意識を少しでも究明するために、比較法研究所の所長をしていた1998年、「自由市場と法的規制」というテーマで、アジア・オセアニア五ヶ国間国際シンポジウムを開催した。本書の第2部で明らかなように、諸外国の名門大学から、すぐれた諸教授の参加を得て、充実した成果を得ることができた。そしてこのシンポジウムの中核を担ったのは、メルボルン大学の比較憲法研究所と早稲田大学比較法研究所との間の、1996年に始まった学術交流である。1997年と2000年にはオーストラリアとニュージーランドを訪れ、1998年には早稲田大学でシンポジウムを行うなど3度の交流を実現することができた。そのさい、国際憲法学会の友人であるCheryl Saunders所長が、大きな役割を果してくれた。

また日本では、英米法学の泰斗である藤倉皓一郎元東京大学教授(当時は早稲田大学教授)が、理論的にも精神的にも率先してこのプロジェクトの実現に、指導的な役割を果して下さった。国際的な学術交流は、その具体的な成果を生み出すまでには、膨大にして煩瑣な手間と時間を必要とする、実に根気の要る仕事である。その仕事を、田口守一教授をはじめとする諸教授が、がっちりと支えてくれた。心から感謝の意を表する次第である。

2001年3月

序　文

藤倉皓一郎

　日本の近代の法制度は，明治維新後，主に独・仏からならって整備されたもので大陸法系に属する。太平洋戦争後，日本の法制度は英米法系，ことにアメリカ法の影響を受けてきた。このような歴史的経過からして，日本の法制度は古来の法伝統へ，あらたに移植された西欧法と英米法との法思考，法技術を加えて独特の発展を遂げてきた。こうした日本法の歴史と経験はきわめて興味深い比較法研究の対象である。

　これまで比較法の分野で，日本法の特性について日本から積極的に外に向かって発信することは少なかった。ますます地球規模になる経済活動，人的，文化的活動のなかで，国境を越える共通課題を抱える国々の間の交流，経験，情報の共有が重要になる。日本の法学者が自国の法的課題への対処，解決について外に向かって発言し，他の国の同様な現代的問題と比較検証することが求められている。

　日本がこれまで行ってきたコモン・ロー諸国との学術交流は，どうしても英米が中心であった。同じコモン・ローの伝統をもつオーストラリアとニュージーランドとの交流が盛んであったとはいえない。しかし，両国とも環太平洋共同体の重要なメンバーとして，日本にとってきわめて身近な存在である。

　本書は，早稲田大学比較法研究所のアジア・オセアニア法制の研究プロジェクトから生まれたものである。1997年12月，早稲田大学法学部の本書執筆メンバーが参加してメルボルン大学法学部とオークランド大学法学部においてシンポジアが開催された。ペーパーを先方の専門領域を同じくする研究者に予め送ったうえで，シンポジア当日の報告，コメント，質疑応答を行った。こうした準備のおかげで，いずれも実質のある討論ができた。シンポジアは，双方の参加者にとってきわめて有意義な交流の機会となり，また後日の相互訪問へもつながった。個人的な感想を加えさせていただくと，私は英米法の研究者でありながら，それまでオーストラリアとニュージーランドを訪れたことがなかった。実際に現地の大学に行き，研究者と対面してのコミュニケーションから，両国がいぜんコモン・ローの伝統を尊重しなが

ら，しかし，現代のさまざまな法的課題に新しい対応を試みている様子を知ることができた。両校の研究者が日本からの訪問者に闊達な知的興味を示し，暖かく歓迎して下さったことも忘れられない。このような学術交流は，さらに1998年9月に早稲田大学比較法研究所が主催した国際シンポジウム「自由市場と法的規制」へと発展した。

　この研究プロジェクトは大須賀明教授が比較法研究所長の時代に企画され実行された。同教授はヨーロッパ，アメリカに有力な研究交流の拠点校を求め，また，それまであまり接触のなかったアジア・オセアニアとの研究交流に着目され，豊かな人脈を活用されてシンポジアを実現された。本書は同教授の洞察と先見と強い指導力の賜物である。

　研究プロジェクトの実行の各段階と本書の編集刊行については，有能な比較法研究所スタッフの全面的な支援があった。ここに記して感謝したい。

2000年11月

序　文

シェリル・ソンダーズ

　本書に収められた論文は3つのシンポジウムの成果であり，主に早稲田大学とオーストラリアのメルボルン大学の法学者からなるが，それに加えて，中華人民共和国，韓国およびニュージーランドの学者も含まれる。その目的は，関連する諸国の法に対する相互理解を，詳細な発表と質疑およびコメントのための時間と機会を用いて，促進することであった。実体法および手続法のみならず法文化における両国間の相当な相違を考えると，このことはより大きな挑戦であった。

　シンポジウムは，疑いもなく，成功であった。その一部は明らかに達成された成果に示されている。それら成功から得られたものには，さらなる対話を通じて成果をもたらし続けるであろう研究者間の交流の確立；シンポジウムに参加することで得られた他の法制度に対する見識；そして，諸論文を収録した本叢書である。諸論文は，財政法から環境法，そして，行政法にまたがる多様な分野に及んでいる。しかし，全体を通してのテーマは，法が必然的に対応する変わり行く社会の期待と要求を含む，20世紀末における日本とオーストラリアの法と政府の役割の変化である。

　明らかであるが，同様に重要な成果は，シンポジウムで用いられた手法である。これは，比較法学の効率性に対する貢献として評価される。グローバル化が進む世界において比較法の重要性は益々認識されている。法制度およびかかる制度が機能する状況における相当な相違のため，他の法分野におけるよりも，より一層方法論が難しくなる。比較法学者が，法が実際にどのように作用しているかを理解するために，法準則を超えて活動しなければならないということは陳腐なことである。より良き理解の必要なレヴェルに達することははるかに難しいことである。

　基本的には，これらのシンポジウムでは3つの方法が用いられた。第1に，日本の研究者が，日本の法および法思想における最近の展開についてオーストラリアで報告された。これが選ばれたのは，対応しうる問題がオーストラリアにおいても出現しているのでないかと思われたからである。各報告に対して，オーストラリア側から研究者が対応し，その後に報告の主題にそって選ばれた専門分野の方々による

議論が行われた。2回目のシンポジウムは日本で行われ，メルボルン大学からの数多くの派遣者を含む，日本と海外からの研究者による報告がなされた。可能な限り，各報告は相互に補完しあう形をとり，全体としては規制と損害賠償のテーマにそって行われた。3番目となる最後のシンポジウムはオーストラリアで行われ，3名の日本人研究者がオーストラリア法の諸側面について報告をし，ここでもまた，オーストラリア側の人々との議論が行われた。

　これらそれぞれの方法は有用で建設的であった。しかしながら，他の2回がある意味で道をつけることとなった第3回目は，最も野心的なものであった。他の国の法制度についてその国の研究者が聞いているなかで報告することは難しいことである。この機会に得られた経験からいえることは，そのような困難を試みる価値があるということである。そこでの報告およびそれに引き続く議論は，法および法準則に関する異なった前提のために相手方の法制度に対する十分な理解が得られない場合に，個々の問題を明らかにする点で極めて効果的であった。そこでの成果は，しばしば比較法学では得られにくいレヴェルの議論と知的交流であった。私の同僚も私同様，この方法を他者にお勧めしたい。

　これらのシンポジウムに参加した諸外国の研究者，そして，特にメルボルン大学から参加した研究者に代わって，私は，この非常に成功を収めた試みを計画し実行した点での見識があった早稲田大学の同僚に感謝したい。将来にさらなる協力がなされることを期待する。（佐野　隆訳）

2000年11月

目　次

はしがき……………………………………………大須賀　明… vii
序　　文……………………………………………藤倉皓一郎… ix
序　　文……………………………………シェリル・ソンダーズ… xi
　　　　　　　　　　　　　　　　　　　　〔佐野　隆訳〕

第Ⅰ部　国家の積極的関与

1　自由主義的な現代憲法のもとにおける国家関与の理論
　　……………………………………………………大須賀　明… 1
2　水俣病被害者の法的「救済」……………………藤倉皓一郎… 9
　　──損害賠償訴訟，行政救済制度，政治決着までの40年──
3　高齢者の財産管理と介護…………………………棚村政行… 19

第Ⅱ部　自由市場と法的規制

(i)　市場経済と法的規制

4　グローバリゼーションと規制改革 ………………土田和博… 29
　　──規制改革の理論と課題──
5　民営化された産業に対する規制の枠組み…マイケル・クロムリン… 39
　　　　　　　　　　　　　　　　　　　　〔大野理彩訳〕
6　中国における現代市場経済と法治 ………………劉　海年… 51
　　　　　　　　　　　　　　　　　　　　〔渠　　涛訳〕
7　韓国における行政規制改革の現状と展望 ………梁　承斗… 65
8　日本における金融ビッグバンの法的側面 ………上村達男… 73

(ii)　規制の諸形態

9　私法上の救済手段による「犯罪」行為の規制：懲罰的損害賠償
　　の場合………………………………………マイケル・ティルベリー… 83
　　　　　　　　　　　　　　　　　　　　〔佐野　隆訳〕

10 厳格責任・絶対責任による法人活動の規制
　　　………………………………ウォーレン・ブルックバンクス…101
　　　　　　　　　　　　　　　　　　　　〔洲見光男訳〕
11 行政規制と刑事制裁………………………………田口守一…113
12 日本における変わりゆく規制形態 ………マルコム・スミス…121
　　　　　　　　　　　　　　　　　　　　〔佐野　隆訳〕
13 規制の新たな諸形態：民主的説明責任と法の支配に対する挑
　　戦？……………………………………シェリル・ソンダーズ…137
　　　　　　　　　　　　　　　　　　　　〔村山史世訳〕

第Ⅲ部　日本におけるオセアニア法制論

14 オーストラリアの統治構造の基本的性格 ……………大須賀　明…153
　　──共和制か，君主制かをめぐって──
15 オーストラリア法における国際法の地位 ……………宮川成雄…161
　　──Teoh 判決が意味するもの──
16 懲罰的損害賠償の非懲罰性 …………………………佐野　隆…169

　あ と が き …………………………………………………田口守一…183

STATE LEGAL INTERVENTION and FREEDOM:
Comparative Studies on Asian Oceanic Legal Systems

CONTENTS ·············· 187

Preface ··· Akira Osuka··· 189
Foreword ·· Cheryl Saunders··· 193
Foreword·· Koichiro Fujikura··· 195

Part I : Affirmative State Interventions

1 The Theory of State Intervention under the Modern-Liberal Constitution——
   ·· Akira Osuka··· 197
2 Litigation, Administrative Relief and Political Settlement for Compensating Victims of Pollution: Minamata Mercury Poisoning after 40 years ···················· Koichiro Fujikura··· 207
3 Care for the Elderly Management of Their Property
   ·· Masayuki Tanamura··· 223

Part II : Free Market and Legal Regulations

(i) Market Economy and Legal Regulations

4 Globalization and Regulatory Reforms :
   Toward A New Model of Law···················· Kazuhiro Tsuchida··· 237
5 Regulatory Framework for Privatised Industries
   ·· Michael Crommelin··· 249
6 Modern Market Economy and the Rule of Law in China: The Past, the Present and the Future ···················· Liu Hainian··· 265
7 Administrative Deregulation in Korea : Now and Future
   ·· Seung Doo Yang··· 283
8 Legal Aspects of the Financial Big Bang in Japan
   ·· Tatsuo Uemura··· 293

(ii) Various Forms of Regulations

9 Regulating "Criminal" Conduct by Civil Remedy: The Case of Exemplary Damages ················**Michael Tilbury**···*307*

10 Regulating Corporate Activity through Strict and Absolute Liability ················**Warren Brookbanks**···*327*

11 Administrative Regulations and Criminal Sanctions
················**Morikazu T**AGUCHI···*343*

12 Changing Regulatory Patterns in Japan :
An Australian Perspective ················**Malcolm Smith**···*353*

13 New Forms of Regulation: A Challenge to Democratic Accountability and the Rule of Law ? ········**Cheryl Saunders**···*371*

Part III : Studies on Oceanic Legal Systems in Japan

14 The Fundamental Nature of Governing Framework in Australia ················**Akira O**SUKA···*387*

15 The Status of International Law in Australian Law: Implications of the *Teoh* Case················**Shigeo M**IYAGAWA···*397*

16 Exemplary Damages, Not Punitive Damages:
A Japanese Perspetive ················**Yutaka S**ANO···*407*

Afterword ················**Morikazu T**AGUCHI···*423*

第Ⅰ部　国家の積極的関与

1　自由主義的な現代憲法のもとにおける国家関与の理論

大須賀　明

　　はじめに
　1　自由主義の変遷
　2　積極的自由論の展開
　3　積極的自由のもつ矛盾の意味
　4　自由の保障と国家の積極的関与
　5　積極的自由権の社会的要因
　6　積極的自由権における権力的契機
　7　国家の民主化

はじめに

　近代市民国家は，いわゆる夜警国家観にもとづいており，人権の保障における国家の役割を極めて限定的にとらえようとする志向の強いものであった。すなわち当時の市民社会は，その価値法則の自律的な展開により市民の生活を確保していたのであり，したがって国家は社会の外縁にとどまり，その内部に干渉することは一切許されていなかった。ただ国家は，社会の自律的なあり方を攪乱する者を排除する役割を与えられていたことから，その任務が治安と国防に限定されていたのであり，かかる国家と社会の関係の法的な反映が，市民憲法における自由権の保障であり，国民の自己統治を基礎とする民主的な統治機構の保障だったのである。
　だがそれにも拘わらず，人権の保障に対する国家の関与は存在していたのであって，とりわけ裁判所は，人権が侵害された場合には，もちろん司法権の範囲内ではあれ，それを救済するために組織的に関与したのであった。しかしそれは，あくまでも人権が侵害された事後に，かつ個別的に行なわれるにとどまり，予防や差止などにより事前に救済される場合は，その人権が侵害されたときにはもはや原状回復が困難となるような例外的な事態に限られていたことなどから，裁判所の関与も全体としては消極的なものにすぎなかったのである。
　ところが現代市民国家になると，国家の積極的な関与による人権の保障が次第に

増大しはじめたのであって，いわゆる20世紀の現代市民憲法において保障された経済的自由の制限と社会権は，その代表的なものであった。前者は，たとえば私的独占の禁止などにみられるように，経済的強者の自由を制限して，自由競争を確保し，正常な資本主義的経済秩序を維持しようとするものであり，後者は，資本主義の弊害を解決するために，要生活保護者などの生活を改善する社会保障や社会福祉を行なうものであって，いずれも国家の積極的な関与を軸に構成されていたのである。まさにそれは，自己の役割を消極的な機能に限定していた夜警国家から，積極的に国民の社会生活の保障に貢献しようとする社会国家への，市民国家の転換を歴史的な背景としていたのであった。

1 自由主義の変遷

　この市民国家の変遷は，それが基本原理としている自由主義の原理的内容の修正を基盤にして展開している。一般に自由主義の立脚する個人主義は，原子論的社会観にもとづいている。この社会観は，国家や社会を個人の集まりと考え，個人を超越した集団の存在を認めないものであるから，個人主義は，個人に最高の価値を認めながら，同時に個人を社会から切り離して原子的存在として抽象化し，絶対的に平等な存在と考える。そして自由主義は，そうした個人に自由を認めるところから，自由の保障は理念的には最大限に確保されるのであった。それはまさに，近代市民憲法が基本原理とする古典的な自由主義であって，そのもとで構想された法的主体は，一般的抽象的な存在としての市民であり，RadbruchのいわゆるPersonにほかならないのである[1]。

　しかし資本主義の弊害により個人の生活が貧困化した時，それを国家が救済することを正当化したのは，社会的存在としての個人が，社会的要因により困窮化しているということを認めることによってであったといえよう。そこから法的主体として，あらたに生活困窮者や失業者などといった，現実に存在する人間の具体的な属性をもった社会的存在，つまりRadbruchのいわゆるMenschが法の世界に登場したのである。ここに個人は社会と結びつけられて，専ら個人を唯一の実在とみる個人主義の考え方が一定の修正を施され，集団主義的思考が導入されて，個人の自由意思にもとづく行為に最高の価値を認めるとともに，そのような志向性をもった社会や国家をも重視することを内容とするようになったのである。まさに個人とともに社会をも尊重する姿勢が組み込まれるとともに，その社会の弊害を是正するのは国

家の当然の役割であるとされ,その社会性を根拠に,国家の積極的な関与がいっそう正当化される社会国家が出現するようになったのである。

2 積極的自由論の展開

この自由主義の修正を権利論において見事に消化した自由論が登場する。それは,19世紀のイギリスの哲学者であるT. H. グリーンが,在来の古典的な自由である消極的自由(negative liberty)に対して,あらたに提唱した積極的自由(positive liberty)であった。近代的自由主義のもとでは,個人的自由と政府の積極的機能とは交叉する領域をもたない,敵対的な関係に立つものと考えられていたので,自由は外的強制のない状態であると,極めて消極的に考えられていた。ところが19世紀後半,失業などの労働問題や社会問題がイギリスを襲い,個人の自由な活動の自然調和の幻想が崩れ去ったとき,秩序の安定のためにも,また個人が好きなようにするための条件を獲得するためにも,調和が人為的努力により達成される必要があり,自由の観念が政府の積極的機能と調和するように再構成されたのである。グリーンの積極的自由の概念は,共同善を志向しつつ自我を実現できる状態を意味しており,自由がそのように解されることにより,「共同善を促進する国家の積極的機能と矛盾しない,むしろ国家の積極的機能によって保障される自由となる」[2]と指摘されている。要するに積極的自由とは,「個人の人格実現のための条件の積極的保障を国家に要求するもの」[3]なのである。

憲法上この積極的自由の範疇に属するものとしては,たとえば社会権の保障をあげることができる。しかしその場合,社会権のなかでも,とりわけ自由権の保障と直接に関連のあるものに限定されなければならず,それが自由権の享受を充分ならしめるための前提条件の確保であって,自由権の保障と間接的に関連性をもつにとどまる単なる物質の供与などは積極的自由にはふくまれない。したがって適正な雇用条件や労働条件の保障,さらには団結権,団体交渉権,争議権の保障などは,勤労権や労働基本権の保障であって,いずれも使用者の契約の自由の制限であり,その制限がなければ財産の少ない勤労大衆の自由と人間らしい生活が侵害されることになるから,その障害を排除するために,国家が自由の保障に積極的に関与してその実現をはかろうとすることはまさに積極的自由であるといえよう。

3 積極的自由のもつ矛盾の意味

　この積極的自由の基軸をなしている国家の積極的関与が，自由という概念と矛盾する側面はどう評価されるべきであろうか。たとえば独占禁止法について，それが自由促進法であるか，それとも自由制約立法であるかについて理解に対立がある[4]。たしかに形式的にいえば，私的独占を制限ないしは禁止する国家の介入は国家からの経済的自由を制限するものであるが，しかしその経済的自由は，公正かつ自由な経済競争を私的独占により阻害している企業の自由であり，しかもその自由の制限により，自由競争への障害を排除して，真の経済的自由の回復をはかろうとするものであるから，独占禁止法は実質的には自由促進法であるということができよう。この種の国家の積極的関与は，自由主義に対し，形式的には矛盾しているものの，実質的には調和を保っているのである。

4 自由の保障と国家の積極的関与

　たしかに市民憲法の制定の由来，国家権力のともすれば権利を侵害しやすい習性などからみて，国家権力と個人の自由が基本的に対立的な関係にあることは否定しえないところである。しかし社会権の具体例からも明らかなように，両者は，全くの敵対的な関係に立ち，妥協の余地なく対峙する存在ではないのである。市民国家が民主主義を基本原理としており，それは個人の権利自由の実現を志向するものであるから，両者は協同の原理に支えられた存在でもあるのであって，個人の自由の保障の実質化に，国家が積極的な役割を果す余地は充分に存在するのである。

　では両者はいかなる範囲，どのような程度で積極的に関わり合うことができるのであろうか。近代市民憲法から現代市民憲法への人権保障の変遷をみれば明らかなように，積極的自由は消極的自由に大きく基礎づけられており，そのため原則としては自由権の対象としての個人の自律的事項の内実に関与することは許されない。それ故国家権力が，個人の能力や人格の実現のための条件の保障をもとめて，自由権の保障の実質化に関与する場合においても，国家は自由権を実現する外枠の確保，つまりその保障のための外的な諸条件の整備に関与することができるにすぎないのである。そして，私はこの自由権の条件整備を国家に対して請求することのできる権利を，積極的自由の概念から切り離して，積極的自由権と称する。

5 積極的自由権の社会的要因

　その第1にあげられるものは，高度情報化社会の出現である。この社会で価値をもつ情報を伝搬する電波メディアなどのニューメディアの飛躍的な発展，それを管理運営する少数の大企業による情報の独占的な支配などにより，少数者による社会の価値観の意図的な操作の危険性が現実化したのであった。そこで，情報の自由な流れを阻害する要因を排除し，思想の自由市場を確保するために知る権利が設定され，アクセス権が主張されたが，いずれも積極的自由権なのである。また体制のいかんを問わず，現代の国家社会に特徴的な支配の傾向はテクノクラシーである。それは，驚異的な発達をとげた科学技術に特徴的な思考に優先的な地位を与え，それにより社会を管理運営しようとするものであるが，とかく人間の尊厳を閑却したところに成立しやすい科学技術の思考方法を利用したり，科学技術的効率を優先させる結果として，人間疎外をひき起こし，非人間的な社会を創出する潜在的な危険性をもっているといえよう。そうした危険に対抗しつつ，個人の自由を確保し，人間性を回復する方途は，積極的自由権の拡大にほかならないのである。

　そのうえ現代は，管理社会化の傾向が顕著であり，管理社会とは，「管理―被管理関係が新しい支配と抑圧の形成として全般化されている社会」[5]といわれる。とりわけ社会の中間領域での管理が肥大化しており，それによる抑圧を縮減するためには，国家の強大な力によって，その中間管理装置の抑圧機能を叩き，自由の領域を創出し，人間性の確保に力を注ぐ必要があるのである。

6 積極的自由権における権力的契機

　積極的自由権は，外的な諸条件の整備ではあれ，自由権自体の実現に国家が積極的に関与するものであるから，その権力的契機のもたらす自由の侵害の危険性は，積極的自由の他の諸形態とは比較にならないほど大きい。まず権力による条件整備と，それにより達成しようとする「人格実現」もしくは「人間諸能力の自由な発展」とは，その実質において密接な関連性をもっているので，権力が条件整備の範囲をこえて，自由の内実に深くかかわり，それを侵害する危険性が極めて大きいことである。さらに積極的自由権が活用されることによって生じる問題は，かような権力的契機自身の自由への禍害とともに，その活用により集積され拡大される権力の肥大のもたらす自由主義への弊害であるといえよう。そうした権力に対抗する存在と

して，多元的な利益集団を創設し，権力分立的な機能を果たさせながら，自由主義の均衡をとり戻そうとしている事例が，アメリカに典型的にみられるのである。

7 国家の民主化

そのような自由主義への弊害を是正したり，あらかじめ防止したりするには，何よりもまず国家権力自体が民主化されている必要があるのである。先ずその理念的な条件としては，権力の担い手である公務員の意識の民主化をあげることができよう。個人主義，自由主義，民主主義などの理念が，権力の意思の形成と実現の担い手の意識の中に定着することである。ついで制度的な条件としては，国民の政治的意思が，国家意思の形成と展開に充分に反映されるような民主主義的な統治のシステムが確立されることである。すなわち議会制民主主義や民主的責任行政の原則や地方自治の原理などが，憲法上明文化されるだけでなく，現実の制度と運用において具体化される必要があるといえよう。さらに積極的自由権の保障にともなって生じる権力の肥大に関しては，国家意思の形成に国民が直接に関与してその内容を構成する憲法的自治を保障し，権力的介入に対し国民の参加や承認を認めることにより，国家の介入に民主的根拠を与え，両者の力の均衡をはかるなかで，自由主義を確保しなければならないのである。

この憲法的自治[6]は，アメリカのニューディール期，その政策を展開する基幹立法であった全国産業復興法や農業調整法などの諸立法において展開されたものであったが，たとえば全国産業復興法が，公正競争規約の作成に関して，産業団体に広範な自治を保障していたことは，公正競争規約の認可など強大な権限を委任された大統領の権力から生ずる自由への障害を是正する役割をになわされていたのである。要するに憲法的自治は，国家が社会的経済的過程に積極的に関与して，経済の混乱を回復し，社会の安定をはかって大不況を克服しようとするために，集中され強化された大統領をはじめとする連邦政府の諸権限に対応して保障されたものであり，いわば鋭角的な権力的規制に対し，それとは裏腹の自由主義の手続を保障し，その弊害を最小限にとどめようとしたものであったのである。

また積極的自由権としての政治的自由が保障されなければならない。それは政治過程への参加の自由であり，積極的な性格をもつので，国民主権の実現と具体化を直接に保障する自由である。その保障が増大すれば，国民の政治的意思が，国家の意思形成の過程により大きく反映されるようになるので，国家と国民の意思の類似

性をますます確保することが可能になるといえよう。一般に積極的自由の保障は，その権力的契機から，権力の肥大をもたらし，国家社会を全体主義化する危険をもつと指摘されるが，国家の民主化は，このように国民の政治への参加を保障することにより，民意の国家意思への反映の道すじを確保するので，全体主義化の危険性に対する自由主義の強力な歯止めとしての意義をもつものなのである。

(1) Gustav Radbruch, Vom individualistischen zum sozialen Recht, 1930, Der Mensch im Recht, S. 36〜7.
(2) 日下喜一「T. H. グリーンの政治思想」行安＝藤原編T. H. グリーン研究86頁。
(3) 藤原保信「イギリス理想主義と『積極的自由』の問題――T. H. グリーンを中心として」渋谷ほか編・政治思想における自由と秩序255頁。
(4) 樋口陽一「自由をめぐる知的状況――憲法学の側から」ジュリスト1991年5月号（978号）。
(5) 見田宗介ほか編・社会学辞典172〜3頁。
(6) 大須賀明「ニューディールと憲法的自治」社会国家と憲法2頁以下。

2 水俣病被害者の法的「救済」
―― 損害賠償訴訟, 行政救済制度, 政治決着までの 40 年 ――

藤 倉 皓 一 郎

  1 水俣病の発生
  2 水俣病被害者による損害賠償訴訟
  3 公害健康被害補償制度の定立
  4 政 治 解 決
   むすび――いくつかの教訓

1　水俣病の発生

　水俣水銀中毒事件は，1950年代半ば，戦後の日本の経済復興期に起こった。1954年，数人の患者が病院に収容されたが，いずれも強い体の震え，視野狭窄，手足のしびれ，運動機能障害などがみられた。入院する患者の数は急速に増え，その多くが熊本の水俣湾の周辺にある漁村の住民であった。水俣病として知られるようになった水銀中毒患者は，はじめ原因がわからないため，伝染病ではないかと怖れられて，その家族まで周囲から差別されることになった。

　水俣病の原因がメチル水銀であると確定されるまでには10年を越える年月を必要とした。1968年，厚生省はメチル水銀を水俣病の原因物質であると公式に認めた。メチル水銀は水俣湾の奥で操業する日本チッソの工場から，アセトアルデヒド製造工程の副産物として排出されていた。チッソは長年にわたってメチル水銀を含む廃水を水俣湾へ直接に放出していた。水銀はじょじょに湾内の魚介類の体内で蓄積され，濃縮され，食物連鎖をへて，ついに汚染された魚介類を食べた住民に水俣病を発症させた。人間の体内に入った水銀は中枢神経を侵し，上記のような症状を引き起こしたのである。

　1965年には，新潟県の阿賀野川流域周辺で水俣病と同様の水銀中毒事件が発生した。その上流には昭和電工の工場があり，チッソと同じ製造工程によってアセトアルデヒドを製造し，廃液を放出していた。

　水俣病の原因物質が科学的に特定される前から，地元の漁民や住民はチッソ工場の廃液が奇病の原因であると直感していた。廃液の広がった湾内では魚が死んで浮かび，魚を食べる鳶や猫が死んだ。住民はチッソ工場に廃液の排出を止めるようく

り返し交渉したが，チッソは応じなかった。漁民はデモ，座り込み，工場への乱入など，抗議行動を重ね，他方で，県当局や委員会などを介して，紛争解決のための調停，仲裁にも望みを託した。しかし，事態は改善されることなく，チッソは一切の責任を認めず，操業を続け汚染行為を止めなかった。

2　水俣病被害者による損害賠償訴訟

　被害者はついに汚染企業に対する損害賠償訴訟に訴えた。1967年，新潟水俣病の被害者(77人)が昭和電工に対して，1969年には，水俣被害者(139人)がチッソに対して，責任を問う賠償訴訟を起こした。賠償請求の根拠は，民法709条「故意又は過失に因りて他人の権利を侵害したる者は之に因りて生じたる損害を賠償する責めに任ず」であった。この条文に基づいて過失責任を追及する原告は，被告の注意義務，被害の予見性，被告の行為と被害との因果関係のそれぞれについて，主張，立証しなければならい。

　新潟と水俣との両訴訟において，裁判所は被告の過失を認定し損害賠償責任を認めた。現代の公害事件へ伝統的な過失責任の要件を適用するに当たって，裁判所は積極的な解釈を示した。第1に，被告はその工場の操業について高度の注意義務を負うとした。第2に，被告は廃水の排出が周辺の住民に被害を与えることを予見すべきであったと認定した。第3に，因果関係について原告に有利な推定を置いた。

　裁判所は判決文の中で各争点につき次のような理由を示した。

　(1)　注意義務。原料や触媒として危険な化学物質を大量に使用する工場は，周辺住民の安全について高度の注意義務を負う。工場廃水中に有害物質が存在する確率は極めて高い。危険な物質が川や海に放出されると，植物，動物，人間への被害は容易に予期できる。したがって，化学工場が廃水を排出する際には常に「最良の知識と技術」を用いて，有害物質の存在とその動植物，人間への影響を確かめなければならない。廃水の安全性を確認することに加えて，かりに被害が現れた場合，または廃水の安全性について疑が生じた場合には，ただちに工場の操業を停止し，必要な最大限の予防措置を採らなければならない。ことに周辺住民の生命と健康に関しては，危険が生じる前に工場はその予防に高度の注意を払わなければならない。

　(2)　予見性。被告は，予見性とは特定の触媒が生む結果の予見に限定されると主張する。廃水中の水銀により水俣病のような水銀中毒を生じるという特定の結果を予見することはできなかった。したがって，被告にはなんらの注意義務違反はない

という。しかし，被告の主張に従えば，環境が汚染され破壊され人の健康が害されて始めて，危険が証明されることになる。その時点まで，危険な廃水の放出は容認されることになってしまう。その結果，住民の生命と健康への侵害は防止できない。それは住民を生体実験に使うのと変わりがない。被告の主張する予見性の理解は明白に不当であると裁判所は判断した。

(3) 因果関係。裁判所は因果関係を3つの部分に分けて判断した。すなわち，(a)病状の特徴とその原因物資，(b)汚染の経路，(c)被告による原因物質の排出である。(a)と(b)については，判決によれば，原告の説明が関連する科学的知見（臨床，病理，疫学，その他の医学専門家の）と矛盾しないものであれば，因果関係は状況証拠の集成によって証明されたといえる。上記のレベルの証拠が得られ，汚染物質の追跡が工場の排水口に至った場合，工場が汚染源であると事実上推定され，法的因果関係は十分に確立されたといえる。

これらの水銀中毒事件において，裁判所は汚染者に厳格責任を負わせたといえよう。判決文は注意義務違反，被害の蓋然性，予見性といった709条の下での伝統的概念を使っているが，汚染者である工場に対して極めて高度の注意義務を課すことによって，実質は無過失責任を認めたといえる。裁判所は因果関係の認定について，原告に有利な推定を置いた。原告がひとたび原因物質とその経路を示せば，挙証責任は被告に転換され，被告が工場から原因物質を排出しなかったことを立証しなければならない。

日本の他の地域においても，大気と水汚染による被害者があいついで訴訟を起こし，勝訴の判決を得た。これらの公害裁判において，法廷は被害者が汚染企業と対決し，その不法な行為を明らかにする場となった。公害の被害者は公害企業に怒りをぶつけ，基本的な意味で人権が侵害されたと主張した。その主張が裁判所によって認められたのである。こうれらの公害裁判の判決が認めた基本原則（因果関係の推定，無過失責任，被害補償など）は，1973年に制定された公害健康被害補償法に採り入れられた。

3　公害健康被害補償制度の定立

1970年の国会では，環境保護に関連する10を越える法律が審議され成立した。1973年に制定された公害健康被害補償法は，公害による健康被害者に対する行政的補償制度を設立した。この法律の成立には主な関係当事者，すなわち，被害者，産業界・

企業，政治家と官僚などが，こぞって賛成した。被害者団体は補償制度の下で，補償金の請求・支払が迅速かつ公平に行われることを期待した。産業界は補償制度の方が費用負担についての予測が可能になり，また費用の総額をも制御しやすいと考えた。将来の多くの訴訟で，裁判所がどこまでの賠償責任を企業に課すか，また賠償額がどれほどになるのかを予測することは難しい。政治家と官僚は補償制度を設定することで，被害者に救済を与え，また訴訟が続発する状態を回避できると考えたのである。

公害被害補償法は大気と水汚染による健康被害者を公的に認定し，被害の程度に応じて定額の補償を支払うことを定めた。大気汚染については多くの工場が集中し汚染度の高い都市部の地域が指定された。硫黄酸化物の濃度を指標として，指定された汚染地域は全国で40を越えた。また，水銀，カドミウム，砒素によって水質，土壌が汚染された7地域が指定された。水質と土壌汚染については，通常，汚染源が特定されていた。汚染地域の住民で定められた症状を示す者は，医師の診断によって公害病患者の認定を受けた。認定患者には医療費，失われた収入，その他の所定の項目について補償金が支払われた。

認定患者に支払われる補償費用は汚染者の負担となった。大気汚染の場合，排出量に応じて定められた賦課金が発生源の工場に課された。自動車所有者も車の重量に応じて賦課金を負担した。前年度の被害補償に要した費用をもとに，固定発生源（工場）が総額の8割を，移動発生源（自動車）が2割を負担して，中央に創設された補償基金へ支払った。この補償基金から地方自治体の窓口を通して，認定患者に補償が支払われた。原因物質と発生源が特定できた水質，土壌汚染の場合には，汚染者がその地域の認定患者へ直接補償金を支払った。

1988年，補償制度が設立されてから15年が経過したところで，108,489人の大気汚染被害者と1,898人の水質，土壌汚染による被害者が認定患者として，補償を受けていた。

健康被害補償制度は2つの目的を果たすために設定された。(1)公害による健康被害の補償，そして，(2)その費用を汚染原因者に負担させる。しかし，この制度はその他の役割をも果たした。(3)公害によって発生した被害を特定する。(4)被害者への補償を公認する。(5)汚染原因者に排出量を減らせるインセンテヴを与える。(6)公害の費用を明らかにする。(7)環境政策上，意味のある重要な情報を生み出す。これら(3)から(7)の機能は，制度設計時には意図されなかったかもしれないが，理論的には興

味を引くものである。

　補償制度の下では，公害の被害の性質と範囲が特定される。原因物質と症状を定めることで，指定地域の住民は公害と自分の健康被害との関連について認識できる。被害の補償を提供することによって，影響を受けている住民が診断を受け認定を申請する動機を与える。補償制度は，公害が存在することを公式に認め，その被害者には補償が支払われることを認める。それまで被害者はしばしば社会的差別を受け，根拠にない体調不調を申立て補償を得ようとしていると非難された。この制度は日本の多くの地域において公害による健康被害が存在し，被害者にはその被害の補償を受ける権利があることを認めた。ひとたび被害者が認定され，補償支払いが公認されると，被害者は公害のシンボルとなり政治的に無視できない存在となった。

　賦課金の負担は汚染原因者に汚染物質の排出を止めるか，排出量を減らせる動機付けを与えた。大気汚染については，固定排出源からの硫黄酸化物の濃度に応じて賦課金が課された。排出基準についての直接規制に加えて，工場は防除装置を設備（賦課金の負担＞除去装置の費用）して，硫黄酸化物の排出量を減らすよう努めると期待された。1989年には，硫黄酸化物による大気汚染が相当程度に改善されたので，すべての汚染地域指定が解除された。その主因は，防除装置の採用よりも，多くの工場が低硫黄原油に切り替えたためといわれる。公害健康被害補償法は大幅に改正され，それ以後，大気汚染について，新たな患者の認定はなくなった。上記の補償制度の付随的な機能も失われた。

　補償制度の下では，毎年の公害による健康被害の費用が明らかになっていた。地域ごとの認定申請者の数，認定患者の数，補償の総額，発生源への賦課金の総額などが，記録され公表された。こうした健康被害に関する情報は補償制度がなければ得られないものであった。大規模な住民の健康調査は，大きな費用が掛かり，組織的，継続的に実施することが困難である。しかし，健康被害についての情報は，住民一般の公害についての認識を広げ，また中，長期の環境政策を定めるうえで，不可欠のものである。

　大気汚染の被害者への補償制度は全般的に問題なく機能していた。大気汚染による喘息，呼吸器疾患などの症状の認定は容易であり，補償費用も多くの発生源への賦課金によって賄われた。この分野で，その後，注目される動きは，各地で認定患者が中心となって，定額の補償を越える損害賠償と汚染物質の排出差止を求める訴訟が起こされ，裁判所の関与の下で，汚染を実質的に減らせる環境政策の実行を約

束する和解が成立したことである。

　しかし，水俣病患者への補償については多くの問題が生じた。第1に，裁判所の判決によってチッソの賠償責任が確定すると，認定申請が急増した。1970年代の終りには，認定判断を待つ申請者の数が数千人にもなった。第2に，年月の経過とともに水俣病の認定基準が不明確になった。申請者の多くは発生初期のような急性の水銀中毒の特異症状ではなく，通常の疾患と区別の難しい症状や，また加齢による障害とも重なる症状を呈した。認定委員会の専門家の中でも，水俣病の典型的な病像について意見が分かれた。裁判所は認定されなかった患者からの請求を審査し，委員会の認定基準が狭すぎると判決した。環境庁もより柔軟な認定基準を提示した。しかし，こうした裁判所と行政機関の努力も患者認定問題を解決できなかった。第3に，認定患者への補償を支払う当事者であるチッソは何度も経済的破綻の危機にみまわれた。その度に，熊本県は公債を発行し，その大きな部分を国が引き受けて，チッソへ低利の融資を行った。チッソを倒産させれば，被害者は補償なしの状態になり，それは政治的にも放置できない事態を招くことになる。

　1995年の時点で，水銀中毒による認定患者は，2,950人（チッソ関係2,260人，昭和電工関係690人）に登った。認定を受けた患者は約180,000ドルの一時金と年間約20,000ドル支払を受けた。チッソは患者当り27,500ドル，総計3,100万ドルを支払，昭和電工は患者当り16,500ドル，総計700万ドルを支払った。1973年，補償制度の発足から1994年まで21年間に，両会社が認定患者に支払った総額は，12億8800万ドルに登った。

　水俣病被害者によるチッソに対する損害賠償訴訟以降も，民事，行政，刑事の分野で公害発生の責任を問う裁判があいついだ。チッソ水俣工場長は業務上過失の刑事責任を問われて，有罪の判決を受けた。被害者は公害病認定委員会による認定の遅れや申請却下の決定を争って裁判所に提訴した。裁判所は認定基準が厳格すぎるとして，委員会に原告の幾人かについては水俣病患者であることを認定するよう命じた。被害者は早急に必要，適切な措置を怠ったとして，国と県の責任を追及する訴訟を起こした。この種の訴訟の主な争点は，(a)国または県は水俣湾での魚介類の捕獲と販売を禁止すべきであったか（県の問合せに対して，国は湾内の総ての魚介類が汚染されているとする明かな証拠はないと回答していた）。(b)国は水質保全法の違反を理由にチッソの操業を停止させるべきであったか（国は水俣湾が同法の規制の対象地域ではないので違反はといえないと主張した）。これらの争点を審理した6つの裁判所

の判断は国の責任を認めたものと否定したものに分かれた。1980年代の終りになっても，これらの訴訟は2,300人が原告となり，11の地方裁判所と高等裁判所においていぜん審理中であった。

1992年，国は県の協力をえて，非認定患者に対する医療プログラムを発足させた。1995年末には，このプログラムの下で4,600人が年間平均2,900ドルの医療を受けていた。1990年代の終わりになると，水俣病認定手続の破綻は明白であった。チッソは恒常的な財政危機にさらされており，訴訟も難しい争点に直面して進展しない状況に陥っていた。政治解決が局面打開の唯一の方途であった。

4 政治解決

1994年，村山内閣は水俣病被害者との間で政治決着を計ることに踏みきった。主な問題は，それまでの救済制度の対象となっていない被害者への措置である。多くの住民が水銀中毒の病状を訴えていたが，認定されず救済制度の外に置かれていた。政府の解決案は次の点を含んでいた。(1)チッソは一定の要件を充たした住民について一時金を支払う。(2)国と熊本県当局は水俣問題への対処が不充分であったことに遺憾の意を表明する。(3)この合意書に加わる当事者はすべての係争中の訴訟を取り下げる。(4)国と熊本県は綜合的医療保障制度を維持し，影響を受けた地域への開発とチッソへの経済支援を継続し，また医療保障支払の手続を再開する。同年五月，水俣病被害者・原告・原告弁護団全国連絡会議とチッソ株式会社とは，政府の解決案を受け入れ，水俣病に関する「すべての問題の最終的，総体的解決」を達成するための合意書に署名した。両当事者とも，あらゆることを考慮して「問題の早期解決を最優先」させる必要があることを認識したのである。この解決案によって，チッソは(1)それまで総合医療保障制度の下で登録され医療を受けている人と，(2)総合医療保障への再開される登録手続で資格を認められた人に対して一時金を支払う。資格ありとされた人には一時金26,000ドルと年間3,000ドルの医療費が支払われる。1997年，すべての登録申請の審査が終了した段階で一時金と毎年の医療費を受給する資格のある人は10,350人に達した。(そのうちには登録手続再開前に資格を認められていた4,400人が含まれる)。資格を認定された人は，平均10年から14年にわたって医療費を受給すると予測され，1人の医療費の総額は29,000ドルから40,000ドルとなり，一時金を合わせると，それまでの判決で認められている賠償額の平均額(58,000ドル)に近い数字となる。

個人への一時金の他に、訴訟に関係した6つの被害者団体へ合計5,000万ドルが支払われた。これらの団体の成員は個人への一時金に加えて、団体からの分配金を受けることになるかもしれない。この団体への配分金はチッソが負担する。医療に要する費用は国と県が公的医療保険の一部として分担する。被害者団体は一時金の受領によりすべての紛争、訴訟を終結し、将来、損害賠償請求訴訟、一切の交渉、被害者補償制度の下での公的認定を求めないことに合意した（チッソ水俣病関西訴訟の原告団は政治解決への参加を拒否し、国の行政責任を問う控訴審訴訟を継続している。2001年春には控訴審判決が下される予定である）。新潟水俣病の被害者も昭和電工と同様の合意に達した。昭和電工は資格の認められた被害者への一時金の支払に加えて、共同体の再生のために250,000ドルの拠出に合意した。

むすび——いくつかの教訓

太平洋戦争後の公害の原型といえる水俣病被害者の救済は、40年間に損害賠償訴訟から行政的補償制度を経て政治解決にまで展開した。しかし、これだけの年月が経過しても水俣病被害の全容が明らかになったわけではない。水俣湾から有明海沿岸の住民の約2万人が健康になんらかの影響を受けたという推測もある。1万7,000人が認定申請を出し、うち4,000人が認定された。約1,200人が水銀中毒により死亡した。賠償訴訟、認定患者への行政補償、政治決着までの40年は、伝統的な共同体を分裂させ破壊した。住民は訴訟派、話合い派、一任派などに分かれ、認定申請する者、しない者、認定された者、退けられた者に分かれた。また政治決着でも登録する者、しない者、登録できた者、否定された者、一時金を得た者、得なかった者に分かれた。一時期、被害者組織は20を越える派に分裂していた。

政治決着は水俣病被害が完全に解決したとの印象を世間に与えたかもしれない。水銀に汚染された魚を閉じ込めるために水俣湾口に張られたネットは、1997年に撤去された。湾内の魚はテストの結果、食べても安全であると宣言された。湾の内外での漁業が可能になった。しかし、地域にはほとんど漁師が残っていない。チッソが激しく汚染した湾内の部分（138エーカー）は埋め立てられ、堆積したヘドロはコンクリートに覆われた。チッソ工場はいぜん操業を続けている。その目的は、水銀中毒の認定患者に今後も補償を支払い続けるためである。

40年間、被害者救済のために、3つの制度的対応がとられた。被害者は抗議、デモ、座り込み、仲裁、調停など、伝統的な紛争対処が満足のゆく結果を生まず、最

後に裁判所に提訴した。裁判は被害者が汚染者と対決し世論を喚起する場となった。訴訟を通して，遠い地方に起こっている水銀中毒事件が，東京にいる政治家，中央政府の官僚の関心事となった。被害者の請求を認めた裁判所の判決は，公害健康被害補償制度を生む理論的な基礎を固めた。補償制度は大気汚染による健康被害者の認定と補償については，ほぼ機能を果たした。認定基準は比較的明確で，また補償費用の原資は全国の発生源への賦課金によって集められ，被害者へ支払われた。これに比べて，水銀中毒被害者の補償については，その病像があいまいになるにつれて，認定手続は破綻し，また補償責任を負うチッソは何度も経済的破綻の危機にさらされた。チッソが倒産すれば認定患者は継続して補償を得られない。40年の歳月の後に政治決着が計られた。それによって，それまで認定を受けていない被害者への補償がおこなわれた。救済の範囲が広げられたのである。また，影響を受けた地域へ総合医療サーヴィスを提供することも救済策の一部となった。このサーヴィスの中には，通常の健康保険の対象とならない治療，療養も含まれる。政治解決の合意書では，対決し分裂し断絶した共同体の復活が強調され，共同体の協同と紐帯を強める施策が求められた。

　大規模被害の賠償を求める訴訟において，最終的には当事者間の和解解決，さらに広く関与者を巻き込んでの政治決着を求める事例が増えている。日本における大気汚染被害者の訴訟，アメリカにおけるエイジェント・オレンジ訴訟，タバコ訴訟，アスベスト訴訟などがその例である。大規模被害の救済には，被害者と被害範囲の確定，原因と責任者の特定，被害額の算出，補償基金の設定または被害補償制度の設立などの対応が必要になる。社会全体にわたる公的健康保険・福祉制度が完備されないかぎりは，大規模被害に対して，訴訟，行政的補償，政治決着などの対処が求められる。いかにして迅速に適切な対応，対処をとり，被害を最小限度に止め，予防に結びつけるかが今後とも法政策の課題である。

　40年を経過した時点で，水俣病事件の記録をたどると，まだ十分に解明されていないいくつもの疑問にぶつかる。廃水中に水銀が発見された段階で，なぜチッソは排出を止めなかったのか。またなぜ停止を命ずる規制が誰もできなかったのか。内部の実験で猫が廃水によって中毒症状を示したのに，なぜチッソは適切な報告・対応をしなかったのか。なぜ水俣湾での漁業は禁止できなかったのか。なぜ訴訟においては賠償請求のみで差止請求ができなかったのか。なぜ規制の責任を負うべき行政官庁は適切な対処を怠ったのか。地方自治体や国には法的責任がないのか。問題

の対処に必要な，裁判所，行政機関，政治決断のもっとも効果的かつ適切な組合せはなにか。なぜ問題のここまでの決着に40年を要したのか。それで水俣病をめぐる問題は解決したのか。こうした疑問は，これからもくり返し問われ，答えを求める努力が続けられなければならない。

　　＊ 本稿は，本書に収録されているKoichiro FUJIKURA, Litigation, Administrative Relief and Political Settlement for Compensating Victims of Pollution: Minamata Mercury Poisoning after 40 Years, Waseda Bulletin of Comparative Law, vol.17 (1996), pp. 24-38から訳出したものである。英文稿作成にあたって参照した文献とその後公刊された文献を注記に掲げた。

［参照文献］

Jun UI ed., Polluted Japan: Reports by Members of the Jishu-Koza Citizens' Movement (1972).

W. Eugene Smith and Aileen M. Smith, MINAMATA, WORDS AND PHOTOGRAPHS: The Story of the Poisoning of a City, and of People Who Choose to Carry the Burden of Courage.1975.

Julian Gresser, Koichiro Fujikura, Akio Morishima, ENVIRONMENTAL LAW IN JAPAN (1981). (水俣病損害賠償請求事件判決をはじめ4大公害事件判決が英文に訳出されている。)

原田正純『水俣病は終っていない』(1985)

富樫貞夫『水俣病事件と法』(1995)

水俣病研究会編『水俣病事件資料集1926—1968』(1996)

小島敏郎「水俣病問題の政治解決」ジュリストNo.1088 (1996) 5頁

＊　＊　＊

宮澤信雄『水俣事件四十年』(1997)

特集・水俣病問題の政治的解決，水俣病研究会編「水俣病研究」1 (1999)

水俣病に関する社会科学的研究会報告書「水俣病の悲劇を繰り返さないために——水俣病の経験から学ぶもの」(1999)

水俣病被害者・弁護団全国連絡会議／『水俣病裁判全史』第1巻総論編 (1998)，第2巻責任編 (1999)

3 高齢者の財産管理と介護

棚 村 政 行

1 日本型高齢社会の特色と現状
2 新しい成年後見制度
3 家族の介護と扶養の責任

1 日本型高齢社会の特色と現状

(1) 日本における高齢化の特徴と傾向

本章では，日本型高齢社会の特色はどこにあるのか，高齢化の進展はどのような問題をもたらすのかを明らかにしたい。その前提として，まずはじめに，日本型高齢社会の特徴と現状はどうなっているのか，日本の高齢化はどのように進んでいるのか。日本では，「高齢化社会」の指標となる高齢者比率（65歳以上の人が総人口に占める割合）が7％を超えたのが1970年（昭和45年）であった。1996年（平成8年）には15％と，欧米諸国と肩を並べる本格的「高齢社会」に突入し，国立社会保障・人口問題研究所の推計では，2000（平成12）年には，17.2％，2015（平成27）年には25.2％と，なんと総人口の4人に1人は65歳以上になると見込まれている。

1998年9月現在の高齢者人口は2,049万人で，高齢者比率は16.2％と過去最高を記録した。また，2020（平成32）年は，26.9％，3,334万人，2025（平成37）年27.4％と顕著な増加傾向をみせる。人口の高齢化のペースは，10％から20％になるのに，フランス95年，スウェーデン66年，ドイツ62年に対して，日本はわずか22年しかかからず，急テンポでの高齢化，高齢化の速度がきわめて早いことが第1の特色といってよい。

第2に，「長生き日本，世界一」と新聞でも報道されたように，日本人の平均寿命は，1999年で女性が84.01歳，男性77.16歳で，男女とも世界一，とくに女性は14年連続世界一を記録した（1999年8月7日付毎日新聞）。厚生省が発表する簡易生命表は，0歳時の平均余命をもとに，男女があと何年生きられるかを計算したもので，65歳を超えた女性の方は20数年は生きられることになる。100歳以上の長寿者も，1998年9月で1万人を超え，さらに1999年には1万1,346人に達しており，鹿児島県

鹿児島市に住んでいる112歳の本郷さん（女性）が最高齢であった。都道府県別にみると，長寿者が多いのが，沖縄県，高知県，島根県で，西高東低の傾向がくっきり。最も少なかったのが埼玉県だった（1999年9月7日付毎日新聞）。

　第3に，厚生省のまとめによると，1993年には，要介護老人は約200万人おり，その内訳は，寝たきり老人は81万1,000人，要介護の痴呆老人約10万人，虚弱老人100万人であるとされる。2025年には寝たきり230万人，要介護の痴呆老人40万人，虚弱老人260万人で計520万人にもなると予測されている。1995年の世帯当たりの平均人員が2.82人と3人を割り込んでおり，65歳以上の高齢者の単身者世帯は220万世帯で，2010年には430万世帯に増えるとみられている。

　家庭の介護能力はますます低下していくのに対して，要介護老人は急増する。要介護老人のうち，在宅は86万1,000人，施設には68万人が収容され，約60％は家族に家で面倒をみてもらっている。寝たきり期間も3年以上が半数を超え，介護者の52.5％が60歳以上のお年寄りで，高齢者が高齢者の介護をするという状態になっていた。寝たきり老人の介護者の85.1％が女性であり，家族の中での女性の負担は一層重くなっている。要介護老人の急増，家族の介護力の低下などで家族の負担が過重になり，それが高齢者の虐待・放置などにつながっているとの指摘もある。

　1996年の総務庁の「高齢者の生活と意識」では，健康への不安53.3％，孤独への不安31.1％，経済的不安は28.4％と高く，アメリカが健康への不安27％，孤独で不安が16.8％，経済が不安で15.3％と，国際的な比較の中でも，多くの高齢者が健康や要介護状態になることに強い不安を感じていることがわかる。

　第4に，高齢者はお金や財産をもっている。たとえば，世帯主が65歳以上で無職の世帯の1998年の実収入は，1か月平均26万830円だった。内訳は，もちろん，公的年金など社会保障給付が85％を占めている。また，65歳以上で働いている勤労者世帯だと，1か月平均48万2,823円となっている。高齢者世帯の平均貯蓄高をみると，有業者世帯で2,686万円，無職者世帯でも2,166万円で，65歳未満の平均貯蓄高1,487万円に比べ，有業者世帯で約1.7倍，無職世帯でも約1.5倍も多い。そして，60歳以上の有業者世帯で3000万円以上もっているのは，29.2％，無職者世帯でも26.6％と，高額な貯蓄高をほこる世帯は少なくない。しかし，意識調査でも，病気や介護など老後の生活に備えて，貯蓄には手をつけないという回答が半数以上を占めている。寝たきりや病気などをおそれて，高齢者の多くは必要以上に貯蓄に配慮し，消費を抑制する傾向が顕著である。

(2) 高齢者の生活不安と人権侵害

　老人には以下の3つの不安がある。1つは，健康に対する不安である。65歳以上になると有病率が高くなり，年をとればとるほど病気との戦いが多くなる。2つ目に，一人暮らしの単身老人世帯が増え，1995年で17.4％にもなる。老人はとかく社会から離れて生活しがちで，孤独という精神的寂しさをいやというほど味会う。老人が社会の中で尊重され，社会との関わりと生きがいをもって生られるようにしなければならない。3つ目に，老人は退職をし経済的にも不安をもつ。平均的な高齢者夫婦の厚生年金（国民年金を含む）月額は20万円くらいであるが，2人の最低生活費として必要な額は23万1,000円を応える夫婦が多く，公的年金月額より約3万円少ない。

　総務庁の調査でも，日本の場合，健康への不安52.3％，孤独で不安が31.1％，経済が不安28.4％と高く，アメリカが健康への不安27％，孤独で不安16.8％，経済が不安15.3％であるのと比べ，多くの高齢者が三つの問題で強い不安を感じていることがわかる。また，総理府の1995年の世論調査によると，自分自身が要介護者となる不安のある者が67.2％，家族が要介護者となる不安を感じている者が72.9％で，多くの人々が不安を感じており，現在の在宅介護サービスへの不満を感じている人が約半数もあった。

　このような高齢者をめぐる厳しい社会状況，経済環境の中で，高齢者は一人の人間として法主体性を尊重され，社会の一員として快適に生きる権利が守られているのだろうか。家族の中で大切にされ，生き甲斐をもって暮らしているのだろうか。高齢者が家族のお荷物や厄介者扱いされたり，尊厳をもって生きる権利を侵害されていないだろうか。心ない人たちの食い物にされたり，判断能力や記憶力が衰えたり，体力がなくなってきたことに乗じて，財産を奪われ相続争いを有利に展開するための手段に利用されてはいないか。高齢者に対する誤解や偏見で誤った法的な判断を導いていないだろうか。ここでは，高齢者の財産管理や介護を通じて日本の高齢化の現状と問題点を考えてみたい。

2　新しい成年後見制度

　つぎに，従来の禁治産宣告・準禁治産宣告制度にはどのような問題点や弊害があったのか，こんど成立した成年後見法は，具体的にどのような内容や特色をもつものかを第2章では検討する。

(1) 禁治産・準禁治産宣告制度の限界

これまでは，判断力が低下した高齢者の財産管理については，障害の程度に応じて禁治産宣告，準禁治産宣告と後見人，保佐人の選任で対応せざるをえなかった。しかし，高齢による判断力の低下は，断続的段階的に能力の喪失や低下をきたし，正常に判断できたり，徐々にくることを考慮していないものであった。また，家庭裁判所の宣告手続には，手間暇がかかり必要な専門医の鑑定は少なくとも20―30万円の費用もかかった。

しかも，禁治産宣告がなされると，官報等の「公告」，家庭裁判所の掲示板に掲示され，戸籍の身分事項欄に「平成10年12月1日禁治産宣告の裁判確定。同日棚村政行後見人に就職」と記載されるので，本人や家族が望まなかったりもした。禁治産宣告や準禁治産宣告を受けると公務員や専門資格取得の欠格に該当するなどの不利益もあった。申立人の中に，公益代表者としての検察官は入っているが，地方公共団体の長など公益代表者を入れるべきだともいわれる。そのため，禁治産宣告の件数は増えているが，利用しにくい硬直した制度との批判がつよかった。

(2) 成年後見制度の導入

そこで，法制審議会民法部会財産法小委員会は，1995年6月から禁治産，準禁治産制度の見直しに入った。一律の硬直化した禁治産制度を緩和し，知的障害者，判断力の低下した高齢者も含んで，幅広く，その者の財産管理あるいは身上監護の能力を補充し，権利擁護をはかろうということで，成年後見制度の立法化が推進された。未成年者の後見に対して，成年者を対象とするため成年後見法，成年後見制度などといわれる。オーストリアの代弁人制度，ドイツの世話人制度，アメリカ，カナダの公後見人制度，イギリスの持続的代理権授与制度など，禁治産宣告のような全面的な行為能力剥奪制度でなく，個別的柔軟に必要な範囲で本人を代理したり保佐する制度が構想され，1999年12月に，ようやく，本人の自己決定を尊重，残存能力の活用，ノーマライゼーションと従来からの本人の保護の理念を調和させる成年後見制度が成立した。改正法は，本人の自己決定を尊重しつつ，ひとりひとりの多様な生き方に個別的かつ柔軟に対応でき，本人の財産の保全管理と身の回りの世話や介護を必要な範囲で行う形である。

(3) 成年後見制度の特色

このように，従来の禁治産宣告・準禁治産宣告制度は，高齢者から一律かつ画一的に財産を管理したり取引する能力を奪ってしまい，弾力性，柔軟性に欠け弊害が顕著になっていた。そこで，民法が改正され，2000年4月から，自己決定の尊重，残存能力の活用，ノーマライゼイション，各人の判断能力に応じた制度の柔軟化，弾力化という観点から，これまでの本人保護の理念との調和をはかる新しい成年後見制度が設けられた。

まず第1に，この制度は，「禁治産者」「準禁治産者」という差別的なマイナス・イメージの言葉をやめ，精神障害の程度に応じて，二類型から三類型に対象者を拡張した。つまり，障害の軽い順に「被補助人」(15条)「被保佐人」(11条ノ2)「成年被後見人」(8条)にし，家庭裁判所が補助人，保佐人，成年後見人を選任することになった。これに対しては，多様な障害者に必要な補助や援助を与える点では，むしろ個別的な対応をすべきで，ドイツののような一元的制度のほうがよいとの批判もあった。しかし，現行制度との連続性，家庭裁判所での処理基準の明確性という点から，三類型が採用されることになった。

新設された①補助類型は，判断能力（事理弁識能力）は不十分だが，まだ②の著しく不十分，③の判断能力を欠く常況に至らない軽度の痴呆，精神障害，知的障害を対象にする。本人の申立または同意を必要とし，当事者が選択した「特定の法律行為」につき，補助人に特定の代理権，同意権・取消権を与える（876条の9，16条）。②保佐類型は，判断能力が著しく不十分な者を対象にし，保佐人に重要な行為についての同意権及びこれに対応した取消権を付与する。また，本人の申立または同意を必要とし，当事者が選択した一定の法律行為につき，保佐人に代理権が付与される（12条）。③の後見類型は，判断能力を欠く常況にある者が対象で，成年後見人には広範な代理権，取消権が付与される。しかし，日常生活に必要な物品の購入等については，自己決定の尊重の立場から，単独で有効にできるようにした（9条）。

第2に，成年後見人等の選任方法や職務につき，柔軟性と弾力性を加え，チェック体制の確立を期した。たとえば，これまでは配偶者が保佐人や後見人に当然に就くことになっていたが，高齢のため配偶者自身も適切な判断ができなかったり，世話ができない場合もあり，家庭裁判所が個別的な事情を勘案して最も適切な補助人，保佐人，成年後見人を選任することができるようにした(876条の7，876条の2，843条)。また，成年後見人等は複数人選任することもできるし，法人でもかまわないと

された（843条3項，同条4項）。

　本人の居住確保を図るため，成年後見人等が本人の居住用不動産を処分するには家庭裁判所の許可を要するものとしている（859条の3）。成年後見人等は，本人の意思を尊重し，その心身と生活の状況に配慮する義務がかせられた（858条）。チェック機能の強化という面から，補助監督人，保佐監督人を新設し，法人も監督人にすることができるようになった（876条の8，876条の3）。

　第3に，自己決定権の尊重の立場から，任意後見制度を新設している。つまり，高齢者等が判断能力のあるうちに事前に，能力喪失時に委任契約を公正証書にしておけば，そこで指定された後見人が契約どおりの事務処理をしてくれる制度である（任意後見契約法1条）。具体的には，自分の将来の生活，療養，財産管理について代理権を与える任意後見契約を公正証書で締結しておき，痴呆が進行したときに，本人，親族，契約相手などが家庭裁判所に後見の開始を申し立て，家庭裁判所が，判断能力が不十分と認めると，任意後見監督人を選任することになる（4条）。そして，任意後見監督人は，任意後見人の事務を監督し，家庭裁判所に定期的に様子を報告することになっている（7条）。家庭裁判所は，任意後見監督人に必要な処分を命じたり，任意後見人を解任することもでき，間接的なチェック機能をはたすことにした（7条3項，8条等）。

　第4に，戸籍への記載に代えて，法定後見及び任意後見契約制度を登録する「成年後見登記制度」が新設された（後見登記法1条）。この登記制度は，登記所において，登記ファイルに，誰が誰の補助人，保佐人，成年後見人になっているか，どのような代理権等を与えられているかなどの所要の登記事項を記録し，公示とプライバシーの保護の調和を図った。本人，成年後見人等一定範囲の者は登記事項証明書の交付をうけ，これにより取引の安全と第三者の保護が図られることになる（10条）。

　新しい成年後見制度は，介護保険制度や地域福祉権利擁護事業などとともに，日本の急速に進む高齢化と高齢者障害者福祉に対応する措置といえる。このようなシステムを活用して，高齢の夫婦も安心して自分たちの暮らしや財産を守ることが可能になろう。

(4) 高齢者社会福祉施策の展開

　高齢者の介護福祉サービスを含む，日本の社会福祉サービスは，租税による公的

福祉財政支出と受益者負担による公的福祉措置に依存してきた。1980年代に入り，高度経済成長政策から低経済成長政策への転換に対応して，社会福祉財政の合理化が課題とされ，自立自助の支援，医療と福祉サービスとの連携，各種社会的資源の整備充実民間活力の導入，家庭介護機能の強化などが推進されることになった。

1989年のゴールドプラン（高齢者保健福祉推進10カ年戦略），1995年の新ゴールドプランが打ち出され，市町村による在宅福祉対策の緊急整備として，ホームヘルパー（1993年約5万人）17万人（1999年の目標），デイサービス（1993年4,300ヵ所）1.7万ヵ所，ショートステイ（1993年約2万床）6万床，在宅介護支援センター1万か所入所施設の緊急整備として，特別養護老人ホーム（1993年20万床）29万床，老人保健施設（1993年11万3,000床）28万床，ケアハウス（1993年1万7,000人）10万人，高齢者生活福祉センター（1993年160カ所）400ヵ所などの増員増設が目指されている。

3 家族の介護と扶養の責任

3では，主として，痴呆高齢者の家族は，身の回りの世話や介護でどのような負担を負っているか，私的扶養と公的扶助はどのような関係にたっているか，介護保険制度はどのような制度かを検討する。

(1) 要介護老人と介護の現状

現在，要介護老人は141万6,000人おり，在宅86万2,000人，施設に55万4,000人（老人福祉施設7万6,000人，特別養護老人ホーム20万人，病院27万8,000人）。寝たきり老人は81万1,000人で，在宅ケアが60％，施設介護は20％，病院が20％と圧倒的に在宅ケアが中心といえる。年齢別での要介護者と寝たきり老人の比率をみると，人口1,000人あたり65歳以上では，49.3人，16.2人，80歳以上では，144.3人，51.2人となって，後期高齢者ほど寝たきり率，要介護率ともに高くなる。

介護者も80％以上が，息子の嫁，老齢の配偶者（妻），娘など女性であり，しかも65歳以上の高齢者が高齢者の面倒をみる（37.5％）という実情がある。寝たきり期間をみても，3年以上が53％と過半数を超えている。65歳以上の高齢者と子との同居率は，1980年の68％から1995年には54.3％と減少し，子夫婦との同居率は1980年の52.5％から1995年には35.5％にまで低下している。

最近の全国400か所の在宅介護支援センターを対象とした調査では，回答があった220カ所から144人，209件の虐待放置が報告されたという。介護疲れで心身ともにく

たくたになった嫁が世話を放棄する例も多く，息子の暴力も目立つ。虐待を受けた70％が女性で，高齢になるほど虐待率も高くなる。専門家は，公的介護サービスが不十分で国や自治体の支援が整わないことが，過度の負担を課された家族に重圧を与え結果的に，弱い要介護老人の虐待につながっているのではないかと分析している。

(2) 私的扶養と介護

ところで，親族間の扶養に関しては，民法877条がある。これでは，直系血族，兄弟姉妹間に扶養義務を認め，例外的に特別な事情がある場合に限って，家庭裁判所が3親等以内の親族に扶養を命ずることができるとする。したがって，民法が家族に扶養義務を課しているのは，親子，祖父母，孫間のように，直系血族か，兄弟姉妹で，伯父伯母甥姪間，息子の嫁と息子の親など一親等の姻族間では余程の事情がないかぎり，扶養義務を課せられることはない。

一般的に扶養義務には，生活保持義務と生活扶助義務の二類型があるといわれてきた。つまり，生活保持義務は，一片の肉，一杯のご飯，一粒の米まで分け合う重い義務であり，自己の生活の一部として自己の生活と同程度の生活を保持する義務といわれる。たとえば，夫婦間の扶養(民法752条，760条)，親と未成熟子の間の扶養(民法766条，877条1項)は生活保持義務の例とされる。

これに対して，成人の子と老親，兄弟姉妹間の扶養などは，自らの生活を確保したうえで，余力があれはそれを振り向ける程度でよい生活扶助義務という。年老いた親を扶養する義務は生活保持義務と解する説もあるが，生活扶助義務とみる説が多い。そもそも，具体的な扶養義務は，扶養権利者の側の扶養の必要性と扶養義務者の資力その他扶養の可能性など一切の事情が勘案されて決定される(879条)。したがって，扶養義務者間で協議ができれはよいし，また調停で第三者に間に入ってもらって合意してもよいし，それでも決まらなければ，家庭裁判所が審判で決めることになる（878条)。

全国の家庭裁判所で申し立てられた扶養事件は，1996年で9,360件だったが，そのうち未成年者に関する事件が8,945件と96％を占め，成年の事件は415件で4％に過ぎない。しかも，調停が成立した事件162件では，金銭扶養が112件で69％，引取扶養が23件で14％，病院や施設収容が9件で6％，金銭扶養と引取扶養そのほかが11％などとなっていた（『司法統計年報1996年』130—134頁)。

老親扶養の問題は，多くは話し合いで解決されており，家庭裁判所の審判で決定される例はきわめて少ない。これは，介護や身の回りの世話が肉親としての愛情や信頼関係に基礎づけられて，はじめて意味をもつサービスであって，嫌々外からの圧力で決定されたり履行されるものではないからであろう。引取扶養は，同居や共同生活を伴い扶養義務の履行の一方法とはみられるが，扶養義務者及び扶養権利者がこれを選択しないかぎり，法的に強制される性質のものではない。まして，寝たきり老人，痴呆老人の介護には24時間を要するケースもあって，望まない子に介護を命じたり，高額な介護費用の負担をさせることは問題であろう。

(3)　私的扶養と公的扶助

　生活に困窮する高齢者，痴呆老人，寝たきり老人の経済問題，介護問題は家族の私的扶養を超える場合がある。私的扶養と公的扶助という国家責任とはどのような関係にたつのか。個人責任，家族責任と国家責任との関係は，一次的には，一定近親者に家族内の生活困窮者，要介護者への支援を私的扶養という形で果たさせ，他方，憲法の保障する福祉国家における生存権保障は，家族によって支えられない人を国家が支えるという構造をもつ。しかし，国家責任の原理はあくまでも二次的補充的なもので生活保護法も謳うように，親族扶養優先の原則が採用され，公的扶助は補充的な保障をする（公的扶助の補足性，生活保護法4条2項など）。

(4)　公的介護保険制度

　これまでの日本の公的介護サービスは，特別養護老人ホームなど老人福祉制度と老人病院などの医療制度によって提供され，その費用も公費（税金）と医療保険料とで別個にまかなわれてきた。しかし，急テンポで進む高齢化のため，従来の方式では公的介護システムを財政的に支えきれないことが明らかになってきた。たとえば，老人医療費の急増で医療保険財政が悪化し，また，厚生省では，2000年に必要な介護サービスの費用5兆円と試算しているが，その財源確保がきわめて困難な状況にある。

　そのため，医療サービスのうち，老人介護の性格をもつ部分を老人医療から切り放して，医療保険とは別個に介護保険を当てて，医療保険財政の立直しを図る。また，老人福祉施設などの提供する介護サービスの不足を増税で補うことは国民の反対がつよいので，介護保険を導入して社会保険化したほうがかえって，スムーズに

財源の確保もできるなどの観点から，公的介護保険構想が生まれてきた。

　1998年6月に，厚生省提出の「介護保険法」案は見送られ，1997年秋の臨時国会で若干修正された法案が継続審議となっていたが，ようやく成立し，2000年4月から介護保険制度がスタートした。介護保険法の内容は，保険者は市町村及び特別区とする（国，都道府県等が支える），被保険者は40歳以上65歳未満の医療保険加入者，65歳以上の高齢者で要介護者，在宅・施設での介護に対する現物給付を行い，要介護認定にもとづく介護給付額の範囲内で給付を受けられるとする。しかし，介護保険制度に対しては，本来国が担うべき社会保障制度の後退を招き，私的保険化で国民の負担を強化するものではないかとか，財源確保の議論ばかりで，実際に提供される介護サービスの質や中身が明らかでないなどの批判があった。

　65歳以上の人が負担する介護保険料に4.4倍の格差があるとか，手続きが面倒だとか，要介護の認定に問題があるなどで，特別対策を講じることにした。

第II部　自由市場と法的規制
(i) 市場経済と法的規制

4　グローバリゼーションと規制改革
―――規制改革の理論と課題―――

土　田　和　博

1　経済のグローバル化に伴う諸改革と理論的基礎
2　規制改革と諸理論
3　規制改革の課題―――一試論―――
　おわりに

1　経済のグローバル化に伴う諸改革と理論的基礎

　(1)　ソ連・東欧における社会主義の崩壊後，1990年代に入って世界の国民国家 (nation states) は国際，国内関係ともに共通ないし類似の事態に直面しつつあるように思われた。「人権・民主主義・市場経済」が新世界秩序の三位一体的グローバル・スタンダードとなり[1]，また国によってバリエーションはあるものの，総じてケインズ主義的福祉国家と呼ばれた国家・社会体制が新自由主義・新保守主義的改革の荒波によって解体ないし再編成に向かいつつあるかにみえたからである。しかし，1997年の東アジアの通貨・経済危機，ロシアのデフォルトのおそれ，日本の長引く不況，理論上損失を招かないはずのアメリカのヘッジファンドの倒産の危機，ヨーロッパにおける社会民主主義の伸長，99年末の「シアトルの悲劇」などを契機として単純な「市場経済ないし資本主義の優位」は明らかに転機を迎えつつある。けれども，この転換がどこに向かうのかは，なお不透明である。

　(2)　新世界秩序のグローバル・スタンダードをどのように評価すべきかは，決して単純な問題でない。例えば「人権」は時代と社会を問わず妥当する普遍的価値であるかに主張されるが，これは基本的には近代西欧の所産であって20世紀末のアジアの社会にそのままの形で妥当するかは必ずしも自明とはいえないし，特に発展途上国においては社会経済的な発展・開発のために市民的政治的人権の制限が許されるかというセンシティブな問題があることも周知のとおりである。そうではあるが，しかし人権の主張には―それが外から行われる場合にも―強権的軍事政権あるいは

開発独裁政権によって抑圧された人民の解放の要求に呼応する側面があることも事実である。また，本稿にとくに関連する「市場経済」についてみると，確かに市場経済化は，日本を含めたアジア諸国にしばしばみられる産業と国家の癒着と腐敗の構造(縁故資本主義=crony capitalism)に変革をもたらし，経済合理性が貫徹する透明な関係に移行させるという側面がないではないし[2]，あるいは自由貿易について時に語られるように，それが経済的ブロック主義を防止しつつ経済的相互依存関係の形成を通じて世界平和に貢献するという一般的抽象的可能性を認められないわけではない[3]。しかしながら，90年代にグローバル・スタンダードとして主張された「市場経済」の実態とは，著しくその経済・政治力を増大させた多国籍企業が世界に生産拠点を設け，地球大の規模で資本と労働を調達し，そしてまた地球的規模で販売するのに適した経済体制であり，その過程で惹起させつつある人権と民主主義と生存の危機あるいは地球環境問題などに目を向けないでは，こうした経済的スタンダードの正当な評価とはいえないと思われる。

　(3)　このような国際的なレベルの変化，とくに経済のグローバル化と国際競争の激化に対応すべく，各国は国内の改革を急いできた。日本では特に93年に成立した細川政権以降，規制緩和・規制改革が急速な進展をみせている。日本の規制緩和政策が到達した原則を確認しておけば，①経済的規制については原則自由・例外規制，社会的規制は自己責任原則を前提として必要最小限化する，②規制の透明化，国際的整合化を図る，③事前規制型行政から事後チェック型行政に転換する，④規制の必要性，妥当性についての説明責任は規制を行う行政庁の側にあるというものである。ただし，現実に進行している事態は単純な規制の撤廃，緩和ではなく，S. K. Vogelのいうように「自由化と再規制(liberalization and reregulation)」，すなわち市場競争の導入と古い規制の廃止および新しい規制・ルールの創出とみる方がより実際に近いと考えられる[4]。また，1997年末，行政改革会議は，中央省庁の再編成，内閣機能の強化，行政の減量と効率化などを柱とする最終報告を決定し，21世紀に向けて「簡素にして効率的で透明な政府」をめざすことを決定した。これらは，国家行政の組織と作用の両面において公領域の縮減と私的自由領域の伸長および負担の軽減を企図する新自由主義・新保守主義的改革である。その底流にある認識を，1998年まで設置されていた行政改革委員会の言葉でいえば，「市場経済下で世界規模の激しい競争」に直面して「国内の高コスト体質」の元凶である政府規制を撤廃緩和し，あるいは国家組織そのものを縮減減量するしか日本に残された道はないとい

(4) 以上のように経済のグローバル化，規制緩和，貿易・投資の自由の一層の拡大を揚言する考え方の底流にある基本的な諸理論にみられる特徴の1つは，例えば規制緩和の効用が，それによって企業，労働者，消費者が享受する利益が，被る不利益を上回り，ネットゲインとなることに存するいう表現にみとめられる。要するに規制緩和は社会全体としてみれば不利益を超える利益をもたらすということである[5]。こうした考え方は，例えば新古典派経済学の影響の強いR．Posnerなどとも親和的である。Posnerは行為や制度の望ましさを基本的にはそれが富，すなわち社会的総余剰を増大させるか減少させるかによって判断するが，総余剰が増加するのはパレート改善の場合，すなわち他者の余剰を減少させないである者の余剰を増大させる場合だけではなく，例えば生産者（売手）余剰の増大が消費者（買手）余剰の減少より大きい場合をも含む。すなわち，ある者の余剰の増大と他の者の余剰の減少を差引計算して残余余剰がある場合もその行為や制度は望ましいとし，この「富の最大化原理」を立法政策上または法解釈上の基本的判断基準としても用いる[6]。これと日本の規制緩和論の背景にある考え方は極めて親和的であるように思われるが，そうだとすればこのような考え方に対しては，ある行為や制度によって総余剰が増加すれば，そのことの方を分配の不平等や個人の権利侵害より重視するものであるとして，功利主義的最大化原理にしばしば向けられる批判が妥当することとなろう[7]。

いま1つのPosner理論の問題点は全面的商品化（市場帝国主義）である。Posnerの理論のままに日本の規制緩和が行われているわけではないが，一部にはそのような傾向と同様な方向の問題が現れてきている。Posnerはあらゆる法領域に経済分析を及ぼし，現存する諸問題の解決策として市場制度の利用を提言ないし示唆する（養子縁組の問題で嬰児の売買を示唆するように）。その理由は，上に掲げた総余剰の増大にあると考えられるが，嬰児の商品化，二酸化炭素や窒素酸化物の排出枠の売買構想だけでなく，身体の一部（臓器，角膜，血液），代理母サービス，選挙権などが商品化候補としてPosnerなどの法と経済学の一部の論者によって主張される。

2 規制改革と諸理論

(1) 本稿は，いわゆる新世界秩序の下における90年代のグローバルな変化とナショナルな改革を新自由主義・新保守主義的な性格をもつものと捉え，これが生み

出す国民国家と国際関係への重大な影響をふまえて，これに対抗・代替するための改革構想にむけて，一試論を理論的側面から展開しようというものである。その際，Posnerに代表されるような新自由主義的競争論の純粋形態が市場帝国主義と功利主義の支配する世界をもたらすにほかならないとすれば，これによらない代替理論に基づいて制度設計を行うべきであるというのが本稿の基本的な考え方である。ただし，現時点で国民国家の理想的な規制制度を細部にまでわたって設計し，その詳細を述べることは困難である。しかし，逆に規制制度の一般原則を透明性，無差別性，最小限性などとして提示するだけのアプローチの仕方も不十分である。その中間のアプローチの1つは，警察，国防，司法など夜警国家が果たす役割に加えて，金融，情報通信，環境，労働，社会保障，国際的投機活動の監視と制限など昨今のトピックめいた分野の規制が必要だと主張することである。しかし，重要な問題はどのような分野で規制を維持すべきかというより，どのような目的で，いかなる内容の規制が必要かがより本質的な問題というべきであろう。ここでは，国家による規制の側から発想するのではなく，社会あるいは世界で，いかなる権利がどのように確保されねばならないかという市民社会から発想する権利論的アプローチを試みたい。

(2) 1971年に公刊されたRawls『正義論』は，個人の権利や自由が多数者の効用によって償われないことを基本的テーゼとする正義の2原理に社会の政治制度および経済制度が適合することを要求し，第1部・理論では自由かつ平等な道徳的人格が社会的協同のうちに自己の生の実現を図るために不可欠な社会的基本財(自由, 機会, 所得, 富, 自尊心の基礎)の分配を規定する主要な社会制度のあり方に関して，無知のヴェールに包まれた原初状態において，いかにして正義の2原理，すなわち，第1原理である平等な基本的諸自由の原理と，第2原理である①機会の公正な平等の原理および②格差原理を選択することに合意するかが論じられる。また第2部・制度では，Rawlsは正義の2原理が制憲議会，立法行為，裁判官，行政官によるルールの適用・市民の遵守という各段階で実現される過程が論じられるが，市場経済との関係で重要なのは次の点である。すなわち，Rawlsは正義の2原理と市場システムの関係に触れ，市場システムは職業選択の自由や経済的権力の分散化，(生産, 資源配分, 財の分配における)効率性，平等な自由，機会の公正な平等と両立するといった利点を有するから，経済制度はその限りでこれに依拠してよいとするが，同時にそれは，① 平等な市民権という自由を保障する基本法，② 機会の公正な平等原則，

③ 家族手当，病気や失業に対する特別給付，等級別所得補助といったソーシャルミニマムの保障など「背景となる制度」に適切に囲まれることを条件とすることも忘れてはならないのである。

　この点に関連して，Rawlsのいう市場経済，市場システム(market system)，さらには自由市場の概念については若干の説明が必要である。すなわち，Rawlsは，これらの用語を必ずしも資本主義経済と同じ意味内容で用いているわけではないということである。すなわち「自由市場の利用と生産手段の私的所有との間には本質的な結びつきがな」く，「社会主義体制といえども，このシステムの利点を利用することができる[8]」のである。換言すれば，市場システムないし市場経済とは「売買に関するある特定の仕組み」ないし流通に関する仕組みであり，「市場の背後にある生産の仕組みについては問わない」のである。それ故，市場システムには社会主義的市場経済あるいは市場社会主義 (market socialism) など，資本制経済以外の経済形態を包含しうるのである[9]。その上で，Rawlsは私有財産制と社会主義体制のいずれが正義の原理によく対応しているかは各国の伝統，制度，社会的諸力，歴史環境によって左右されるから一般的には答えられないとして，体制選択の問題は棚上げにする，というより当該社会の歴史や社会的諸関係の具体的あり様を離れて，一般的に私有財産制と社会主義体制の優劣を問うても無意味であるとするのである[10]。

　(3) さてPosnerなどの全面的商品化論に抗して，商品化(市場)領域と非商品化(市場)領域の共存を認めるという多元主義の立場に立ちつつ，非商品化の方向に向けてプラグマティックに非市場的側面・要素を漸進的に拡大するという構想を示すのがM.J. Radinである[11]（漸進的多元主義）。その一環として，Radinは市場領域における非市場的要素の維持・拡大という構想を示し，その１つの具体化として人格構成的財産関係（人格と密接に結合すると客観的に判断される人と物の関係，たとえば賃借人とアパートの関係，愛情を抱き合う夫婦と結婚指輪の関係）が代替可能財産関係（貨幣との交換以外には意味をもたない人と物との関係，たとえば賃貸人とアパートの関係，宝石商とその店頭にある指輪の関係）よりもエンタイトルメントにおいて強いと考え，前者を後者に優先させることを挙げる。そして，裁判所や立法府は黙示的に，あるいは直接にこの問題に焦点を合わせることなしにこれを行いつつあるという[12]。

　全面的商品化に対するRadinのもう１つの対抗戦略は，地位不可譲性，コミュニティ不可譲性，社会的禁止による不可譲性および市場不可譲性という４種類の不可譲性 (inalienability) を区別すること[13]，および商品化に対する判断を現実世界にお

ける力関係の非対称性をふまえて，プラグマティックに行うことであるが，この点は後述する。

3 規制改革の課題——一試論——

(1) 以上のような諸理論は，あるべき規制システムの法モデルにどのような示唆を与えるのであろうか。以下では2つの問題，すなわち市場の外延の限定と市場の内包の権利論的構造化を課題として提示したい。前者は全面的商品化傾向にどのように歯止めをかけることができるかであり，後者は功利主義的最大化原理にかわるいかなる公準を提示することができるかである。要するに，以下では主権国家レベルにおいて市場の外延を限定しながら，市場内に含まれる諸利益を権利として整理し，これに優先順位を設定して国家はこれを擁護すべきことを試論として述べたい[14]。

(2) 前述のごとく日本の規制緩和論は社会全体において規制緩和による利益が不利益を上回るからこれを肯定するという点において功利主義的な富の最大化原理と矛盾しない性格をもっている（総和主義）。これに対して，以下に述べる試論は社会ないし市場における諸利益を量的に差引計算するのではなく，むしろその質的差異に着目する市場の内包の権利論的構造化という課題を提示する。

具体的には，主権国家における市場の内包を，①人の生存(生命)，健康，安全に対する権利などの基底的人権，②商工自営業者，農林漁業従事者，消費者などの人権としての財産権，③中小企業法人の人権でも独占財産でもない財産権，④資本主義の制度的保障にとどまる独占財産にわけ，国家はこの順序で保障を確保しなければならない。①，②は前国家的自然権を憲法上確認したものであるから最優先され，③は憲法上の保障ではないが法律によって権利性を付与されている限りで次に優先され，④は憲法上の人権ではなく資本主義の制度保障に過ぎないため最劣後することになる。そのため主権国家は，a 市場参加主体，b 取引対象たる財，c 市場の過程，d 市場の帰結に関して，経済的規制，社会的規制および独禁法による規制などを行うわけであるが，①や②を③や④より優先して保障する以上，当然ながら従来の官僚主義的，独占保護的性格を人権擁護的，国民志向的な方向へ転換することが前提となる。

以上の整理から政府の規制緩和措置の評価・峻別のための原則を導くこともできる。すなわち，(i)①，②の保障を目的とし，これに積極的に作用する規制は維持・

強化されるべきであり，これに消極的に働く規制は撤廃・改革すべきである。(ii)④に対する制限を目的とし，制限に積極的に作用する規制は維持・強化すべきであり，消極的に働く規制措置は撤廃・改革すべきである。

(3) 市場の外延の限定，すなわち，全面的商品化傾向にいかに歯止めをかけることができるかという課題については，4種類の不可譲性に関して，その根拠，内容，範囲がそれぞれ異なるということが重要である。例えば，選挙権の譲渡が禁止される理由は，それが権利であるとともに一種の社会的義務でもあることに求められるが，他方，年金の受給資格の譲渡禁止は，年齢，掛け金などの条件を満たすことによって発生する一身専属的な資格であるからであろう。また，4種類によって不可譲性の内容が異なる例としては，選挙権は有償譲渡も無償譲渡も許されないが，臓器はRadinによれば無償譲渡はむしろ推奨されるべきものである。不可譲性の範囲が異なるという意味は，麻薬は販売のみならず生産そのものも禁止されるが，電気は生産（自家発電）は許されるが，日本では小口の需要者に販売することはできないという対比によって明らかとなろう。この問題は，社会保障，参政権，医療倫理，環境などさまざまな分野で個別具体的に検討せざるを得ず，これ以上の観念的抽象的一般化は避けるべきであるが，いずれにせよ，現実世界における力関係の非対称性を直視し，このような現実世界を前提として全面的商品化の禁止，無償譲渡のみの許容，不完全な商品化などによって，商品化問題への対応を検討することが重要である。

おわりに

本稿は，無制約な市場経済をコントロールするために，「平等主義的市場システムの法構造モデル」の提示を試みたものである。無制約な市場経済は資本主義のグローバル化と世界的競争と繋がっており，その意味では国民国家間の協力と連帯がこのモデルに基づく法の実現には不可欠である。グローバルな資本主義のコントロールに向けて，諸国民の地域的なネットワークの形成が重要な第一歩となろう。

(1) 桐山孝信「冷戦終結と新国際秩序の模索」神戸市外大・外国学研究32巻1頁。
(2) 坂本義和「世界市場化への対抗構想―東アジア地域協力と「市民国家」―」世界1998年9月号61―2頁。ただし，坂本の力点は国家と市場の「合理化」がそれらの「民主化」に結びつくかという点にある。また，同『相対化の時代』(1997年) も参照。

(3) Ernst-Urlich Petersmann, Paul Krugman and Brian Barry, "The Feasibility and Desirability of Global Free Trade", in Gerain Parry, Asif Qureshi and Hillel Steiner ed., *The Legal and Moral Aspects of International Trade* 7 (1998).
(4) S.K Vogel, *Freer Markets, More Rules* 3-4 (1996). Vogelは，自由化と再規制を推進しつつあるのが，一般に指摘されるように規制の拘束を受けてきた企業ではなく，むしろ国家機関 (state institutions) であるとする（日本については，この点は疑問の余地があろう）。その上で再規制を，①競争促進的再規制（電気通信事業でみられるように新規参入者と既存業者の間で競争を促進させるために行われる非対称的規制など），②法化的再規制 (judicial reregulation, 暗黙のルールを法典化することなど），③拡張的再規制（自由化の過程で官庁の権威を維持するために新規制を創出し，権限を拡張する場合），④戦略的再規制（外国会社の参入を抑制するなど）に分類する (pp. 16-24)。
(5) 例えば，川本明『規制改革―競争と協調―』135頁（1998年）をみられたい。
(6) R．ポズナー（馬場孝一・国武輝久監訳）『正義の経済学』94頁以下（1991年）。
(7) 詳細は，拙稿「規制緩和と新自由主義的競争論」静岡大学法政研究1巻2・3・4号138頁以下（1997年）を参照されたい。
(8) John Rawls, *A Theory of Justice* 271 (1973, Oxford paperback), ジョン・ロールズ（矢島欽次監訳）『正義論』211頁以下（1979年）（翻訳は若干変更した）。
(9) 高橋洋児『市場システムを超えて』52―5頁（1996年）。また，国分幸『デスポティズムとアソシアシオン構想』（1998年）によれば，第2次大戦前にO．ランゲやH.D.ディキンソンらの「競争的社会主義」は，職業選択の自由や消費選択の自由（すなわち，労働市場と消費財市場）を認めるとともに，資本財，生産資源については国家が「計算価格」を設定するという理論的構想をもっていたし（同書336頁），また戦後には現実にユーゴスラビアの「自主管理市場経済」やハンガリーのNew Economic Mechanismと呼ばれる改革（生産物市場を容認し，資本市場を禁止する）など，社会主義の基盤の上に市場経済を導入するという実験を試みている（同書318頁以下）。こうした東欧社会主義国の実験は不完全に終わったが，市場社会主義 (market socialism) の理論的営為は英米において現在も継続している（例えば，David Miller, *Market, State and Community* (1989))。
(10) Rawls, supra note 8, at 274. 『正義論』213頁。ところでRawlsは『正義論』においては，正義の2原理の適用範囲を「他の社会から隔離された閉じたシステムと暫時考えられる社会の基本的構造」，すなわち端的には「国民社会」に限定していた。C．Beitzによれば，Rawlsがそのように考えた理由は，国民社会が他のそれと些細な形でしか相互作用を及ぼさず，それぞれの国民社会は自給自足的であると前提されたためである。しかしながら，今日の世界は貿易・投資その他の関係において著しく相互作用を強めており，1国で自給自足的な社会は稀というべきであっ

て，Rawlsの理論的前提は，21世紀初頭の今日の状況からあまりにもかけ離れている。Rawlsの議論が現下の国民社会ないし世界にも適用可能なように修正を施す必要があるわけであり，これを試みる1人の論者がBeitzである（Charles Beitz, *Political Theory and International Relations* (1979)）。私はBeitzによる拡張について要旨次のように述べたことがあった（拙稿「規制改革の理論と課題―規制緩和への対抗戦略―」静岡大学法政研究3巻3・4号（1999年））。

　Beitzの理論的修正によれば，まず原初状態の参加者は国民社会からに限らず国際社会からということになる。そこは無知のヴェールに包まれているから，例えば天然資源の何がどこにどれだけ埋蔵されているかは知らないが，不均等な分布それ自体は知っていると考えられること，あるいは原初状態の参加者が生まれつく社会が，高度に工業化され情報化された裕福な社会なのか，それとも単一農産物の輸出に自己と家族の命運をかけざるをえないような発展途上の社会なのかを知らないことなどから，最もましな最悪を選択するという保守的なマキシミンルールに従って，格差原理を含む正義の2原理に合意することになる。ここにおいて正義の2原理は，国際上の分配的正義を含む地球的原理となるわけである。また，Beitzの理論の法制度論的含意についてみると，必ずしも具体的に語られているわけではないが，次のような国際的正義の2原理の適用関係が考えられる。まず言論集会の自由や身体の自由，個人財産を所有する権利など，正義の第1原理上の権利が国際関係においても最優先され，ついで第2原理の機会の公正な平等の原則によって，人が同じ才能と能力と意欲をもつ限り，カースト制などの社会環境の影響をうけることなく同じ社会的経済的機会を持つことを確保し，さらに国際的格差原理によって天然資源の不均等な分布や人の生来の才能の違いなど自然的要因が人間の社会経済的状態に及ぼす影響を除去しようとするものと考えられる。天然資源や人の才能はまさに人類共有の資産であって，それを分かち合うことを含んだ格差原理に国際的原初状態の参加者は合意していると考えられるからである，と。

　しかしながら，Rawlsは近著 *The Law of Peoples* (1999)においてBeitzとは異なる仕方で国際関係への拡張を試みているようであり，これを含めた検討が不可欠であるが，現時点ではその準備がない。従って国際的正義の原理に関しては本稿では触れることをせず，この点は他日を期したいと思う。

(11) M.J. Radin, "Market-Inalienability," 100 Harv. L. Rev. 1849 (1987). M.J. Radin, "Justice and Market Domain," in J.W. Chapman & J.R. Pennock, ed., *Market and Justice* 165 (*Nomos* 31, 1989)も参照。

(12) M.J. Radin, *Reinterpreting Property* 18, 53-55 (1993).

(13) 地位不可譲性（status-inalienability）の例としては年金など社会保障給付の受給資格の不可譲性が，コミュニティ不可譲性（community-inalienability）の例としては選挙権の譲渡禁止が，社会的禁止による不可譲性（prohibition-inalienablity）の例としては麻薬の禁止が，また市場不可譲性（market-inalienability）の例として

は労働や住居の自由取引の制限がそれぞれあげられる（Radin, "Market Inalienability", 100 Horn. L. Rew. 1849, at 1854)。

(14) 対抗理論モデルをどのようなタイムスパンで構想するかは，1つの問題である。50年，100年というパースペクティブでみれば，社会主義の道が本格的に復権する可能性はありえよう。しかし，本稿はこのような(半)世紀的タイムスパンではなく，せいぜい2, 30年を視野に収めて，どのような法モデルが対抗・代替理論として可能かを論じようとするものである。

＊ 本稿は，「規制改革の理論と課題──規制緩和への対抗戦略」静岡大学法政研究3巻3・4号（1999年）に若干の加筆・修正を行ったものであることを付記する。

5 民営化された産業に対する規制の枠組み

マイケル・クロムリン
[大野理彩 訳]

 序
1 競 争 政 策
2 競 争 法
3 インフラストラクチャーへのアクセス
4 経済的規制
 結 論

序

　オーストラリア経済において政府は常に主要な役割を担ってきている。19世紀には，政府は，運輸，通信，エネルギーといった社会的インフラストラクチャーストラクチャーの主要な部分を提供する任務を担ってきた。これらの事業は民間の手に委ねるには規模が大きすぎた。20世紀に入ると，政府は，これらの領域において支配的であり続け，さらに，銀行業，保険業といった他の分野にも参入した。このことは，しばしばイデオロギーによるよりも実務上の理由により正当化されてきた。規模が小さく，孤立している経済においては，独占の危険が高かったが，公的独占の方が私的独占よりも望ましいとされた[1]。

　政府による経済への参加には様々な形態がとられてきた。政府の省の欠点はすぐに認識され，省の能力を超えると思われる機能を果たすために，各種委員会や制定法上の機関が設置された。効率性を求めることと責務を負わせることの双方を追求することにより，様々な公的機関が生み出されたが，それはこれら二つの目的が本来相対するものであるという関係を映し出すものであった[2]。

　オーストラリア行政法には，政府がその権限行使について責務を負うことをより確実にすることを意図したいくつかの方策が設けられている。それらのなかには情報へのアクセス権[3]，不正な行政行為に対する請求についてのオンブズマンによる調査[4]，審判所による行政審査[5]，裁判所による司法審査[6]，および立法議会による全般的な監視が含まれる。これらの方策は，多かれ少なかれ，政府の職員および省に対してのみならず，各種委員会および制定法上の機関に対する規制の枠組みを構

成する。

　近年，効率性の追求が責務を負わせることに優先されている。それは，政府の機関の「コーポラタイゼーション」がなぜ進められきたかの説明となる。「コーポラタイゼーション」という用語は，一機関を（議会の制定法により設置される）制定法上の機関構造または（内閣により設置される）省構造から，民間セクターに適用される企業法に従った企業構造に転換することを示すために造られた言葉である[7]。この転換により，政府はかかる企業の株主となる。政府機関のコーポラタイゼーションの結果の1つとしては，政府企業のほとんどの決定から行政法にそった精査と審査を取り除くことが挙げられる[8]。

　しかし，コーポラタイゼーションは何かの終わりというよりも始まりを表しているようだ。ファラーとマッカビーを以下に引用する[9]。

　　「コーポラタイゼーションは，1つの視点からは，所有権を維持しつつ，公的セクターにおける効率性を追求する動力の拡大とみることができる。他の視点から見ると，コーポラタイゼーションは民営化のお粗末な代わりにすぎない。」
さらに[10]，

　　「コーポラタイゼーションは商業化政策の一環であり，その商業化政策とは自由化政策または経済の規制緩和の一環である。コーポラタイゼーションは，民間セクターを効率性の手本とし，可能な限り民間セクターの会社を模倣することを目指している。しかし，模倣は模倣にすぎない。低価で監督できないことおよび政治的干渉の存在のため，コーポラタイゼーションされた組織は，民間セクターにあるそれに相当する組織と比べて，その組織運営費の観点から見てほぼ不可避的に効率性の面において劣る。」

　民営化は企業体を行政法に従った精査と審査の最後の残滓から解放する。民間セクターの新しい構成員となった民営化された企業体は，その商業活動に対して適用される一般法に服する。ある場合には，それで十分でありうる。競争市場の原則により望ましい効率性が得られる場合がある。しかし，市場が停滞した場合，効率性を期待できる理由はない。私的独占の結果を緩和することをもくろんだ新しい形態の規制を作ることを考慮しなければならない。

1　競争政策

　1995年4月11日にオーストラリア政府評議会（以下，COAGとする。）[11]は，フレッ

ド・ヒルマー教授が議長を務めた独立諮問委員会によるオーストラリア経済に関する詳細な勧告[12]に従い，全国競争政策を採択した。全国競争政策は，オーストラリア経済における効率性は，競争に対する障害を取り除くことにより高められるという哲学に基づいている。この政策の主要な要素には以下のようなものがある。

- 1974年（連邦）通商慣行法第四編の反競争的規定の範囲の拡大；
- 主要なインフラストラクチャーへアクセスする権利を認める全国的アクセス制度の確立；
- 競争に馴染み易い事業とそうでない事業を分離することで，政府による独占状態を再編し，前者には競争法を適用し，後者に対しては新しい規制制度を設ける；
- 公的および民間事業を同じ土台の上に置く（競争的な中立性）；および，
- 政府事業がかなりの程度の市場におけるシェアを保持している分野における政府事業の価格の監視。

全国競争政策のもとでは，オーストラリアの民営化された産業に対する新しい規制的枠組みの根幹は，競争法であり，それをインフラストラクチャーへのアクセスを認める新しい規定と「自然的独占」という残りの領域を扱うことを意図した経済規制上の新たな方策が補完している。

2 競 争 法

1974年（連邦）通商慣行法第四編は四つのタイプの制限的通商慣行を取り扱う。これらの規定は民営化された産業および，政府企業に対して通常適用される。

- 同法第45条は，実質的に競争を低下させる目的を持つまたは影響を与える契約，取り決め，合意を禁止する。
- 同法第45A，47および48条は，再販価格維持および価格差別を含む広範な価格協定慣行を禁止する。
- 同法第46条は物品およびサービスの市場で相当程度の力を有する企業による市場における力の濫用を禁止する。
- 同法第50条は，市場における集中を規制する。同条は，ある企業の株式または資産の取得が，その取得する側の企業に，オーストラリアにおける物品またはサービス市場を支配させるか，または，物品またはサービス市場での既存の支配を強化させる場合には，かかる取得を禁止する。

同法は，取り決めまたは取得から生じる公的利益が，それにより生じる公的損失を上回る場合には[13]，競争を低下させる取り決め（第45条），排他的な取り決め（第47条），および，合併および取得(第50条)を認める権限をオーストラリア競争および消費者委員会（以下，ACCCとする。）に付与している。ACCCの決定は，オーストラリア競争審判所による審査に服する[14]。

同法は「競争」に対する包括的な定義を与えていない。そこでは，当用語は輸入された物品およびサービスからの競争をも含むと述べられているにすぎない[15]。競争に関するいかなる事項を定義するにも，関連する「市場」の特定を要する。第41条は，「市場」とはオーストラリア市場を意味し，審査対象の代用となる物品およびサービスを含む，と規定する[16]。関連製品およびオーストラリア内でのかかる製品の市場の地理的広がりを特定することは，実際上の大変困難である[17]。

市場の構造もまた競争に関連する[18]。市場構造の二つの重要な側面は，集中と参入である。集中には，市場参加者の数，規模，配分および重要性の検討を要する。市場における集中が強ければ強いほど，いかなる取り決めまたは行為であっても競争の障害になる可能性が高くなる。参入は，ある市場に参加していない部外者がその市場で事業を開始することのできる可能性，あるいは，市場参加者がかかる市場においてその事業を拡大することのできる可能性のことをさす。参入に対する障壁となるあらゆる取り決めや慣行は競争を低下させることとなる。

民営化された産業はしばしば，集中と参入障壁で特徴付けられる市場と関わっている。1974年通商慣行法第四編はかかる市場でのそれら産業の行為を規制する。

3 インフラストラクチャーへのアクセス[19]

3.1 基本的設備理論

アメリカ合衆国の裁判所は，インフラストラクチャーの独占支配から生じる参入障壁に対処するために，シャーマン法第2条に基づいて基本的設備理論を発展させた。同理論は，（経済的な理由であれ，実際上の理由であれ）同様のインフラストラクチャーを築くことができず，かつ，かかるインフラストラクチャーへのアクセスが市場参入のために必要とされる場合は，新規参入者になりうる者に合理的な条件でアクセス権を与えるというものである。

オーストラリアでは，合衆国において基本的設備理論を生じさせた自然的独占の特徴は，送電網，天然ガスパイプライン，通信網，鉄道，港湾および空港の分野に

おいてにみられる。ヒムラー報告書は多くの産業においてインフラストラクチャーへのアクセスが欠けているために競争が阻止されているとした。しかし同時に同報告書は，現行の競争法（特に1974年通商慣行法第46条）は，合衆国における基本的設備理論に相当する基本的設備理論を包含していないと記した。したがって，同報告書はアクセス制度の規定を含むよう1974年通商慣行法を改正するよう勧告した。

勧告は1995年（連邦）競争政策改正法により実施され，同法は1974年通商慣行法に第三A編を挿入した。第三A編は，鉄道網，送電網，および，天然ガスパイプラインといった基本的設備によって供給されるサービスへのアクセスを認める三つの仕組みが定められている。それら3つの仕組みとは，アクセス宣言，アクセスの保証および効率的なアクセス制度上の手続きである。これらの仕組みは相互に排他的である。つまり，基本的設備はいかなる場合であってもこれらの3つのうち2つ以上の制約を受けることはない。

3.2 アクセス宣言

アクセス宣言は，指名された大臣，通常は連邦の大臣であるが，時として州機関により提供されるサービスに関する場合には州の首相により宣言される[20]。アクセスを求める者は，全国競争評議会（以下，NCCとする。）に対してサービスを宣言する勧告を求めて申し立てをなすことができる[21]。そのような勧告を出す前にNCCは以下の条件が満たされていることを確認しなければならない。

- サービスに対するアクセスが，求められているサービスの市場以外の市場における競争を促進するであろうこと；
- サービスを提供するためにもう一つの設備を作る事がいかなる者にとっても不経済であること；
- 設備が，その規模，国内または国際貿易・通商に対する重要性，または国内経済に対する重要性の面で，全国的な観点から見て重要であること；
- アクセスが健康および安全に不当な危険を生じさせないこと；および，
- アクセスが公益に反しないこと[22]。

指名された大臣に対してNCCからアクセス勧告が出された場合，大臣もまた，宣言をなすか否かを決める際に上記事項を検討しなければならない[23]。サービスに対するアクセス宣言が出されれば，アクセスを求める者は設備の所有者とアクセスに関する交渉に入ることができる。合意に至らない場合は，ACCCによる拘束力ある仲

裁を求めることができる[24]。ACCCは，サービスに対するアクセスの条項および条件を決定する際に以下の事項を検討しなければならない。
  ・サービス提供者の正当な事業利益および設備に対する投資；
  ・競争による公益；
  ・サービスを利用する権限を現に有している者すべての利益；
  ・アクセスを提供するために直接かかる経費；
  ・アクセスの拡大の費用がサービス提供者以外の者により出される場合，かかる拡大がかかるサービス提供者にもたらす価値；
  ・設備の安全かつ信頼に足る運用のための要件；
  ・設備を経済上効率的に運用するための要件；および，
  ・ACCCが関係があると考えるその他のすべての要因[25]。
連邦の大臣およびACCCの決定はオーストラリア競争審判所の審査に服する[26]。

3.3 アクセスの保証

アクセスの保証は，現存のまたは予定されているサービスに関してサービスの提供者によりなすことができる[27]。そのような保証が効果を持つのは，ACCCが承認した場合だけであり，ACCCは以下の事項を検討する事を要する。
  ・サービス提供者の正当な事業利益；
  ・競争による公益；
  ・サービスへのアクセスを望むであろう者の利益；および，
  ・ACCCが関係があると考えるその他のすべての要因[28]。

3.4 効率的なアクセス制度

効率的なアクセス制度上の手続きは，あるサービスのための既存のアクセス制度を認識するためのものである。この手続きには，NCCによる勧告および指名された大臣による決定が関わる[29]。NCCおよび大臣の双方は，連邦，州および準州により1995年に締結された競争原則合意第6項に定められている関連原則を適用しなければならない。それらには以下のものが含まれる。
  ・同様の設備を築くことが経済的に実行可能か否か；
  ・他の市場での効率的な競争を促すためにサービスへのアクセスが必要か否か；
  ・設備が，その規模，国内または国際貿易・通商に対する重要性，または国内経

済に対する重要性の点において，全国的な観点からみて重要であるか否か；
- 安全なアクセスが可能か否か；
- 設備が州境または準州境を越える影響を有するか否か；
- 設備の位置関係からかなりの困難が複数の領域で生じるか否か。

　州のアクセス制度が1974年通商慣行法第三A編の目的から鑑みて効率的なアクセス制度ではない，と指名された大臣が決定した場合は，かかる決定は，オーストラリア競争審判所による審判に服する[30]。

3.5　天然ガス全国第三者アクセスコード

　1997年11月7日に，連邦，州および準州は，天然ガスパイプライン制度のための全国第三者アクセスコード（以下，コードとする。）の創設を規定する天然ガスパイプライン合意を締結した。かかる合意に従って，南オーストラリア州議会は，1997年（南オーストラリア）ガスパイプラインアクセス法を制定し，コードに立法上の根拠を与え，連邦議会は同計画を実施するために1998年（連邦）ガスパイプラインアクセス法を制定した。

　同コードは，天然ガスの輸送および配給のための統一的な枠組みのもとで適用されるアクセスの原則を定めている。コードの適用を受けるパイプラインの所有者または運営者は規制当局とアクセスについての取り決めをしなければならない。輸送パイプラインの場合，規制当局はACCCである。アクセスの取り決めは，1974年通商慣行法第三A編のアクセス引き受けに類似しており，ガスの輸送と配給サービスに対するアクセスを可能とさせるための条項および条件が定められている。これらの条項および条件には，パイプラインの所有者または運営者により提供されるサービスの内容の記述，競争入札手続で決定されるか，コードの第8条に含まれる原則に従って定められるサービスに対する価格表，サービスに適用される条項および条件，および，パイプライン輸送量の管理に関する政策，パイプライン輸送量の取引に関する政策およびパイプライン輸送量のアクセスの優先順位に関する政策，が含まれなければならない。パイプライン輸送に関わるアクセスの取り決めはACCCの承認を得なければならないが，ACCCが承認を与えることができるのは，アクセスの取り決めがコードに規定されている最低限の要件を満たしているとACCCが認めた場合のみである。ACCCの決定はオーストラリア競争審判所の審査に服する。

3.6 ヴィクトリア州草案決定

　トランスミッション・パイプライン・オーストラリア社により提供される輸送サービスに対するアクセスに関して，1998年5月にACCCが出した草案決定は，天然ガスアクセス制度の重要性を明らかにした。同社はヴィクトリア州政府により保有されている。同社はヴィクトリア州の既存の高圧輸送パイプラインを所有し，維持管理している。この草案決定以前，ヴィクトリア州政府は，ヴィクトリア州のガス産業の民営化の一環として同社を売却する意思を示していた。草案決定では減価償却され最適化される代替費用100％ベースに対して税引き前の7％の返却率を提示した。これは，ヴィクトリア州政府によって示された10.16％をかなり下回るものであった。草案決定がもし採用されたなら，それはトランスミッション・パイプライン・オーストラリア社の予定していた歳入を約17％減少させるものとなり，同社の売却価格に約8億ドルの減少をもたらすであろう。ヴィクトリア州政府は，この問題が解決するまで，同社の民営化を延期している。

4　経済的規制

　ヴィクトリア州電力産業は，政府による独占の民営化とかかる産業への民間の参加者に適用される新しい規制の枠組み作りのケース・スタディとして役に立つ。1995年まで，電力産業はヴィクトリア州電力委員会（以下，SECVとする。）により政府による独占事業として運営されていた。SECVは，発電，送電，配給および販売に責任を持ち，さらに，技術面および安全面に対する規制にも責任を負っていた。

　1993年（ヴィクトリア州）電力産業法は，民営化に伴う電力産業の構造と規制に関して州政府の目的に効力を与えた。同産業の自然的独占要素を潜在的な競争要素から切り離すことを意図して構造上の変化がもたらされた。SECVは以下の組織にとってかわられた[31]。

- 発電にかかわる五つの個別の事業部門からなるジェネレーション・ヴィクトリア；
- 高電圧網を所有，維持，管理するために設立された送電網組織であるパワーネット・ヴィクトリア；
- 電力卸市場を監視，支配し，電力供給の安全を確保するための独立体であるヴィクトリア・パワー・エクスチェンジ；
- 以前のSECVの電力配分資産からなる，企業法に基づき形成された五つの地域

民間電力配給会社，および11の地域の電力引き受け会社；および
・限定された範囲での既存の契約上の責務を履行するヴィクトリア州電力委員会。

1993年電力産業法第12編は，当産業の規制を定めるが，電力産業は1994年（ヴィクトリア州）規制長官職法に服する規制産業であると規定する。さらに，第12編は，規制長官により運営される，発電，送電，配給，供給および販売に関する認可制度を確立した。

1994年（ヴィクトリア州）規制長官職法で宣言されている目的とは，
「競争および公正で効率的な市場行為を促進し保護する，また，競争的な市場が存在しない場合は，競争的市場行為への刺激と独占力の悪用の回避を助長する，規制産業に対する経済的な規制の枠組みの創設である。」
1933年電力産業法に基づく規制長官職の目的は以下の通りである[32]。
・発電，電気の供給および販売における競争の促進；
・発電，送電，電気の配給，供給および販売の効率的で経済的なシステムの維持の確保；
・電力価格，および，電力供給の安全性，信頼性並びに品質に関する消費者の利益の保護；および，
・財政的に実行可能な電力供給産業の維持を容易にすること。

換言すれば，電力産業に対する規制の枠組みは，電力産業の参加者とその顧客が商業上の成果を交渉することを促進している[33]。競争または顧客の利益のために市場力の濫用を正す必要がある場合にだけ，規制長官職が介入することとなる。

1994年規制長官職法第11条は，同職はヴィクトリア州議会の制定法に規定される場合を除いて，同職の機能の遂行に関して大臣の指示または支配に服さない，と規定している。

電力産業に関する規制長官職の主な権限は，電力サービスおよび電力供給の水準および条件，認可および市場行為に及ぶ[34]。同職は，かかる事項につき調査を行い，報告書を公表することができる[35]。また，決定および認可条件を実施にまで拡張して権限を及ぼせることができる[36]。政府および規制長官職の両方が，電力に関する料金表，課金および価格を規制する権限を有している[37]。1995年6月20日に，政府は料金表命令として知られる評議会命令の方法でその権限を行使し，その結果，当面規制長官職はかかる機能からはずされている。

ヴィクトリア州電力卸市場（以下，VicPoolとする。）の参加者の行為は，電力産業

により設けられ規制長官職により承認されたプール・ルールにより規制されている。同ルールは，参加の申請および参加者に対する許可，勧告要件，紛争解決，プールへの入札，発電者予定作り，発電者への支払い決定，顧客への課金，および，プール手数料を含む領域に及ぶ(38)。

　規制長官職はまた，電力産業により設けられたいくつかのコードも承認している。そのなかには，（電力システムの安全で確実な操業に関する）システム・コード，（プール参加者の中で移転される電力の算出を確保する）卸量測定コード，（安全で効率的で信頼できる送電制度の確保を図る）送電コード，（顧客にフランチャイズ権を与えるための電力販売条件を定めた）供給および販売コード，および，（新しい測定機の設置を規制する）小売料金表測定コードが含まれる(39)。

　1999年7月1日に全国電力市場が創設されることで，ヴィクトリア州の電力産業にもう1つの規制が適用される。1995年4月のCOAGの会合で連邦，州および準州政府により承認された全国競争政策には，全国送電網管理評議会により実行される電力の取り決めが含まれていた。それに続き，1996年5月には，ニューサウスウェールズ州，ヴィクトリア州，クイーンズランド州，南オーストラリア州およびオーストラリア首都準州の各政府は全国電力市場立法合意に至った。同合意に従って，南オーストラリア州は1996年（南オーストラリア州）全国電力法を制定し，それに引き続き，合意参加各州はそれぞれの法域で同法を採用した。同法は全国電力コードに効力を与え，コード参加者がコードの規定に違反したという事項を扱う全国電力審判所を設置した。

結　　論

　オーストラリアにおける政府による独占の民営化は規制緩和を伴うものではなかった。その代わりに，新たな課題に対応するために新しい規制制度が考案された。新しい制度は競争，市場および価格という概念に基づいている。時として「手際良い」と記されるが，これら制度はその性質および効果の点で決して単純なものでない。複雑さが，以前の制度と同じほど，新しい制度での特徴となっている。かかる制度の効果を判断するには早すぎる。しかし，明らかなことは，これら新しい方法はオーストラリアにおける政府に対する態度の根本的な変化を反映していることである。今まで政府による独占にゆだねられていた産業において，政府は適切に行為していなかったという前提の上に，これら制度は築かれた。それらは，自然的独占

に固有な問題を認識する一方で，政府による独占という解決策より，規制された私的独占という解決策を好んだのである。とりわけ，これら制度が示していることは，オーストラリアの公共政策のおいては，責務を負わせることよりも効率性の追求の方が優先されているということである。

(1) 例えば，Crommelin, M and Hunter, R, "Monopoly and Competition in Energy: Australia" *Journal of Energy and Natural Resources Law* (December 1989 Supplement) 135参照。
(2) Wettenhall, "Corporations and Corporatisation: An Administrative History Perspective" (1995) 6 *Public Law Review* 7.
(3) *Freedom of Information Act 1982* (Cth).
(4) *Ombudsman Act 1976* (Cth).
(5) *Administrative Appeals Tribunal Act 1975* (Cth).
(6) *Administrative Decisions (Judicial Review) Act 1977* (Cth).
(7) Wettenhall, R, "Corporations and Corporatisation: An Administrative History Perspective" (1995) 6 *Public Law Review* 7, 11に引用されている，Michael Howard, Statement before the Industrial Relations Commission of NSW (IRC No. 789 of 1993)。
(8) Allars, M, "Private Law But Public Power: Removing Administrative Law Review from Government Business Enterprises" (1995) 6 *Public Law Review* 44.
(9) Farrar, J and McCabe, "Corporatisation, Corporate Governance and the Deregulation of the Public Sector Economy" (1995) 6 *Public Law Review* 24 30.
(10) Ibid., 42.
(11) オーストラリア政府評議会は連邦，州および準州の長からなる。
(12) Independent Committee of Inquiry (Hilmer Committee), *National Competition Policy Review*, AGPS, Canberra, 1993.
(13) Section 88.
(14) Section 101.例えば，*Re AGL Cooper Basin Natural Gas Supply Arrangement* (1997) ATPR 41-593参照。そこでは，クーパー盆地採ガス地からの天然ガス合同マーケティング事業の認可を打ち切ったACCCの決定をオーストラリア競争審判所は破棄した。
(15) Section 4 (1).
(16) 物品およびサービスの代替性に対する決定の際には，価格および所得などの変化に応じて需要が変化する度合いが関連要因となる。
(17) 例えば，*Queensland Wire Industries Pty Ltd. v. The Broken Hill Proprietary Company Limited* (1989) 167 CLR 177参照。

(18) Rose, "Resources Joint Ventures and the Trade Practice Act 1974" (1991) 9 *Journal of Energy and Natural Resources Law* 95, 100-1.
(19) 本節は, McDonald, "Access to Gas Trunk Pipelines in Queensland" (1998) 17 *Australian Mining and Petroleum Law Journal* 138を利用している。
(20) *Trade Practices Act 1974* (Cth), s. 44H.
(21) Ibid., s. 44F.
(22) Ibid., s. 44G.
(23) Ibid., s. 44H.
(24) Ibid., s. 44V.
(25) Ibid., s. 44X.
(26) Ibid., s. 44K, 44L, 442P.
(27) Ibid., s. 4422A.
(28) Ibid.,
(29) Ibid., s. 44M.
(30) Ibid., s. 44O.
(31) *The Office of the Regulator-General Act 1994*第10条に基づく命令, Statement of Government Policy, 29 September 1994.
(32) Office of the Regulator-General, Electricity Regulatory Statement, 1 September 1995; *Electricity Industry Act 1993* s.157も参照。
(33) Ibid.
(34) *Office of the Regulator-General Act 1994*, s. 26.
(35) Ibid., ss. 28, 33.
(36) Ibid., ss. 35, 36.
(37) *Electricity Industry Act 1993*, ss. 158, 158A.
(38) Office of the Regulator-General, Electricity Industry Regulatory Statement, 1 September 1995.
(39) Ibid.

6 中国における現代市場経済と法治
―――過去の歩みと将来

劉 海 年
[渠　涛訳]

　　はじめに
　1　一般的考察
　2　中国の歩み
　3　目標，機会と挑戦
　　むすびにかえて

はじめに

　現代的市場経済体制及び法治制度は，いずれも人類社会の発展する過程において形成され打ち立てられたものである。これらの体制と制度の成立は人類が自然発展法則と社会発展法則に対する認識を向上させ，客観世界と主観世界を改造する過程において自ら運命を定める能力を向上させること，及び人類文明が新しい水準に到達したことなどを示している。

1　一般的考察

　歴史の発展過程を見れば，経済と法律とはいつも相互依存の関係にあり，経済は法の生成の基礎であり，反対に成立した法律は経済に反作用を及ぼす。つまり，「どの時代の経済生産及びそれによって構成された社会構造も，その時代の政治的ないし精神的な歴史の基礎である[1]」ので，これらの，経済基礎によって産出した上部構造と称される政治，法律，哲学及びその他の形の精神的なものはいったん成立すると，経済基礎に対する反作用，ならびにそれに対する奉仕が始まるものなのである。
　今日までの人類社会にはおよそ三種類の経済形態，すなわち，自然経済，生産品経済，市場経済が現れている。自然経済は農業を中心とする自給自足の閉鎖的経済であり，生産品経済，つまり計画経済は工業及び農業の生産水準が自然経済より高くなっているものの，全体的には低い水準にとどまっており，国家の経済計画によって生産が組織され，また，生産品が分配される経済体制である。市場経済は，近代的市場経済と現代的市場経済という二つの類型に分けることができる。近代的市場経済においては資本，労働力及び商品の分配などのすべてが完全に市場に委ねられ

ているのに対して，現代的市場経済においては国家が意識的，計画的，また一定の目的を持って市場をある程度指導しコントロールする役割を発揮している。このような役割は経済のマクロコントロールの手段として一定の役割を果たしているが，主導的な地位にあるものではない。

　上記の３種類の経済形態に相応して，３種類の性質が異なった法律制度が成立したのである。自然経済においては，生産は主に家庭，荘園または村を基本単位としていたため，そこにいる人々は生産者であると同時に生産品の消費者でもあり，また，作業の専門化，分業化が進んでいなかったため，各種経済組織の間の連携が緩やかで，人々は狭い閉鎖的な環境の中で生活していた。そこにおける人々の社会的関係を調節する規則は主に血縁関係をきずなとする同族支配の制度とそれを基礎に成立した法律であった。そのいずれも独断性，階級性及び残忍な刑罰手段を伴っており，これによって多数を占める生産者が少数の支配階級に依存するという関係を維持させていた。一方，生産品経済は，自然経済が崩壊し，市場経済が西側諸国に形成し始めたにもかかわらず，数多くの弊害も同時に現れたという情勢のもとで世界の東方，たとえば旧ソ連，東ヨーロッパの旧社会主義諸国及び中国などの国で現れた経済形態である。これらの国々では，革命という手段によって自然経済から脱出しようとしているものの，経済の発展水準が未だ立ち後れていたため，また，自国の現代化過程において西側諸国の発展過程に現れていた生産の無秩序，残酷な競争，貧富の極端な分化及び経済・政治の独占などの弊害を回避するために高度集権的な計画経済体制が作り出されたのである。この体制は，農業の協同化，私営工業・商業の公有化，及び国家所有制経済を基礎とし，生産と分配が高度集権的な計画に基づいて行われるものである。このような体制設計の初志はすばらしいものであるというべきであろうが，これらの国々での実践過程においては次第に自国の発展条件を無視するようになり，「政治と経済が一体化し，経済が政治の付属品になる[2]」といった本末転倒の現象が現れるようになったのである。このようになった社会においては，上から下までへの経済計画及び生産品分配を貫徹する行政命令と行政指示がむやみに膨張し，「法治」といったところか，簡単な法律制度でさえ邪魔物としか扱われてなくなり，その結果としては，人々に忌避される正真正銘の「人治」が出現するようになったのである。

　しかし，現代的市場経済は法治の「陣痛促進剤」である。つまり，現代市場経済の法治に対する要求はその質からいっても，量からいっても以下のように自然経済

または生産品経済よりはるかに上回るということである。
① 生産品経済のもとでは，憲法及び法律に自由に関する規定が設けられているものの，農民，労働者ないし企業の一般従業員，国家幹部ないし政府機関の従業員は，それぞれその所在の地域，企業または政府機関に対する依存度が高いため，それによる自由の制限を受けざるを得ない。しかし，現代的市場経済は，商品交換経済であるため，市場に進出するものが自己の商品と労働力を商品として自由に販売できる市場を必ず必要とし，また，自然経済及び生産品経済の社会の大多数の人にとっては考えられないほどの人の自由が要求される。つまり，独立した人格を有する人の自由が確実に保障されなければならないということである。
② 市場に進出し，自由に取り引きをなすものがその販売する目的物に対して所有権を有するものでなければならない。したがって，法主体たる資格ばかりではなく，明晰な財産権関係も法律によって確立されなければならないということである。
③ 商品交換の実現と市場の経済の健全な運営には，良好な契約関係と相互信頼関係を欠かすことができない。これらの経済的関係を超えたものは完備した債権法によって保護されなければならない。
④ 現代的市場経済は利益の獲得を中心とする経済である。このようなハイテク時代の今日の複雑な社会環境の中では，いかなる投資者にもその投下資本の収益，また新しい技術の導入に対する関心が高まっているので，競争の過激化が予想され，また，各分野での競争が公平に行われるように，血縁や親族友人等の関係の公平競争に対する影響を除去し，さらに権力と経済の独占による経済の崩壊を防ぐために，公平競争を保障する法律が不可欠である。
⑤ 競争は発展と利益をもたらすが，その反面，優勝劣敗という原則のもとで必ず一部分のものが淘汰される。社会の継続的発展，また発展に安定的で良好な環境を獲得するためには，競争に失敗したもの，及び社会における弱者に対して有効な社会的保障を提供しなければならない。つまり，社会保障に関する法制度を整備する必要がある。
⑥ 現代的市場における各種法主体が激しい競争の中で利益の最大化を追求するため，私人相互間のいがみ合いが避けられないばかりではなく，場合によっては国家または社会的利益を損するまで私的利益を求めることも現れるであろう。

このようにさまざまな利益の衝突を生じることは完全に回避できないが，その衝突の拡大化，過激化は押さえられなければならない。そのため，市場に進出する法主体の行為規範を定め，衝突する各方面の利益的要求に対して公正に裁決することが必要である。つまり，これによって，現代的市場経済の発展に必要な秩序を整備しなければならない。

⑦　現代的市場経済が計画経済に代替することは計画を完全に拒否するという意味ではない。それは，「計画も市場もあくまでも手段であるに過ぎない[3]」ので，市場経済における競争の盲目性，資源と社会労働力の浪費，及び社会の不安定等の副作用を回避するためには，国家の経済発展に応じたマクロコントロール及び計画による関与は必要である。したがって，国家は市場に対するマクロコントロールに関する法律を制定しなければならない。

⑧　市場経済の発展は，市場に密接な関係のある民事法，経済法及び関係行政法規を必要とする以外に，市民の基本的な権利の保護，政府行為の規範，社会秩序の維持，及び環境資源の保護などの法律も必要である。これらの法律をもって，現代的市場経済の運営に良好な外部条件と社会環境を提供し，経済の安定的かつ秩序のある発展を保障する。

現代における各国の市場経済の発展は，国際市場に密接な連係を必要とし，また，グローバル化も進んでいるところである。これは，国際取引において共通の規則の遵守を要求するばかりではなく，政治，文化などの分野の法律も国際的一致性が要求されるようになっている。これが各国における市場経済の発展の外部的条件であると同時に，外部からの一種の促進力でもある。

2　中国の歩み

中国の歴史上では，小農制農業を基礎とする自然経済が長期にわたって存在し，かつて輝かしい時代もあったものの，この200年来の発達してきた西側資本主義国家に比べて，中国の経済がいつも立ち後れた状態に陥っている。1949年の革命が成功した後，短期間の経済回復期を経て，生産品経済体制が打ち立てられた。この体制はかつて経済発展にある程度の活気を引き起こし，また，自然経済よりはるかに進歩したものであるにもかかわらず，一時期は，経済発展に関する自然法則が完全に無視されたため，盲目的に経済の躍進をはかり，高い投下のかわりに収益が低く，大量の資源と労力を浪費して最終的には窮地に陥ってしまったのである。「文化大革

命」の終息,特に1978年以降,中国は過去に対して深く反省し,「左」の指導思想の誤りを是正して「事実求是」という指導思想と路線を確立した。それと同時に,経済建設を中心とする方針を打ち立てる一方で,現代的法律制度の整備にも力を注いできた。この20年の過程をおよそ以下のように3段階に分けることができる。

1 第1段階(1978年～1992年)

1978年の中国共産党第11期第3回中央委員会全体会議では,1950年代以来のいわゆる「階級闘争をかなめとする」という政治路線が終息し,全国の活動の重点が経済建設に移されるようになり,また,過去の硬直した計画経済体制も放棄されるようになった。改革は,最初に農村で家庭を基本単位とする生産量運動の請負生産責任制が行われたが,農村で一定の成果を収めた後,都市へ推し進められていった。改革の実践によって,現代化を実現させるには,商品経済を発展させなければならないと認識されるようになって,経済界でも「計画経済を主とし,市場調節を補助とする」命題や「計画経済と商品経済との結合」,さらに「商品経済を主とし,計画経済を従とする」などの理論,観点が提起され,そのいずれも国家政策に援用された。中国の経済は模索しながら進んでいるが,それに相応して法制建設も急速に展開している。法制建設の初期段階では,社会全体に「文化大革命」で権利が恣意的に侵害されたことについて記憶に新しいので,自己の権利が法律に保障されるよう,社会の秩序が少なくとも50年代の水準に回復されるように期待していた。1978年,鄧小平は「有法可依,有法必依,執法必厳,違法必究(依るべき法があるべし,法がありて従うべし,法の執行は厳しくすべし,違法に対し追究すべし)[4]」という16文字の方針を提起した。この方針は重要であり,中国の法制建設に深く影響している。しかし,この方針の中の「依るべき法があるべし」は立法の緊急性のみが強調されているので,この立法の最初の段階に成立した法律については「大雑把に制定し,そして逐次に完備していく[5]」しか選択の余地がないように思われる。この段階では,憲法の改正が行われたほか,刑法,刑事訴訟法,及び経済関係を調整する法律,たとえば,民法通則,経済契約法,渉外経済契約法などが制定された。しかし,立法者は,これらの法律をできる限り経済発展の需要に応えうるよう努力はしたが,従来の計画経済体制からの影響が完全に除去されていなかった時代であったので,一部分の法律は制定されてまもなく,さらに公布された時から改革の現状との間に齟齬が現れていた。

2　第2段階（1992年〜1997年）

　中国が社会主義市場経済の建設を正式に打ち出したのは1992年である。また，この年に開かれた中国共産党第14期全国代表大会は，改革開放，特に社会主義市場経済の本質が社会主義か，それとも資本主義かに関する論争に対し，鄧小平によって提出された「社会主義社会の生産力の発展，社会主義国家の総合的な国力の増強，人民生活水準の向上という3つに有利であるか否かによって決められる[6]」という基準をもって判断を下した。これによって，中国の改革開放の目標は社会主義市場経済の建設であると一層明確になったのである。このような情勢に応じて，第8期全国人民代表大会常務委員会は社会主義市場経済に適応する法律体系の構築に関する構想を打ち出し，また，具体的な立法計画も制定した。結果としては，第8期全国人民代表大会の任期内には，全国人民代表大会及びその常務委員会が採択した法律は85件，法律関係の問題に関する決定（日本の「通達」に相当——訳者）33件，計118件であった[7]。社会主義市場経済という目標の明確化，またこの目標を実現させるために尽力する人々の自覚性の向上によって，この時期に制定された法律の水準が明らかに高まっており，法制建設全体もすばらしい成果が収められている。また，経済関係，政治関係，行政関係，刑事関係，司法関係等の立法にはいずれも現代国家の有すべき法治の原則が数多く取りいれられている。しかし，「市場経済に適応する法律体系」は立法指針として，過去の「依る法があるべし」よりは具体的になっており，また，立法機関により明確な基準を与えているとはいえるが，完全なものであるとはいえないように思われる。つまり，この「市場経済に適応する法律体系」の範囲については，法学者と実務家との間が従来から一致した認識にいたっておらず，これが法制建設という歴史的任務の全体に対する認識，また法制建設の具体的な作業に影響しかねないと考えるからである。

3　第3段階（1997年〜現在）

　1997年に開かれた中国共産党第15期全国代表大会では，社会主義初期段階の経済，政治，文化等に関する基本路線と綱領を制定し，社会主義体制の下で中国の経済を発展させることを再度強調した。また，「民主の強化，社会主義法制度の整備，『依法治国（法に基づいて国を治める）』，社会主義法治国家の建設」などが強調された。さらに，「立法作業の強化，立法の水準の向上をはじめ，2010年に中国の特色のある社会主義法律体制を打ち立てる[8]」という目標を定めたのである。これは，中国の法

制建設の趣旨が単に「社会主義市場経済の法律体系」のみではなく,「中国の特色のある社会主義法律体系」であることを示したのである。この法律体系は,社会主義法治国家に不可欠な一部分であり,現代の法治原則に基づいて構築されなければならない。現在,中国の法制建設は,まさにこの第3段階の起点から出発したところである。

4 小 括

20年来,中国では,現代的市場経済を構築するという目標のもとで,経済改革と法制建設が協調した歩みですすめられてきた。ここ十数年来の中国経済が継続的な高速成長を維持しえたのも,この二者の協調関係を重視したことに深く関係するものである。このように,中国が未だに社会主義初期段階にとどまっているという認識を前提にした二者の協調関係こそ,経済の発展を維持させることができたばかりでなく,社会の安定も同時に維持でき,さらに,一部分の国で改革の過程において現れた経済の崩壊,社会の動乱,及び政局の不安定を回避することができたと考えられる。いうまでもなく,安定を前提にしていたため,法律による政治体制改革の推進のプロセスがうまく機能しておらず,全体からいえば,政治体制の改革が経済体制改革より立ち後れている。つまり,「人治」から法治への転換の歩みは幅が小さく,速度も遅いものであった。今日,中国社会の世論の関心を集めた腐敗現象もこれに関係がないといえないであろう。このような現象に対して迅速に認識を高め,自覚を強め,断然とした措置を取らなければ,今後は思わぬ重大な代償を払わなければならなくなるであろう。

3 目標,機会と挑戦

1996年に開かれた第8期全国人民代表大会第4回会議,及び中国共産党第15期全国代表大会は,改革開放以来の経験を総括して,まもなく到来する21世紀における中国の発展に壮大な目標を立てた。この目標を実現させる過程においては,良い機会にもめぐまれるであろうが,厳しい挑戦となることも予想される。中国人民にとって,いかに機会を逃さず,挑戦していくかが今後の5年,10年,20年ないし50年の光栄の歴史的任務である。

1 目標——今後の発展に関する全体的設計

(1) 経済建設に関する目標

1996年の第8期人民代表大会第4回会議では、「中国国民経済と社会発展の第9回5か年計画と2010年までの長期目標に関する綱要」が批准され、その主な内容は以下のようなものである[9]。つまり、①第9回5か年計画期間内に、現代化建設に関する第2段階のマクロプランを全面的に実現させることで、②2000年の時点に、人口が1980年に比べて3億人が増えるという状況のもとで、1人当たりの国民総生産を1980年より4倍増にすること、③基本的に貧困を消滅させ、人民の生活を「小康[10]」という水準に到達させること、④現代企業制度の建設を早め、初歩的な社会主義市場経済体制を完成させること、国民総生産は2010年の時点に2000年の2倍増にし、人民の「小康」という生活水準をさらに豊かにし、比較的に完全な形の社会主義市場経済体制を完成させ、さらに、次の世紀の中葉に現代化を基本的に実現させるための基礎を打ち立てる、などということである[11]。

このような経済的目標は中国に以下のことの実施を要求する。つまり、「社会主義公有制を主体とする多種類所有制の経済が共に発展できるような基本的経済制度を堅持し、完備させなければならない。また、社会主義市場経済体制を整備し、資源の配置が国家のマクロコントロールのもとで主に市場によってなされるようにし、労働に応じた分配を中心にすえるが、同時に多種類の分配方式も完備させ、一部分の地域または一部分の人が率先して豊かになることを認め、それによって社会全体が豊かになることを徐々に実現させる。さらに、改革開放を堅持し、国際社会での協同関係、及び競争に積極的に参与する[12]」などということである。

(2) 政治及び行政改革に関する目標

この人民代表大会の会議ではこのような経済体制改革及び中国の発展に関する任務が提出されたと同時に、政治体制の改革に関する目標も提出されている。つまり、「民主の強化、社会主義法制度の整備、『依法治国(法に基づいて国を治める)』、社会主義法治国家の建設」であり、「人民が国家の権力を掌握し管理するため、民主的選挙、民主化した政策の決定、民主的管理、及び民主的監督を実現しなければならず、人民が法に依り幅広く権利と自由を享受することを保障し、人権を尊重し保護しなければならない[13]」。これらの政治、及び経済の目標の実現は、憲法に定められた「中国を富強、民主、文明の社会主義国家に建設する」という歴史的任務を遂行することに重要な役割を果たすものである。

一方、政府機関に対して、法に基づく行政の執行、市場経済の要求に応じた政府

機能の転換,機構の簡素化,効率向上を推進,国家機構の組織,定員,活動プロセスなどの法定化の実現,人民へのサービス水準の向上,公民の権利の確実な保障など,が要求されている。

(3) 法制建設に関する目標

経済及び政治の改革に関する上記の目標を達成するには,制度の改革と整備はもちろん,政治経済制度を調節し制御する手段なる法律も必要であり,つまり,法治が実現しなければならない。したがって,上記の政治経済改革の目標とともに前述した「立法作業の強化,立法の水準の向上をはじめ,2010年までに中国の特色ある社会主義法律体制を打ち立てる」という法制建設に関するの目標も打ち出されている。また,司法改革について,専門人員の育成および制度の完備を通して,司法機関が法に基づいて裁判権または検察権等を公正かつ独立して行使できることを保証する。さらに,全人民の法律意識および法制観念を高め,特に高級幹部の法制観念及び法に基づいて日常政務を執行する水準を高める一方で,民主監督の制度,及び法に基づく権力の行使メカニズムの整備が重要であり,つまり,公平,公正,公開という原則を堅持し,憲法と法律による監督を強化し,国家法律の統一を保たなければならない。

2 機会——現在の有利な条件

上記の目標を達成するには以下のような有利な条件が備えられていると考える。

① 「依法治国」及び社会主義法治国家の建設はすでに国策と目標として定められており,また全国の人民大衆に深く浸透している。全国各地の至るところでは,「依法治省」,「依法治市」,「依法治県」,「依法治郷」,「依法治廠（工場）」,「依法治水」,「依法治山」などのスローガンが掲げられ,また,民間の支持が得られている。

② 法律普及の教育及び市場経済発展の実践を通して,公民の権利意識が日増しに強くなり,自己の経済,政治,文化社会,及び身分的な各種権利と自由の保護を法律に求めることは一般的になっている。

③ 香港はすでに1997年に中国に回帰し,マカオは1999年12月に回帰する。また,台湾も最終的に平和的な統一が実現するであろう。この3つの地域の法律は中国大陸の法律とは,性質上,さらに形式上(たとえば,香港とマカオはコモン・ローである)が異なっているが,そのいずれも基本的には現代法治社会が形成されて

いる。これらの地域の回帰，及び平和統一によって，これらの地域と中央政府及び内陸の各地との間の関係が一層密接になることが予想され，また，これによって国家全体の法治水準が高められていくと思われる。

④ 中国の市場経済の発展は，国際市場と一層緊密に連携していき，さらに，国際市場との一体化がある程度実現すると考えられる。中国は，国連安全保障理事会の常任理事国として，これまで，国際上の事務に積極的に参与して正義を主張してきた。かつて17件の人権に関する条約を含む一連の国際条約に加入し，また，1997年には「経済的・社会的および文化的権利に関する国際規約」に加入し，さらに，最近，銭其琛副総理と江沢民主席が相前後して，中国が近いうちに「市民的および政治的権利に関する国際規約」に加入することを宣言している。いかなる国際条約への加入も加入国が一定の国際的義務を負うことを意味するものである。このような国際市場との経済上の密接な関係，及び政治上の国際的義務の負担は，その国の国内法に対して数多くの内容に関し，国際社会との一致性，先進国の立法経験の借用などを要求する。その結果としては，中国の法律が必然的に国際上通用する法制度と同一方向に帰していくであろう。このような傾向は私法領域にとどまらず，公法の領域にも及び，そのうち，人権保障も中国法の重要な内容の一つとなるであろう。

⑤ 中国は，この20年の弛まぬ努力を経て，憲法を中心とし，行政，民事，経済，刑事，及び社会保障関係の基本的法律を支柱とする法律体系の枠組みが打ち立てられている。その中には，確かに改正され，または改めて制定しなければならないものが一部存在するものの，数多くは中国社会主義初期段階の経済，政治，及び文化の発展に相応するものである。今日の中国では，法律面からいえば，20年前，ないし10年前のような「依るべき法がない」，または法律が不備な状況よりはかなり改善されている。また，各分野において依るべき法規定が存在することはいうまでもなく，法律の制定及び実施を通して，法治に関する新しい情報を得ており，法治に関する豊富な経験を積んでいる。

⑥ また，長年の努力によって，中国では立法，司法，弁護士，及び法学研究と教育などの方面の人材が数多く育成されている。これらの人材は新しい世紀における中国の現代的法治建設の中堅になると思われる。

3 挑戦——解決すべき問題

中国では，現代的市場経済に相応する法治制度の建設が，数多くの有利な条件と機会に恵まれているものの，以下のように数多くの問題（＝挑戦）に直面している。

① 中国の歴史は，小農業を中心とする自然経済である。1840年から半封建半植民地に陥って以降，民族資本の発展が一部見られ，官僚と深く係わりのあるいわゆる官僚資本も登場して，社会全体が半自然経済の状態になっていった。新中国が成立した1949年以降，生産品経済が実行され，生産と分配においては国家が主導的地位を占めていた。このような社会基盤の上で現代的市場経済を発展させるには，既存の社会的条件に依存することができなく，経済発展の法則の認識に基づいて政府主導で経済発展を推し進めていかざるをえない。これは，経済発展の漸進性を決めると同時に，法律によってこの種の経済形態を形成させる基礎が打ち立てられることを求めなければならない。現在農村で実行している家庭を基本単位とする生産量運動の請負生産責任制と村民自治の制度，及び市・町における個人工商業経営者の権利の保障，国有企業の所有権と経営権との確実的な分離の実現などは，市場経済の形成と発展の基礎であるので，国家がこれらを十分重視しなければならない。

② 中国は2000年以上の封建専制主義の歴史を有する国であり，長期にわたって「人治」が隆盛し，そのような時代の法律は，統制を中心にして義務が重視される反面，権利は軽視されており，あくまでも支配者の道具であったに過ぎない。封建帝王の独断専行で，その言葉が法であり，また，全国では，そのような法が家族の家訓と融合して施行されていた。このような状況は1949年以降かなり変わってきているが，生産品経済体制のもとで，国家の主な活動の内容は経済計画の制定及び執行であったため，法律の内容は依然として統制と義務を重視するものが存在していた。このようなものが今日の現行法にも一部残留している。現代的市場経済を発展させるには，如何に立法の民主化を実現させ，権利を基礎とし権利と義務を有機的に結合した法律を制定し，さらに，その法律を如何に国家の指導者，官僚・役人から人民大衆まで同等に遵守される行為基準にするかは，今後解決しなければならない問題である。

③ 中国は13億の人口，56の少数民族，広大な国土を有する大国であるため，経済，政治，文化の発展が大変不均衡な状態になっている。中国で現代的市場経済の発展，及び法治国家の建設には，各民族，各地域，各級の幹部及び人民大

衆の一致した認識と協同した行動が不可欠であり，また，中央政府と地方政府がともに努力することが必要である。中央と地方との関係，各政府部門の内部と外部の関係を如何にうまく処理するか，また，一部分の政府部門また地方政府が立法，司法，及び法の執行を自己の権力への保護と拡大の道具にして法律の有効性，及び統一した市場の形成に悪影響を及ぼすことを如何に防ぐか，なども今後解決しなければならない問題である。

④　中国では，経済体制改革が絶えず深化している中，政治体制改革も徐々に進められているため，社会関係の多くは変化しており，また引き続き変化していくことと思われる。しかし，法律制度としては安定が望ましく，朝令暮改は法律の権威を揺るがすに違いない。一方，改革は必ず変化を伴っており，さもなければ，経済と政治の発展が阻害されるに違いない。したがって，この両者の関係を如何に処理するかも今後真剣に研究し解決されるべき問題である。

⑤　中国の改革は上から下へ，つまり，政府の統一した指導のもとで進められてきたものである。この偉大な改革を成功裏に収めるためには，常に政府の指導を強化しなければならない。しかし，現在の指導体制の基盤は生産品経済体制の強い影響のもとで打ち立てられたものである。したがって，改革に対する指導を強化するためには，現行の指導体制に対する改革も必要であり，これをもって政府機能を転換させ，市場経済の発展に適応させる。

⑥　生産品経済体制下の社会分配関係は，実質的にはその体制での地位によって決められていた。今日に至っても，公共権力機構には，職位が分配の主な基準とされている。指導体制に対する改革は，必ず一部分の職位の高い改革者の個人的な利益にも影響を及ぼし，この部分の人からの改革に対する抵抗が予想される。したがって，改革を引き続き，順調に推し進めるには，如何にこの関係をうまく処理するかも今後研究し解決しなければならない問題である。

⑦　中国の市場経済と国際市場に連係し一体化する過程は，ばら色の平坦な道ではなく，種々の良い機会もあるものの，危険ないし落とし穴も存在するに違いない。これは，われわれの国際市場に関する知識の不足によるものだけではなく，一部分の国が自己の市場に他国の進出を拒絶することや，さらに一部の巨大な国際的投機集団が中国を含む発展途中の国における現代化の実現を好ましく思っていないことによるものであるように思われる。このような国際情勢のもとで，中国にとっては，大胆に良い機会を利用して開拓すると同時に，如何

に危険ないし落とし穴を避けるかが重要な課題である。つまり，この過程において，如何にわが国における市場経済の保障メカニズムを整備し，また，他の国と連携し，すでに発生または発生が予想される経済的危機に対して経済的または法律的措置を事前に備えて，国際市場が健全に運営され，世界経済の持続的発展に貢献することも真剣に考えなければならないことである。

むすびにかえて

現代的市場経済及び法治の建設を目的とする今日の中国の改革は，古今に未曾有な事業であるが，波瀾万丈に展開されている。この改革の過程において種々の困難，及び厳しい挑戦に直面しているにもかかわらず，改革への決意が固められ，方向も明らかになっており，成功への道も開けているため，中国各民族の協同の奮闘によって必ず予期した目的に達成すると固く信じている。

(1) 『マルクスエンゲルス著作集（中国版）』第1巻232頁。
(2) 張文顕著『法学基礎範疇の研究』（中国政法大学出版社）309頁（1993年）。
(3) 『鄧小平文選』第3巻373頁。
(4) 『鄧小平文選』（1975〜1982年）136頁（括弧内の訳は訳者によるものである）。
(5) 同上137頁。
(6) 『鄧小平文選』第三巻372頁。
(7) 田紀雲「全国人民代表大会常務委員会での工作報告」『人民日報』1998年3月25日。
(8) 『中国共産党第15期全国代表大会資料集』人民出版社33〜34頁（1997年）。『国民経済と社会発展の第9回5か年計画及び2010年までの長期目標綱要に関する報告（単行本）』（人民出版社，1996年）14頁。『中国共産党第15期全国代表大会資料集』（人民出版社，1997年）19頁。『中国共産党第15期全国代表大会資料集』（人民出版社）31〜32頁（1997年）。
(9) 以下の内容は，『国民経済と社会発展の第9回5か年計画及び2010年までの長期目標綱要に関する報告（単行本）』（人民出版社）14頁（1996年）参照。
(10) 中国では，古代から生活の豊かさが「貧困，温飽，小康，大同」といった4段階に分けられている。
(11) 『中国共産党第15期全国代表大会資料集』（人民出版社）19頁（1997年）。『中国共産党第15期全国代表大会資料集』（人民出版社）31〜32頁（1997年）。
(12) 『中国共産党第15期全国代表大会資料集』（人民出版社）31〜32頁（1997年）。
(13) 同上31〜32頁（1997年）。

7 韓国における行政規制改革の現状と展望

梁　承　斗

　はじめに
1　韓国の行政規制改革の現状
2　展　　望

はじめに

　この小論は，早稲田大学比較法研究所創立40周年を記念する，『自由市場と法的規制』との主題の国際シンポジウムで報告した，1998年8月現在の，「韓国においての行政規制改革の現状と展望」を略述するものである。

1　韓国の行政規制改革の現状

1　行政規制改革の推進経緯

　1980年代のはじめから世界各国では過渡なる規制は経済活動の公正性と効率性を沮害するとの認識から規制に対する批判的視覚が強くなり規制を廃止または緩和すべきであるとの議論が活発に展開された。
　韓国においても経済発展がめざましい成功をおさめるにしたがって社会・経済的構造が多角化され，ことかさなる国際的貿易摩擦を克服するための国際化・開放化の要求と必要性が認められた。1980年代後半におよんで政府はこの方向に向っての発展を模索しはじめた。また政府は政府による度を過ぎる規制がむしろ国家競争力を沮害する障碍要因として作用するとの認識をもとに政府みずから行政規制を緩和ないし改善する努力をせざるを得なかった。
　このような努力の一環として金泳三政府は「企業活動規制緩和に関する特別措置法」(1993年) と「行政規制および民願事務基本法」(1994年) 等を制定・公布して規制改革の法的基盤を設けるとともに，行政刷新委員会・経済行政規制改革委員会・企業活動規制審議委員会等の規制改革機構なる行政委員会を設けて規制緩和の努力を本格化した。
　しかしこのような政府主導型の規制緩和作業ではいろんな種類の個別的な規制改

革推進機構が多元的に規制改革作業を推進した結果，総合的で一貫した作業が出来ないとの欠陥を露呈した。たとえば1つの工場を設立するには金融，土地，工場設立許可，労働力の確保等かずかずの側面の行政過程が総合的にスムーズに進めらるべきであるのに，政府主導型規制緩和努力はこのようなプロジェクトに対する核心的規制に対する本質的検討作業が出来ない物足りなさがあった。のみならず既に在る規制を改革する作業と同時に，新く導入される規制に対する事前統制装置が不充分で客観的な検証作業なしに新しい規制がたやすく導入されるという問題点があった。

このような問題点を解消し既に在る規制の正当性とその成果を総体的に検証する作業をすると同時に常設的な民間主導型の規制改革システムを導入して規制改革を一貫的に，また，体系的に推進させるために金泳三政府は1997年8月22日に「行政規制基本法」を制定・公布し，引き続く金大中政府は相次いで「行政規制基本法施行令」を制定・施行した。また規制改革業務を専担させるために国務総理室の国務調停室に規制改革調停官室を新く設けた。ただ，産業資源部にある企業活動規制審査委員会は独自的に活動を続けるように存置している。

2 行政規制基本法の主な内容と規制改革推進現況
(1) 行政規制の原則

行政規制の基本原則――行政規制基本法は行政規制の基本原則として比例の原則と社会的規制の合理化を規定している（5条）。すなわち，国家または地方自治体は国民の自由と創意を尊重して規制を設ける場合にもその本質的内容を侵害しないようにすると同時に規制の対象と手段は規制の目的を実現する最少限の必要な範囲でもっとも効果的な方法によって客観性・透明性・公正性をたもつように「行政規制比例の原則」を定めている。また国民の生命・保健と環境等を保護するための規制に実効性を与えるように「社会的規制の合理化」を命じている。もう一つの画期的な原則はいわゆる5年間の「規制日没制(sun-set)」を採択したことである。したがって規制は原則的に5年間を限ることになった。

規制法定主義――また規制はかならず法律にその根拠をもたなければならず，その内容も理解しやすい言葉で具体的・明確に規定すべきであることを定めている（4条）。細部的な規制に関しては法律が具体的に範囲を定めて大統領令・総理令・部令又は条例・規則に委任する事が出来るのは勿論である。

ただ，専門的・技術的事項や軽微なる事項の場合には，業務の性質上委任すべき事項に関しては，具体的に範囲を定めて委任する場合に限って告示で定める事にした。

(2) 規制の範囲

改革すべき規制は，国家または地方自治体たる行政主体が特定の行政目的を実現するために法律・大統領令・総理令・部令とその委任によって定められた告示等（訓令・例規・告示・公告），または，条例・規則等を根拠として国民の権利を制限し，または，義務を賦課する行為と規定している（2条）。

ただ，次の事項には適用しないことにしている。即ち，

 1．国会，法院，憲法裁判所，選挙管理委員会および監査院が行う事務，
 2．刑事，刑法および保安処分に関する事務，
 3．兵役法，郷土予備軍設置法，民防衛基本法，非常対備資源管理法に依る徴集，召集，動員，訓練に関する事項，
 4．軍事施設，軍事機密保護および防衛産業に関する特別措置に関する事項，
 5．租税の種目，税率，賦課および徴収に関する事項，

等に関しては行政規制基本法を適用しないことに定めている。

(3) 規制の登録・公表

政府の中央行政機関の長は各各の中央行政機関別に所管の行政規制を規制改革委員会に，規制の根拠となる法令の公布または発令された日から30日以内に登録しなければならない。既に在る規制は規制改革委員会の要請があった日から90日以内に登録しなければならない。規制改革委員会は登録された規制事務目録を作成して公表するように定めた（6条）。規制事務目録は毎年2月の末まで規制改革委員会が官報に掲載，または，コンピュータ通信等を利用して国民に公表することになっている。

規制改革委員会が職権によって調査し，登録しなかった規制を発見した場合には関係中央行政機関の長にこれを遅滞なく委員会に登録させるか，または，その規制を廃止する法令等の整備計画を提出させることにしているし，関係中央行政機関の長は要求を受けた日から30日以内に登録するか，又は，整備計画を提出しなければならない。

(4) 規制の新設・強化に対する審査

意見収斂──中央行政機関は規制を新く設けるか，または，強化する場合には，

行政節次（手続）法が定める手続きによって公聴会，行政上立法予告の方法で民間団体，利害関係人，研究機関，専門家等の意見を十分に収斂しなければならない（9条）。

規制の存続期間の明示――規制を新設・強化する場合には規制を継続する明白な理由がない限りかならず規制の存続期間を明示するように定めている。存続期間は必要な最短期を設けるべきであり，その期間は5年を超過することが出来ないことにしている（8条）。

規制影響分析――中央行政機関の長は規制を新設・強化する場合には規制影響分析をしなければならない。

規制影響評価の要素（7条）は
① 規制の新設，または，強化の必要性，
② 規制目的の実現可能性，
③ 規制の代替手段の存在，および，既存規制との重複与否，
④ 規制の費用と便益の比較分析，
⑤ 競争制限的要素の有無，
⑥ 規制内容の客観性と明瞭性，
⑦ 行政機構・人力，および，予算の所要，
⑧ 関連民願事務の具備書類・処理節次等の適正性等

各項目を分析・評価することになっている。

自体審査――中央行政機関の長は規制影響分析の結果を基礎に規制の対象，範囲，方法等を決めてその妥当性に対して審査する。

規制審査請求――中央行政機関の長は新く設けられるか，または，強化される規制に関する規制影響分析，自体審査結果，行政機関・利害関係人の意見を添附して行政規制委員会に審査を要請しなければならない。すべての規制は法令にその根拠がなければならないので規制審査請求は法制処の法令案審査請求の前に規制審査を請求することになる。

行政規制改革委員会の審査――行政規制改革委員会はまず分科委員会において規制が重要規制であるかを審査（予備審査）する。重要規制の場合には全体会議において，重要規制ではない場合には分科委員会で審査する。

行政規制改革委員会は国民の日常生活，および，社会・経済活動に及ぶ波及効果が強い場合，即ち，
① 規制影響の年間費用が100億オン以上の規制，
② 被規制者の数が年間100万名以上の規制，
③ 明白に競争制限的な性格の規制，
④ 国際的基準（WTO，OECD等が設定した基準）に照して規制の程度が多過ぎるか，または，合理的でない規制等

は重要な規制としている。

行政規制改革委員会は審査の結果，承認または改善を勧告する。改善は規制の新設・強化を撤回するか改善することを勧めるのを意味する。この勧告を受けた機関の長は撤回または改善措置を行ってこれを委員会に報告する。

(5) 既存規制の整備

既存規制に関しては次の方法によって整備する。

意見提出による整備——大韓民国に居住する内・外国人はだれでも既存の規制の廃止または改善に対して各級行政機関，公共団体，民間団体（貿易協会，全経連等）に意見を提出することが出来る。これらの意見は規制改革委員会に回附され委員会は審査の必要があると認める場合には審査して改善を勧告する。

自体整備——中央行政機関の長は所管規制をみずから整備して，毎年1月10日まで既存整備に対する前年度の自体整備結果を委員会に提出する。

現在行政規制改革委員会が把握している規制件数は約11,000件である。

大統領は既存規制の50％を整備することを指示し，行政規制改革委員会はこの規制の50％を今年の年末まで整備するように各中央行政機関の長に要求している。各各の中央行政機関の長は整備計画を樹立して整備に着手しており，今年の9月の初めまで国税庁，調達庁，統計庁，警察庁，関税庁等の庁級中央機関が整備結果を行政規制委員会に報告しており，行政規制委員会はこの報告を基に予備審査，分科委員会審査，全体委員会の審議・議決で正当性が認められない規制を改革している。

規制整備総合計画の樹立・施行——行政規制改革委員会は汎国家的な次元で規制整備のマスタープランを樹立し，これを国民に公表することになっている。委員会は既存規制の整備指針を作成し国務会議の審議を経て毎年10月の末まで各各の部処に送付する。この指針を受けた各部処は12月の末まで規制整備計画を作成，規制改

革委員会に提出し，委員会は提出された計画を総合して規制整備総合計画を樹立し，国務会議の審議と大統領の承認を得て，官報，PC通信等を通じて公表する。その後，各部処は毎年1月10日まで前年度規制整備総合計画の推進実績を委員会に提出することになっている。

現在，規制改革委員会は所属の専門家グループに核心規制改革課題及び優先推進課題等約100余件を選定させ，これらの改革法案を研究させており，まもなく，これらの規制改革課題は各各の中央行政機関に送られ，整備が推進される予定である。

企業活動規制緩和に関する特別措置法に依る整備——企業活動規制審議委員会は独自的に企業活動に関する規制の改革作業を推進することになっている。企業活動規制審議委員会と行政規制改革委員会との関係は特別・一般委員会関係である。企業活動規制審議委員会は企業活動に関する規制を定める法令の改廃，規制制度の改善のための法令の制定等に関して行政規制改革委員会に勧告をすることが出来る。行政規制委員会はこれらの勧告事項の審議のみならず企業活動規制審査委員会の審査事項に関しても企業活動規制委員会に優先して審議を行う道が開かれている。

(6) 訓令・告示等の再検討

訓令・告示等を根拠として規制に関しては法令に根拠が有るかを基本法施行後1年以内に再検討することを基本法が定めており，法令に根拠が無い場合にはその規制を廃止するか，または，存続の必要が有る場合には関係法令にその根拠を置くように定めている。

(7) 行政規制改革委員会

政府の規制政策を審議・調停し規制の審査・整備等に関する事項を総合的に推進するために大統領の所属下に行政規制改革委員会を設置している。この委員会は国務総理と民間人の2人の共同委員長，15人以上20人以内の委員で構成し，全体委員の過半数は民間委員を委嘱するようにしている。現在には財政経済部長官，行政自治部長官，産業資源部長官，国務調停室長，公正去来(取引)委員会委員長，法制処長の6名の政府委員と12名の民間人で構成され総員は20名である。分科委員会は経済第1分科委員会，経済第2分科委員会，一般規制分科委員会が設けられており，民間委員が分科委員長を務めている。

委員会は，

① 規制政策の基本方向と規制制度の研究・発展に関する事項

② 規制の新設・強化等に対する審査に関する事項

③　既存規制の審査，規制整備総合計画の樹立・施行に関する事項
　④　規制の登録・公表に関する事項
　⑤　規制改善に関する意見収斂および処理に関する事項
　⑥　各級行政機関の規制改善実態に関する点検・評価に関する事項
　⑦　其の他委員長が委員会の審議・調停が必要だと認める事項
等の審議・調停を行うのをその主な業務としている。
　行政規制改革委員会は，現在，月2回召集されている。
　行政規制改革委員会は専門委員・調査委員を任命し，委員会の業務に関する専門的な調査・研究業務を担当させている。

2　展　　望

　以上で韓国での行政規制改革に関して，行政規制改革委員会の機能を中心に，略述した。
　現在までの規制改革活動は事業者に負担となる環境規制，産業安全規制，消費者保護次元での規制等の社会的規制の緩和等に関しての規制改革を行っており，市場競争の促進のための競争制限的規制の緩和という根本的な規制の構造的改革はいまだ実現されていないのが現実である。
　今後の韓国の競争制限的な核心的規制緩和の対象領域は，金融（銀行，保険，証券，外換等），土地利用（首都圏人口集中抑制施策等），労働関連の規制等，生産要素的市場規制と，物価規制，経済力集中抑制等に関する規制であると云わなければならず，これらの規制の緩和は高度の政治的決断を必要とする政策的問題であると思う。

8 日本における金融ビッグバンの法的側面

上 村 達 男

1 バブルの崩壊と法的視点の欠如
2 第3の近代化——法的システムの壁
3 金融ビッグバンと規制理念の転換
4 金融制度改革の動向
5 金融法制の整備と法的総合力の強化
　おわりに

1 バブルの崩壊と法的視点の欠如

　日本では1990年初頭に証券市場における巨大なバブルが崩壊し，その後遺症の大きさに苦しんでいる状況ある。バブルの怖さはそれが弾けて元の木阿弥になることではなく，バブルのピークを前提にした，裏付けのない過大な経済構造が出来上がってしまうところにある。こうした経済構造を前提とした経済活動は，バブルが崩壊したときに破綻する。裏付けのない過大な経済構造の破綻は，企業倒産・失業・景気悪化・犯罪等の不幸の源泉であり，その矛盾の解決を海外に求めれば戦争の原因ともなりうる。バブル形成期の幸福はバブル崩壊時の不幸に較べたら，比較にならないほどに薄っぺらな一時的幸福である。しかも過大なバブルの経験は人間の精神構造をも蝕む。厳しい自己管理を避けて，バブルの復活を常に夢見ることになりやすい。
　ではこうした巨大なバブルを生んだ原因とは何か。日本ではこれをもっぱら金融政策ないし経済政策的な問題に求める傾向がきわめて強いが，これといった説得的な説明と処方箋が経済学の立場から提示されているとはいえず，むしろ経済学不信の声が大きい。私見によると，日本が戦後ゼロからの経済発展を，法的なチェックシステムを欠いたままに遂行してきたところに大きな原因があるように思われる。もとよりこのことは，官僚と経営者による開明先制君主的な上からの強力な指導と裏腹の関係にあるため，戦後の急速な経済発展を可能とした要因と見ることも可能である。しかし，そうした経済発展のある段階で，理性的な法的枠組みを構築し，そのことで自ずとバブルの芽を摘んでいくようなシステムを導入しなければならな

かった。しかしそれができなかったことを正面から認識しなければならない。

　日本は世界経済の牽引車と目された時期もあったが，今やそれもローカルルールの恩恵であったにすぎないのではないかとの見方が強く，むしろ日本の金融システム・企業システム全体に対して国際的な不信の目が寄せられている。日本の経済的な成功を，日本のシステムの長所によって説明してきた日本文化論・日本的経営論・日本的風土論・日本人論はいまや跡形もない。それどころか，日本の金融機関というだけで上乗せ金利が課せられる（Japan premium）。金融不正や企業不正に対する日本の法的な対抗力の弱さに対する認識もきわめて大きくなっている。日本企業の情報開示や財務諸表に対する信頼は地に落ちている。日本の監査法人の監査証明もまったく信用されていない。日本の大企業が依然として総会屋（経済マフィア）と手を切っていないことも明らかにされた。

2　第3の近代化——法的システムの壁

　上記のように日本の現在の状況は，企業制度・証券制度・金融制度が成立する制度的な基盤，すなわち法的条件を維持するための強固なシステム（ブレーキ）を欠いたままにアクセルばかりを踏み続けてきたことの咎が一度に噴出している姿である。日本は会社制度も証券市場制度も金融制度も諸外国並に有しているようで，それらの制度が内在する危険や怖さに対する本能的な皮膚感覚を有していない。これらに対する十分な警戒心を持たないままに経済的成果のみを追求してきた。欧米において，こうした制度の発展史は失敗と挫折の繰り返しである。幾度に及ぶ深刻な失敗を経験する毎に，多くのシステム防護装置が標準整備されてきた。法定資本制度・配当規制・情報開示制度・業務監査制度・会計監査制度・厳格な市場不正禁止規定・市場監視機構の構築・厳格責任制度等々である。しかし，日本はこうした制度の有する切実さを知らずに，これら制度を運営し，案の定諸外国が過去において経験した失敗を素朴に繰り返した。法人による株式保有や株式の相互保有，金融機関の株式保有が大きな危険と背中合わせであることにも注意を払わなかった。日本の金融機関は株式の含み益をBISの自己資本比率の算定基礎に加えてしまったため（含み益の45％—経済界が当時90％を主張したことなどまったく忘れられている），株価によって経営が左右される体質を作ってしまい，経済の悪化を率先してより悪化させる機関になり下がっている。アメリカの金融機関が株式保有を禁じられていることの意味を理解することもできなかった。巨大な経済力を持ちながら，それを維持し運営す

るにふさわしい十分なシステムと運営ノウハウを備えていない日本，今，日本はそうした局面に立たされている。

日本は130年前に開国したが，当初の国家目標は「富国強兵」「殖産興業」という言葉に示されているように軍事力と経済力を高めることで列強と肩を並べることにあった。53年前の敗戦を機に，国家目標は経済力の増強1本に絞られた。いわば「富国強兵『財』」である。そして現在こうした目標は一応達成されたかに見えるが，非西欧国家日本が真の近代国家たるための第3の大きな壁が残されている。それは法による規律，rule of lawの確立，「富国強『法』」である。もとより日本社会の習俗にも及ぶ全ての分野を欧米流の解決方法に委ねることがいいとはいえない。文化論が通用する分野も存在する。しかし，とりわけ金融・証券・産業の分野はグローバルな基準が支配する分野であるから，第1に，法制面での共通性なしには対等な業務展開をなしえない。第2に，この分野で諸外国に伍して業務展開を行うためには諸外国の企業が行う違法・不正行為に対する強力な対抗力を有していなければならない。しかし，そのためには外国企業に対してのみ妥当するルールを設定することは出来ず，国内企業に対しても妥当するものでなければならない。現状は日本企業が制裁金・司法取引・損害賠償・罰金の名目で取られるだけであり，取ることの出来ないシステムである。LME（ロンドン金属取引所）での銅の不正取引を理由に，住友商事はアメリカのCFTCに130億円余の支払いを余儀なくされた。第3に，金融市場という生き物ともいえる対象に対して，時々刻々ルールを設定し機動的に法運用を行うという市場規制に特有の規制の在り方自体が，日本としてことさらに経験の乏しい分野である。しかし早急にこれを達成しなければならない。第4に，日本の司法制度それ自体が，こうした分野に対応できるだけの強い司法足りうるかという根源的な問題が存在する。日本ではそもそも物事を司法で解決するという発想そのものが乏しい。

3　金融ビッグバンと規制理念の転換

戦後，日本が経済復興をめざす段階において，金融は強い統制下にあり，要は国民に対しては低金利・低配当を，産業分野に対しては重点的な資金提供を，というのが政策の基本であった。とにかくも当面は国民に我慢を求めつつ，早急に世界に通用する各産業分野での大スターをつくろうとしたのである。大スターが出来てしまえば海外で獲得してきた富により国民は潤うことができる。これはある程度成功

したが，大スターを作る過程のルール・システムは何も変わっていなかった。

1948年，GHQの影響下に証券取引法が制定された。この法自体は大恐慌後のアメリカルールを基本とするものであり，その理念は大衆参加状況下の証券市場を想定した法制であった。しかし，日本では証券市場もゼロからの出発であったため，出発段階で実体と法との大きな乖離が存在した。証券規制の第1段階は，証券市場や証券会社に不慣れな国民大衆を警察的な観点から保護するというところに置かざるをえない。日本も当初の規制理念は産業警察的な取り締まりに置かれた。企業金融の主役はあくまでも銀行融資であり，銀行は融資を通じて企業を支配し，各企業にはメインバンクが存在した。証券規制の第2段階は証券会社・証券市場の育成・投資者の保護という，政策的な保護育成行政である。銀行融資中心から証券市場へと資金調達チャネルが多様化しつつある過程でもあった。銀行行政も含めて日本ではこうした行政中心の在り方を，大蔵省を長とする「護送船団方式」というが，こうした規制方式がバブル崩壊直前までの日本の金融・証券規制の理念だったのである。

上場株式の時価総額630兆円，1年間に，イタリアの1年分のGNPに相当した130兆円も時価総額が増加するという，バブルのピークを示した狂乱怒濤の1989年（日本全土の地価はアメリカ全土の地価の4倍であり，東京の地価でアメリカ全土が買えた）が終わり，1990年はじめにバブルが全面的に崩壊した。そしてそれとともに発覚した証券不祥事は全国民的な批判の対象となり，大蔵行政も大きな批判を受けた。日本の証券市場がすでにきわめて巨大なものとなっていたにもかかわらず，依然として保護育成型行政を続けたことが，あたかも親が子供の非行をかばうように，行政による証券会社不正の隠蔽をもたらし，なれ合いともいえる関係を作っていたことも次々と明らかにされた。

かくして，大蔵省も証券・金融規制の理念を市場中心型に転換すべきことを正面から認めざるを得ないこととなった。市場中心型規制とは市場メカニズムが有する長所を最大限に発揮させるために，市場の成立条件を整備し，市場の運営状況を監視し，市場が有する病理を排除することで，市場の自律的な運動能力を高めることを目標とする規制の在り方である。ここでは主役は行政ではなく市場メカニズムそれ自体であるから，行政は脇役に回る。行政の形態も政府が市場に直接的に介入できない形態，たとえば独立の行政委員会方式が求められる。日本では1992年に大蔵省の外局として証券取引等監視委員会が設置され，さらに今年の5月には独立行政委員会としての金融監督庁が発足した。ここでは銀行規制・保険会社規制・証券規

制が一体化され，従来の証券取引等監視委員会は金融監督庁の一部局となった。行政介入型規制からルール型規制への転換である。日本はわずか50年余の間に，証券市場規制の3段階をすべて経験することとなった。

1996年11月に，時の橋本龍太郎総理大臣は「我が国金融システムの改革」と題する指示を発表し，2001年を目途に金融システムの大規模な改革を実現することを宣言した。その際の指導理念は，freeでfairかつglobalな国際的な通用する金融市場を構築することにおかれた。いわゆる金融ビッグバンの始まりである。

4 金融制度改革の動向

かくして，金融にかかるあらゆる領域にまたがる制度改革へ向けて，検討が一斉に開始された。各省庁の各種審議会からは続々と報告書が公表され，項目に応じた実施時期を明示しつつ，金融ビッグバンの具体的なスケジュールが明らかにされた。

私見によると，金融ビッグバンは4段階の制度改革から成るものと思われる。第1段階は証券不祥事以前から検討されていた金融制度改革と不祥事後の対応に係るものである。

1993年の，損失補塡(注)を違法とする証券取引法改正，1994年の証券取引等監視委員会の設置に係る関係法律の改正は後者に関する。銀行が子会社による証券業務を行えるものとする等の内容を含む大改正である。1994年証券取引法・銀行法等の改正は前者に関する。不祥事以前の制度改革論議は，単に金融自由化ばかりを強調する楽観的な理念による部分が大きく，前者もそうした色彩を有しているが，現在の理念から見ても，その先取りと考えられる要素があることは確かである。

第2段階は，明白に金融ビッグバンを目標としつつも，現行法体系そのものには手を加えずに，早急に可能なところから国際水準を達成しようとするものであり，本年の6月5日に成立した金融システム改革関連法がそれに相当する。同法はきわめて多くの法律の改正を総称するものであり，証券取引法・銀行法・証券投資信託法・保険業法等の大改正である。証券取引法だけを見ても，有価証券市場概念の拡大（従来は取引所市場だけを有価証券市場とし，法律上店頭市場は業者の慣行取引にすぎなかった），証券業としての店頭デリバティブ取引の認知，証券会社の登録制（従来は免許制），私設取引システム運営業の認可制，証券会社の専業制（証券業をなしうるのは証券会社だけという原則―ただし，例外は多数存在した）の緩和，顧客財産の分離保管義務の撤廃，証券会社の自己資本比率規制の強化，証券会社倒産対策としての投資

家保護基金制度の創設，売買委託手数料の自由化，不公正取引規制の強化（市場間相場操縦の禁止，フロントランニングの禁止等），市場集中原則の緩和，等々を広範に内容とする。こうした金融システム改革関連法と同時に，金融の証券化（securitization）のための受け皿会社たる特定目的会社（special purpose company-SPC）の法的根拠を提供するSPC法，証券化のために集合債権群の一括譲渡にかかる簡易な対抗要件を定める債権譲渡特例法，金融機関が破綻した場合におけるスワップ取引の一括清算の合法性を定める特別法，も制定された。これらの膨大な改正法は，どの一部をとっても日本にとっては大きな改正だが，欧米にあってはいずれも既に実現を見ているものである。

このように第2段階の改正は大規模なものであるが，これは銀行法・証券取引法・保険業法・商品取引所法といった現行法制のシステム（それぞれに所管官庁ないし部局が異なっている）を前提にしつつ，可能な限り共通法理を模索し，必要な改正を行ったものである。第3段階は，こうした法制の枠組みを超えた金融サービスに関する横断的な包括法の制定である。大蔵省に設置された，多彩な専門家と多くの省庁の代表から成る「新しい金融の流れに関する懇談会」は，本年6月17日に「論点整理」を公表したが，これは英国の金融サービス法に倣った横断的包括的な金融法制の制定を提言するものである。まだ具体化するには至っていないが，早急な実現が望まれる。

第4段階は完全な私見であり，何ら具体化されていないが，証券取引法や銀行法が当然に前提にしている個々の概念自体を全面的に見直しつつ，日本版モデルを世界に問うという段階である。英国が金融サービス法を制定した際に，彼らは旧来の個々の概念を捨てて新たな概念を自分たちの頭で時間をかけて作ることで，金融サービス法を構想した。日本も時間をかけて日本版モデルを模索すべきである。もとより，すぐにでもできることは第3段階の金融サービス法に反映させるべきである。しかし，概念の根本にまで遡った理論モデルづくりには時間がかかるので，理論上は第4段階を考えておいた方がよいように思われる。

問題はそうした作業に見込みがあるかであるが，私見は大いに見込みがあると考える。たしかに，日本の金融制度改革は始まったばかりである。欧米のモデルを追いかけるしか道はないかにも見える。しかし，欧米の規制水準を謙虚に学ぶことと，理論構成について欧米の理論モデルしか選択肢がないと考えることとは一体の事柄ではない。アメリカの規制水準はきわめて高い。しかし，州にしか会社法がなく連

邦会社法を有しない稀れ連邦国家であるアメリカでは，事実上の連邦会社法を形成するために証券諸法が事実上会社法の代わりをしなければならないとの特殊な事情がある。証券関係法をトータルに市場規制法として純化しにくい事情にある。英国も沿革上の理由から，マーケット法については証券取引所の自主ルールに委ね，詐欺防止や目論見書規制・インサイダー取引規制を会社法に委ね，多くの業者規制を自主規制に委ねてきた。包括的な業者法ができたのは1986年の金融サービス法が初めてである。

　ここで詳しくは述べられないが，日本は1つの目的規定を有する証券取引法の下に，マーケットと行為規制と業者規制を一体として包括的に位置づけている貴重な立法例であるために，こうした諸規制を，普遍的な理念である「市場」機能の充実強化・市場における公正な価格形成の確保という，統一的な目的の下に，包括的な資本市場法制として体系化することで，真に市場機構を守り抜くことのできる普遍的な理論モデルを世に問うことも不可能でないように思われる。金融システムを一つの巨大なダムに喩えると，小さなひび割れも見逃さずに修復し，つねにシステムの状況を監視し，あらゆる手段を駆使してそれを守り抜くための法体制を構想することは，とりわけ日本にとって重要であるが，それは普遍的な意義を有する作業でもある。少なくともそうした意気込みで日本版モデル構想に取り組むことが必要であろう。

5　金融法制の整備と法的総合力の強化

　(1)　市場機構の確保と大目的とした新たな包括的資本市場法制構想の具体的な内容をここで示すことはできないが，取引の客体たる金融商品の開発・上場等の迅速化，多様な市場の開設・運営，市場の担い手としての仲介業者規制，間接規制の担い手たる自主規制機関規制，情報開示規制および不正取引規制等の行為規制，政治に左右されない独立の行政機関による証券・金融行政等，がその内容となる。ここでは高度に組織的な市場だけではなく相対的な取引市場も，公正な価格形成の追求という市場規制としての目的を共有するものとして扱われる。

　こうした体制の下では，金融・証券犯罪は公共財たる市場メカニズムに対する抽象的危険犯として位置づけられるため，重罪として認識される。また，市場阻害行為は，行為に対する非難という性格を有する通常の刑罰のように，単に1回罰すれば済むものではなく，市場への影響の排除・事前の予防措置・反復行為の防止といっ

た措置が重要であるから，こうした目的に適う行政処分の多様性（利益の吐き出し，排除措置等）・民事制裁・課徴金といった規制手段が多彩に用意されている必要がある。その際，規制の漏れに対応できないために肝心の市場が破壊されても何もできないのでは市場規制の意味をなさないため，法令の定めは可能な限り要件等を事前に明示すべきであるが，市場の状況に柔軟に対応するために，機動的なルール設定や，事前の問い合わせへの対応（アメリカのno-action letter）・ガイドラインの設定等により，最後に残らざるを得ない包括規定をも，十分に使いこなせるだけのシステムを確立する必要がある。市場規制にあっては法運用の安定性・確実性・透明性は，すべての要件を事前に示すことによってではなく，最終的には柔軟な法運用システムが確立することによって担保される。

　なお，金融法制を支えるためには，会計・監査制度の信頼性を著しく高めることが不可欠の要件であるが，そのためには会計・監査理論自体が証券市場を支える公益性への認識を正面から受け止めるものになっていなければならない。

　(2)　一般に金融ビッグバンを目指す法制度改革といえば，このような金融・証券法制の改革のみを思い浮かべる。しかし，とりわけ我が国において大事なのは，こうした金融・証券法制は一般私法すなわち民法・商法・手続法（訴訟法）の充実とともに存在しなければならないことである。これには2つの意味がある。1つは金融・証券法制自体が機能するために一般私法の充実が必要という問題であり，1つは金融・証券法制から外れても，すれすれのところまで一般私法が待ちかまえているという問題である。前者は，例えば証券取引法上の損害賠償制度が機能するためには，市場での違法行為・因果関係・損害が区認定に横たわる立証上の困難が克服されなければならないといった問題である。市場適合的な柔軟な理論が存在しなければならない。後者は日本では特に注意を要する点である。もともと，金融・証券法制に固有の概念も一般私法の概念を，市場取引に適合させるために徐々に形成されてきたものである。相場操縦は不法行為ないし詐欺の観念から出発して，流通市場の犯罪として構成された。インサイダー取引も詐欺ないし信任義務の観念を母体とする。したがって，アメリカでは証券諸法の適用が仮になくても，こうした概念を作ってきた一般私法法理で賄おうと思えば賄える程度のものが存在している。日本には金融法制を支えるこうした広大な一般私法法理の体系が金融法制と連続的に連なっていない。金融・証券法制から外れる場合には，あたかも「何でもあり」の世界に放たれたかに思う向きが多い。

(3) 金融機関や証券会社は，金融機関の証券会社である前に上場会社であり，その前に株式会社である。金融・証券法制がいかなる規制を用意しようとも，まずはそれが株式会社として全うであることを前提とし，次に一般上場会社として全うであることが前提となっている。例えば金融機関に対する日銀考査や，証券会社に対する大蔵検査は，本来少なくとも一般企業に要請される程度の，会社法上の監査制度，証券取引法上の公認会計士監査制度くらいは機能していることを前提としているはずである。しかし，日本では実はこのレベル自体が心許ない。日本のコーポレート・ガバナンスを根本的に見直し，実効性のある経営監督体制を基本に立ち返って構築しなければならない。

その他に，discovery制度やclass action制度の導入，仲裁制度等の非裁判手続きの充実等の，手続法制上の課題も山積している。司法自体についても，長すぎる裁判・法曹の数滴地域的充実等の裁判制度の改革も，ルール型規制の時代における最重要課題である。要は，金融法制の根本的な充実は日本の法的な総合力を高めることで支えられなければならないのである。

おわりに

日本は現在不良債権問題を中心とする金融危機の最中にある。景気もきわめて悪化している。金融制度改革はこうした緊急課題への対応と平行して着実に遂行されなければならず，きわめて難しい舵取りを必要としている。当面の緊急対策を実行しながら，もっとも理性的な作業を進めることができるのか，私個人としてはかなり悲観的ではあるが，これを実行することこそが，日本の対外的な信用を基本的な部分で高める，根本的・究極的な景気対策でもあることを認識すべきであろう。さもなければ日本の企業社会はいつまでも安心してアクセルを力強く踏むことはできないだろう。

(注) 証券取引で損失を被った大口投資家に対して使用権会社が損失の穴埋めを行う行為。大証券会社を中心に公表されただけでも2,000億円を超える損失補塡が行われていた。私は，これを当時から違法であった事前の損失保証の実行行為であったと今でも確信しているが，事後の損失補塡についてはこれを違法とする明文規定がないことを理由に違法行為ではないとして処理され，裁判所もこれを追認した。

(ii) 規制の諸形態

9 私法上の救済手段による「犯罪」行為の規制：
懲罰的損害賠償の場合

マイケル・ティルベリー

［佐野　　隆訳］

1　背　　景
2　懲罰的賠償の定義および用語法
3　規制緩和，刑事法および懲罰的賠償
4　主要な障害：デュー・プロセス
5　懲罰的賠償の付与に対する制限
6　懲罰的賠償をより広く利用できるようにすること
　　結　　論

1　背　　景

　大変一般的に言えば，刑法が存在するのは，ある時点における社会が一定の行為を反社会的で受け入れがたいと考え，かかる行為を非難し，抑止し，罰したいと考えるからである[1]。現在においては，それは国家の規制的な枠組みを通して行われている。しかし，このことが常に当てはまった訳ではない。初期の段階においては，受け入れがたい行為を罰することは，集団の復讐の問題であったことが知られている[2]。復讐は集団（拡大家族であれ，クランであれ，一部族であれ）により，その集団の基準に従わない行動をとった集団内のメンバーに対して，あるいは，問題が生じた集団間の関係を律する慣習上の受け入れられている規範に従わなかった他の集団に対して，集団として，あるいは，そのメンバーの1人を通して，強制された。いずれの場合も，［強制を行うという］集団行為をとらないことは，無秩序の暴力の危険を冒すものであった。集団が，民族としての，そして後には国民としての一体性を帯びるにつれて，行動を規制する役割は，当然，新たに生まれた組織に委ねられ，今日では，それは国民国家に明らかに与えられている。しかしながら，少なくともコモン・ローの制度の下では，「犯罪」と呼ばれる行為を規制する責任が国家の排他的領域であると考えられるようになったのはわずかにこの200年ほどの間である[3]。このことが生じたのは，近代の官僚制，特に犯罪を捜査し犯人を裁判所へ送ること

のできる警察の発達によるものである。犯罪捜査から起訴の過程で犯罪の被害者およびその者と社会的に密接な関係にある者の役割は小さく，伝統的には，関係当局の関心を犯罪に引きつけることにかぎられている。

「犯罪」に分類される行為とそのようには分類されない行為との区別を付けることが難しいのはよく知られている。このことは驚くべきことではほとんどない。なぜなら，根本的には，この区別は，公に罰すべき行為と，そうではない行為の分類に対する社会的な合意をあらわすものであるからである。かかる合意は，宗教，道徳，哲学，社会認識および経済学の中のあい対立する見解が入り混ざるるつぼの中で鋳造される。その区別を付けることは，安定している単一文化の社会においても十分に難しい。ましてや，現代の民主的で多元的な社会においては，なお一層難しい。したがって，おそらく，同様に言えることは，今日の視点から見れば比較的同質的であった社会においては，基本的な合意は得られていたということである。そこから我々に授けられたものが，我々が犯罪と分類する行為であり，それらの授かり物なくしては，我々の社会の中でこのトピックについて多くの合意が得られたとは信じがたい。

我々が犯罪と理解していることの多くが歴史を通して判断されてきたものである[4]。例えば，不動産に対する妨害(不動産に対するトレスパス)を刑事上の制裁により抑止することが適切であるかどうかという問題を考えてみよう。原則的には，その答は，「被害者の」不動産との関係に対して社会が置く価値と，不動産がその社会のすべての富の中で果たしている役割によって変わってくる。土地およびその所有から生じる力は，今日でさえ，貴重な政治的，経済的，社会的財産となりうる。その価値は歴史的には今日以上のものがあった。偉大な行政官であったノルマン朝の王たちが，1066年の征服以後イングランドを支配し，地方の領主から自身の手に権力を集中させることでイングランドを一つの国家へと作り始めたとき，王たちは次の問題に直面した。すなわち，いかなる基準で法的事件を，新しい国法体制(それは後に「コモン・ロー」となるが)と地方の有力者が支配する既存の裁判所との間で配分すべきか，という問題に直面した。彼らが出した答は，「平和を破る恐れのある事件」すなわち「国王の平和」であった。なぜなら，その当時，臣民に対して，少なくとも暴動や私的暴力に訴えることを避ける，平和的な生活を伴う最低限の社会的水準を保障することは君主の役割であったからである。最初に出された考え方が「平和を破る」という概念であったことは，公的秩序に対する重大な侵害であることを示

し，国王の裁判所は「犯罪行為」に関与すべきであるというきっかけを含んでいる。実際，国王の裁判所はそうしたが，しかし，犯罪と不法行為との間で区別はなされなかった。不動産における権利に対する妨害は平和を破る恐れがあり，したがって，それが国王の裁判所の管轄権に服するようになったことは，驚くべきことではない。そして，国王の裁判所では，科される責任は，刑事および民事の双方を含むものとなった(5)。

したがって，犯罪行為を定義することの内在的な難しさは，我々の法における多くの行為が民事上の違法行為(6)と犯罪(7)の双方であることを確保する歴史的な事情と結びついている。このことは，そのような行為は刑法および私法の両方の対象となるべきなのか，あるいは，いずれか一方のみによりより適切に扱われるのかという問題を問う最初の理由となる。

その問題を問うもう1つの理由も存在する。すでに示したが，どの行為が犯罪と分類されるべきかに関する合意を得ることの内在的な難しさは，多元的な民主主義社会においては増幅されている。裁判所が民事訴訟において，犯罪と分類されるべきだと考えるが，そのように分類されていない行為に直面したと考えよう。1つの例として，既存の詐欺罪に当てはまらないコンピュータ技術を用いた取引きにおける「詐欺」の新たな出現が考えられる。なぜならこれらの考えられるそれぞれの犯罪では，何らかの重要な要素が欠けているからである。そのような行為が最初に現れたときに，裁判所は民事手続においてその行為を「処罰」することができるべきであろうか。そのような行為が常に裁判所に持ち出されるようになり始めたにもかかわらず，国会がかかる行為を含む新しい犯罪を認める立法をしていない場合にはどうなるであろうか。

本稿は，これらの2つの問題を，民事訴訟において裁判所が懲罰的賠償を科すことが適切であるか否かという問題を提起することで論じる。また，この問題が規制緩和の議論とどのように関連しうるかをも示す。この問題自体の解決は後日に期したい(8)。

2 懲罰的賠償の定義および用語法

合衆国においてpunitive damagesとして一般に知られている懲罰的賠償（exemplary damages）は，被告を罰し，被告および他の者が将来類似の行為をなすことを抑止することを目的とする賠償金である(9)。懲罰的賠償金は，コモン・ロー体系の一

つの特徴であるが，大陸法系では見られないものである(10)。もっとも，両体系の影響を受けた法体系の中には(11)，時として制定法による導入を通して(12)，いくらかの影響が見られる。

しばしば区別を付けることは難しいものの，懲罰的賠償金は加重的賠償金（aggravated damages）と区別されなければならない(13)。加重的賠償金は填補的(compensatory)である(14)。加重的賠償金が与えられるには，原告の「尊厳上の利益(dignatory interests)(15)」に対する侵害を含む事件であり，その場合は被告の行為の邪悪さ（outrageousness[＝著しく正義に反すること]）により原告の被る損失が増大したと考えられうる場合である(16)。したがって，加重的賠償は，それを与えるきっかけが被告の行為にあるので，懲罰的賠償に類似している。名誉毀損は加重的賠償の対象となりうる不法行為の一例である(17)。加重的賠償金の付与を招きうる被告の行為には，事件のあらゆる状況からして，謝罪がなされるべきなのにも，名誉毀損となる主張に対して被告が謝罪しない場合(18)，あるいは，時として（例えば，真実であると嘘の主張を繰り返す）訴訟中の被告の態度(19)などが含まれる。

オーストラリアにおいて懲罰的賠償が機能している仕方に関して，現実を示す4つの点が記されなければならない。第1に，懲罰的賠償は，現実には，合衆国において見られるほど，多くの事件において認められるものではない。第2に，最近まで，懲罰的賠償は，実際には原告に対する故意の侵害を含む事件に限定されていた傾向があった。しかし現在では，被告の行為が著しく悪い場合(20)――例えば被告である使用者が長年にわたり従業員を健康の危険にさらすことに対して無配慮で過失があった場合(21)――には，過失（negligence）の事件でも認められるようになってきている。第3に，懲罰的賠償が認められる場合，その賠償額はあまり高くない傾向にあり，合衆国において通常見られる巨額な懲罰的賠償金はオーストラリアにおいては断じてありえない(22)。このことの一つの理由は，ヴィクトリア州を別にすれば，オーストラリアの民事事件で賠償審理が行われるのは極めてまれであるからである。第四に，オーストラリアにおけるほとんどの名誉毀損訴訟が行われるニューサウスウェールズ州では(23)，制定法により［名誉毀損訴訟では］懲罰的賠償が認められなくなっている(24)。つまり，同州における名誉毀損訴訟では加重的賠償金が非常に重要である。

3 規制緩和，刑事法および懲罰的賠償

　政治上，「規制緩和」は現在流行である。規制緩和へと駆り立てる哲学は，本質において，より多くの善が自己利益を増進させることで得られ，そして，自己利益の増進は経済的効率性を生み，小さな政府を求めるものであると考える。刑事法に関する国家の独占は規制緩和の哲学とは相容れない。このことから，少なくとも，主張できることは，国家の独占を切り崩すことで，そのことから生じるより多くの効率性のために，刑事法の規制緩和が行われるべきであるということである。民営刑務所の創設はこの主張が一定の成功をすでに収めていることを示している。政治的な視点からすれば，民営刑務所は大変魅力的である。それは，単に政府の予算から費用のかかる項目を減らすのみならず[25]，収監者は納税者の負担で面倒を見られているのではないという事実を政治家たちは指摘することもできるのである。そうではなくて，刑務所は営利企業（commercial enterprises）として運営されている。しかし，収監者たちの時間と労働を用い，差し出がましい国家の規制から独立して運営されている民営刑務所は，国家の刑務所では上手く行かなかった効率性によって，社会の純益（net social benefit）を達成しえたかどうかを言うには，あまりにも尚早すぎる。もちろん「社会の純益」がパレード[26]であれカルドー－ヒックス[27]であれ彼らの視点[28]を通して見ても単に経済上のものだけではない。

　それでは，刑務所は民営化によりより効率的になりうるなら，刑事裁判制度の他の側面についてはどうであろうか。例えば，行為が刑事と民事の双方の色彩を帯びる場合，処罰の費用は民事訴訟へと移すことがより効果的であると言える場合が少なくともあるのではないか。結局は，舞台から国家を取り除くことが直接の経済上の利益をもたらし，かかる利益は，起訴するかどうかの決定の費用，証拠収集の費用，刑事訴訟審理の費用，刑事上の制裁を執行する費用を減らすことから生み出されうる。これらの主張は直ちに2つの主要な障害に出会う。第1はデュー・プロセスの懸念であり，そして，第2は，民事事件における適切な（つまり，刑事型の）制裁の限られた利用可能性である。我々の目的にとって，これは懲罰的賠償の限られた利用可能性のことである。

4 主要な障害：デュー・プロセス

　民事手続と刑事手続とは極めて異なっている。刑事手続は共同体の公序（social

policy) を強制 (enforce) する。国家は公序に違反したと認められた者に刑罰を科すことでかかる公序を強制する。そのようにする国家の目的は様々に表現されている。つまり，有罪と認められた者を処罰すること，彼らが再度犯さないための警告として行為すること，他の者が犯罪を犯さぬように抑止すること，公序に違反した者を非難することで法に示される正当性を示すこと，違反により侵害を受けた者のために復讐し，侵害を被った者が自らの手で制裁を加えることを回避すること，そして，違反をなした者を社会復帰させること，というように[29]。対照的に，民事手続の目的は，原告に対して違法な行為を行った被告から，原告が塡補，原状回復(restitution)または何らかの形で強制的な救済を得ることを可能にさせることである[30]。民事手続において塡補に圧倒的な力点が置かれていることがその本質を強く示している。つまり，被告の行為により作り出された状況を，被告が問題とされる行為をしなかったのなら，原告が占めていたであろう立場へと原告を置かせることを被告に求めることで，治癒させることである。

　刑事手続も民事手続も，結局は，特定の型の行為に対する制裁を含むものであるが，刑事手続における制裁は，典型的には，民事手続における制裁よりも厳しい。私法上の制裁は，特に塡補は，単に矯正的正義 (corrective justice) の観点から正当化されているに過ぎない。しかし，刑法上の制裁ははるかにそれを上回る。刑事上の制裁に伴う重大な結果には，特に，収監による人身の自由の剥奪が含まれる。

　この理由により，刑事手続には「デュー・プロセス」の観点で，その用語を最大限に広範囲に用いて，厳格な制限の下に置かれる。それらの制限には以下のものが含まれる：

- 刑事手続の後に処罰が加えられうる犯罪の国家による明確な定義；
- 国家自身による刑事訴追の開始，追行およびそのコントロール；
- 訴追のあらゆる段階での被告の保護，特に，無罪の推定，黙秘権および被告の有罪を合理的な疑いがないまで国家が立証しなければならない要件；
- 犯罪に対する最高刑の立法による規定；
- 刑事上の制裁の国家による強制，あるいは少なくとも，制裁の強制に対する国家の責任。

　国家が刑事手続のあらゆる段階で関与していることが理解できる。伝統的にはこれは排他的な関与であった。しかし，以下の修正が必要である：

- 国家が刑事法違反を起訴しないと決定した場合には，違反が生じた法の強制に

利害を有する者は，訴えを提起するために法務長官（Attorney General）の名において関係人訴訟（relator action）を提起することができる場合があるが[31]，その場合には法務長官の同意が必要である[32]。

- 犯罪の被害者は刑事手続の様々な段階で介入できる場合がある。特に，今日では，被害者には量刑の段階で「被害者影響説明書（victim impact statement）」を提出する権利が広く与えられている[33]。法制度の中には，起訴するかしないかの決定の際に，被害者の発言が許される場合もある。
- 犯罪の被害者には，犯罪を犯したとして有罪とされた者を直接相手方として，あるいは，より一般的には国家を相手方として，塡補を強制する権利が与えられる場合もある。これらの権利は別個の手続で執行される[34]。

これらの修正にもかかわらず，刑事訴追においては国家が主役であることにはかわりがない。実際，このため，国家の公務員の行為が無能であったり腐敗している場合は，被告に与えられる保護はまったくかほとんどない場合がある。さらに，思い出されなければならないことは，刑事手続においては，特に，手続を開始するか否かの決定においては，国家が広範な裁量権を有していることである[35]。

5 懲罰的賠償の付与に対する制限

処罰と抑止という目的は，懲罰的賠償および刑事手続に共通している。その結果，懲罰的賠償と刑事法との間の重複の可能性は大きい。しかし，実際は重複の幅は民事件でどれほど広く懲罰的賠償が利用されるかに左右される。

何世紀もの間，コモン・ローは，exemplary, punitive, vindictiveと様々に記された賠償金を民事件で認めてきた[36]。そのような賠償金の役割とそれが利用できる状況は，イギリスの貴族院が*Rookes v Barnard*事件判決[37]を下す1964年までは明確には示されていなかった。同事件でDevlin貴族院裁判官は，その偉大な判決の中で，懲罰的賠償は刑事法と民事法を混同させるものであり変則（anomalous）であり，将来，懲罰的賠償は3つの明確に定められる状況において認められるに過ぎないと判示した。すなわち，それらは，

- 政府の公務員が強圧的(oppressive)，恣意的(arbitrary)または非立憲的(unconstitutional)な行為に従事した場合；
- 被告の行為が原告に対して支払われるかもしれない賠償金を上回るであろう利益をもたらすであろうと被告が計算した場合；そして，

・懲罰的賠償が制定法により認められた場合[38],

である。これらの分類は，法原則と政策と先例との間の妥協を示すものであった。法原則と政策は，懲罰的賠償は，処罰と抑止を目的とするので，それは民事法と刑事法の目的を混同させるので，あらゆる民事事件において認められるべきでないとする。すなわち，懲罰的賠償は変則なのである[39]。他方，処罰と抑止を目的とする賠償金が認められたことを立証する「混沌」とした先例の一群が明らかに存在していた[40]。懲罰的賠償は一定の型の訴訟でしか認められないということをその妥協が求める限りで，その基準は，他の点におけると同様に，非論理的である[41]。なぜなら，その基準は被告の行為に目を向けていないが，法原則上被告の行為のみが懲罰的賠償が認められる状況を決定すべきであるからである[42]。

これらの理由により，Devlin貴族院裁判官による懲罰的賠償に関する法の説明はオーストラリア[43]，ニュージーランド[44]，そしてカナダ[45]では従われなかった。そのため，それらの法域における懲罰的賠償に関する法は1964年以前の「混沌」とした状態のままであった。しかし，私が他の所で論じたように[46]，実際は懲罰的賠償が認められるべきか否かの問題にとって関連する4つの要因が存在している。それらは，

・被告の行為の質
・原告の訴訟原因の質
・原告が被告の行為の被害者でなければならないという事実，そして，
・事件のあらゆる状況の中で懲罰的賠償がその目的を果たすことができるかの可能性，

である。

被告の行為

懲罰的賠償を認めるか否かの決定の中心にあるのが不法行為者の行為である[47]。オーストラリア法においてかかる行為は「原告の権利に対する傲慢な無視による意識的な違法行為 (conscious wrongdoing in contumelious disregard of the plaintiff's rights)[48]」に相当しなければならない。この表現の元は偉大な不法行為学者であり法学に関する優れた著書を残したSir John Salmondの書の中にある[49]。

この描写に関して2つの点を頭に入れておくべきである。第1は，犯意 (mens rea)，すなわち，行為の心理的要素が，刑事法と一致する用語で表現されていること

である。被告は，少なくとも，意識的な行為者でなければならない。そして，被告の行為に対する動機が考慮に入れられる場合がありうる[50]。例えば，被告が最善の動機で原告の最高の利益であると考え行為したという事実が認められれば，懲罰的賠償は認められない場合がありうる[51]。第2には，犯罪行為(actus reus)，すなわち，行為の客観的描写が，極めてあいまいであることである。行為は「傲慢(contumelious)」でなければならない。しかし，母国語として英語を話すほとんどの人はcontumeliousという語を耳にしたことがないであろう。もしあったとしても，前後の文脈からそれが非常に悪いという意味に違いないということを別にすれば，その意味を知る者がいないことはほとんど確実である。裁判所が示す所では，行為は裁判所による単なる不承認よりもそれ以上のものが求められなければならない[52]。しかし，諸事件で示されるものは，いかなる事実状況が懲罰的賠償を認めることによって裁判所がなす非難に値するか，あるいは，値しないかを示す個々の例示に過ぎない。

原告の訴訟原因

*Rookes v. Barnard*事件判決以前の「混沌」たる状況の中に懲罰的賠償に関する法が存在していた時点で，懲罰的賠償を認めることに関連する要因の一つが原告の訴訟原因であった。その理由は，イギリス法が数多くある特定された訴訟原因を通して定型的なシステム(formulary system)として発展してきたからである。したがって，原告の訴訟原因が懲罰的賠償が利用できる（そして利用できない）場合を決定する基準となることは，驚くべきことではない。この状況はイギリスにおいて今も続いている。そこでは，懲罰的賠償は，*Rookes v. Barnard*事件判決以前に利用できた事件[＝訴訟原因]にしか利用できないということが確立している[53]。イギリスの法律委員会(Law Commission)は，この状況を，懲罰的賠償が原則的にはほとんどの違法行為に対して利用できるように変えるべきであると，正しく，勧告した[54]。簡単に記せば，*Rookes v Barnard*事件判決が，懲罰的賠償の質と目的とを特定した以上，もはや懲罰的賠償の利用可能性を原告の訴訟原因に結び付けて考える必要はなかった。これが現在のオーストラリア法[55]およびカナダ法[56]における状況である。*Paragon Properties Ltd. v. Magna Envestments Ltd*事件アルバータ州控訴院判決におけるClement上訴裁判官が述べるように[57]，

「法原則を発動させるのは違法行為者の非難されるべき行為であり，填補的賠償

金を生じさせ，生じた行為が関連をもつ違法行為の法的分類ではない。法原則の適用に対して恣意的な制限を設けることは，根底を成している原則を切り崩すことになり，また，原則を不確定で議論の余地のある法体制に置き換えることになる。」

被害者としての原告

*Rookes v. Barnard*事件判決において[58]，Devlin貴族院裁判官は，原告が処罰されるべき行為の被害者である場合のみ原告に懲罰的賠償が与えられるに過ぎないと述べた。したがって，何らかの理由で(例えば，感覚の鈍さのために)被告のとんでもない行為の影響を受けない原告には懲罰的賠償は認められないであろう。

オーストラリアにおいては，この主張を支持するものがある。すなわち，このことが実際意味していることは，懲罰的賠償が利用できるのは，原告が塡補的賠償金を請求できる権利を有している場合だけであるということである。つまり，いわば，懲罰的賠償は塡補的賠償に「寄生(parasitic)」しているのである[59]。しかし，ニュージーランドの判例法は，この考え方が狭すぎることを示してきている[60]。ニュージーランドにおける身体傷害（personal injury）の事件におけるように制定法がコモン・ロー上の損害賠償請求権を廃止してしまった場合，懲罰的賠償を求める独立した請求を認めるよう制定法を読んではならない理由はないように思われる（つまり「損害賠償金（damages）」を塡補的賠償金に限定されていると読むことである）[61]。

懲罰的賠償の目的を果たすことの可能性

懲罰的賠償は，その目的，つまり処罰し抑止することが達成されない場合には，利用することができないであろうと述べることは，明らかであろうと思われるかもしれない。しかし，実際にはそう言うほどたやすいものではない。例えば，被告の行為に保険がかけられている場合を考えよう。そのような場合に，懲罰的賠償はその目的を実際達成しうるであろうか。極めて明らかに，被告は「痛み（sting）」を感じないであろうから，懲罰的賠償で被告を罰することはできないであろう。しかしながら，それでも懲罰的賠償で他の者を抑止することができると主張しうる。この理由および他の理由でオーストラリア連邦最高裁判所（High Court of Australia）は，後に*Gray v. Motor Accident Commission*事件判決[62]において承認された*Lam v Cotogno*事件判決[63]において，自動車の使用の際の被告の傲慢な態度が原告に身体

傷害に与えた被告に対して，たとえその被告には第三者自動車強制保険がかけられていても懲罰的賠償を利用することができる，と判示した。Luntz教授はこの判決を「不条理(absurd)」と言うが⁽⁶⁴⁾，私も彼に同意する。(同様に第三者強制保険をかけている)他の自動車運転者が，被告の行ったような行為をひかえるであろうと言うことは，想像力を働かせすぎているに過ぎないし，さらに，そのような運転者は懲罰的賠償が科せられる危険や，そのことが保険料にもたらす影響を知っていると仮定してみることも同じである。連邦最高裁判所が示した他の理由は，懲罰的賠償を認めることで原告の復讐への衝動が和らぐであろうというものであった⁽⁶⁵⁾。しかし，原告の復讐への衝動は，おそらく，懲罰的賠償を認めることに伴う処罰と抑止で和らげられるべきであるが，まず第1に被告を処罰し抑止することがなお適切であることに違いないことは確かである。

　このことは，被告が保険をかけている場合は，すべて懲罰的賠償を排除すべきであるということを意味しない。例えば，最近イギリスでは，警察が原告の権利を侵害したいくつかの事件で，懲罰的賠償が認められた⁽⁶⁶⁾。そのような賠償は抑止を達成するということで正当化しうるように思われる。そのような賠償がいくつか認められれば，警察の支払う保険料が高騰し，ついには，保険がかけられなくなる危険のため，警察が侵害行為を止めようとする圧力となるであろう。しかし，この規範に訴える議論が前提とするのは保険料を決定する要因であるが，その要因は，正当化される場合もあればされない場合もある——例えば，増大する危険は，効果的な再保険契約を通して保険業者が負担するに過ぎない場合がありうる。

　被告が保険をかけている状況を別にすれば，懲罰的賠償がその目的を果たさないかもしれない状況がほかに2つある。1つは，原告が受ける塡補賠償額が非常に高いため，それ自体が十分な処罰と抑止となる場合である⁽⁶⁷⁾。2番目の場合は，被告がすでに処罰されている場合である⁽⁶⁸⁾。*Gray*事件判決⁽⁶⁹⁾で，Gleeson長官およびMcHugh, Gummow, Hayne各裁判官は以下のように述べた。

　　「違法行為者に関連し，刑事法が適用され，相当な処罰が加えられている場合には，懲罰的賠償は付与されえない(may not)と我々は考える。『えない』というのは，民事手続の対象となっている行為と実質的に同一の行為を理由に相当な処罰が科されていることは懲罰的賠償の付与を妨げるものであると考えるからである。この判断は，それぞれの個々の事件の事実関係および状況に左右される裁量の問題として達した判断ではない。」

この法準則の根底をなす原理は，先ず第1に，刑事法により相当な処罰がなされれば懲罰的賠償を付与する理由が完全に達成されたという考えであり[70]，第2に，二重の処罰を避けようとすることである[71]。この法準則の根底をなす原理は明快であるけれど，連邦最高裁判所のその意見には，同裁判所自体が認めているように，多くの問題に答えが与えられていない[72]。それらの問題には，刑事上の処罰が「相当」か否か；どのような場合に刑事手続と民事手続との間に「実質的な同一性」が存在するのか；関連する刑事手続での無罪判決が懲罰的賠償を求める民事手続に及ぼす効果；および，刑事手続の存在またはその可能性が民事手続に与える影響の決定という困難を含んでいる[73]。オーストラリアでは，これらの問題は後の判例法においても依然解決されないままで残されている[74]。一方，ニュージーランドの控訴院は，より広い準則を述べることでこれらの困難の多くを回避した。*Daniels v Thompson*事件判決[75]において控訴院は，被告の行為が刑事訴追の対象になっているかなりそうな場合には，懲罰的賠償を求める請求は起こし得ないと判示した。

*Gray*事件判決で示された策，そして（なおのこと）ニュージーランドで採用された策の双方とも処罰を執行する点での刑事法の，したがって，国家の第1次的役割を強化するためのものである。*Daniels*事件判決において，ニュージーランドの控訴院の多数意見（Richardson P, Gault, Henry and Keith JJ.）は，次のように述べた[76]。

「犯罪行為を扱う国家の役割には優先順位が与えられ，私的利益による介入はかかる役割が完了するまで延期される……このことはまた，犯罪行為を理由に処罰を科すことは，そのあるべき姿のように，第一次的には刑事法にあることを確実にするものである。」

これらすべての実際上の効果は，懲罰的賠償の利用可能性を，オーストラリアおよびニュージーランドが*Rookes*事件判決におけるアプローチを採用した場合よりも恐らく制限するものである。なぜなら，被告の行為は，懲罰的賠償が利用可能なほとんどの事件で恐らく刑事法のそしてその制裁の対象となるからである。このことは，実際上，懲罰的賠償が重要となる唯一の場合は，現に犯罪と定義されていない，あるいはいまだ犯罪と定義されていない行為を非難することを裁判所が望む場合に限られる，ということを意味しているのかもしれない。

6 懲罰的賠償をより広く利用できるようにすること

　懲罰的賠償はより広く利用できるようにすべきで，訴追と処罰の費用を刑事訴訟から民事訴訟へと移すべきなのか。純粋に経済的な考慮理由を別にすれば，私には以下の際立った点で原告に利するのでこの主張が支持されると思われる。

- 原告は「訴追」するかしないかの問題および事件の進行をコントロールすることができる。この点は，——性的虐待事件における家族関係のような——原告と被告との間に以前から続く関係がある場合には重要となりえよう。
- 刑事手続と民事手続との関係に対するニュージーランドで採られたアプローチが採用されるなら，訴追が遅れているかあるいは訴追の判断が避けられている場合には，裁判所には訴追の裁量権に対する何らかの，もちろん僅かな，指揮権が与えられる。それは，訴追権者に裁量権を行使することを求めることで，裁判所が訴追権者の怠惰に圧力をかけられるからである。
- 国家でなく原告が「罰金」を手にする。伝統的には，これは原告に対する「タナボタ（windfall）」であるとみなされている。「タナボタ」と言うことは，原告は本当は金を受け取るべきでないことを暗示するものである。しかし，この主張は，処罰に対する国家の独占を前提としている[77]。

　これらの主張に反対するものとして，すでに論じたデュー・プロセスの問題点がある。私が特に重要であると思う3つの点を示す。

- 第1の点は立証責任である。被告が処罰されうるには，立証は民事での証明水準を上回るものでなければならない。解決策は，懲罰的賠償を認めることに伴う重大な結果を考えると，明確で揺るぎ無い証拠が存在しなければならないということかもしれない。オーストラリアにおいては，これは*Briginshaw*事件における基準の下で可能である[78]。
- 第2の点はより難しい。すでに見たように懲罰的賠償の付与を正当化する行為の描写が不確定であり，そのためReid貴族院裁判官は，かつてそれは「刑法典という名に値する法律に載せられないほどあいまいな用語」[79]で表されていると述べた。このことがより一層断言できるのは，問題とされる行為が，実際，刑法による非難の対象となっていない場合である。懲罰的賠償を呼び起こす行為の性質を決めずに，懲罰的賠償を認めることは，現代の市民生活における刑法典の根底をなしている原則——つまり，事前の刑法上の規定がなければ犯罪も処罰も存在すべきではないという

原則[80]——に違反していると見ることができる。さしあたり，私には，懲罰的賠償に値する行為の定義における現在の不明確さをどのように克服することができるか理解に苦しむ。

・第3に，立法またはコモン・ロー上の原則の発展により，処罰として与えられる賠償金の額をコントロールする必要があり，その額が一定の一貫性を得る必要がある。懲罰的賠償の額の決定を，裁判官の，そしてなおさらのこと，陪審の完全な裁量に任せることはできない。この点で，節度［ある賠償額］を求める最近の忠告は十分ではないであろう[81]。

結　論

懲罰的賠償に対して大きな信頼をよせ刑事訴追に関する国家の独占を切り崩すことを求める揺るぎ無い主張がなされようと，最後のパラグラフで示した点には，重大な注意が向けられる必要があろう。刑事裁判制度の規制緩和の状況の中で，それらの問題点に答が与えられないままでいることは，裁判官および原告の手にあまりにも大きな権限を与えることとなろう。実際，懲罰的賠償が民事法の中で正当化しうる役割を有していることに我々が納得ゆくまでは，おそらく，我々は規制緩和という考え方を抱くべきではないのかもしれない。そして，私はBurrows教授同様[82]懲罰的賠償が民事法の中で正当化しうる役割を有しているとは，断じて確信していない。

少なくとも当面は，懲罰的賠償は民事上の救済手段の枠組みの中で例外的な救済手段[83]としての現在ある変則的な地位を保つべきである。

(1) J. Smith and B. Hogan, *Criminal Law*, 8th ed., Butterworths, London, 1996) Ch. 1参照。

(2) A.S. Diamond, *Primitive Law Past and Present* (Methuen, London, 1971)p. 18, Ch. 18.現存している共同社会からの例では，さらにE Adamson Hoebel, *The Law of Primitive Man: A Study in Comparative Legal Dynamics* (Harvard UP, Cambridge, 1961)参照。

(3) 特に，A H Manchester, *A Modern Legal History of England and Wales* 1750-1950 (Butterworths, London, 1980) pp. 226-230参照。

(4) イギリス刑事法の発展の簡単な歴史に関しては，J.H. Baker, *An Introduction to English Legal History* (2nd ed., Butterworths, London, 1979) Ch. 24.

(5) T.F.T. Plucknett, *A Concise History of tne Common Law* (Butter-

worth & Co (Publishers) Ltd., London, 1956) pp. 463-482参照。
(6) 通常は不法行為であるが契約違反も犯罪となりうる場合がある。
(7) *Uren v. John Fairfax & Sons Pty Ltd.* (1966) 117 CLR 118 at 149 per Windeyer J.（不法行為と犯罪の源は大変混同している）参照。また、*Gray v. Motor Accident Commission* (1998) 158 ALR 485 at 489 per Gleeseon CJ, Mchugh, Gummow and Hayne JJ.も参照。
(8) 懲罰的賠償の経済的分析に関しては、A Ogus, "Exemplary Damages and Economic Analysis" in K Hawkins (ed), *The Human Face of Law: Essays in Honour of Donald Harris* (Clarendon Press, Oxford, 1997) Ch. 4参照。
(9) *Whitfeld v. De Lauret & Co. Ltd.* (1920) 29 CLR 71 at 81; *Uren v. John Fairfax & Sons Pty Ltd.* (1966) 117 CLR 118 at 149; *Australian Consolidated Press Ltd v. Uren* (1967) 117 CLR 221; *Lamb v. Cotogno* (1987) 164 CLR 1 at 9.
(10) R. Zimmermann, *The Law of Obligations: Roman Foundations of the Civilian Tradition* (Juta & Co. Ltd., Cape Town, 1990) p. 909 n. 54参照。
(11) 例えば、P.J.Visser and J.M.Potgieter, *Law of Damages* (Cape Town, Juta & Ltd., 1993) pp. 156-157（南アフリカのローマン・ダッチ法）参照。
(12) D Gardner, "Reflexions sur les Dommages Punitifs et Exemplaires" (1998) 77 *Canadian Bar Rev* 198（ケベック州の著作権違反を理由とする賠償）参照。
(13) M Tilbury, "Factors Inflating Damages Awards" in P.D. Finn (ed), *Essays on Damages* (Law Book Co. Ltd., Sydney, 1992) at 92-96参照。
(14) *Uren v. John Fairfax & Sons Pty Ltd.* (1966) 117 CLR 118 at 149 per Windeyer J.
(15) *BHP Ltd. v. Fisher* (1984) 38 SASR 50 at 66.
(16) M.J. Tilbury, *Civil Remedies* (Butterworths, Sydney, 1990) vol. 1 para 3208（感情に対する侵害の場合に増大された損害に特別なラベルを貼ることの正当化理由は、そのような損失が裁判所が是認しない被告の行為を引き合いに出すことにより黙示されることである。）参照。
(17) 完全な分析は、M.J. Tilbury, *Civil Remedies* (Butterworths, Sydney, 1990) vol. 2, paras. 11012-11023参照。
(18) Ibid., para. 11019.
(19) Ibid., para. 11015.
(20) 例えば、M.J. Tilbury, "Exemplary Damages in Medical Negligence" (1996) 4 *Tort L. Rev.* 167により論じられた*Backwell v. A* [1997] 1 VR 182参照。
(21) M. Tilbury, "Exemplary Damages in Negligence Claims" (1997) 5 *Tort L. Rev.* 85により論じられた*Trend Management Ltd. v. Borg* (1996) 40

NSWLR 500参照。
⑵ M. Tilbury and H. Luntz, "Punitive Damages in Australian Law" 17 *Loyola of Los Angeles Int'l and Comp LJ*. 769 at 791-792 (1995)参照。
⑵ シドニーは世界の中の名誉毀損の首都であると呼ばれている:R Pullan, *Guilty Secrets: Free Speech and Defamation in Australia* (Pascal Press, Glebe, 1994) at 3参照。この記述は,利用できる経験的証拠により支持されない:New South Wales Law Reform Commission, *Defamation* (LRC 75, 1995), para 3.25参照。ロンドンのほうがそのようにみなされるのにふさわしい:E Barendt, L. Lustgarten, K. Norrie and H. Stephenson, *Libel and the Media: The Chilling Effect* (Clarendon Press, Oxford, 1997) p. 16参照。
⑵ *Defamation Act* 1974 (NSW) s. 46 (3)(a).
⑵ ニューサウスウェールズ州における収監費用については,New South Wales Law Reform Commission, *Sentencing* (LRC 79, 1996), paras. 1.18-1.21。
⑵ 非常に簡単に示せば,生じたことにより誰もがより大きな負担を負わされてはならない。
⑵ 非常に簡単に示せば,生じたことによりより富んだ者がより負担を負う者に対して保障をさせなければならない。
⑵ 一般的には,R. Posner, *Economic Analysis of Law* (4th ed., Little Brown & Co., Boston 1992) Ch. 1参照。
⑵ New South Wales Law Reform Commission, *Sentencing* (DP 33, 1996) paras. 3.2-3.24参照。
⑶ 前出注⑯ Tilbury, paras. 1028-1029参照。
⑶ 有名な例は,*Gouriet v. Union of Post Office Workers* [1978] AC 435である。
⑶ M. Aronson and B. Dyer, *Judicial Review of Administrative Action* (3 rd ed., LBC Information Services, Sydney, 1996) pp. 917-920; C. Lewis, *Judicial Remedies in Public Law* (Sweet & Maxwell, London, 1992) pp. 21-22参照。
⑶ 前出注⑵ New South Wales Law Reform Commission, Ch. 11参照。
⑶ Ibid., Ch. 10.
⑶ J. Fionda, *Public Prosecutors and Discretion: A Comparative Study* (Clarendon Press, Oxford, 1995)参照。
⑶ 特に,H McGregor, *Mayne & McGregor on Damages* (12th ed., Sweet & Maxwell, London, 1961) para. 207参照。
⑶ [1964] AC 1129.
⑶ Ibid., at 1226.
⑶ 特に,*Broome v. Cassell & Co. Ltd*. [1972] AC 1027 at 1086-87 par Lord Reid参照。
⑷ *Broome v. Cassell & Co Ltd* [1972] AC 1027 at 1070 per Lord Hailsham

of St. Marylebone.
(41) Ibid., at 1087 par Lord Reid.
(42) *Gray v. Motor Accident Commission* (1998) 158 ALR 485 at 493を検討。
(43) *Uren v. John Fairfax & Sons Pty Ltd.* (1966) 117 CLR 118; *Australian Consolidated Press v. Uren* (1967) 117 CLR 221.
(44) *Taylor v. Beere* [1982] 1 NZLR 81; *Donselaar v. Donselaar* [1982] 1 NZLR 97.
(45) *Vorvis v. Insurance Corporation of British Columbia* [1989] 1 SCR 1085.
(46) 前出注(16) Tilbury, Ch. 5。
(47) *Gray v. Motor Accident Commission* (1998) 158 ALR 485 at 493.
(48) *Whitfeld v. De Lauret & Co. Ltd.* (1920) 29 CLR 71 at 77 par Knox CJ *Gray v. Motor Accident Commission* (1998) 158 ALR 485 at 489 per Gleeson C.J., McHugh, Gummow and Hayne JJ.も参照。
(49) J. Salmond, *A Treatise on the Law of Torts* (5th ed, Sweet & Maxwell, London) p. 129参照。
(50) 前出注(16) Tilbury, paras 5005-5007参照。
(51) 例えば, *Proprietary Schools of Western Australia Ltd v. Crown* (1943) 46 WALR 37.
(52) *Uren v. John Fairfax & Sons Pty Ltd.* (1966) 117 CLR 118 at 153 per Windeyer J.参照。
(53) *AB v. South West Water Services Ltd.* [1993] QB 507.
(54) Law Commission of England and Wales, *Aggravated, Exemplary and Restitutionary Damages* (Law Com., No. 247, 1997) paras 5.49-5.77.
(55) 特に, *Lamb v. Cotogno* (1987) 164 CLR 1 at 8。
(56) *Vorvis v. Insurance Corporation of British Columbia* [1989] 1 SCR 1085.
(57) (1972) 24 DLR (3d) 156 at 167.
(58) [1964] AC 1129 at 1227.
(59) *XL Petroleum (NSE) Pty Ltd. v. Caltex Oil (Australia) Pty Ltd.* (1985) 155 CLR 448.
(60) 特に, *Donselaar v. Donselaar* [1982] 1 NZLR 97参照。
(61) これは, 正当化できないはずの, 塡補の賠償金を懲罰的賠償金であると詐称して認める機会を裁判所に与えることになった:J Smillie, "Exemplary Damages for Personal Injury" [1997] *NZ L. Rev.* 140.
(62) (1998) 158 ALR 493 par Gleeson CJ., McHugh, Gummow and Hayne JJ.:しかし, at 505 per Kirby Jと比較。

⒃ (1987) 164 CLR 1.
⒁ H. Luntz, *Assessment of Damages for Personal Injury and Death* (3rd ed., Butterworths, Sydney, 1990) para 1.7.6.この不条理さは保険会社が保険契約者に対して求償権を持つときには小さくなる:*Gray v. Motor Accident Commission* (1998) 158 ALR 485 at 494参照。
⒂ *Lamb v. Cotogno* (1987) 164 CLR 1 at 9.
⒃ 特に, *Thompson v. Commissioner of Police* [1997] 2 All ER 762 (CA)。
⒄ 例えば, *Backwell v. A* [1997] 1 VR 187。
⒅ *Gray v. Motor Accident Commission* (1998) 158 ALR 485; *Watts v. Leitch* [1973] Tas SR 16参照。
⒆ (1998) 158 ALR 485 at 494.
⒇ Ibid., at 495.
(71) Ibid.
(72) Ibid., at 495-496.
(73) Ibid.
(74) 例えば, *McDonald v. State of New South Wales* [1999] NSWSC 350 (20 April 1999) (拘留を伴わない量刑でも相当な処罰とみなされうる)。
(75) *Daniels v. Thompson* [1998] 3 NZLR 22. 十分な議論に関しては, J. Smillie, "Exemplary Damages and the Criminal Law" (1998), 6 *Torts L.J.* 113参照。
(76) *Daniels v. Thompson* [1998] 3 NZLR 22 at 53.
(77) さらなる批判に関しては, N.J. McBride, "Punitive Damages" in P. Birks (ed), *Wrongs and Remedies in the Twenty-First Century* (Clarendon Press, Oxford, 1996) p. 196参照。
(78) *Briginshaw v. Briginshaw* (1938) 60 CLR 336, 特に, at 362-363 par Dixon J参照。および, *Backwell v. A* [1997] 1 VR 182参照。
(79) *Broome v. Cassell & Co. Ltd.* [1972] AC 1027 at 1087.
(80) *Nulla crimen nulla poena sine praevia lege poenali*.
(81) 例えば, *XL Petroleum (NSW) Pty Ltd. v. Caltex Oil (Australia) Pty Ltd.* (1985) 155 CLR 448 at 463参照。*Thompson v. Commissioner of Police* [1997] 2 All ER 762 (CA)と比較せよ。
(82) A Burrows, "Reforming Exemplary Damages: Expansion or Abolition?" in P Birks (ed), *Wrongs and Remedies in the Twenty-First Century* (Clarendon Press, Oxford, 1996) Ch. 7.
(83) *Gray v. Motor Accident Commission* (1998) 158 ALR 485 at 490-491 per Gleeson CJ. McHugh, Gummow and Hayne JJ.

10　厳格責任・絶対責任による法人活動の規制

ウォーレン J. ブルックバンクス

[洲 見 光 男 訳]

　　はじめに
　1　ニュー・ジーランドにおける犯罪の分類
　2　ニュー・ジーランドにおける厳格責任の範囲
　3　厳格責任と環境犯罪
　4　量 刑 方 針
　5　代理人の行為についての本人の責任
　　おわりに

は じ め に

　現代社会の複雑性とそれが私たちの社会環境や自然環境に与える影響は，否応なしに強力な規制手段を必要としてきたが，規制目的の1つは，居住環境を保護する必要と経済発展を促進し経済を繁栄させる必要との間に適切なバランスをとることにある。

　ニュー・ジーランドを含む多くの西欧諸国は，こうした規制方法の一つとして，新しい種類の犯罪を設け刑法を適用するという戦略を採用してきている。ここにいう新しい種類の犯罪とは，厳格責任(strict liability)を問う犯罪と呼ばれているもので，真の意味の犯罪ではなく，伝統的に認められてきた刑事法上の諸原則が限定的に適用されるにすぎない犯罪である。そこで，こうした犯罪は，行政法の領域に属し，法執行の経済性と効率性を理由に刑罰が科せられる犯罪であると見る方がより適切である。そのような手続きで被告人となるのは，大部分が法人であり，特殊な規則ないし制定法に違反する態様でその通常の業務を行ったに過ぎないという場合が多い。

　厳格責任を問う犯罪は，道路運送，食料品・薬物の管理，労働安全，環境管理を含む広範な領域の社会活動に浸透し始めている。規制が重要視される理由は，有罪判決を得るための厳格な証明基準を充足しなくても，個人や法人に対して，高度の行動基準を強制しうることにある。しかし，問題を広く捉えると，刑法が拡大適用され，その一方で，伝統的に認められてきた刑事法上の保護が次第に失われている

のではないかという点を指摘しうる。

　本稿の目的は，特に環境立法上の犯罪に関して，「厳格」責任および「絶対」責任(absolute liability)の範囲を検討することにある。厳格責任の正当化根拠は，厳格責任を問う犯罪には汚名(stigma)が伴わず，また科せられる制裁が比較的重くない点にある，というのが伝統的な考えであった。しかし，実際には，多くの場合において重い刑事制裁を科すことが可能であって，被告人が個人であるか法人であるかを問わず，起訴は被告人に対し重大な結果をもたらすことを明らかにしたいと思う。厳格責任・絶対責任という強力な法執行の手段が，実際に，とくに環境犯罪の領域において法人による犯罪を抑止しているのかどうかは明白でなく，さらに研究が必要とされる分野である。

1　ニュー・ジーランドにおける犯罪の分類

　ニュー・ジーランドの現行法は，「真の」犯罪，「厳格」責任を問う犯罪および「絶対」責任を問う犯罪の3つのカテゴリーの犯罪を認めている。第1のカテゴリーの犯罪と後2者のカテゴリーの犯罪とは，規制目的が全く異なるとされる点で，両者には重要な概念上の区別が存在する。

　いわゆる「真の」犯罪は，通常，故意または過失の形態でのメンズ・レアの証明が要求される犯罪で，主として，刑法(1961年)および軽犯罪法に規定されているほか，運送法(1969年)や薬物乱用法(1975年)にも見いだすことができる。

　真の犯罪については，個々の違法行為を処罰し，適切な制裁を加えることによって将来の犯罪から公衆を保護することに，その目的がある。制裁は，「犯罪者に向けられた」(offender-facing)ものであって，応報，抑止，権利剥奪を量刑目標として，社会の不承認(disapprove)を表明するはけ口(outlet)を提供する。このカテゴリーに属する犯罪についてとくに重要なのは，被告人が犯罪の挙証責任と証明の基準について伝統的に認められてきた保護を受けるため，検察側は，コモン・ローの一般原則に従って，個々の事件においてメンズ・レアを含む犯罪の構成要素すべてについて合理的な疑いを越える証明をしなければならない，ということである。

　他方，「厳格」責任および「絶対」責任を問う犯罪は，たとえば，殺人や強盗の有罪判決に随伴する公の非難(public condemnation)といったものに依存するものではなく，「行為に向けられた」(conduct-facing)犯罪である。真の犯罪の有罪判決には，「犯罪行為のもつ不名誉」(disgrace of criminality)ゆえに公の汚名が伴うが，厳

格責任ないし絶対責任を問われる犯罪には，汚名はほとんどあるいは全く伴わないといわれている。こうした理由から，公衆の健康と安全を守る上で違法な活動に対し制裁を科す必要はあるが，「真の」犯罪の有罪判決に内在する非難を加えることが適切でないと考えられる場合においては，厳格責任ないし絶対責任を問う犯罪（「準犯罪」(quasi crimes)）が，法人活動を規制する手段として，多くの西欧諸国の立法者にとってますます魅力ある存在になりつつあるように思われる。

ニュー・ジーランドでは，増大する「規制」立法によって禁止されることとなった新しい形態の行為を規制するため，立法府はますます「厳格責任」を問う犯罪を規定するようになってきている。前述したとおり，厳格責任は，たとえば，道路運送や環境管理について典型的に認められるものであるが，工業機械の取扱い，アルコール飲料の醸造・販売や不法入国についても認められるようになってきた。これらの「行政」犯─公共福祉規制犯罪（public welfare regulatory offense）と呼ばれることがある─は，メンズ・レアを犯罪の構成要素としておらず，そのため検察側に利点をもたらし得る点に，その本質がある。

しかし，刑事法上の原則を貫徹しようとする立場からは，厳格責任を問う犯罪は，挙証責任および被告人の抗弁に関し認められてきた基本的な原則に反するものである。「厳格」責任を問う犯罪については，主観的要素の証明が必要とされず，メンズ・レアの欠如に基づく伝統的な抗弁が排除されている。ただし，被告人は，「自分にまったく過誤（fault）がなかった」ことを証明して刑事責任を免れることができる。これと対照的に，「絶対」責任を問うものと特徴づけられている犯罪については，検察官がメンズ・レアを証明する必要がないことはもちろんのこと，被告人は過誤がなかったことを抗弁として主張することも認められていない。

「厳格」責任ないし「絶対」責任を認めて刑罰を科すというやり方が，多くの西欧諸国においてますますポピュラーになってきているが，これは，立法上の要求に反するおそれのある業務を行う法人に重大な影響を及ぼす。法人の経営者に過誤がなくても，刑事責任の認められる場合があるので，この形態の刑事責任は，厳罰的（draconian）であり，経済の発展に寄与する法人活動を不必要に圧迫しかねないものということができよう。

ニュー・ジーランドの裁判所は，こうした問題について，環境管理といった一部の分野に適用される量刑原則を示すことによって検討を加えてきたが，この点は後述する。

2 ニュー・ジーランドにおける厳格責任の範囲

　厳格責任がニュー・ジーランドにおいてどのように発展してきたかを検討する前に,「厳格」責任という用語について, 若干の予備的考察をしておくべきだと思われる。「厳格」責任という概念は, イギリスのコモン・ローに由来するが, その法域では「厳格」責任と「絶対」責任という用語は, ほとんど相互に交換可能なものとして用いられている。そのため混乱の生ずる可能性があり, 実際, ニュー・ジーランドにおける厳格責任の法理の発展に混乱が見られたのである。裁判所は厳格責任と絶対責任という2つの概念を明確に区別してきたのに対し[1], 残念なことに, 立法府は裁判所ほど明確な区別を行っていないのである[2]。

　厳格責任ないし絶対責任を問う犯罪は, 産業革命後に生じた急速な社会的・産業上の変化に対処する重宝な手段として, 19世紀にイギリスで発展した。こうした犯罪は, たとえば, 混ぜ物をしたタバコ[3]や腐った肉の販売[4], 未成年者・酩酊者へのアルコール飲料の販売[5]といった, 公衆の健康と安全にとって有害な行為を規制対象とするものであった。この新しいタイプの制定法犯罪は, 公衆を保護する必要があるときには, 被告人に過誤がない場合であっても, 有罪の言渡しが正当化されることがあり得るという考え方を反映するものであった。厳格責任ないし絶対責任を問う犯罪は, ほとんどの場合, 規制目的に反する特殊な行為から生ずる害悪を規制することに, そのねらいがある[6]。こうした犯罪の取締りは, 警察ではなく, 専門の機関 (特定のタイプの活動が, たとえば環境汚染や労働安全に与える影響を監視・コントロールするために創設された機関) によって行われることが多い。

　それでは, 厳格責任を問う犯罪と絶対責任を問う犯罪とは, 実際にどのように区別されているのであろうか。また, 両者はどのような社会目的を達成するのであろうか。両者の区別は, 実体のあるものなのか, それとも形式に過ぎないものなのか。これらについてカナダの刑事法学の発展から若干の指針を得ることができる。

(1) カナダにおける発展

　イギリス法は, 伝統的に2つのカテゴリーの犯罪を認めてきたに過ぎない。行政犯は, それが「真の」犯罪としてメンズ・レアを要求されていない限り, つねに「絶対的」である。ここでは,「厳格」責任は「絶対」責任を意味しており, 中間のカテゴリーは存在しない。カナダの最高裁判所は, 1978年のR v. The City of Sault Ste

Marie判決[7]において，メンズ・レアが要求される犯罪と絶対責任を問う犯罪との間に，新しいカテゴリーに属する犯罪の存在を認めた。起訴は，河川への汚染物質の違法排出による環境汚染に関するものであったが，最高裁判所は，メンズ・レアは犯罪の成立に不可欠な要素ではないが，絶対責任に代わるものがあり得たという判断を示した。被告人は「自分に全く過誤がなかったこと」を申し立てることによって（この点の立証責任は被告人にある），刑事責任を免れることができるという，全く新しいカテゴリーに属する犯罪を考えることによって，このような判断がなされたのである。後に公共福祉規制犯罪として知られるようになる，新しい第3のカテゴリーに属する犯罪は，「厳格」責任を問う犯罪としても知られている。最高裁判所は厳格責任の特徴について次のように述べた。

「……当該禁止された行為を行うことは，犯罪を構成するものと推定される。ただし，被告人は，合理的な注意を尽くしたことを証明することによって，責任を免れることができる。その際，道理をわきまえた人であれば，当該状況の下でどのように行動したであろうかを検討することが必要である。事実を誤認し，そのため作為あるいは不作為が犯罪とならないと誤信したことが合理的であること，あるいは，特定の事態を回避するために合理的な措置をすべて講じたことは，抗弁たり得る。」[8]

最高裁判所は，「公共福祉」犯罪について，それによって公衆の健康と安全を守るのに必要な高度な基準を維持することができるのであり，その点にその存在理由があると述べた。「公共福祉」犯罪は，司法による便宜的な創造物であり，高度の注意義務を課すことによって社会の利益を保護しようとするものであるが，これが正当化されるのは，不知や錯誤があっても免責されないことを知っている場合の方が，注意義務を遵守する可能性が大きいからである[9]。

(2) **厳格責任の論拠**

前述したとおり，メンズ・レアの要件を放棄する理由の一つとして通常挙げられるのは，公衆を保護するためには危険な行為を行う者には高度の注意義務を課す必要がある，ということである。危険な行為を行う者は，適切な注意を払う必要があるのであるが，過失責任を問われることがないため，危険を小さくしたり排除した

りするインセンティブが欠如している場合には，自己の過失のコストを社会に転嫁し得ることになる[10]。高度に危険な行為を行う者は，刑事責任を問われる可能性があれば，一層注意を払うよう動機づけられるものだと考えられている。

ニュー・ジーランドでは，厳格（および絶対）責任は，人身に対する損害を原因とする不法行為責任に部分的に代替するものであり，事故保証立法 (accident compensation legislation) が不法行為責任にとって代わっている。ニュー・ジーランドでは，事故により生じた人身に対する損害について訴訟を提起することはできない。そこで，民事責任を問われるおそれがないため，過失による事故を回避する経済的インセンティブを欠く事業主間で，不注意が助長されることにもなりかねない。そこで，法人活動を規制することに主眼が置かれている場合には，厳格責任はとくに適切な規制手段であると考えられている。その理由として，第1に，法人に言い渡される有罪判決には，通常，個人の場合と同じ程度の汚名が伴わないこと，第2に，法人の活動は，個人の活動と比べ，はるかにスケールの大きいものであって，それが社会に与える脅威もより大きいこと，第3に，これがもっとも重要であるが，法人については，メンズ・レアの証明が特に困難であることを指摘し得る。

(3) 絶 対 責 任

「厳格」責任がその性格上，過誤がなかったことの一般的な抗弁を許すのに対して，「絶対」責任はそのような譲歩を認めず，責任は絶対的である。これは，被告人は自分に全く過誤がなかった場合であっても責任を問われるということである。この意味で，絶対責任は，常軌を逸した (aberrant) ものであって，例外的な場合にのみ認められるべきものである。ニュー・ジーランドの裁判所は，公共福祉規制犯罪という新しいカテゴリーの犯罪が登場し，過誤がなかったことの被告人の証明が抗弁として認められることにより，裁判所が絶対責任を問う犯罪と判断せざるを得ない制定法犯罪の数は減少するであろうという見方を示している[11]。しかし，立法府は，制定法犯罪が「厳格」責任を問うものであるとしながらも，過誤がなかったことによる抗弁の許される（限定的な）範囲を制定法自体で宣言することによって，事実上「絶対」責任を問うことができるようにしてきている。被告人が制定法上認められた狭い範囲（たとえば，緊急避難（ないし不可抗力）であったこと，かつ，被告人の行為が合理的であったこと，かつ，行為のもつ影響力を減殺したこと，これらすべてについて証明を要求する形で典型的に表現されている）の抗弁を主張できない

限り，責任は絶対的であり，有罪判決が言い渡されることとなる。これが，ニュー・ジーランドの環境立法で通常用いられているモデルである[12]。そのような制定法に定められた抗弁は，立法府が被告人に過誤のなかったことによる一般的な抗弁を採用し法典化した範囲を示すものであるというのが，裁判所の判断である[13]。法典化された段階で類似の抗弁が排除されたと解釈することができるため，実際には，過誤のなかったことが抗弁として認められる余地はまったくないこととなる。

次に，ニュー・ジーランドの裁判所が環境犯罪について下した若干の判決を参照しながら，法人の活動を規制するために厳格責任・絶対責任がどのように採用されているかを説明したいと思う。また，この分野で採用されている量刑方針についてもコメントを加えることとしたい。

3 厳格責任と環境犯罪

ニュー・ジーランドにおける主たる環境立法は，資源管理法（Resource Management Act 1991。以下，「RMA」と略称）である。RMAは，同法の定める義務に違反する程度によって刑罰の階層を構成している[14]。もっとも重大な犯罪については，2年以下の拘禁刑および20万ニュー・ジーランド・ドル以下の罰金を科すことが可能である。他方，RMAの与えている権限の行使を故意に妨害する犯罪など，軽微な犯罪については，1,500ニュー・ジーランド・ドル以下の罰金刑が定められている。

裁判所は伝統的に，環境立法に違反する行為を，真の犯罪というより「軽罪」(misdemeanor) とみなしてきた[15]。ニュー・ジーランドの初期の環境立法については，まさにその通りであった。Hastings City v. Simons判決[16]において，Cooke裁判官（現在はLord Cooke of Thorndon）は，旧水質・土壌保護法（1967年）に定められた犯罪は，「公共福祉規制のカテゴリー……に属し」[17]，それゆえ適切にも真の意味での犯罪には分類されず，刑事法上の伝統的な諸原則の適用が限定される行政法の領域に属する犯罪と見る方が妥当であると，述べた[18]。

しかし，RMAの下では，もっとも重大な犯罪につき非常に高額な罰金刑および拘禁刑の言い渡される可能性があることから，環境に対し重大な損害を与える行為あるいは環境管理上の諸原則に反する行為を犯罪化して，これに刑罰を科すという立法府の意図が窺える。しかし，拘禁刑の可能性がなく，財産刑が定められているに過ぎない犯罪については，真の意味での「犯罪」とはいえず，単純な行政犯と見るべきであるとされている[19]。

先に指摘したとおり，立法府がある制定法犯罪を「厳格」責任を問うものと称することがますます慣例化してきているが，公衆の健康と安全にとって有害な行為あるいはその可能性のある行為を規制することに立法目的がある場合には，とくにそうした傾向を認めることができる。環境犯罪はこのカテゴリーに属するものと考えられているが，例としてRMA341節を挙げることができる。同節は，同法第3部に定められた義務の違反に対し厳格責任を規定している。検察側は，被告人の刑事責任を立証するためにメンズ・レアを証明する必要はない。しかし，RMAは，行為が「［緊急避難として］必要であった」こと，あるいは，行為が被告人の支配を越える事態の発生（不可抗力）によることを証明して，責任を免れることができる，と規定している。さらに，被告人は，抗弁を主張するにあたっては，自己の行為が「合理的であった」こと，および，自己の行為あるいは事態の与える影響を十分に減殺したことを証明しなければならない。

　ニュー・ジーランドにおける厳格責任を問われる犯罪は，一般に，コモン・ロー犯罪ないし裁判所により創造された犯罪であるが，これは，そうした犯罪は過誤がなかったという一般的な抗弁の許される犯罪であることを意味する。しかし，RMA341節の規定する犯罪は，過誤がなかったことの抗弁の範囲を制限しようとする立法者の企図を表すものか，あるいは，環境犯罪について過誤のなかったことに関する一般原則の適用範囲を法典化したものである[20]。341節が排他的・自己完結的であり，同法の定めるもっとも重大な犯罪との関係では，制定法上の狭い例外にあたる場合を除いて，実際上「絶対」責任を課していると解されてきた[21]。このように考えると，もっとも重大な犯罪について，かなり長期の拘禁刑（2年以下）を科すことが可能であるとしても，メンズ・レアは，無謀であろうが過失であろうが，必要でないということになる。

　厳格責任・絶対責任の発展には，伝統的に認められてきた刑事法上の諸原則が掘り崩され，刑事責任それ自体の認定にではなく，単に犯罪者が禁止された事態を「惹起した」かどうかに依拠するプラグマティックなモデルが是認されることになってしまうという問題がある。訴追側には，処罰効果を高めながら，起訴のコストを削減し得るという利点があるが，これに反し，行為者にとっては，犯罪事実についての重要な認識を欠き，結果を意図することも予見することもなかったにもかかわらず，犯罪を犯したものとしての烙印を押されてしまうという問題がある。

4 量刑方針

　RMAは，環境犯罪に関するまったく新しい量刑制度の先駆的存在となっている。もっとも，RMAそれ自体は，量刑上考慮すべき事項について何ら規定していないので，大部分は広範な立法目的を検討することによって推論しなければならない。
　RMAは環境への有害な影響を回避することを強調しており，これは刑罰に対するより厳格なアプローチに現れていると考えられてきた。適切な注意を尽くさなかったことの証明を要件として，会社の取締役 (director) および経営者 (manager) は拘禁刑および罰金刑を科せられる。こうした事情は，刑罰目的だけでなく，経済目標および教育目標を達成するためにも，量刑について柔軟で斬新なアプローチが採用されるべきであるという立法府の裁判所に対する指示を示すものと，ニュー・ジーランドの裁判所は解釈してきた[22]。
　高等裁判所 (High Court) は，ある会社が液体貯蔵庫に貯蔵しておいた有毒廃棄物を河川に流出させたという事案に関するMachinery Movers v. ARC判決[23]において，汚染の「外部的」(external) コストは誰が負担すべきかという観点から，環境汚染が経済に与える影響を検討した。高等裁判所は，規制がなされていない場合において，社会が経済的アウトプットと環境の質との間に適切なバランスをとることができない経済上の理由は，汚染者でなく，それ以外の者が汚染のコストを負担しているからである，と判示した。そうした汚染の「外部的」コストは，汚染を惹き起こした者によって一般に考慮されることはない。汚染のコストが，実際に汚染を惹起した者によっても，また，その者の生産した物を購入する者によっても負担されない限度で，経済活動から生ずる総利益のいくらかが汚染の犠牲者から社会の他の集団に誤って再分配されているのである。高等裁判所は，市場の失敗 (market failure) を是正するためには，外部的コストを汚染者に戻すために，政府が介入し，汚染者に経済的コストを負担させたり，刑罰を科したりする必要があると判示したが，このような内容の原則を示すにあたって，環境と開発に関する国連会議で採択された「環境と開発に関するリオ宣言」の原則16を引用した (Riode Janerio 3-14 June 1992, 31 ILM 874 (1992) 879)。
　高等裁判所は，Machinery Movers v. ARC判決において，環境犯罪についての重要な原則を示すにあたって，オンタリオの裁判所 (Provincial Division) がR v. Bata Industries Ltd判決[24]で明らかにした原則を承認し，環境犯罪に適用し得る

「一般的事項」と，環境犯罪で有罪判決を受けた法人に関連する事項とを区別した。第1のカテゴリーに含まれるのは，①影響を受けた環境の性質，②加えられた損害の程度（範囲），③犯罪の計画性および，④被告人の態度であり，第2のカテゴリーには，①法人の規模，資産，業務の性格，②法遵守への努力度，③悔悟，④犯罪による利得および，⑤犯罪歴などが含まれる。

Bata Industries 判決は，「一般予防」について，刑罰威嚇により法を遵守させるという通常の消極的な意味においてではなく，社会の不承認を強調し，行為が非難すべきものであるとの公の烙印を押すことによって，公衆の保護がもっとも図られるという考え方を示したが，ニュー・ジーランドの高等裁判所もこれに同意した。また，高等裁判所は，科せられる刑罰が重く，そのため同様の状況下にある他の会社が環境に対する損害の排除に協力するのを抑止されることがあってはならず，この意味で，抑止という概念には「奨励」の要素が含まれていることにも賛成した。つまり，刑罰は，「抑止しすぎる」ものであってはならないのである。

現在までのところ，RMA上の犯罪の起訴は，大部分が汚染物質の不法排出や動植物の保護地域の破壊に関するもので，科せられた罰金は，5,000から80,000ニュー・ジーランド・ドルであった[25]。この罰金額は，決して小額ではなく，重大な「真の」犯罪で通常科せられるよりもはるかに高額である。「厳格」責任・「絶対」責任を問う犯罪と名づけられたからといって，それだけで個人であろうと法人であろうと，重い刑を言い渡される可能性がなくなるわけではないことを，そうした罰金額は示している。

5 代理人の行為についての本人の責任

RMAは，代理人の行為について本人の起訴を認めている。本人は，自ら犯罪を犯したかのように扱われるわけである[26]。ただし，犯罪が行われていることを知らなかったことあるいは知ることを合理的に期待できなかったこと，または犯行を防止するための合理的な手段をすべて講じたことを本人が証明すれば，抗弁となることを制定法は認めている。同様に，被告人が法人である場合には，取締役も「法人の経営（management）に携わっている」いかなる者も，犯罪が行われていることを知らなかったこと，および，会社が犯行を防止するための合理的な措置をすべて講じたことを証明して抗弁を主張することが許されている[27]。当該規定によって，法人の役員が犯罪について実際何も知らなかったとしても，検察側が当該状況の下で知

るべきであったことを証明できれば，法人役員の責任が認められることになる。このことは当該規定のもつ重要な効果である[28]。

おわりに

厳格責任・絶対責任を用いることが，西欧の多くの法域でますます一般的になりつつある。こうした形態の責任のもつ主たる利点は，有罪判決を勝ち取るのに必要とされる検察側の挙証責任が免除され，そのため検察官にとっては有罪判決を得る見込みが高まるということである。しかし，厳格責任・絶対責任が実際に，より効率的な業務の遂行を可能にし，自然環境に与える損害をより小さくし，職場環境を一層保護し得るものとして，社会に利益をもたらすものであるかどうかは分かっていない。厳格責任・絶対責任は，刑事責任に関する確立された諸原則に対する妥協という高い代償を強いるものであるから，こうした利益を確保し得るものであることが望まれる。

厳格責任・絶対責任は，法人を主たる対象として認められるものであるが，これは，法人・その代理人の活動が性格上そうした責任を問われる行為に含まれることが多いためである。

厳格責任は，環境を保護し，環境汚染を最小限に食い止める政策目的と合致するものではあるが，いかなる代償を払っても追求すべきものではない。関係者の法の支配に対する敬意が失われてしまってはならないからである。刑事制裁を科す伝統的な手段と厳格責任・絶対責任のような他の手段（限定された状況の下で一定のタイプの行為を規制するもっとも有効な手段）との間に適切なバランスを保つことが必要なのである。

(1) See *Civil Aviation Dept. v. MacKenzie* [1983] NZLR 78.
(2) 詳細に「厳格責任」を問う犯罪規定を検討すると，立法府は「厳格責任」という表現を用いながら，絶対責任を問う犯罪を規定していることが明らかとなる。
(3) See R. v. Woodrow (1846) 15 M & W 404.
(4) *Hobbs v. Winchester Corporation* [1910] 2 KB 471, CA.
(5) *Cundy v. Le Coq* (1884) 13 QBD 207.
(6) Simester, A & Brookbanks, WJ, Principles of Criminal Law (Brookers', Wellington, 1998) 124.
(7) (1978) 85 DLR (3d) 161.

(8) *R. v. City of Sault Ste Marie* (1978) 85 DLR (3d) 161, 181.
(9) Ibid., 170.
(10) Simester & Brookbanks, supra. 128.
(11) *Civil Aviation Dept. v. MacKenzie* [1983] NZLR 78, 85 per Richardson, J.
(12) See *Mc Knight v. NZ Biogas Industries Ltd.* [1994] 2 NZLR 664 and see *Canterbury Regional Council v. Doug Hood Ltd.* 30/6/98, Judge Skelton, DC Christchurch, CRN 7076006424.
(13) Ibid., 669.
(14) See D. Grinlinton, "Liability for Environmental Harm in New Zealand" [1997] Env. Liability 106, 108.
(15) Ibid., 109.
(16) [1984] 2 NZLR 502.
(17) Ibid., 506.
(18) *Civil Aviation Dept. v. MacKenzie* [1983] NZLR 78, 85 per Richardson, J.
(19) Grinlinton, supra, 109.
(20) *Mc Knight v. NZ Biogas Industries Ltd.* [1994] 2 NZLR 664, 669.
(21) Grinlinton, supra. 110.
(22) *Machinery Movers v. ARC* [1994] 1 NZLR 492, 500-01.
(23) Ibid.
(24) (1992) 9 OR (3d) 329.
(25) Grinlinton, supra. 110.
(26) Resource Management Act 1991, s. 340 (1).
(27) RMA, s. 340 (2).
(28) Grinlinton, supra. 111.

11 行政規制と刑事制裁

田 口 守 一

はじめに
1 経済犯罪に対する行政制裁
2 経済犯罪に対する刑事制裁
3 手続法的問題
むすび

はじめに

(1) 規制緩和と経済犯罪の抑止

　経済犯罪とは，個人の利益を超えた経済秩序または経済利益を保護法益とする犯罪である。経済活動の複雑化・広域化にともなって，経済犯罪の態様も複雑化・広域化している。詐欺，横領，背任などの伝統的小規模犯罪から，企業単位・国際単位で行われる独禁法違反，証券取引法違反などの大規模犯罪へと巨大化している。

　ところで，このような経済犯罪を抑止するためには，行政規制や企業の自主規制による事前的コントロールと刑罰などの制裁による事後的コントロールとが，ともに必要である。このうち，事前の行政規制を緩和するいわゆる規制緩和は，2つの効果をもたらすことになる。すなわち，①事前的コントロールのうちの自主規制の比重を重くすること，および②制裁による事後的コントロールの役割が重くなること，である。

　このようにして，経済犯罪の抑止という観点からすると，規制緩和は，企業の自主規制と制裁のあり方の検討を要請することになる。以下では，主に制裁システムを中心に検討する。

(2) 制裁のシステム

　経済犯罪に対する制裁として，まず，自主的制裁と法的制裁とを区別することができる。企業の自主的制裁としては，証券取引法における過怠金制度，業界団体による除名処分，違反企業の公表，あるいは，企業内部における解雇，降格，配置転換，減俸などの制裁がある。このような自主的制裁が的確に実施されれば，有効な

犯罪抑止効をもたらすこととなる。しかし，そのためには，企業がその社会的責任を自覚することが必要であり，今後ますますこの側面は重要な課題となろう。さらに，非法的制裁として，いわゆる社会的制裁にも触れておく必要がある。マスコミによる弾劾や市民による違反企業の商品不買運動などである。このようなインフォーマルな制裁は，時に大きな効果をもたらすこととなる。しかし，あまりインフォーマルな制裁に期待すると，制裁の行き過ぎのみならず法的制裁制度の発達を遅らせることになることに注意すべきであろう。

次に，法的制裁としては，民事制裁，行政制裁および刑事制裁がある。民事制裁としては，民法上の不法行為責任としての損害賠償責任が代表される。ただ，民事制裁は，原告の立証責任や裁判費用などの問題があり，必ずしも有効な抑止システムとはなっていない。以下，ここでは，とくに行政制裁および刑事制裁について，その相互関係を整理し，刑事制裁の役割りを中心にして考えてみたい。

1 経済犯罪に対する行政制裁

(1) 行政制裁の意義

経済法規（行政法規）違反に対する行政制裁として，刑罰（行政刑罰）が科される場合と狭義の行政制裁が科される場合とがある。ここでは，狭義の行政制裁を取り上げる。行政制裁として，金銭制裁とその他の行政処分を区別することができる。

まず，金銭制裁として，過料，反則金，課徴金がある。過料は，行政上の義務違反に対して科されるものであり，その行為自体が当然に反社会的性格を有するわけではないが，行政上の秩序維持のために科される制裁金である。反則金は，刑罰に替わる行政制裁であるが，罰金もしくは科料に相当する金額等を納付すべきことを通告し，犯則者がこれを納付したときは，公訴を提起されないという制度である。また，独占禁止法は，事業者の不当な取引制限等の行為について，その行為を行っていた期間の売上高に一定の比率を掛けた額を課徴金として納付することを命ずるものとしている（法7条の2第1項）。不正に得た利益を剥奪することによって，違反の抑止を図ることを目的とする制度である。

これらに対して，その他の行政処分としては，営業規定に違反した場合に，「営業許可の取消し」，「営業停止」等の措置がとられることがある。また，行政庁が，義務の不履行あるいは行政指導に対する不服従があった場合に，その事実を「公表」する制度もある。以下，各論的に2つの犯罪態様について検討する。

(2) 独禁法違反と証券取引法違反

独禁法違反行為としては，不当な取引制限（いわゆるカルテル行為や談合【刑法の談合罪では法人は処罰されないので，ここでは独禁法上の談合を念頭におく】など）などがあり，これに対する刑罰としては「3年以下の懲役又は500万円以下の罰金」（独禁法89条）が定められている。公正取引委員会は，1990年に「独占禁止法違反に対する刑事告発に関する方針」を公表し，積極的に刑事告発を行うことを明らかにした。しかし，刑事告発は，1991年から1997年までの間に，4件しかなされていない。

他方，1990年から1995年までのカルテルおよび入札談合に関する等の法的措置件数は107件であり，主として，勧告，審決，警告，注意等の行政処分がなされてきた。1977年の改正で，課徴金制度が導入され，カルテル事件の重要なものは課徴金で処理されてきた。例えば，1985年から1994年の10年間で，事件数109件，納付命令数（対象事業者数）1,592件，課徴金額285億円となっている。

課徴金額は，不当利得分であって，制裁金は含まない。したがって，課徴金に加えて制裁としての罰金も可能である。しかし，課徴金も違反の抑止効はあり，さらに罰する必要はないと一般に考えられている。これは，後述する刑罰権行使の最終手段性にも由来する。したがって，刑事告発は，特に悪質な違反事件や消費者被害が大規模な事件についてなされることになる。

証券取引法違反の態様としては，相場操縦（法197条）やインサイダー取引（法166条，167条）などがある。ここではインサイダー取引にふれておく。インサイダー取引犯罪規定は，いわゆる日米貿易摩擦が引き金となって，1988年に証券取引法に導入された。また，1992年には，証券取引等監視委員会が設置されて，積極的な刑事告発が期待されたが，その摘発件数は，1997年まで6件のみとなっている。さらに，法定刑は，3年以下の懲役もしくは300万円以下の罰金であり（同198条15号），また，法人に対しても5億円以下の罰金が科せられる（同207条1項2号）こととなっているが，実際に言い渡された刑罰は，執行猶予付き懲役刑が1件あるほかは，すべて略式手続による20万円から50万円の罰金である。ここでは刑罰による犯罪抑止力はほとんど無きに等しいといえよう。

他方，インサイダー取引に対する刑事制裁以外の制裁をみると，①監督官庁による証券会社等に対する免許の取引や業務停止等の行政処分（証券取引法35条）。②大蔵大臣の申立により，裁判所の行う証券取引違反行為の禁止または停止命令（差止命令・192条）。③虚偽有価証券届出書提出や相場操縦等の行為によって損害を蒙った私

人による損害賠償請求の制度(21条等，160条)。④証券取引所および日本証券業協会は，自主規制措置として，会員が法令等に違反した場合には，5億円以下の過怠金の賦課や，会員権の停止または除名等の処分を行うことができる。このうち，裁判所の差止命令や私人の損害賠償請求は，立証の困難さから，現実には行われていない。免許取消や業務停止処分も，影響が大きいのでこれも実際には行われていない。1997年の証券取引法改正で，法人に対する罰金の上限が5億円に引き上げられたのに伴って，過怠金の上限も5億円に引き上げられており，過怠金の意義は大きなものとなっている。しかし，それにしても莫大な不当利得に較べれば低額であることは疑いがない。したがって，不当利得の剥奪処分である独禁法上の課徴金の制度を，証券取引法にも設けるべしとの意見も強い。

2 経済犯罪に対する刑事制裁

(1) 刑事制裁の最終手段性と責任主義

刑事制裁の意義を考えるに当たっては，その最終手段性と責任主義について考えておく必要がある。「刑法は生活利益保護のための最後の手段(ultima ratio)である」と言われるが，それは「刑罰は物理的強制力によって人の自由や財産等を剥奪するものであって，多くの弊害を伴うから，その発動は，民事的・行政的制裁等，刑法以外の社会的統制手段では充分出ない場合に限られる」という意味である。この刑罰の最終手段性を実体法的に担保するのが責任主義といえよう。

民事責任については，公害問題を契機として，不法行為責任の無過失責任化が進み，いわゆる民事責任の客観化という現象をもたらしている。これに対して，刑事責任は，依然として主観的なものと理解されている。すなわち，刑罰の本質を，過去の行為に対する法的非難として捉えるかぎり，それは，他に適法行為の可能であったこと，従って，行為者に故意または少なくとも過失のあったことを前提としている。このように，行為者に故意または過失がない限り処罰しえないという考え方を責任主義(Schuldprinzip)と呼んでおり，わが国刑事法の大原則となっている。この責任主義は，かっての故意・過失を要件としない結果責任(Erfolgshaftung)あるいは厳格責任（strict liability）の克服を通じて形成されてきた原則とされている。

(2) 業務主（法人）処罰の根拠

経済法規違反の経済犯罪については，いわゆる両罰規定により，行為者のほか業

務主(法人)も処罰されることが多い。そこで、このような法人に対する刑事罰の根拠が問題となる。かって、無過失責任説は、法人の責任の根拠を他人の行為による無過失責任とした。しかし、刑罰としての罰金は損害か賠償とは異なり、その内容は、違法行為に対する法的非難であるとすれば、このような考え方は責任主義に反することになる。

そこで、通説・判例は、過失責任説をとり、両罰規定は、業務主の監督義務違反の存在を推定するものであり、業務主は、従業者の違反行為が不可抗力になることを立証しない限り、自己の過失行為に基づいて処罰されるとする。

しかし、過失推定説を根拠にしても、法人の過失は自然人のそれとは異ならざるを得ない。すなわち、法人の過失に、違反行為との因果関係が必要であるとすれば、業務主に要求される注意義務の内容は特定されていなければならない。そうすると、注意義務の内容は、違反行為を防止するための管理義務とそのための監督義務ということになる。この場合、具体的な違反行為に対する予見可能性は不要であり、当該業務の性質から、その種の違反行為が抽象的に予見可能であれば、それを防止するための監督義務を認めるべきこととなる。言い換えれば、法人の過失は具体的予見可能性を内容とする刑法犯の過失より若干ゆるやかなものとされており、その限度で責任主義の原則も修正されているといわねばならないであろう。

(3) 罰金刑の改善

法人に対する刑罰は罰金ということになる。しかし、罰金額が低ければその抑止力も乏しいことになる。また、罰金の手続が略式手続によって科されていることも刑罰の感銘力を低下させている。そこで、罰金刑の抑止力を高める一つの方法は、罰金刑の上限を引き上げることである。このような観点から、例えば、証券取引法の罰金額の上限は、1997年の改正で300万円から500万円に引き上げられた（197条）。さらに、両罰規定のもとでの法人に対する罰金額が、自然人行為者に対する罰金と同額という従来の考え方を改めて、法人に高額の罰金を規定すこととした。証券取引法は、1992年の改正で法人の罰金額上限をそれまでの300万円から3億円に引き上げ、1997年の改正でさらに5億円にまで引き上げた（207条1項1号）。その他、例えば、独占禁止法が1億円（95条1号）、廃棄物処理法が1億円（30条1号）、商標法が1億5,000万円（82条1号）、銀行法が3億円（64条1項1号）の罰金額上限を、法人に対して規定している。

このような法人に対する重罰化は，法人処罰を過失推定説に基づくものと考える立場からは，一応の理論的根拠をもつこととなる。法人は，一般的にいって，自然人よりも資力が大きく，また，自然人に科すことの出来る自由刑を科すことができないのであるから，刑罰の抑止力を保つためには，自然人よりも高額の罰金刑を定めておくことも適切な措置といえよう。

3 手続法的問題

(1) 経済犯罪の捜査の困難性

刑事制裁の発動に関しては，さらに，手続法的な分析も加えておく必要がある。すなわち，経済犯罪は，適法な経済活動の形態を装って行われることが多く，また，その経済活動が複雑な経済ルールの下で行われるので，適法行為の裏に潜む犯罪を探知することが困難となる。このような困難性を克服するためには，強い捜査権限を捜査機関に認めざるをえないこととなるが，強い捜査権限は同時に市民の人権制約や企業の自由な活動を制約することともなる。したがって，このような手続法的困難さからも，刑事制裁の発動が制約されざるをえないことにも注意すべきである。

(2) 調査と捜査

大型経済犯罪の捜査については，別の国家機関が最初に調査を進め，その告発をまって捜査機関が捜査を開始するという2段階のシステムがとられている。例えば，独占禁止法については，その運営にあたる行政委員会として公正取引委員会が設けられている。公正取引委員会は，内閣総理大臣の所轄に属するが（法27条），準司法的機能を与えられているため，その職権行使には独立性が与えられ，行政府から干渉されることはない。その結果，公正取引委員会が，当該企業に対して勧告，警告，注意，裁判所への緊急停止命令の申立等の司法手続以外の措置をとる場合がある。

しかし，悪質事件であって刑事事件とすべきものについては，検事総長に告発をすることになる。独占禁止法は，公正取引委員会は，私的独占・不当な取引制限の罪など独占禁止法違反の罪があると思料するときは，検事総長に告発しなければならないと規定しており（同73条1項），この告発は訴訟条件とされている（同96条1項）。したがって，検察官としては，公正取引委員会の告発がないかぎりこの種事件を訴追することはできない。この点については，消費者・企業の経済的・財産的利益の保護もまた独禁法の保護法益といえるから，立法論としては，関係者の告発権

も肯定すべきであろう。

　つぎに，証券取引法違反事件について，インサイダー取引はむろん秘密裏に行われるのであるから，その摘発にも当然困難が伴う。そこで，インサイダー取引を取り締まる機関として，1992年に大蔵省に証券取引等監視委員会が設置された。委員会は，強制調査権や刑事告発権を有する(法210条, 226条参照)。この場合には警察・検察も独自に摘発することができるが，犯罪認知の困難性から，実際上は委員会の活動に依存している。これまでの摘発件数の少なさから考えると，インサイダー取引の摘発のためには，当該取引システムに関与している関係当事者の取締機関に対する協力が必要であろう。

む　す　び

(1)　刑事制裁と行政制裁

　規制緩和は，取引の自由化とともに，経済犯罪に対する事後的コントロールの強化をも要請する。その際，今後如何なる事後的コントロールを中核に考えるべきかについて，①インサイダー取引処罰の強化などの刑事制裁の強化を考える説，②営業停止，課徴金などの行政処分を活用すべしとする説，あるいは、③経営の合理化や危機管理体制の整備などの企業の自主的努力および企業内司法（コーポレイト・ジャスティス)に期待すべきであるとの説などが提唱されている。いずれの説もそれぞれの正しさを持っていると考えるが，アプローチの順序としては，第1に企業の自主的規制を促進させ，第2に行政制裁の充実を図り，そして第3に，真に悪質な犯罪については刑事制裁を発動していくという考え方が妥当と思われる。なお，ここでは，触れることができなかったが，不正利益の剥奪制度や民事制裁の制度も当然視野にいれなければならない。

(2)　全体的考察の必要性

　差し当たりの結論として，今後の経済犯罪の抑止策としては，以上のような刑事制裁，行政制裁，そして企業の自主規制などを全体として考察することが重要と考える。従来，一方で，犯罪に対する制裁としては刑罰的制裁が唯一であるとの固定的な考え方が強く，しかし，同時に，刑法の謙抑性から過度に刑事制裁の発動を抑制しすぎる側面もあった。今後は，各種制裁の全体的考察の中で，刑事制裁の適正な役割りを見定めなければならないと考える。

12 日本における変わりゆく規制形態

マルコム・スミス[1]

[佐 野　隆 訳]

　は じ め に
1　アメリカ行政モデルの諸要素
2　アメリカ型への道の主要な階段
3　日本の規制官は何を規制するのか
4　オーストラリアにおける行政権限対他の政府機関の間に見られるいくつかの傾向
　結　　論

は じ め に

　ほぼ30年前の1969年に私が日本法の研究を開始した時，第一の問題関心は，「日本との合弁事業」[2]であった。この研究には，日本への外国投資の規制に対する当時の制度の研究，および，企業法，証券規制法ならびに独占禁止法に関する初歩的な研究を必然的に伴った。これらの領域すべてに行政規制がかかわっていた。次の大きな研究は，ハーヴァード・ロー・スクールで行なったオーストラリア，日本およびアメリカにおける国際貿易規制の行政裁量に関するものであった[3]。その際に，日本の行政法の知識を高める必要があった。今日まで，関心は持続しているが，その焦点は資本および金融市場の規制へと移った。オーストラリアの視点から見た日本の制度についての印象を共有し，オーストラリアの制度の興味ある特徴を紹介したいと思う。そして，両国における行政規制に関する共同研究のために今日の議論を，そして，将来の関心を喚起することを希望する。

　1969年に，オーストラリア人が行なった日本の制度に関する表面的な検討は広範な比較研究を伴うものであった。当時のオーストラリアはイギリス流の考え方に非常に影響を受けており，そのことは行政および行政法についても言えた。当時のオーストラリアは，アメリカの制度と対比をなす，イギリス型のキャリア・シヴィル・サーヴィスを連邦および州レヴェルで持っていることを誇りにしていた。行政法はイギリス法を直接採用した。我々は，イギリス型に近く，アメリカおよびヨーロッ

パの制度を比較のために利用する，と考えていた。

　私が研究を開始するほんの5年前の1964年に，イギリスの貴族院は有名な*Ridge v. Baldwin*[4]事件判決を下し，行政決定に対する自然的正義の原則を確立した。私の学部時代の授業は，古臭いイギリスの令状あるいは手続方式を通じての行政官の司法コントロールに集中していた。それらの手続は高度に技術的で，一般的には，私の教官たちは，それらの技術性に集中し，全体的な令状制度の単純さを偽装していた。当時は，司法的偏向に対するコントロール，および，いわゆる私的条項[5]により裁判所から争点を奪う議会の権限にも目を向けていた。行政判断がほとんど裁判所に持ち込まれなかったので，本案に対する審査という概念はなかった。行政上の規則作成に対する事前のコントロールという我々の概念は，議員が変更の可能性を求める議会の中で作られる新しい規制により行なわれた。議会による行政官への権限委任を規制する，判断基準を明確化することによる立法上のコントロールはほとんど，あるいは，まったくなかった。情報の自由は知られていなかった。我々の制度は，イギリス型の制度で，アメリカの手続を参照することはほとんど，あるいは，まったくなかった。

　対照的に，1969年には，日本の行政法について書かれた英文の僅かばかりの資料は，日本の行政法がドイツ法に基づいており，占領時代に由来するアメリカのいくつかの重要な原則が加えられていることを述べていた。当時の，そして残念ながら今でも，文献のほとんどが，行政のための司法制度の詳細ではなく，「行政指導」の現象に集中している[6]。明らかなことは，行政指導の評価が書かれたのはアメリカの法律家のためか，あるいはアメリカの法律家によったことである。実際，1950年代および1960年代において，オーストラリアは日本に見られるのと類似の規制構造を示していた。日本に関する1960年代後半の文献は，裁判所による行政上の決定の審査を得ることの難しさと，官僚が行使するコントロールを受けない裁量の範囲を強調していた。状況はオーストラリアにおいても類似していた。

　1998年の時点で振り返って見ると，双方の制度は，技術上の詳細さではなく手続の重要な要素の点で，1960年代以来アメリカ型に向けて劇的に展開してきたと言えると思う。しかし，両国の発展の過程には意味ある相違があると言いたい。オース

トラリアでは，その発展は経済法をアメリカ流に改革すること（例えば，証券および貿易慣行法）で得られた国内的選択により行なわれた。その発展は，1950年代以来，オーストラリアの法律家がアメリカの法的訓練を受けることにより補強された。オーストラリアは，15年にわたって，わが国の２大政党に共通で，両党により強力に進められた，規制緩和と民営化を経験している。行政法の改革はこの過程の中の必要な一部分である。日本における行政改革は，貿易および投資紛争と結びついてたアメリカからの外圧により密接に結びついているように私には思われる。オーストラリア人の目には，日本の行政改革は，前向きというよりは受身の，自ら進んでというよりは不承不承のもののように思われる。

1 アメリカ行政モデルの諸要素

　詳細な法準則には触れないで，アメリカ行政モデルの主要な要素を特定しようとすれば，1990年代後半においては以下の要素が重要であると思われる。

- すべての政府の行為は法の支配に服すべきである。
- 憲法が法制度の頂点で，関係制度上の相互作用および国民と政府との間の関係を規定する主要な原則を提示する。
- 権力分立の理論により，行政は，立法における行為のための基準を特定することで認められる権限の範囲において議会の指示の下にあり，委任されている決定権限の行使の点で司法府の監視の下にある。
- 法の支配は，あらゆる行政上の活動が，適用される規則および手続が事前に公表され知れ渡っているという意味において，透明であることを求める。
- いかなる行政上の規則作成権限も，規則を発展させる過程において立法府と公衆の精査を可能にする点で明確な基準により制約を受けなければならない。
- すべての行政上の決定は審査の基礎を形成しうる明確な基準に帰すことができなければならない。
- すべての行政上の決定は個人の権利を保護する適切な過程を経て到達されなければならない。
- 個人は個人の権利に関連する政府保有のファイルにある資料にアクセスする権利を持つ。
- 独立したエイジェンシーが主要な規制手段である。

2 アメリカ型への道の主要な階段

　上記した基本原則の要点は過去50年にわたりオーストラリアおよび日本において模倣されてきたことは，明らかなことであると思う。両国とも，法の支配を追随すると公言することで20世紀に入った。事実，両国とも年が進むにつれそれへの関与を強めていった。両国とも，立法および行政活動の合憲性に関してアメリカ型の司法審査を採用した。両国とも行政権限の制限を記す憲法を有している。もっとも，日本の憲法はこの点についてより明確に示している。オーストラリアでは，かかる制限を明確に示すには，司法判断が求められた。日本には，国民の権利および義務を規定する憲法第3章という付加的な要素がある。オーストラリアは権利章典を持っておらず，したがって，行政官に対する類似した制約は，憲法の特定の規定に基礎をおく，立法により，あるいは，暫定的には裁判所により，科されてきた。

　過去50年の間の目覚しい発展は以下の領域で起こっている。
・行政審査過程の確立。
・委任される規則に適用される明確な基準を含むように委任をする際の立法のあり方の変化。
・規則作成過程を示す行政手続法。
・情報の自由制度。
・経済上の規制エイジェンシーの確立。

　順にそれぞれについて簡単に触れ，本シンポジウムの全体的なテーマに対する重要性を説明したい。

(1) 行政審査過程の確立

　占領中の改革により，1948年に初めて日本に基本的なアメリカ型の行政審査過程が導入された。それらは1960年代前半に行政不服審判法および行政事件訴訟法という形で拡充した。当時の，そして現在でも，これらの法の弱点は行政組織内での独立した審査という問題であり，裁判所に問題を持ち出そうとすることが簡単に退けられてしまうことである。このことの理由は，付随的な差し止め請求が法廷で首尾よく主張されない限り，苦情対象の行政活動を続行することを法律が認めているからである。内閣が直接行動することで覆されうる差し止めが認められた場合でも，

あるいは，差し止めが認められない場合でも，そして，主たる訴えが，通常は数年を経て，審理へと至った時には，行政活動は完了しており，原告は何らの損害も示しえないという現実に直面する。

　オーストラリアのやり方は，行政審査を促進するために，1975年以来新しい行政審判所構造を作り上げることに基礎をおいている。日本国憲法第76条3項はそのような発展を日本で行なうことを難しくしているかもしれない。オーストラリアでこれら発展の成功は，おそらく，難民請求といった一定の事項を一般的な制度から切り離し特別な審判所の下で扱おうとする政府による最近の試みにより最もよく計ることができる。

　市場に対する行政の介入と行政行為に異を唱える容易さの関係は，外国投資，外国貿易およびより最近の資本市場に関する規制を調べた私のすべての研究の中で明らかになっている。行政の濫用に対する異議が迅速・安価に，そして効果的な救済の合理的な可能性を持って行なえるなら，規制権限の濫用が幅を利かすことはない。しばしば，異議が成功するかは次の点，つまり，委任される権限への制限に左右される。

(2)　委任される規則に適用される明確な基準を含むように委任をする際の立法のあり方の変化

　1969年，オーストラリアおよび日本は1つの明確な立法上の特徴を共有した。両国とも，行政機関に対して規則作成権限の無制限な委任をなすということを常としていた。委任に何の基準も含まれず，後に作られる行政規則自体に明確な基準を含むよう求めていなければ，善意の決定であるかのように見えることに裁判所が介入を差し控えるお膳立てをしたことになる。この点の重要さは，同じ領域におけるアメリカ型の立法委任について私が詳しく研究するまでは，はっきりと認識していなかった。これらの委任が持つ影響は，経済規制，特に，外国貿易の分野で顕著であった。私がよく使う比較は，市場規制の重要な部分である輸出入規制の領域であった。オーストラリアおよび日本では，委任は完全に無制限であった。オーストラリアの場合，最初の1900年（連邦）関税法は，単に，「参事会における総督は（輸入または輸出を）禁止する規制をなすことができる」[7]，と述べられていたにすぎなかった。同

法には，委任に基づき決定をなす点で行政官を制限する何らの基準も規定していなかった。日本の外国為替および外国貿易管理法の規定も同様であったが，第１条は一定の基準を科しているように思われ，それは有名なココム事件で地方裁判所の関心を引き付けた[8]。しかし，ほぼ半世紀の間で外国貿易権限の行使に対する数少ない司法上成功した異議の１つであった，原告にとって有利な認定であっても，実務における変化をもたらすことはなかった。最終的には，法は1987年にこの問題に対応するため改正された[9]。他方，アメリカは同じ領域において行政機関に対する立法上の非常に多くの制約があったので，片手を背中で縛られた形で貿易紛争に取り組んでいるように思われた。

オーストラリアにおける今世紀の最も重要な行政上の改革へと導いたキール委員会は，明らかに，適切な審査過程が確立されれば，裁量を制限する必要はない，と考えていた。日本の役人もこの考えに同意すると私は感じている。しかし，私は常に，もう一人のオーストラリアの一流の専門家であり，以前の関税表委員会の委員長であったヘンリー・ブランドの見解を支持している。裁量に関する彼の報告書は以下のように主張する。

「決定をなしうる状況を述べている詳細がより詳細であれば，市民は自身の権利についてより明確になり，行政上の裁量に基づきなされる決定に対する審査過程を求める要求はより少なくなる。」[10]

(3) 規則作成過程を示す行政手続法

裁量を規則の中に規定する方法に対する私の関心は，アメリカの行政手続法の中の規則作成の点への関心を生じさせた。1994年に新しい行政手続法により日本に導入された変化[11]，および，かかる変化をもたらす原因となったアメリカのモデルは将来の研究にとって実り多い分野となっている。日本における行政行為の将来の改革に対して行政手続法が有している重要性は，おそらく，同法の適用から特定的に排除されている多くの領域を検討することで最もよく評価できる[12]。簡単に記せば，日本の行政活動の鍵は，常に，一括した白紙委任の下で自己の活動領域を定める行政官の権限である。規則作成および決定行為が適切な監督に服さない限り，真の改革は起こらないであろう。

(4) 情報の自由制度

　この分野が，過去15年間のオーストラリアにおける行政官・規制官と規制を受ける者との間のバランスを変えた改革のうち，最も最近に起こったものである。オーストラリアでは，情報の自由法[13]は，野党の好む政策であり，政府に対抗するために使われる有用な情報を得るために野党によって好んで使われる武器である。オーストラリアにおけるこれらの法の成功はその適用を制限しようとする政府の試みの程度により計ることができる。

　一方で，情報の自由法第3条1項a号は，その目的を「可能な限り連邦政府が有する情報にアクセスするオーストラリア社会の権利を拡大すること」と，非常に広範な表現で述べているが，同法第3条1項b号は，この一般的アクセス権利に対して適用除外を作ることで制限を科している。これらの適用除外は，主要な公的利益の保護のため，および，省ならびに公的機関により収集され保持されている情報の対象者の私的ならびに事業上の事項のために，存在している。しかし，オーストラリアの裁判所は，開示の方向に向け，第3条1項b号を幅広く解釈している[14]。情報の自由法は，1980年代半ば以降，オーストラリアでは連邦および州のレヴェルで，そして，日本では地方レヴェルで，存在しているが，日本では全国レヴェルでの法は，やっとその兆しが見え始めたにすぎない[15]。日本における新しい法の影響は，数年のうちに，比較研究のためのもう1つの実り多い分野になるであろうが，これらの法は新しい規制の概念の設計にとって不可欠なものである，と主張したい。

(5) 経済上の規制エイジェンシー

　これは大きなテーマであるが，私は，日本もオーストラリアも経済の領域においてはアメリカ型の規制エイジェンシーを採用している，と指摘するにとどめたい。日本は，占領により，公正取引委員会と証券および為替委員会を持つことになった。公正取引委員会は，その後も途絶えることなく活動を続けている。証券委員会は，1950年代に廃止され，一連の証券スキャンダルに対処するために，1990年代初旬になってやっと復活した。オーストラリアの対応する組織が今日ある姿になったのは，1960年代後半，貿易慣行構造の合憲性を認めた連邦最高裁判所の重大判決の後であった。1970年代には，全国的な企業および証券に対する規制組織ができた。オーストラリア競争および消費者委員会は，現在では，最も強力な経済規制者であると

言うことができよう。企業規制組織は，証券市場および企業に対する広範な規制権限を伴う，オーストラリア証券および投資委員会へと発展した。

3　日本の規制官は何を規制するのか

　過去30年にわたる日本の行政過程を検討する点で重要な第二の点は，規制を受けてきた活動の種類である。前川リポートにおいて見られるように，日本で行政改革を語るとき，それは，行政官が行為する「やり方」および彼らが規制する「事柄」について語っている。オーストラリアでは，この点では後者を「規制緩和」と呼ぶ傾向が強い。私が手がけた最初の研究である外国投資規制，次の研究である外国貿易規制，そして，より最近の研究である資本市場規制が示していることは，日本の行政官はミクロ経済の活動に深くかかわっているということである。彼らは，何をすることができるかを，そして，どのようにそれをするかを語り続けてきた。これは適切な規制の役割であろうか？

　日本における資本市場の規制緩和に関する標準的な業績を集めてみれば，しばしば20頁を超える，緩和される個々の決定のリストを見ないことは稀である[16]。緩和される決定は，非常にしばしば，取引の性質に関してか，取引の規模に関するビジネス上の決定になり，その枠内で決定が下される枠組みにはならない。

　現代の規制の概念は，参加者が市場に有する力を濫用することができない公正な市場に向けての一般的な枠組みを含むものである，と私には思われる。それらの枠組みには以下のものが含まれる。
・反独占法
・公正取引法
・消費者保護法

　金融市場のような特定の部門では，規制の焦点は，個々の取引に対する介入，あるいは，特定の型の取引の禁止から，市場内で活動する者の支払能力を確保することにより，あるいは，支払能力の水準を満たさない者を迅速に退場させることを確保することにより，システムの安定性と一体性を維持することに移行している。

この点は，現在の日本における銀行危機という進行中の問題における鋭い解答となる。銀行に対して，過去50年の間，利率を定めるとか，コマーシャル・ペーパーの商品開発を制限するといった，非常に数多くのビジネス決定をどのようにするかを述べる点で，規制官は本来すべき仕事，すなわち，銀行の支払能力を確保するために適切な手続を作ることを確保すること，をしていなかった。評釈者は，規制官は日本の制度の慎重に考慮すべき要件を，あるいは，日本の財政制度の外部的作用を，適切には監視していなかった，という点で合意している。

　システム自体は脅威にさらされておらず，したがって，規制官は彼らが対象とするビジネスの日々の取引に介入することに忙しくしているべきでありまたそうすることができた，と考えられていたように思われる。このことと，行政上の方法，すなわち，はっきりと規定され周知されている原則に照らし合わせることのできない行政指導あるいは「窓口」指導とが混ざり合った。不幸なことに，システムは不安定化し，公衆を裁量の濫用から守る任に実際にあたる官僚は腐敗しやすく，したがって，監視システム自体が効果的ではなかった。

　最も重要なことは，政府による金融部門の規制に対する戦後のアプローチの不可欠な原則，つまり，国庫はシステム内の主要なプレーヤーを後押しするものと考えられなければならないということが，逆の結果を生じたのである。システムの一体性を確保する代わりに，システム内のモラルハザードを極点まで高めてしまった。実際に存在した数少ない思慮ある規則を執行しなかったことに加えて，政府は，銀行の取締役会が承認した取引の危険を適切に算定するという取締役会の義務を逃れることを認め，銀行の役員が危険の算定に基づかない理由で貸出しを承認することを認め，預金者が彼らの資金を預ける機関の健全さを見極める彼らの義務を逃れるのを認め，そして，株主が取締役に責任を採らせる彼らの義務を逃れるのを認めた。換言すれば，官僚は，支払能力を保証していると思い，そして次には，銀行が実際に支払能力があることを確保するための正しい質問をしないことで，通常の市場管理のあらゆる仕組みを無効にした。

　このような背景の下で，大変に目に付くことは，提案されている銀行改革は，評釈者の間では，官僚による介入を規律する明確な規則を導入し銀行業に対する官僚

の介入を制限するものとして，歓迎されているということである[17]。行政改革は，市場の責任追及の仕組みを強化する平行して行なわれる法の強化の一部として見られなければならない。資本の適正比率，不動産といった部門に対するマキシマム・エクスポージャー，関連企業に対する貸出し等に関する分別ある規則は，企業の財務状態の適切な開示により，そしてまた，自己の義務に違反する取締役を相手方とする株主または債権者による訴訟を促進する法により，支えられなければならない。将来に向けてのこれらの法構造の発展は，日本の主要な金融機関が抱えている既存の不良債権という差し迫った問題を解決するのと同じくらい重要であろう。

4 オーストラリアにおける行政権限対他の政府機関の間に見られるいくつかの傾向

最後のこの章で将来の比較研究にとって興味深いものとなるかもしれない，オーストラリアの規制における3つの傾向を示す。

(1) 立法を効率的に変える行政上のエイジェンシーの権限

私が1973年に日本で研究をしていた時，オーストラリア政府は全国レヴェルで初めての企業および証券法案を提出した。オーストラリアおよび日本で多大な関心を引き付けた一つの特徴は，提案されている全国レヴェルの規制委員会に与えられた立法自身を変更することが可能となる委員会自身の規則を作成する権限であった。この特徴は，それ以来，全国レヴェルの企業および証券構造の一部分をなしており，現行の一例は，企業法7.12編に見られる。同編は企業が証券の購入の申し込みをしている場合，企業に対する指針および規則を示している。同法は，オーストラリア証券および投資委員会に対して，同法の「すべてまたは一部の遵守をある者に対して免除[18]」する権限を与えている。この規定の結果，委員会は特定な事例に応じて裁量的な免除により法を改正することになり，規制を受ける側はこの領域における現実の法が何であるかを見出しにくくなっている。

日本における法が，憲法第41条の国会が「国の唯一の立法機関である」という要件に従って，同じことができるであろうか？

(2) 司法審査の排除または制限[19]

　近年オーストラリアにおいては移民関連書類は，通常の行政法上の原則が適用されない特別な制度の下にある。

　1994年に発効した1958年移民法に対する1992年の改正は，「ヴィザ申請に関する公正な決定をなすために何が求められるかについての不確定さ」を取り除くことを目的としていた（1992年法案に付けられた説明文書）。しかし，ヴィザ申請に関連する手続から自然的正義の準則を完全に除去する際に（同法第2編第3章ＡＢ節），立法府は，移民決定に関する責任は司法府ではなく行政府が負うべきであるという政府の考えを反映させた。これらの改革は，本案審理の制度を改善するよりは，申請者に対する政府および行政の管理を増加させている。

　改革の主要な特徴である第476条は，いくつかの判決の中で連邦裁判所による分析を経ている[20]。全員一致の意見は，第420条は，決定を審査する際に難民審査審判所に自然的正義の準則に従うように義務付けているが，第476条1項は連邦裁判所に司法審査をなす権限を与えている，というものである。しかし，第476条2項および3項は審査の根拠を大幅に削っている。第476条2項ａ号「難民の地位を求める申請者に対して，決定を下すことに関連して自然的正義の準則違反が生じていることを理由に申請を拒絶した難民審査審判所の決定に異議を申立てる権限を明示的に否定している[21]。」さらに，第476条2項ｂ号は，「いかなる合理人もそのような権限行使をしえないほど不合理な」権限行使に基づく決定に異議を申立てることを否定している。

　第476条3項は不適切な権限行使を狭く3つの理由に制限しており，以下の事由を明示的に排除している。
・関連ある考慮事由を考慮しないこと，または，
・関連のない考慮事由を考慮したこと，または，
・悪意での行為。

　同様に記すに値することは，いくつかの連邦裁判所の判決では，第420条の内容が何であれ，同条は裁判所に本案に関する決定を審査することを認める審判所が従う

べき手続を何ら規定していない，と結論付けたことである[22]。

さらに，同条は，同条の適用がなければ，1977年（連邦）行政決定司法審査法および1903年（連邦）司法法に基づき可能となる審査を制限もしている。したがって，法は難民審査審判所に自然的正義に従う義務を科している状況にあるが，これらの規則に対する違反が生じた場合に，申請者に対するいかなる救済も否定されている。

この分野において，法により与えられているもう一つの行政裁量の例は，同法第417条であり，同条によりそれに基づきなされる決定は第485条の効力により司法審査を受けないことになる[23]。第417条は，申請者にとってより有利であるとして，大臣が審判所の決定を別の決定に変更することを認める。*Minister for Immigration & Ethnic Affairs v. Ozamanian*事件大法廷判決[24]は，第485条は審査の権利を制限しているものの，基本的な権利，事由あるいは免責を廃止あるいは削減しているものとしてみなすべきではない，と判示した。

ここでもまた私は，司法審査に対するこの種の制限は，裁判所に最終的な司法権限を委ねている憲法第76条2項に鑑み，日本においては困難であろうと考える。

(3) 司法審査と行政審査の単一審判所への併合

規制者と規制される者との関係は最近の政府の改革により再度影響を受けるかもしれない。1997年5月，連邦司法長官は，内閣は連邦レヴェルの5つの主要な事案審理を行なう審判所を統合する点で原則として合意したことを，公表した。行政上訴審判所，社会補償上訴審判所，退役軍人上訴審判所および難民審査審判所である。単一の審判所，行政審査審判所が設置されるであろう[25]。

ヴィクトリア州政府は，1998年8月に，審査審判所の制度を再編し，民事および行政審査過程を同一構造内の司法審査へと統合した。新しい審判所には3名の司法職がおり，彼らは，あたかも裁判所への上訴のごとく，司法職の身分で審判所において行政パネルからの審査を法的視点で審査することができる。審判所長は最高裁判所の裁判官であり，2人の副審判所長は県裁判所の裁判官である。

ヴィクトリア州法務長官はこの新しい構造を以下のように描写した。
「ヴィクトリア州民事および行政審判所は今日までのオーストラリアにおけるこの分野での最も包括的な改革であろう[26]。」

結　論

私が論じたことは，オーストラリアと日本の行政法制度には，双方ともアメリカモデルの影響を受け，過去30年にわたりはっきりとした同一性があるが，しかし，重要な相違も存在する，ということである。英米の研究者は，日本の行政法の基盤の大部分をなしているドイツの理論をほとんど無視している。また，日本の憲法は，オーストラリアの憲法にはない，手続的権利を明記している。日本の憲法はまた，権力分立に基づくより明確な統治構造を規定しており，かかる構造により，オーストラリアで発展した司法審査に対する立法上の制限を行なうことはより困難であろう。戦前に存在した行政裁判所を禁じる意図で作られた第76条2項における特別裁判所の禁止により，最近のヴィクトリア州での実験を真似ることは問題となろう。最後に，我々は我々自身の長く確立された慣行に対してアメリカのモデルを押し当てるので，両国それぞれに経済規制の運用という比較研究の実り多い領域がある。

(1) 私の研究助手である法学部4年生のKerry Liu BA (Hons) に，本稿の準備を手伝ってもらったことに感謝する。
(2) 1971年メルボルン大学法学部修士号論文。
(3) 1976年ハーヴァード・ロー・スクール博士号論文"Administrative Discretion in Foreign Trade Regulation: United States, Australia and Japan".
(4) [1964] AC 40.
(5) 言い換えると，特定の状況での司法審査を明示的に制限する立法。
(6) 遠藤教授の"Administrative Law Theory During the Thirty Years after the War" (1981) 14 *Law in Japan: An Annual* 82，または，塩野教授の"Public and Private Law" (1986) 19 *Law in Japan An Annual* 15といった，日本の行政法理論の英訳は1980年代になるまで現れなかった。行政法上の問題に当てられた特集号Law in Japan 第19巻も参照。
(7) 第50条
(8) 一般的には，松下満雄 "International Trade and Competition Law in Japan" (Oxford 1993) 218—241頁参照。
(9) 同221—223頁。

⑽　Committee on Administrative Discretions, *Final Report*, October, 1973, para 191.
⑾　1993年法律88（宇賀教授による総務庁訳）
⑿　Boling, D., "Administrative Procedure Law Makes Inroads on Bureaucracy but Leaves Web Largely Intact" (1994) *East Asian Executive Reports* 7参照。
⒀　1982年（連邦）情報の自由法，各州および準州にも対応する法律が存在する。
⒁　例えば，*Accident Compensation Commission v. Croom* [1991] 2 VR 32, per Young CJ; *Sobh v. Police Force of Victoria* [1994] 1 VR 41, per Ashley J参照。このアプローチはアメリカ連邦最高裁判所で採られているものと一致しているように思われる。
⒂　Repeta, L. and Chafee, J., "Japanese government Information: New Rules for Access" *Japan Information Access Project Special Report*: June 1988, www.nmjc.org.jiap/specrpts/joho.html
⒃　例えば，Kaufman (ed.) Banking Structure in Major Countries (Kluwer, 1992) Appendix: Chronology of Major Changes in the Japanese Financial and Monetary Environment, 1975-1990, Khoury, The Deregulation of the World's Financial Markets (Pinter, 1990) 114, Exhibit 4.6 Chronology of Money and Credit Market Deregulation in Japan 1984-89.
⒄　鹿野"Prospects for Financial Reforms in Japan" The 21st Century Policy Institute Symposium, March 5, 1998, New York, http://www.keidanren.or.jp/21ppi/english/symposium/19980305/shikano.htmからの引用。
⒅　第1084条2項。
⒆　この部分は，Kerry Liuに負うところが大である。
⒇　例えば、*Thanh Phat Ma v. Billings* (1996) 142 ALR 158, per Drummond J: *Zheng v. Minister for Immigration & Ethnic Affairs* [1996] ACL Rep 77 FC 8; *Yao v. Minister for Immigration & Ethnic Affairs* [1997] ACL Rep 77 FC 45; *Eshetu v. Minister for Immigration & Ethnic Affairs* [1997] 142 ALR 474, per Hill J参照
(21)　Drummond J, *Thanh Phat Ma v. Billings* (1996) 142 ALR 158, 163.
(22)　*Velmurugu v. Minister for Immigration & Ethnic Affairs* (Fed Ct, 23 May 1996, unreported), per Olney J; *Zakinov v. Gibson* (Fed Ct, 26 July 1996, unreported), per North J.
(23)　連邦最高裁判所の専属管轄権がそれら決定の審査に及ぶ範囲を除く。
(24)　(1996) 141 ALR 322, Jenkinson, Sackville & Kiefee JJ.
(25)　J. Barnes, "From the AAT to the Federal Court: Treading the Path of Reform" (1998) 26 *Aust Bus LR* 205, 211.
(26)　Hon. Jan Wade, MLA (A-G), 2nd Reading Speech, VCAT Bill, Hansard,

9 April 1988, p. 975.

補償：立法の抜粋

1998年ヴィクトリア州民事および行政審判所法
第98条　一般的手続
(1)　審判所は，
　(a)　自然的正義の準則に拘束され，
　(b)　記録裁判所に適用される証拠準則または慣行または手続に，審判所がそれぞれ準則，慣行または手続を採用した範囲を除いて，拘束されず，
　(c)　適していると思われるいかなる事項も手がけることができ，
　(d)　本法の要件および授権立法および同審判所下にある事項の適切な考慮事由が許す可能な限りで，形式性および専門性を取り除きそれぞれの手続を追行し，迅速さを持ってそれぞれの手続を決定しなければならない。
(2)　1項b号を制限することなしに，審判所は，いかなる文書の内容も，いかなる時間制限またはかかる文書もしくはその送達に関連する規則に特定されている他の要件の不遵守にかかわらず，証拠に採用することができる。
(3)　本法，規則および準則の制約内で，審判所はそれ自身の手続を規制することができる。
(4)　1項a号は，本法または授権立法が，明示的であれ黙示的であれ，自然的正義の準則から離れることを認めている範囲で，適用されない。

1982年情報の自由法
第8編
第29条　決定理由の陳述
　決定者は，1982年情報の自由法に基づいてなされた決定に対する理由の陳述を求める要求に関連して，決定者が同法第27条に従う通知を要求をなした者に対して与えるか，すでに与えている場合は，第46条に従う。

第30条　情報の自由手続における審判所の情報の検査のための非公開性
　第146条におけるいかなる相反事項にもかかわらず，1982年情報の自由法に基づく手続において同法に基づき主記録官が保持する情報は，いかなる者による検査または複写のためには公開されない。

13 規制の新たな諸形態：民主的説明責任と法の支配に対する挑戦？

シェリル・ソンダーズ

[村山史世訳]

　はじめに
1　伝統的諸制度と諸原理
2　変化の時代
3　司法審査とその他の形態の外部審査
4　民主的説明責任
　結　論

はじめに

　このペーパーで問題にすることは，サービスの提供，政策の実行，公共資金調達においてオーストラリア政府が用いている―それはオーストラリア以外でも同様に用いられている―新たなメカニズムのオーストラリア法制および憲法体制への影響である。このメカニズムには，政府機関の株式会社化および民営化，契約したプライベートセクターを通じての政府サービスの提供，そして税に代わる利用料金やその他の料金の賦課を含む。極端に言えば，これらは，政府それ自体―少なくとも地方レベルの政府―の必要性についての疑問を生じさせる。

　これらのメカニズムの利用はいくつかの要因によって突き動かされてきた。1つはパブリックセクターの効率性・応答性（responsiveness）について信頼が失われたことである。これは部分的にはイデオロギーに，部分的には経験に基づいている。これに関係したもう一つの要因は，自由貿易の流れへと明らかに傾倒を深めながらますます競争的になった世界において，よりいっそう競争的となることの必要性および限られた資源を最大限に活用することの必要性である。

　このペーパーにおける私の議論は以下のようなものである。民主的かつ法的説明責任のための伝統的な手続は，理論上も実務上も，これらの変化に対してまだ適応していない。裁判所において適応プロセスは進行中であるが，これはオーストラリアの憲法的・制定法的枠組という制限内である。しかしながら，代表制それ自体の

本質を根本的に変更するなしには，民主的プロセスへの適応はさらに難しいかもしれない。

1 伝統的諸制度と諸原理

オーストラリアの憲法体制は，英国とアメリカ合衆国に依っている。しかしながら，目下の目的に特に関係があるオーストラリアの憲法体制の諸相は，大部分は英国の制度をモデルにしている。

特にオーストラリアは，ウエストミンスター型あるいは議会制の政治体制を連邦でも州レベルでも採用している。政府は，選挙で選ばれた代表者によってほぼ完全に指揮される[1]。国会議員を有権者の代理人と考えることに否定的なエドモンド・バーク的な考えが優勢になっている。議員は「思慮と良心に基づいた最も明確な確信」を議会に持ち出すべきであるとバークは論じたが，それは今や政党の部屋へと差し出され，そこでの決定が優勢になってゆくだろう[2]。政治文化と選挙制度の構造は，両方とも2つの主要な政治グループによる議会支配と高度に対立的な政治スタイルを確かなものにしている。執行府の権力は議会から導き出され，政策と行政について議会に対して責任を負う。この関係は十分に確立された憲法の諸原理によって補強されている。すなわち，議会のみが新たな法を創設できるし，創設する権限がある。また既存の法を変更できる。議会のみが税を課すことができる。議会だけが公的資金を支出する権限がある。歴史的に，独立公共サービス部局（independent public service departments）は，それら事体は独立した法的存在ではないが，それらの活動に対して固有の責任を有する大臣に対して助言する。

一連の同じ傾向を持った諸原理は，100年前にA.V.ダイシーが明確に述べた法の支配とほとんど同じものの一つの型をオーストラリアに適用していると言える[3]。政府は法に従って活動しなければならない。政府とプライベートセクターは同様に同じ法に服し通常裁判所で裁判を受ける。この法の内容を指し示すものは憲法上ほとんど存在しないが，コモンローの諸原理は，自然的美徳あるいは民主的に選挙された議会の自己保全本能と一体になって個人の自由を尊重するであろうという自画自賛的な信念が多少存在する。

ダイシーの時代以来これらの諸原理は，はっきりと認識できるような行政法の発

展を通じて粉飾されてきた。行政法をダイシー自身はあざ笑っていたが，しかし実際はダイシー自身の命題と広く一致していた。政府の諸決定が適法であることは裁判所によって決定される。この目的のために裁判所が依拠する根拠は，判決する権限を与えている制定法から権限の範囲や手続的公平について議会の意思を引き出すことあるいは推論することで求められた。オーストラリアでは，司法審査は現在，以下のような他のメカニズムによって補足されている。すなわちそれらには，「実体的事項」に関する決定に対する審判所の審査手続[4]，オンブツマンによる不当な行政についての苦情調査手続，政府情報[5]や決定理由[6]の義務的開示手続，プライヴァシィー保護手続[7]などが含まれる。

応答性ある政府の諸原理と法の支配に結びついた諸原理の両者は以下のことを前提としている。すなわち新たな政策は，立法を通じて実施され，法律の下で諸個人に影響を与える諸決定がなされる；資金は課税で調達される；法は大臣に対して責任を負う機関によって執行されるし，大臣もまた議会に責任を負う。しかしながら，同時に，コモンローは，議会への問合わせることなしに，執行部が単独でいくつかの活動を引き受けることを受容している。固有の執行権には，あらゆる法的人格が持つ能力，すなわち法人の創設，契約の締結，サービスに料金を課すこと，資金を使うことが含まれている。それらにはまた，主権の行使により密接に結びついた諸機能やある時はその本質として"大権的（prerogative）と言われる諸機能が含まれる。これらのうちで最も重要なものには，条約の署名および批准，宣戦布告および講和が含まれる。これらの諸機能を立法部よりは執行部のものとみなすことの合理的理由は，部分的には他の法的人格の地位との対比によっているし，また部分的には機能的であるしあるいは歴史的である。議会と国王の間の主要な闘争を終局させた1689年の権利の章典以来，立法権と執行権の間の境界について重要な変更はない。議会は，執行権の行使を無効にできるが，しかしそのようなことをほとんど行わないのが，責任ある政府の原動力である。

2 変化の時代

オーストラリアの法域では，公共サービス部門の機能を補うために，制定法によって創設された準独立機関が絶えず用いられている。しかし他の点では，政府のプロセスにおける執行部の構造および立法部が中心の位置を占めること―それに応答責

任ある政府と法の支配の諸原理は基づいている―という前提が広く採用されている。しかし,近年変化が始まった。これらの諸変化の本質とその諸変化が突きつけている難問は以下で述べる。ペーパーの残りでは,難問に対して政府,立法府そして裁判所による応答を論じる。

(a) 制定法で創設された機関

オーストラリアにおける責任ある政府の伝統的モデルに対する歴史的上の例外である,制定法で総説された独立機関の役割からはじめるのが都合がよいだろう。独立した公共部門が大臣に助言をしながら行政を行い,その大臣が今度は議会に対して責任を負うのは,前提として決して正しいものではなかった。公共部門は,重要な役割を担っているし,常に担っていた。しかしまた,政府の執行部門からの独立の程度に変化をつけながらある目的のために行政機関を制定法で特別に創設するという政府機能遂行に関する長い伝統があった[8]。そしてほとんどいつでも,この種の行政機関に関係して応答性ある政府の諸原理の有効性について論議や討議があった。法的には,このような機関に対する大臣の権力は,このような機関を創設する制定法によって,程度は異なりながらも,制限されている。しかし実務的にも政治的にも,大臣は,幹部職員達の任命,資金の抑制,法律修正の提議等の権利,その他の巧妙な方法を通じて広範な影響を行使できる。この議論に対する最近の貢献としては,オーストラリア連邦裁判所のフィン判事のものがある。判事は「制定法に規定された(したがって,おそらく,相応して制限される)大臣の指揮権に従う制定法で創設された諸法人の,わが政府組織における憲法上の地位および立場」を「オーストラリア法域における二つのかなり大きな亀裂」の一つであると述べている[9]。

問題は継続しているが,どちらかと言えば諸機関に商業的原理で操業することを求めるという最近の傾向によっていっそうひどくなっている。このことを達成するために,プライベートセクターにおける良く似たものを真似て機関を再編成することがますます追求されている。これは様々な方法によって行われるだろう[10]。しかし,もっとも極端な形としては,一般会社法のもと機関が創設され,その取締役会は,パブリックセクターと政府から引き抜いて構成する。

このような構造によって,憲法上の諸原理及び手続の妥当性についてたくさんの疑問が起こる。政府企業体の運営を構成している一般的あるいは個別的立法に服す

るような会社の取締役会および株主総会によってめいめいなされた諸決定を規制するのは，会社法であろう。外見上は少なくとも司法審査は全く適用されない。たとえ大臣達が政府株式の名目上の保有者だとしても，彼らが株主の権利および責任を行使することについて議会に説明責任を負わなければならないことが，（例えそうであっても）全く明白であるとは言えない。企業体が少数のあるいは過半数の株式をパブリックセクターに売却することで部分的に民営化される場合には，より問題は難しい。政府が少数株主の場合には，それは現実に起こっていることではあるが，公的資金の利用を審査するメカニズムでさえもはや適用できない。

(b) 委託契約─外部調達

だんだんとオーストラリア政府は，オーストラリア以外の政府同様，プライベートセクターとの契約を通じて政府の諸機能をますます外部調達している。近年これは，例えば刑務所の管理，救急車サービス，そして発電および売電などに影響を与えている。

外部調達は，パブリックセクターが以前所有していた産業を私的所有へと転換すること，あるいは民営化と同時に起こる場合は，政府は規制的な枠組みを賦課することによって支配手段を保持することを求めるだろう。これは私の同僚であるクロムリン教授の主題である。この場合の民主的説明責任の問題は，規制者と大臣そして大臣と議会の間の規制メカニズムの透明性および関連性に依拠している。裁判所や他の機関による外部審査の問題も同様に生じるだろう。とりわけ，有効な審査体制が稼働しており他方産業が公共的に行われている場合は。例えばこれは，電話産業の場合であり，それが株式会社化され部分的に民営化される以前は，連邦オンブツマンにたくさんの苦情をもたらした。

また政府サービスの外部調達は，別の諸論点を提出する。すなわち民主的説明責任と審査である。ある意味これらは新しいものではない。その程度を別にすればだが。政府は，いつも執行権の行使において契約を結ぶ。まさにその本質によって，政府契約は議会が審査することは難しいし，裁判所による審査からほとんど免責されている。しかし，部分的には人々に対して公共サービスを私的に提供するということの含意の故に，また部分的には事実上の規制にとって契約を用いたメカニズム

の可能性の故に，最近の外部調達の規模は伝統的な憲法慣習に対する難問の重大さを目だたさせている。

　人々に対するインパクトは少なくとも2つの形態をとる。第1のものは，政府と契約者との関係についてである。政府の規模と関連ある財産は，ある契約者の実行可能性を決める点までそのビジネスを価値あるものとする。採択が不当でありその説明責任も適切に果たされないままの契約手続きにおいて，公正な取り扱いがどのくらい保障され得るだろうか？一般的に想定されている答えは，手のこんだ入札手続きである。しかしながら，これらが効率的で透明でかつ公正でなければ，問題を解決する代わりに，さらにこじらせてしまう。それは，相当数の入札申込みの準備に必然的に捧げられる時間と資源の故である[11]。

　影響を受けるもう1つのグループは，最終的にサービスの提供を受ける人々であるが，そのサービスは公的資金を利用しながらプライベートセクターによって提供される。もしこれらのサービスがパブリックセクターによって供給されているならば，受益者は裁判所，審判所，あるいはオンブツマンによって決定を審査してもらう権利があるだろうし，彼らに影響ある決定がどのようになされたかについての情報にアクセスする権利があるだろう。少なくとも理論的には，議員個人や議会自体を通じて，このようなサービスの供給に対してもまた民主的説明責任を確保する方法があるだろう。このような新たな仕組みのもとでは，パブリックセクターによって提案された複製物にも審査のメカニズムは導入されるべきか，あるいは市場のメカニズムは十分なものか？プライベートセクターの機関が行うサービスの供給についての苦情に，議員はどのような立場をとるべきか？どのように応答するよう政府は期待されるべきか[12]？

　第3の，そしてまだ比較的まだ未探求の争点は，政府による事実上の規制を目的とした契約の可能性に関わる。Dainithは，1989年にこの現象に注目し，政策への服従を確保するために，命令権（imperium）よりも所有権（dominium）をますます利用していると彼は分析する[13]。もしもサービスの基準を課したり，社会的あるいは経済的規範の発展を促進したり，あるいは，例えば囚人の社会復帰と刑務所の安全確保の間でどちらを優先するかを確定するために契約が利用されるならば，政府は

そのような選択にたいして説明責任があるどうか,そしてどのように説明責任を有するかについて問題が生じる。

(c) 利用者払い

　政府が商業慣習によりいっそう依拠していることの別の側面,すなわちDainithの言葉で言えば,命令権以上に所有権を利用することは,税金よりも利用料金を課して公共サービスの資金にすることである。またこれも新しい現象ではない。その目新しさは,その程度と,その根底にある原理についての争点がよりはっきりしてきたことである。

　オーストラリア憲法自体は,免許料金やサービス料金を課税の定義から除外している[14]。この定義は裁判所によって精密にされている。そして裁判所は,以下のように判決している。すなわち,税金（tax）は公共目的のために公的機関によって強制的に金銭を取り立てることで,法によって強制出来るものであり,「行われたサービスに対する支払いではない[15]。」裁判所は,特典やサービスに対する料金と偽っている税（imposts）を注意深く審査する傾向があるが,実際に一般的強制的な徴税に対してはそうではない[16]。この区別は重要である。税金を課すには議会の権威が要求されるが,少なくとも他の種類の料金に対してはそうではない。これは数年前に図式的に描かれた。すなわち一定の政府決定の審査に対する料金の支払いが行政実務によって強制的に要求されたが,それは上院が料金賦課の委任立法を却下した後であった。問題は,税（imposts）は税金（tax）かどうか,そしてオーストラリア憲法のもとで議会両院各々の権限と関係があるかどうか,である[17]。

　しかし,憲法上の争点は広範な範囲で未解決のままである。税金収入の多くが,特定の目的に献じられているし,あるいは「担保とされている」。例えば,道路税は,道路維持の担保であるのかもしれない。タバコ税は,タバコと関係ある病気から生じるヘルスケアの担保であるかもしれないし,あるいは喫煙を推奨しないキャンペーン広告の担保であるのかもしれない。このような税金を,これらあるいはそれ以外のサービスに対する利用料金から区別することは難しいかもしれない。強調されている論点は,税金の定義の限界である。もしも料金が道路や病院や学校のような一般的なコミュニティサービスを提供する施設の利用に対して課されるとした

ら，これらは，その適用の一般性という理由からあるいは利用者には他に有効な手段がないし実際に徴税が強制的であるという理由からに税金と見なされるべきであろうか？もし見なされるならば，その施設が公的に所有されている場合と，施設が私的に所有されてはいるが政府の権威の下で利用可能な場合と，どんな違いが生じるか？

(d) 政府のない統治

　最近の動向が生みだした諸論点の最後の例は，ジ・オールド・メルボルン埠頭 (the old Melbourne Docklands) の再開発の経験から引き出せる。その埠頭の経済的条件は，大阪ウォーターフロント開発になぞれえられる。もっとメルボルンの方がスケールは小さいが。地理的に，その地域は，メルボルン市当局という地方政府の管轄権内にある。しかし今のところ計画及び開発は，州政府の後援の下，制定法で創設された機関によって行われており，市議会が全く関わっていない。これはある部分では争いがあるが，他方再開発の最初段階に生じる多くの複雑な部分を効率的に処理する必要性から，そしてこの地域に人が住みつくまではともあれ民主的代表制は現実的でないという理由で，全般的には受け入れられている。

　将来の統治に対する仕組みは明確ではないけれども，それは意見の衝突をより多く引き起こすだろう。この地域の諸計画で描かれていることは，おおよそ15,000の居住者，オフィススペース，スタジアム，エンターテイメント区域そしてテーマパークである。各々の区域は，その地域のすべての快適な生活のための施設(amenities)の提供に責任を負う個々の入札者によって，全体として開発されるだろう。再開発された埠頭全体へのインフラストラクチャー——それには道路網も含まれる——は，同様に入札者によって提供されるだろう。インフラストラクチャーは最終的に公的所有に復帰するのかどうか，復帰するとしたらいつ復帰するかについて契約は秘密にされているので，今の段階では，確かではない。

　メルボルン市は，この地域の統治を出来るだけ早く再開したがっている。民主的正当性のある機関によって提供されるべき，そして選挙による代表者によって地方のコミュニティー——それに対して代表者は責任を負う——に課された地方税によって資金を出されるべき社会的，経済的，環境的サービス範囲の必要性に対して

部分的に論及しながら、メルボルン市はこのケースを論じている。彼らの要求の帰結は誰も知らないが、それは成功するかもしれない。しかし、開発が完遂するまでその要求は抵抗にあいそうであるし、完遂までは30年位かかるだろう。その時でさえも、地方代表制が州政府によって容認されるかどうか、あるいは非典型的で歴史の浅くかつ専門的であると思われているこの地域の全住民が地方代表制を要求するかどうかという問題さえある。オータナティブなシナリオは、以下の通りである。その地域では、私人である株式会社 (private corporations) が住民との契約関係に基づいてサービスを提供し、実際に私的に所有されている社会共同の施設の利用に料金を課す。

3 司法審査とその他の形態の外部審査

商業化、株式会社化、そして外部調達へという傾向が明白になって以来、司法審査の伝統的メカニズムおよびそれ以外のより新しい手続きで不平の除去や決定の透明性を十分にするためのものはどの範囲まで適用されるべきか、あるいはどの範囲まで拡張されるべきか、ということに対して多くの研究が行われている。これらの研究に含まれるものは、政府企業体についての行政審査評議会による審査[18]、情報自由化法[19]、政府間相互サービス提供プログラム[20]、そして委託契約[21]などである。

これらの報告書において露わになっているものは、その程度は異なっているものの、いずれも競合的な公法的アプローチと私法的アプローチとの間の緊張と、この新しい文脈においてどちらが機能する見込みがあるかについての不確かさである。中心的な問題は以下の通りである。会社法、取引慣習あるいは競争法と契約法を含み、また市場の力学とおそらく自主的な行動規範[22]と結びついているプライベートセクターの救済手段は、パブリックセクターである機関が商業的サービスを提供することに対して、あるいは私人である請負人が公共サービスを提供することに対して相応の説明責任を備えるかどうかである。しかし、根本的な諸論点が同様に存在するし、それらの諸論点はそれら自身で緊張を作りだしている。一つは、ある場面における公法上の手続と救済手段に対する敵意の程度であるが、この敵意は、公法上の手続と救済をパブリックセクターに適用する場合でさえ見られる。これらを説得するために、新たな私人の顔をした政府は行政法を抑制するあるいは引っ込める

(wind back）機会を提供している。これに反対の立場であり他の場面においては同じくらい有力な見解は，政府は政府以外の者すべてが模範とするようなモデルを提供するべきだという見解である。この見解の支持者は，権限授与書（precept）は絶対的かどうか，あるいは政府のサービスがプライベートセクターと競争している場合に権限授与書は適正に変更できるとするかどうかで分かれる。

　これらの争点に対する政府からの政策上の反応は限られており，一般的には，断片的でばらばらである。既存の手続が株式会社化された機関及び民営化されたサービスまで及んでいるその範囲内では，全体的にそれらの手続は適正である。しかしそうでなければ，サービスと機関に対する公的及び法的責任は，根本的な首尾一貫した諸原理が持ち上がらないような仕方でプラグマチックに取り組まれる。少なくともレトリック上は，公法上の諸原理及び制度の拡大よりもむしろ自己規制を含む市場を通じた規制を政府は明らかに好んでいる。珍しい例としては，単純な個別の産業を行う公的および私的機関の両方に対する苦情を取り扱うために，専門的な紛争解決メカニズムが確立されている。

　対照的に，司法審査の射程はこの新しい分野へとだんだん拡張されはじめてきた。それは，歴史的な前提と原則によって，そしてある程度は制定法によって抑制されていた。伝統的には，裁判所は，大権的あるいは固有の執行権力の射程を明確にする準備はなされていたが[23]，しかしその行使を審査することについては用心深かった。そのようなことをするのは以下のような事実からあらゆる場合において難しいとされてきていた。すなわち，手続上の公正さあるいは極端な権力の集中（ultra vires）のような審査理由は，制定法によって授けられた権威のもとで行われ議会の意思に言及することによって正当化される，諸決定に対する審査と結びついて発展してきた。部分的にはこれらの理由で，ここ数十年間立法のおかげで司法審査はもっと利用されやすくなったが，その立法においてはまた，制定法に言及しながら裁判所の管轄権を明確にしている。例えば連邦の諸決定に対する審査の原理的な手段として1977年の行政決定（司法審査）法（the Administrative Decisions (Judicial Review) Act 1977）は，「法律の条項によって」行政機関のような性格を取得している機関が行った諸決定を審査するための管轄権を連邦裁判所（the Federal Court）に与えている[24]。

様式は今や崩れつつある。まだいくつかの反対意見は存在するが，裁判所は，固有な執行権行使としてなされた諸決定に対して審査する用意は出来ている。手続的公正さは最低限適用されるだろうし，また状況次第で，過度の権力集中という理由も適用されるだろう[25]。オーストラリア連邦裁判所は，最近以下のような判決を下した。すなわち，公共団体は，部分的には契約の文言に基づいて，しかし部分的にはまた公共団体が「道徳的模範（moral exemplar）」であらねばならないという理由で，入札を公正に行う義務がある，と[26]。少なくとも自ら規制的機能を遂行する一私的団体がパブリックセクターの救済手段を適用することを，イギリスの裁判所は認めさえしている[27]。オーストラリアでは，少なくとも連邦レベルでは，裁判所に管轄権が与えられているという点から見て，そのような発展は不可能であろう[28]。

4 民主的説明責任

執行部の議会に対する責任及び議会を通じた有権者に対する説明責任において政府の実務が変化しつつあることのインパクトは同様に強烈である。これもまた重要である。執行部と立法部の関係は，その実務上の効率性についての冷笑にもかかわらず，オーストラリア憲法制度の基本的要素である。

議会制は，政府の主要かつ新しい政策は立法に基づくことを前提としている。統治の新たなアプローチはすべて一つの特色があるが，それは立法を要求することがだんだんと少なくなっているということである。既存の法は，政府機関を法人の地位へと変換するために改められる必要があるだろう。それを越えてしばしば枠組みとなる立法が行われる[29]が，団体に合法的な規制機能や特権が与えることができなければ，その立法は本質的ではない。一般法のもと法人格付与によって設立された団体は，さらなる立法による支援を全く必要としない。

株式会社化と民営化の時代においては，政府が用いるその他のテクニックについても同じであることは間違いない。外部調達は慣行通りに契約に基づいている。多くの場合立法的枠組みすら全く存在しない。利用者払いの料金の地位はあいまいであるが，少なくともそれらのいくつかは議会の権限を伴わずに課すことが出来ることは疑いない。

立法が存在しない場合でさえ，議会が政府の活動を監視することを憲法理論は前提とする。困難なのは，このようなことを行うための手段が限られているということだ。ほとんどの政府団体が議会に年間報告書を提出することを要求されているが，それは干渉のための一つの方法である。歳出手続を通じて支出を承認することを議会に要求することは，特定の契約あるいは契約一般が増加するかもしれないという状況に備えている。この目的のために議会が効率性を発揮できるように，独立機関である会計検察長（Auditor-General）および公的会計の監視に責任を有する議会の諸委員会が補佐している。これに関して注目に値することは，政府と会計検査院との間で近年対立が増えつつあり，後者の権限の独立性と射程を脅かしていることである。同様に注目する意義あることとしては，この種の契約の重要な細目を，商業上の機密であるという理由で，議会は知らされえなかった。

議会がこの困難に立ち向かうためには，現在行われている統治とは異なった方法を承認する新たな手続がデザインされねばならない。例えば，行政審査評議会はそのような一つの手続を検討した(30)。一般外部契約法 (a general Contracting Out Act) が最低限の要求として課すものとして契約の監視，契約者の実績評価，契約を結んだ機関が契約の細目を年間報告書への掲載要求が望ましいものかについての見解を評議会は求めた。また契約者の活動によって影響されるサービスの受給者およびその他の人々に対して救済を提供するのにその法律が有益であることを，評議会は示唆した。この提案に対する政府からの反応は完全に好意的というわけではなかったし，評議会は最終報告書でこの勧告を続けなかった。

外部契約法に対する比較的斬新な示唆が，連邦レベルで議会を条約締結の決定に参加させるという近年の別な手続と類似している(31)。条約締結と批准は，またオーストラリアのシステムでは執行権の一つであるが，その地位はだんだんと疑問視されている。現在の手続では，制定法に基づいていないものの，条約は議会に上程されることが要求し，かつそれらについて公の見解を求めるための議会の委員会を設けることになっている。この手続は条約締結手続により多くの透明性をもたらしたことは疑いない。議会の役割は限定されていて，緊急性や機密性を要する条約の場合にはその手続は完全に差し控えられるという領域は存在するが。

議会が執行過程によりいっそう参画できるようオープンにして行くことの難しさは，議会自体の特徴に内在している。議会は遅く扱いにくい。議会の行うべきことが減らされた帰結として，議会がよりいっそう課題を実現できなくなっているとしたら，皮肉にも議会はもっと遅く扱いにくくなってゆきそうである。そしてこれは高度に二項対立的である。議論の余地はあるが，提案されているような政府とその対抗者との間の争いに関係して提案された新法をじっくりと検討するには議会は適切ではあるか，しかし型にはまりすぎている。しかしながら，対立する方法は，第三者や政府の他の機関が参加したり，本案についての注意深く時として機密性をもってじっくりと検討するに値する手段としては，より受入れがたい。

結 論

20世紀終わりの西側諸国において市民は消費者へと変容し，人々と政府との関係はだんだんと仕事と依頼人のそれへとなってきたという見解は，陳腐なものとなった。この現象は，機関が対処している人々を消費者として描くという政府のレトリックをしばしば反映している。その動機は，もともとは非人間的な官僚制においてサービス文化を奨励することであったのだろう。もしそうであるなら，それはシチズンシップの概念および市民と国家との関係についての悲しむべき反映である。というのは，人々を舞台中央に据えるために市場に訴えかける必要があるからである。しかしそうなった場合は，市場の類似物は，メカニズムとしてだんだん適したものとなってゆき，そのメカニズムを通じて政府は政策を作成・実行し，サービスを変化させながら提供する。

これは多くの点で，憲法的そして法的意味において同等の対応を要求している一つの革命と言える。現在のところ対応は断片的で，ケースバイケースに基づいて発展している。いくつかの面白いアイデアが現れ始めているが，それらには底辺を支える首尾一貫した哲学がない。この哲学がなければ，そしてこの哲学が生じるまで，消費者国家に向かうゆっくりとした流れは，シチズンシップの結びつきを弱めることおよび代表機関の悪評を増やすことを助長しながら，続くだろう。

21世紀の憲法学者にとって1つのプロジェクトは，新たな統治の現実を受けとめて，その行使についての諸制度と諸原理を発展させること，そしてもし必要ならば，

民主的政治形態それ自体の基礎のいくつかを再び構想してみることである。比較研究は本質的となろう。これらの争点について日本の学者とのさらなる交流に期待している。

(1) 国の憲法を変更するためには選挙人の承認が要求される（憲法第128条）。
(2) Edmund Burke, speech to the electors at Bristol, in Jack Lively and Adam Lively (eds) *Democracy in Britain*, Blackwells, 1994, 62-63より
(3) A.V. Dicey, The Law of the Constitution, extracted in Lively and Lively, op. cit., 178-180.
(4) 例えば1975年行政上訴審判所法
(5) 1982年情報自由化法
(6) 1977年行政決定（司法審査）法第13条
(7) 1988年プライヴァスィー法
(8) R Wettenhall, *Corporations and Corporatisation: An Administrative History Perspective* (1995) 6 PLR 7.
(9) *Hughes Aircraft Systems International v. Air Services Australia* (1997) 146 ALR 1, 24.
(10) Dominic McGann, "Corporatisation, Privatisation and Other Strategies – Common Legal Issues" in Bryan Horrigan (ed.) *Government Law and Policy: Commercial Aspects* (Federation Press, 1988) 55
(11) Dan Young, "Current Issues in Government Tendering and Contracting Practice" in Horrigan, op. cit., 69, 74-5.
(12) これらの疑問，またそれ以外の疑問は，オーストラリア政府あるいは行政法の事柄についての第一の勧告機関である行政審査評議会（the Administrative Review Council）によって現在調査対象となっている（*The Contracting Out of Government Services*, Issues Paper, February 1997.）。
(13) Terence Dainith, " The Executive Power Today: Bargaining and Economic Control" in Jeffrey Jowell and Dawn Oliver(eds) The Changing Constitution, Clarendon Press, Oxford (2nd edition 1989), 193.
(14) 第53条
(15) *Air Caledonie International v. The Commonwealth* (1988) 165 CLR 462, 467.
(16) このように*Air Caledonie*事件自体で，オーストラリアに到着したすべての乗客が支払うべき「入国手続き料金」が税金であると判決された。
(17) 第53条。税を課すような信用証券の出どころは上院であってはならない。また，第55条も参照。
(18) *Government Business Enterprise and Administrative Law*, Report no. 38.

⑲ *Open Government: A Review of the Federal Freedom of Information Act 1982*, with the Australian Law Reform Commission, Report no. 40.
⑳ *Administrative Review and Funding Programs*, Report no. 37.
㉑ *op. cit.*
㉒ これらは「憲章 (Charters)」という形式をとることがだんだん増えているが，英国の「市民憲章 (Citizen's Charter)」の利用から啓発を受けたことは明らかである。the Administrative Review Council, *The Contracting Out of Government Services*, op. cit., 41-43; Robin Creyke, "Sunset for the Administrative Law Industry?" in John McMillan (ed.) *Administrative Law Under the Coalition Government* (1997) 20, 57.
㉓ *Barton v. Commonwealth* (1974) 131 CLR 477.
㉔ 第3条
㉕ *Council of Civil Service Unions v. Minister for the Civil Service*. (1985) AC 374.
㉖ *Hughes Aircraft Systems International v. Air Services Australia* (1997) 146 ALR 1, 41.
㉗ *R v. Panel on Take-overs and Mergers; ex parte Datafin p. lc* (1987) 1 QB 815
㉘ 1977年行政決定（司法審査）法の目的に照らせば，団体は制定法のもと裁決できない。また，憲法第75条（v）によって連邦最高裁判所 (the High Court) に与えられ，1903年裁判法 (the Judiciary Act 1903) 第398条によって連邦裁判所に与えられた管轄権の目的に照らせば，団体は「連邦の一機関 (officer)」でもない。
㉙ 例えば，1997年連邦機関および会社法 (Commonwealth Authorities and Companies Act 1997)
㉚ *The Contracting Out of Government Services*, op. cit.
㉛ Daryl Williams, "Treaties and the Parliamentary Process" (1996) 7 *Public Law Review* 199.

第Ⅲ部　日本におけるオセアニア法制論

14　オーストラリアの統治構造の基本的性格
――共和制か, 君主制かをめぐって――

大須賀　明

はじめに
1　オーストラリア憲法の君主制的要素
2　オーストラリア憲法の共和制的実態
3　オーストラリアの統治構造の基本的な仕組み
　　――欧米諸国のそれと比較して――

はじめに

　本論文の研究をはじめた直接の理由は, オーストラリアの国家体制は, 君主制なのか, それとも共和制なのか, そして憲法はそれをどのように規定し, 現実にはどのように運用されているのかを知りたいということであった。本論文はもちろんその課題の究明を行なってはいるが, 同時に, それを契機にオーストラリアの統治構造全体の具体的な仕組みを把握してみたい, 正確にいえばそのための最初のステップを踏んでみたい, という考えをもっている。だが残念なことに日本にはオーストラリアの法制に関する文献も, 法学書も極めて少ない。日本の英米法学では, オセアニア法制の研究が, 今なお欠落しているとさえいわれるほどの現状にある, と云われている。しかし私には共同研究を遂行するなかで知り合うようになった多くのすぐれたオーストラリアの友人たちがいる。しかも私たちは, オーストラリアで最も有力なメルボルン大学のLaw Schoolと学術交流を行なっている。それならば私たちにはオーストラリアの法制を研究し, それを日本の学者をはじめとする多くの人たちに知らせる道徳的な義務があると思い, 私たちのプロジェクトはこの研究を始めた。

1　オーストラリア憲法の君主制的要素

　オーストラリア憲法は, 英国議会法律の9ヵ条とオーストラリア連邦憲法法律 (the Commonwealth of Australian Constitution Act) から成っている。前者の法律の前文と最初の8ヵ条は通常冒頭条項 (covering clauses) と呼ばれ, 後者の憲法の条項とは区別されている。そしてその総体としてのオーストラリア憲法の内容をみて

みると，随所に君主制的要素が散見される。

たとえば，前文は，オーストラリア国民は，「大ブリテンとアイルランド連合王国の国王のもと，ひとつの永続的な連邦共和国において結合する」と述べている。また冒頭条項の第3条は，女王に対し，オーストラリア連邦共和国を実現する権限と最初の総督を任命する権限を与えている。さらに第Ⅰ章議会の第一部総説の第1条では，立法権は連邦議会に与えられているが，その議会は女王と上院と下院から成るとして，女王は議会の部分であると規定している。また第2条は「女王によって任命される総督は，連邦共和国においては，女王陛下の代表でなければならない。そして女王陛下が喜んで彼に割り当てるような女王の諸権力と諸機能を，女王の慈悲深い要請のある間はこの憲法に従って，共和国のなかで，所持しなければならないし，行使することができる」と定めている。そしてさらに第4条が，総督が何らかの理由で，行動することができないような場合には，女王に，行政官(administrator)を任命する権限を与えていること，126条により副総督を任命する権限を，女王は総督に与えることができること，などなど[1]を定めていることにあらわれている。

2 オーストラリア憲法の共和制的実態

以上述べた君主制的要素の指摘は，1900年に制定された英国議会法律とオーストラリア連邦憲法法律の条文の内容をそのまま分析したものである。しかし20世紀の100年の間に，憲法の文言は変更されなかったものの，オーストラリアの統治構造には，実質的に大きな変化が生じた。新しい法律の制定や様々な運用の変更や裁判所の判決などにより，とりわけ国王と総督の性格や役割が変わり，総督の任命のあり方が変化するなかで，英連合の枠組みのなかではあれ，オーストラリア連邦の独立が大きく進展したのであった。

まず冒頭条項の第3条は，その条文の内容からみて，現在では，もはや歴史的な意味しかもっていないことは明らかであろう。ついで女王もまた議会の部分であるという第1条の規定についても，それは真の権力(real power)が国王から議会に移ってしまったという，英国における歴史的な発展の帰結を反映しているが，だがそれとて国王を全く排除してしまうというものではなく，現在でも国王が議会の部分として演じている役割が残っており，それは，その他の立法過程を通過した法案に裁可(assent)を与える権限である，という指摘がある[2]。この裁可という法的行為は，立法過程を通過した法案に具体的な法的効力を与え，確定的に成立させる行為

なのか，それともすでに立法過程で現実的な法的効力を与えられており，単にそれを儀礼的に追認するにすぎない行為なのかは問題になろう。もし前者であれば，女王は政治的実権をもつことになり，統治構造は君主制に傾斜することになるが，後者であれば共和制に傾斜することになるであろう。全体の法的な仕組みから考えると後者の見解が正しいのではなかろうかと思われるが，そうだとすればこの規定の実質的な意味はすでに全く失われているということができる。

また，1973年の法律で，女王はオーストラリア女王と改められた。このことのもつ法的な意味について，この改正により女王は，オーストラリアの問題については，オーストラリアの閣僚からのみ助言を受けるのであって，英国の閣僚は一切関係のない存在になった，という指摘がある[3]。まさに憲法制定当時に比較して，この点でも君主制のあり方は大きく変化したのであって，オーストラリアの独立度の達成は顕著なものがあるように見受けられる。

さらに総督は，オーストラリアにおいては，女王の代表であるという第2条の規定についても，なるほど憲法が施行された1901年には，女王が元首であり，総督はその女王の代理をする者であった。その時点ではオーストラリアは自治領という特別な地位を得たものの，基本的には英国の植民地であったので，初期の総督は，英国人であって，英国の首相の助言にもとづいて，英国の君主により任命されており，オーストラリア政府は全く関与することができなかった。ところが1930年にはじめて，オーストラリア政府は，オーストラリア人（オーストラリア出身でかつ在住の市民）を，総督として国王に推薦し，国王も不承不承ながら総督に任命した。この時オーストラリア政府の総督の推薦権は確立したといわれているが，このオーストラリア市民の指名が慣行化したのは1960年代半ば以降だといわれている[4]。この変更に伴なって，総督は法的にはオーストラリアの政府にのみ接点をもち，国外の権力には接点をもたない存在となり，女王には責任を負わない存在となった。

いずれにせよ，慣例により，女王がオーストラリアとの関係で演じている唯一の役割は，総督を任命すること，さらには必要なら解職することであるが，その権限さえもオーストラリアの首相の助言にもとづいて行使されているのである。しかも第2条では総督の職務の期間が「女王の慈悲深い要請のある間（during the Queen's pleasure）」と規定されているが，それとても通常5年間と決まっている。さらに総督はすべての必要な執行権（executive power）を憲法61条にもとづいて保持しているといわれており[5]，今日では，元首の重要な機能はすべて，現代的な意味での総督

により行使されているのであって、女王によっては行使されていない。そして第4条の定める女王の任命権限などもオーストラリア首相の助言にもとづいて行使されている。また1986年のオーストラリア法律により、UK（英連合王国）政府は、州のことはすべて州に委ねたし、UK議会は、立法する権限をすべて、連邦と州と準州に引き渡した。さらに女王は、州知事を州の首相の助言にもとづいて任命する。しかもその知事はオーストラリア人であるので、女王は州知事に対してもっていたかっての植民地の権能をすべて放棄してしまったのである。

一般に共和制については「選挙によって選ばれた代表者を通じて統治が行われる体制」[6]とか「国民の意思に基づいて政治の運用がなされる国家形態。政治の運用が君主でなく、貴族のような少数の門閥者ないし国民全体によって行われる場合、これを共和制（republic）と呼んだ」[7]などと定義されている。

これに対して、伝統的に君主とされるものの要件を一般的に整理してみると、a．世襲的にその地位が継承される独任機関で、b．統治権の重要部分を掌握し、少なくとも行政権の主体ないし調整的権能をもつ存在であって、c．対外的に国家を代表する権能を有し、d．国家的象徴性を備えるもの、とされている[8]。日本国憲法における天皇は、「国政に関する権能を有しない」（4条）とされており、天皇の行う国事行為も内閣の助言と承認にもとづく、名目的かつ儀礼的な行為であるから、まずbの要件を欠いている。さらにまた憲法上条約の締結や外交関係の処理は内閣に委ねられており、天皇にはそれに関する名目的な権限すらない。天皇の権限は、全権委任状、大使・公使の信任状、批准書その他の外国文書の「認証」に止まるのであって、それらの文書の付与権があるわけではない。したがってcの要件を全く欠いているといえよう。それ故天皇は伝統的な意味での君主ではないと云えるのであって、そのうえ国民主権主義のもと三権分立のシステムを採り、議院内閣制により政治が行なわれることになっているので、日本国憲法は明らかに共和制を採用しているということができるのである。

オーストラリアの場合も、すでに述べたように、元首の重要な機能はすべて女王から総督に移行しており、対外的に国家を代表する権能も、総督と政府と議会によって行使されていることからみて、bとcの要件を欠いており、オーストラリア女王も伝統的な意味での君主でないことは明らかである。そのうえ総督はオーストラリア政府の首相の推薦にもとづいて任命され、最高裁（High Court）の判決で明らかなように、三権の分立という憲法のレイアウトのもと[9]、議院内閣制によって政治が運

用されている点からみて，明らかにその統治の基本構造は，実質的に共和制であるということができよう。

　しかし君主制を採用する国においては，世界史的にみて，君主が，絶対君主から立憲君主へ，さらには議会主義的君主へと移行しており，それとともに次第に君主の権限が縮少されている。そして最後の議会主義的君主制は，すでに国民主権に基づく君主制である[10]。その種の君主は，国民代表としての資格を有し，憲法上何らかの政治的権限を行使しうるかたちになっている。とりわけその場合行政権が対象になるが，イギリスやベルギーの両憲法では，立法権の一翼をも掌握するかたちになっている。もちろんこれらの国々では，議院内閣制の発達により，国王の権限はほとんど名目化されている。そうしたことから現代では君主制の観念自体が変質しているということと，したがって共和制と区別することが困難になっているという指摘がなされている。こうした指摘を背景にしながら，今日君主の観念が流動的になっていることを理由に，さきの君主の要件のうちaとdの要件だけで君主と認めてもよいとする学説が多数になっている。日本の天皇がaの要件をみたしていることはいうまでもないが，憲法は１条で「天皇は，日本国の象徴であり，日本国民統合の象徴であって，この地位は，主権の存する日本国民の総意に基く」と定めていることからdの要件も充足していると云えよう。したがって天皇はこの種の君主であることは明らかであるが，この学説の場合には君主が存在するからといって，君主制か共和制かの二者択一を迫られるといった性格のものではない。その統治構造が共和制であることを前提として，そのなかに，この種の限定的な意味の君主が共和制を害することなく，しかし共和制と一定の緊張関係を保ちながらどのようなかたちで，存在しているかの問題がつきつけられるにとどまるのである。

　日本の場合には，基本的には共和制をとりながら，部分的に象徴天皇制が採用され，憲法上，日本国と日本国民の統合に，天皇が象徴的に貢献することが期待されている，そうした仕組みになっているといえよう。またオーストラリア女王はaの要件を充足していることは明らかである。さらに，シンポジウムのなかで，マイケル・スミス教授は，女王は象徴であり，その意味するところのものは第一に，英国の伝統に対するきずな（絆）であり，第２に，英連邦諸国に対するきずなであり，第３に変更する必要のない，確立され，安定した統治の体系の象徴である，と述べた。まさにdの要件をも充足することが明らかである。したがってオーストラリアは，日本同様，部分的には象徴君主制を採用しているが，基本的には共和制の国家形態

3 オーストラリアの統治構造の基本的な仕組み
――欧米諸国のそれと比較して――

つぎのような一文がオーストラリアの法学書にのっている。「君主は事実上の共和国の影であるにすぎない。総督は公選の首相によって任命される事実上の大統領であり、この首相に対して責任を負い、ほとんど必ず彼の助言にもとづいて行動する。そして同じ種類のことが州知事と州首相に対しても云えるのである」[11]

このように総督を大統領であるといっても、それは厳格な三権分立をとりながら、間接的にではあるが公選され、強大な政治的権限を集中的に保持しているアメリカの大統領に類似しているものではない。何故なら総督は、議会に対して重要な権限をもっている。たとえばそれは、第5条が定めているように、議会の会期を決定したり、下院を解散して選挙を行うことであったり、議会を停会する権限であるが、それらは首相の助言にもとづいて行使されることになっている[12]。また61条は、連邦共和国の執行権（executive power）が女王に与えられており、それは女王の代表としての総督によって行使することができるものであると定め、法的には総督の権限とされているものの、それもまたすべて政府の助言にもとづいて（on government advice）行使されることになっている[13]。このように総督の権限は重要かつ広範であるがその実質的な決定権は、そのほとんどすべてが首相や政府をはじめとする他の統治部門に掌握されていて、かなりの程度に名目的なものであるように思われる。

しかも議員として公選されている首相によって実質的には任命されるシステムになっていることからみても、ヨーロッパ諸国の大統領に類似しているように思われる。その場合でも直接公選され強大な政治的権限をもつフランスの大統領[14]ではないことは明らかである。しかしそれよりは権限が弱いものの、軍隊の指揮権、最高国防会議の主宰、戦争状態の宣言など軍事に関する権限や両議院の解散権などをもち、名目的元首ではなく国政に実質的な影響を及ぼす権限をもつ、イタリアの大統領[15]に類似しているとも考えられない。どちらかといえば、「ほとんど権力はもたないが、しかしそれでも権力の点で欠けているものを個人的な権威によって埋め合わせることが期待しうる人」であると云われ、条約締結権、首相候補者の推薦、首相の提案に基づく連邦大臣の任免、法律の認証と公布など総じて形式的なものに限定されているドイツの大統領[16]に近似していると考えられるのである。

またヨーロッパ諸国の統治構造を，国家元首（国王または大統領）と首相それぞれの役割や機能との関連において概観してみると，まずコアビタシオン期（保革共存政権）のフランスを除いて大統領を国家元首とする諸国においては，程度の差はあるものの，議院内閣制的な政治の運用が行われている。つまり民意を反映する議会の信任にもとづいて統治が行われなければならない仕組みになっている，と云えよう。また立憲君主制を採用する諸国においても，国王の権限は殆ど形式化・名目化しており，実質的な政府の首長の役割を首相が担い，そこでもまた首相の活動は議会の信任にもとづいたものでなければならない仕組みになっている。

オーストラリアも議院内閣制をとっているという点ではヨーロッパ諸国と類似しているということが言えると思うが，女王の元首としての権限や機能が総督に移行しているということを除けば，やはり宗主国であるイギリスの，国家元首ではあるが名目的な存在となった国王のもとで，強力な地位をもつ首相を中心とする（「首相政治」）議院内閣制がとられている統治構造に，実質的には一番近似しているように思われるのである。

(1) *The Australian Constitution*, at 25.
(2) *id*. at 23.
(3) Zelman Cowen, The Legal Implications of Australia's Becoming a Republic, *The Australian Law Journal*. vol. 68 at 589.
(4) *id*. at 590.
(5) *The Australian Constitution*, at 24.
(6) 田中英夫編・英米法辞典722頁。
(7) 末川博・法学辞典966頁。
(8) 樋口陽一・憲法Ⅰ，128頁。
(9) *The Australian Constitution*, at 23.
(10) 佐藤功・君主制の研究，40〜1頁。
(11) P.H. Lane, *An Introduction to the Australian Constitutions*, at 263.
(12) *The Australian Constitution*, at 26.
(13) *id*. at 69〜70.
(14) 今関源成「第五共和制の基本的枠組み」・奥島ほか編フランスの政治35頁以下。
(15) 井口文男「共和国憲法」・馬場ほか編イタリアの政治43頁。
(16) 渡辺重範「ボン基本法体制の成立・展開と連邦諸機関」渡辺編・ドイツハンドブック65〜6頁。

15 オーストラリア法における国際法の地位
―― *Teoh* 判決が意味するもの ――*

宮 川 成 雄

　はじめに
　1　連邦最高裁のテオ判決
　2　変形理論における「正当な期待」の意義
　3　変形理論をとるオーストラリアの理由
　4　より広い文脈でのテオ判決の意義

はじめに

　本報告で私は，オーストラリア法制における国際法の地位について検討したい。私は特に1995年にオーストラリア連邦最高裁により下された *Teoh* 判決に関心を持っている。その正式名称は *Minister of State for Immigration and Ethnic Affairs v. Ah Hin Teoh* (以下，テオ判決)[1]である。
　連邦議会はテオ判決の意義を否定する動きをみせたことがあるが，その試みは数度にわたり失敗に終わっている[2]。連邦議会が覆そうとしたテオ判決の判旨とは，国内法化されていない条約を，オーストラリア行政府が遵守すべきことを示唆する判示部分である。そのような法律案がもし成立したとしても，オーストラリア国内法秩序における国際法の地位を理論的に考察するに際して，テオ判決が提起したことの重要性は否定されることはないと考えられる。
　テオ判決は，オーストラリア法における条約の国内的効力に関する変形理論の立場を一歩踏み出すものであり，ある意味で，条約を法律による変形なくそのまま「国法（Law of the Land）」[3]とする，アメリカ合衆国の立場への接近を示唆するものともいえる。またテオ判決が，オーストラリア法への国際人権法の影響を示すものであることは否定できない。このようなテオ判決の理解は，オーストラリアの法学者には耳障りに聞こえるかも知れないが，以下で示す私の議論が意味のあるものと受けとめられるように願う次第である。
　私の議論の要点は次のとおりである。オーストラリア法秩序においては，条約はたとえオーストラリア政府によって批准されようとも，議会によって法律化されなければ国内法としての効力をもたない。しかし，テオ判決において，オーストラリ

ア連邦最高裁は児童の権利条約の批准が[4]、行政活動における公正な手続への「正当な期待 (legitimate expectation)」[5]を生じさせると判示した。つまり、行政府は児童の権利条約の規定を適正に考慮して行政決定をなさねばならないとしたのである。このことは、アメリカ合衆国において、非自動執行条約が実施立法の制定を待たねば「法的効力」を認められないにもかかわらず、行政府が当該非自動執行条約の規定を遵守しなければならない、とされていることに類似するように思われる。

テオ判決は、オーストラリア法への国際人権法の重要な影響を示すものでもある。テオ判決は、国内法と国際法との峻別が従来ほど意味をもたなくなった現代の法状況を反映しているといえる。国内法と国際法とを峻別することは、国内事項と国際事項が明瞭に区別されえた時代においては、一定の意味をもちえていた。しかし、今日のグローバリゼイションの時代において、国境を越えた関心事項である人権問題は、国家の枠にかかわらず個人に対してより直接的な影響をもつ問題である。

1 連邦最高裁のテオ判決

まず、テオ判決そのものを検討してみよう。オーストラリアの教授陣にとっては無用な繰り返しであると承知しているが、私の議論の要点を明瞭にするために、テオ判決の判旨を以下にまとめておく。

事実の概要は次のとおりである。被上告人であるテオは、マレーシア国民であり、オーストラリアでは一時入国許可により滞在しており、1988年にオーストラリア国民たる女性と婚姻した。同女には前夫との間になした4人の子があったが、被上告人との間に3人の子が生まれた。被上告人は永住許可を申請したが、同申請への決定が下される前に、被上告人は麻薬犯罪を犯し、6年の拘禁刑の判決を受けた。同人の永住許可申請は棄却され、同人に対し退去強制命令が下された。同人は連邦裁判所に対し、これら2つの行政決定に対する審査を求めた。第一審判決は訴えを棄却したが、第2審判決は永住許可申請の棄却を取消し、退去強制命令については永住許可申請の再決定がなされるまで、その執行停止を命じる判決を下した。

移民民族問題担当大臣は2審判決を不服とし、連邦最高裁に上告したが、最高裁は4対1で上告を棄却し、原審判決を維持した。最高裁の多数意見は、Mason主席裁判官とDeane裁判官による共同判決と、Toohey裁判官およびGaudron裁判官のそれぞれの個別意見から構成されている。なお、McHugh裁判官は反対意見を付している。

多数意見の判旨は以下の5点に要約できる[6]。第1，条約の批准は，オーストラリア政府が当該条約の規定にしたがって行動をなすことを，世界とオーストラリアの全ての人に対して表明してしたことに他ならない。この積極的な表明は，「これに反対する立法上又は行政上の指示がない限り (absent statutory or executive indications to the contrary)，行政決定権者が条約を遵守して措置をなすという正当な期待 (legitimate expectation) の適正な基礎」[7]となる。第2，「正当な期待」が生み出すものは，手続的公正という概念の下で，行政府が条約に従わないことを意図しているときは，利害関係人はそのことについて告知され，そのような政府の決定に反論をなす適正な機会が与えられるべきであるという要請である。第3，本件で問題となるのは児童の権利条約第3条1項であり，当該条項は「児童に関するすべての措置をとるに当たっては，……児童の最善の利益が主として考慮されるものとする。」と規定している。第4，移民不服審査委員会と移民民族問題担当大臣は，被上告人の犯罪の重大性と，彼が退去強制された場合に妻子が陥る苦境とを比較衡量した上で，前者が後者より重きをなすと判断した。しかし，行政府が児童の権利条約で要請されている児童の最善の利益を，「主として考慮」したかについては立証がない。第5，行政府は条約の非遵守について，告知をしておらず，またそのことについて反論をなす適正な機会を与えてもいない。したがって，本件の行政決定においては自然的正義，すなわち手続的公正が欠けている。

　Gaudron 裁判官の個別意見は，多数意見を構成するものではあるが，その特徴は本件で問題となった子がオーストラリア国民であることを強調している点である。同裁判官は，本件では児童の権利条約が2次的な重要性しかもたず，本件では子が国民たる地位を有するがゆえに，子及び親のコモン・ロー上の権利として，行政府のあらゆる裁量的決定において，児童の最善の利益を第一の考慮事項として尊重すべきことが要請されると判示した[8]。同裁判官は児童の権利条約が，他の文明諸国と同じくオーストラリアにおいて当然とされている基本的人権を表現しているものとして，その意義を認めるものでる。このように児童の権利条約の意義を限定した上で，同裁判官は「同条約に効力があるとの期待を論ずることが合理的である」[9]とした。

　連邦最高裁の多数意見は，児童の権利条約のオーストラリアにおける法的地位について，大変慎重な見解を示している。例えば，Mason 主席裁判官と Deane 裁判官の共同判決は，「正当な期待が存在するからといって，それは必ずしも［決定権者］

に一定の行政決定をなすべきことを義務づけるわけではなく」、「[その点]が正当な期待と拘束力ある法規範との差異である」と述べている。さらに続けて、同共同判決は次のように述べる。

　「正当な期待により決定権者は一定の行政決定をなすべきことが義務付けられると考えれば、それを法規範と扱うことと同然になってしまう。そのことは国内法化されていない条約規定を、あたかも裏口から国内法に組入れることである[10]。」

　連邦最高裁の多数意見は、変形理論の枠を踏み外さないように大変に慎重である。しかし、事件の実際の処理の観点から見れば、「正当な期待」を1つの選択肢と扱ってはいても、「正当な期待」に法的拘束力を与えていることと何ら差異はないといえよう。行政府は被上告人の犯罪の重大さと、彼の退去強制後の子の苦境を比較衡量したことにおいて、子の利益に何らかの考慮を払ったわけではあるが、連邦最高裁はそれだけでは子の最善の利益が第1の考慮事項とされていないと判示しているのである。判決の重要なポイントは、どのような考慮がなされれば、"a primary consideration"がなされたこととなるのかということである。連邦最高裁は、本件において行政府の考慮が"primary"と評価しえない理由を説明していないように思われる。また、最高裁は「正当な期待」を1つの選択肢として扱いながら、行政府が「正当な期待」にしたがってなしたと考える決定を、裁判所がそれを満たすものではないとして取消している。しかし、行政府は「正当な期待」を満たしたと考えたのであるから、行政府が「正当な期待」に従わないことを選択した場合の手続的保護までも要求するのは、いささか無理な要求のように思われる。

2　変形理論における「正当な期待」の意義

　次に、テオ判決が示す1つの重要な意義について論じたい。すなわち、それはテオ判決において、国際法の国内的効力に関する変形理論が1つの修正を受けている、とみることができるということである。一般的に理解されている変形理論は、条約に2重の制約を課すものである。第1は、条約の法的拘束力に関するものであり、条約の国内的効力を否定する制約である。第2は、条約が国内法秩序に組入れられる方法に関するものであり、イギリス議会やオーストラリア議会といった、本来の立法機関が条約の諸条項を実施する法律を制定しなければならないわけである。したがって条約は、国内法秩序において法的効力をもたないのであるから、行政府に

対して国内法化されていない条約規定に従うべしとする義務を課すことは、一般的な変形理論からすれば変則的な要求を課すことになる。条約の実施立法の制定をまたずに、条約が行政府の決定を規律すると考えることは、一般的な変形理論の枠を踏み越えることになる。

もし変形理論が、条約はそれ自身の効力として、行政府に条約を遵守して決定をなすべしとする義務を課すという内容をもつのであれば、ある意味でこの理論は、条約の国内的効力に関する受容理論においていわれるところの、非自動執行条約の性質に類似する要素を認めることになる。

条約の国内的効力に関する受容理論においては、自動執行条約と非自動執行条約の区別が知られているところである。非自動執行条約は、実施立法がなければ国内法秩序において「法的効力」をもたないと考えられている。しかしながら、アメリカの著名な国際法学者である Henkin 教授の見解によれば、非自動執行条約が司法府だけでなく、立法府や行政府に対しても法規範たりえないという理解は誤りである、ということが指摘される。非自動執行条約は裁判所によって直接に適用されることはできないが、行政府がその権限行使にあたって遵守すべき法規範であり、また、立法府がその立法活動において適切な配慮をなすべき実体的基準なのである[11]。

国際法の国内的効力に関する受容理論をとるアメリカでは、非自動執行条約は裁判所において直接適用されえないが、行政府と立法府に対しては法としての役割を果たしうるものといえる。オーストラリアでは変形理論がとられているのであるが、テオ事件において連邦最高裁は、議会によって立法化されていない児童の権利条約が、行政府の側でそれに従うべき「正当な期待」を生じさせると判示した。このことは受容理論と変形理論との融合、あるいは接近を示しているように思われる。このことが冒頭で私が述べた、国際法の国内法秩序における地位に関して、オーストラリアがアメリカ合衆国の立場へ接近していると評したことである。

3 変形理論をとるオーストラリアの理由

次に、オーストラリアにおいて国際法の国内的効力について変形理論がとられる理由を、少し検討してみたい。

オーストラリアはイギリス法を継受したといわれる。イギリス法において国際法の変形理論がとられる理由は、議会主権の強い伝統との関連で説明される。しかし、

オーストラリアが変形理論を実践する背景には、イギリスの伝統とは異なったオーストラリア特有の2つの理由が存在すると思われる。その1つは、オーストラリア憲法第51条(29)号が規定する、対外事項に関して立法をなす連邦議会の権限である。1901年にオーストラリア憲法が施行されたときには、外国と条約を締結する権限はイギリス国王の大権の1つとされていた。しかし、1931年ウエストミンスター法[12]を1つの画期として、オーストラリアの国家として独立性が成熟してくるにしたがい、条約締結に関する国王の大権は、オーストラリア憲法第61条の連邦行政府の権限に服するものとされるに至る。同条は明文では条約締結に言及してはいないが、連邦最高裁は憲法を次のように解釈している。すなわち、憲法第61条の権限により連邦行政府が締結した条約を、連邦議会は憲法第51条(29)号の権限によりそれを実施する法律を制定することができるとした[13]。

変形理論をとる第2の理由は、立法権と行政権の権力分立原理に根ざすものである。連邦議会は行政府の条約締結権限に対する抑制手段として、助言同意の権限を確立してはいない[14]。したがって、条約の国内的実施について議会立法を要件とすることが、条約締結権による立法権の侵食を防止する機能をもつのである。またもう1つの意味でも権力分立原理は重要である。つまり、連邦政府と州政府との間の権力分立である。連邦政府が締結する条約の国内的効力を否定することにより、州政府は連邦権限による州権限の侵食を防止することができるのである。

4 より広い文脈でのテオ判決の意義

オーストラリアの法秩序の枠内で考えれば、テオ判決はオーストラリアで実践される変形理論に1つの変化を示すものである。それは変形理論と受容理論の接近ということもできよう。またそれは、国際人権条約の実施立法を制定しない連邦議会の不作為に対して、裁判所が示した対応策とみることもできよう。もっとも、児童の権利条約について連邦最高裁がテオ判決で示した態度は、変形理論の枠を踏み外さないように大変注意深いものであった。この最高裁の自己抑制的な態度は、連邦政府の権力分立構造を混乱させず、そして州権と連邦権限の関係を乱さないための、司法部の思慮深さを示すものである。

最後に、より広い文脈でのテオ判決の意義について言及しておきたい。テオ判決は国際人権法のオーストラリア法への重要な影響を示すものといえる。国際法の射程は国際問題の領域を越えて国内領域に及んでいる。国内法制が国際人権法の発展

から孤立したままでいることはありえない。テオ判決は国際法の規律する事項が質的に変化していることを如実に反映している。トランスナショナルな関心事項は、個々の人間の利害に、より直接的な影響を及ぼすようになってきている。国際法が人権問題を規律するようになるということは、国境という壁に風穴があけられることを意味する。国際法と国内法の区別は曖昧なものとなってくる。両者の区別が明瞭であった時代には、条約の多くは2国間条約であり、条約当事国の権利義務を規律するものであった。現代のグローバリゼイションの時代にあっては、条約は多国間条約の形式で締結されるものが増大している。また、トランスナショナルな関心事項は、人権保障の分野に限られることはない。例えば、地球環境の良好な質の保全は、国家並びにトランスナショナルな行動主体による協力が実効を挙げている法分野の一つである。遺伝子組換え技術の分野では、例えば農作物などへのこの技術の応用について、トランスナショナルな法規制の枠組みが、新たに形成されるよう求められている。テオ判決は現代のグローバリゼイションの時代に下された判決である。それゆえに、この判決はオーストラリア法の枠の中で重要性をもつだけでなく、国際法の新たな発展においても重要な判決なのである。

(1) (1995) 183 CLR 273, *reprinted in* 69 AUSTL. L.J. 423 (1995).
(2) 連邦最高裁の判決以来、労働党政権及び保守連合政府はテオ判決の意義を否定する声明をおこなっているが、その趣旨の法案は議会において成立していない。*See*, GEORGE WILLIAMS, HUMAN RIGHTS UNDER THE AUSTRALIAN CONSTITUTION 20-21 (1999); Gillian Triggs, *Australia's Indigenous Peoples and International Law: Validity of the Native Title Amendment Act 1998 (CTH)*, 23 MELB. U.L. REV. 372, 396 (1999).
(3) U.S. CONST. art. VI, cl. 2.
(4) The Convention on the Rights of the Child（児童の権利条約）はオーストラリア政府により1990年12月17日に批准され、翌年1月16日からオーストラリアに対して効力を発生している。
(5) *Teoh*, 69 AUSTL. L.J. 423, 432 (1995).
(6) テオ判決の判旨の分析につき、村上正直「オーストラリアに対する人権条約の影響——同国裁判所の動向を中心に」『国際法外交雑誌』98巻1・2号206-10頁(1999年)参照。
(7) *Teoh*, 69 AUSTL. L.J. 423, 432 (1995) (Mason, C.J. and Deane, J.).
(8) 人権条約がコモン・ローの発展に影響を与えることは、Mason, C.J.を含めた多

数意見の四人の裁判官に共通した立場であると指摘される。Kristen Walker & Penelope Mathew, Case Note, Minister for Immigration v. Ah Hin Teoh, 20 MELB. U.L. REV. 236, 244 (1995)

(9)　*Teoh*, 69 AUSTL. L.J. 423, 440 (1995) (Gaudron J).

(10)　*Id.* at 432-33 (Mason, C.J. and Deane, J.).

(11)　LOUIS HENKIN, FOREIGN AFFAIRS AND THE UNITED STATES CONSTITUTION 203-04 (2 nd ed., 1996).

(12)　The *Statute of Westminster 1931* (UK) was adopted by Australia in 1942 by the *Statute of Westminster Adoption Act 1942* (Cth.), and given retrospective effect to 3 September 1939.

(13)　Senate—Legal and Constitutional References Committee, *Commonwealth Power to Make and Implement Treaties—Report*, paras. 4.6-4.22, *at* http://www.austlii.edu.au/au/other/dfat/tort 4.html.

(14)　*Id*. paras. 7.1-7.2, *at* http://www.austlii.edu.au/au/other/dfat/tort 7.html.

＊　本稿はメルボルン大学比較憲法研究所と早稲田大学比較法研究所の共催により，2000年3月17日にメルボルン大学で開かれた学術交流会議において，筆者が発表した原稿を補訂し訳出したものである。

16 懲罰的損害賠償の非懲罰性

佐 野 　 隆

　　序
　1　背　　景
　2　オーストラリア
　3　ニュージーランド
　4　日　　本
　　結　論

序

　コモン・ロー系諸国と大陸法系諸国との法制度には大きな違いが多くある。言うまでもなく，オーストラリアおよびニュージーランドは前者に属し，日本は後者に属す。それらの違いのなかの1つが，民事手続における懲罰的損害賠償の利用可能性であると言われている。歴史的理由により，コモン・ロー系諸国では，「変則」[1]であるとみなされているものの，懲罰的損害賠償が利用されてきている。他方，日本は，他の大陸法系諸国と同様に，民事手続で懲罰的損害賠償を利用するという考えを採らない。

　本稿では，先ず特に，オーストラリアおよびニュージーランドにおける近年の発展を中心に懲罰的損害賠償を説明する。次に，日本の状況に触れ，最後に幾つかの提案と残された問題を含む現時点での結論を示す。

　確かに，オーストラリアおよびニュージーランドにおける法制度と日本の法制度との相違は非常に大きいので，それら法制度の間の比較をすることは無用で不毛であるかもしれず，あるいは，有害でさえあるかもしれない。しかし，Atiyah教授が指摘するように，「法学者の1つの役割は時として考えられないことを考えることである[2]。」本稿では，民事手続における懲罰的損害賠償の利用可能性を検討することで紛争解決の際の裁判所の役割を考える。

1　背　　景

　不法行為法が現在ほど原則に基づくものではなかったころには，不法行為者を処

罰するとともに犠牲者に補償をすることは異常だとは考えられていなかった。有名な *Wilkes v Woods* 事件判決[3]においてPratt主席裁判官は陪審に対して以下のように説示した[4]。

> 「損害賠償金の目的は，侵害を受けた者に対する賠償のみならず，加えて有責な者への処罰，将来の同様な行いの抑止，そしてかかる行為自体に対する陪審が抱く憎悪の証でもある。」

しかし，現代においては不法行為上の救済の主要な目的は犠牲者に対する補償であると考えられている。懲罰的損害賠償の利用可能性は，*Rookes v. Barnard* 事件[5]において貴族院により詳しく検討された。同事件判決においてDevlin貴族院裁判官は以下のように述べた[6]。

> 「懲罰的損害賠償は本質的に通常の損害賠償とは異なる。損害賠償という語の普通の意味における目的は，補償をすることである。懲罰的損害賠償の目的は処罰することと抑止することである。このことは法の民事上の機能と刑事上の機能を混淆するものと考えられうるし，実際私の知る限り，懲罰的損害賠償という考えはイギリス法に特有なものである。」

懲罰的な原則がどの程度，そして，どのような事件で認められているかを明らかにするために先例を検討した後で，Devlin貴族院裁判官は懲罰的損害賠償が認められうる3つの有名なカテゴリーを示した。それらは，1）政府の公務員の強圧的，恣意的，または，非立憲的な行為[7]，2）被告の行為が，原告に支払うべき補償を超える利益を被告にもたらすと計算されてなされる場合[8]，3）懲罰的損害賠償が制定法により明示的に認められている場合[9]，である。

Rookes v. Barnard 事件でDevlin貴族院裁判官は，懲罰的損害賠償の付与が検討されている場合に常に頭に入れておかなければならない3つの考慮事由をも表明した。第1に，原告が処罰可能な行為の被害者でない限り，原告には懲罰的損害賠償を与えられない[10]。第2に，懲罰的損害賠償を付与する権限は，自由を守るために使われる一方で，自由と対立する形でも使われうる[11]。第3に，当事者の資力は，補償の算定の際には無関係であるけれど，懲罰的損害賠償の算定の際には関連する。被告の行為をさらに悪くするもの，あるいは軽減するあらゆる行為が関連する[12]。これらの考慮自由を検討し，上訴人により引き合いに出された先例を検討した後で，Devlin貴族院裁判官は，加重的損害賠償と懲罰的損害賠償の間にある混乱の源を法から取り除くことが出来る，と結論付けた[13]。

*Rookes v. Barnard*事件判決以降，イギリスでは懲罰的損害賠償は上記3つのカテゴリーに厳格に限られていた[14]。しかし，他のコモン・ロー系諸国はイギリス流のアプローチに従わなかった。

2　オーストラリア[15]

　1966年，オーストラリア連邦最高裁判所は*Rookes v Barnard*事件貴族院判決に従うことを拒んだ。*Uren v. John Fairfax & Sons Pty Ltd*事件判決においてTaylor裁判官は以下のように判示した[16]。

　　「懲罰的損害賠償が付与されうる状況のより正確な定義の余地が恐らく存在したということに私は同意する。しかし，Devlin貴族院裁判官が提案し，同事件に加わった他の貴族院裁判官が同意したような広範囲に及ぶ改革が，処罰は刑事法の事項であると主張することで正当化できるとは思わない。確かに刑事法は，犯罪でもある違法行為について刑罰を規定するが，犯罪とされていない違法行為については処罰を規定していない。しかし，わが国の裁判所は，そしてあえて言えばイギリスの裁判所も，どちらのタイプにおいても，被告の行為を裁判所がはっきりと非難することを認めるような状況または様態でなされた違法行為に対する実際上の罰としての懲罰的賠償の原理を認めてきた。

　*Rookes v. Barnard*事件でDevlin貴族院裁判官が検討した先例を考慮した後で，Taylor裁判官は続けて以下のように述べた[17]。

　　「私の考えでは，*Rookes v. Barnard*事件で明示的に行なわれた『法から変則を取り除く』試みは，そのねらいを達成していない。また，私の見解では，そのような試みは，罰という形で損害賠償金を付与することを認めることは民事法の機能ではないと主張することで正当化しえない。」

同裁判官は続けた[18]。

　　「*Rookes v. Barnard*事件で検討されたことで示される見解は，当裁判所が同事件で述べられたよりも広いカテゴリーでしばしば懲罰的損害賠償を与えてきているという，わが国における法発展を考慮に入れていない。」

　結局，オーストラリア連邦最高裁判所は，貴族院には従わずに，*Whitfeld v. De Lauret & Co Ltd*[19]事件判決により確立された法状況を維持した。同事件でKnox長官は以下のように判示した[20]。

　　「損害賠償は塡補的か懲罰的である場合がある。塡補的損害賠償は原告が被っ

た実質的損失に対する補償として与えられ，かかる損失により算定される。懲罰的損害賠償は，他人の権利に対する放漫な無視による意識的な違法行為の場合のみに与えられるにすぎない。」

これらの事件が示すように，オーストラリアでは懲罰的損害賠償はイギリスよりも緩やかなかたちで与えられると言われている。しかし，懲罰的損害賠償が与えられるべきか否かの問題に関連するいくつかの要因が存在する。1つの要因は，事件のあらゆる状況の中で懲罰的損害賠償がその目的を果たすことができるかどうかであると言われている[21]。懲罰的損害賠償が処罰と抑止というその目的を達することができないと思われる場合が少なくとも3つある。それらは，1）被告の行為に対して保険がかけられている場合，2）原告に支払われる塡補賠償が非常に高額で，十分に処罰と抑止に相当する場合，および3）被告がすでに処罰されている場合である。

第1の場合については，オーストラリアにおける以前の先例は*Lamb v Cotogno*事件[22]であった。同事件でオーストラリア連邦最高裁判所は，原告に身体傷害をもたらす被告の邪悪な行為に対して第三者強制自動車保険がかけられている場合であっても，被告に対して懲罰的損害賠償を利用することができる，と判示した。このような場合の懲罰的損害賠償は被告を処罰していないことは明らかである。*Lamb*事件判決において懲罰的損害賠償を認めたもう1つの理由は，懲罰的損害賠償を与えることで原告が抱く復讐への衝動を緩和させるというものであった[23]。*Lamb*事件判決は現在では，*Gray v. Motor Accident Commission*事件オーストラリア連邦最高裁判所判決[24]により支持されている。*Gray*事件判決は，*Lamb*事件判決を支持したのみならず，1つの点で懲罰的損害賠償の利用可能性を拡大している。というのは，*Gray*事件の被告は原告に身体傷害を生じさせた不法行為者ではなく，第三者強制保険の保険者であったからである。Gray事件の不法行為者は，制定法上の規定により訴訟手続から外された。この点に関しては，すぐ後でふれる。

第2の場合に関しては，ここでは，不法行為法の通常の塡補的救済手段が，ある場合には，懲罰的損害賠償が認められない場合であっても，塡補的賠償金が高額なため，処罰と抑止として機能する場合があるとだけ指摘しておく。

第3の場合に関しては，最も重要な判決は*Gray v. Motor Accident Commission*事件オーストラリア連邦最高裁判所判決[25]であると言える。同事件の上訴人であるGrayはBransdenが運転する車にはねられ傷害を負った。Bransdenは，原告を含む

アボリジニーの青年たちのグループに向けて、原告を轢き重傷を与える意図で、車を運転した。同車は、（南オーストラリア州）自動車法の第三者強制規定に基づき保険がかけられていた。Bransdenは、上訴人に対する重傷を意図的に負わせた刑事上の罪で起訴され[26]、同罪で陪審による有罪確定の後[27]、7年の禁固刑が言渡された[28]。

原告は、先ず第1にBransdenを相手取り、ネグリジェンスを理由とする損害賠償を求め、南オーストラリア州地区裁判所に訴訟を提起した。事実審理において、ネグリジェンスを理由とする責任は争われなかった。原告の請求の中で、特に懲罰的損害賠償が求められた。1995年に、訴訟手続が修正され、被告が州政府保険委員会に変更された[29]。

第1審判決は原告勝訴であった。しかし、懲罰的損害賠償請求に関して第1審裁判官は、懲罰的損害賠償が請求される理由となった行為と同一の行為で相当期間の禁固刑ですでにBransdenが処罰されているので、懲罰的損害賠償を与えるべきではない、と結論付けた。原告は、懲罰的損害賠償が認められなかったこと、および塡補的損害賠償が低すぎることを不服とし、南オーストラリア州最高裁判所に上訴した。同裁判所大法廷は原告の主張を双方とも退けた。そこで、Grayは、オーストラリア連邦最高裁判所に上訴した。

連邦最高裁判所は、塡補的損害賠償金が低すぎるという原告の主張を認めたが、懲罰的損害賠償に関する主張は退けた。同裁判所は以下のように判示した[30]。

「本件のように、違法行為者に関連し、刑事法が適用され、相当な処罰が加えられている場合には、懲罰的損害賠償は付与されえないと我々は考える。『えない』というのは、民事手続の対象となっている行為と実質的に同一の行為を理由に相当な処罰が科せられていることは懲罰的損害賠償の付与を妨げるものであると考えるからである。この判断は、それぞれの個々の事件の事実関係および状況に左右される裁量の問題として達した判断ではない。」

これらの点に加えて、Gray事件判決のなかではいくつかの重要な意見が表明された。第1に、すでに示した通り、連邦最高裁判所は、Lamb v. Cotogno事件判決[31]を支持し、不法行為者が訴訟当事者でない場合であっても、適切な事件では保険がかけられている行為を理由とする懲罰的損害賠償が認められうる、と判示した。第2に、同裁判所は、ネグリジェンスで構成されていても、原告もしくは原告の立場にある者の権利を放漫に無視して意図的に被告が行為したことが証明されうる場合

があると述べることで，ネグリジェンスを理由とする事件で懲罰的損害賠償が認められる可能性があることを表明した。第3に，同裁判所は*Watts v. Leitch*事件タスマニア州最高裁判所判決[32]を支持した。Kirby裁判官は以下のように述べた[33]。

「懲罰的損害賠償金の部分は権利ではなく，陪審が与えることも差し控えることも選べる損害賠償金の要素であった。*Broome v. Cassell & Co*事件判決においてHailsham貴族院裁判官は，懲罰的損害賠償は『裁量的』であると記した。類似の記述がカナダの先例およびオーストラリアの先例の中にある。実際，裁量権の存在は，何らかの要因が懲罰的損害賠償を退けることを適切にする場合，事実審裁判所がそうすることを許す『安全弁』であると記されている。」

3 ニュージーランド

よく知られているように，ニュージーランドの不法行為法は，1974年以来の事故補償制度のもとで身体傷害を理由とする訴権を廃止しているので，極めて特殊である。

ニュージーランドでは，*Rookes v. Barnard*事件でのイギリスの判決以前は，悪意訴追や名誉毀損を理由とする事件で懲罰的損害賠償は認められていた。*Rookes*事件の影響が，*Taylor v. Beere*事件[34]においてニュージーランドの控訴院により検討された。控訴院は懲罰的損害賠償に対する制限的なアプローチに従うことを拒んだ。Richardson裁判官は，不法行為法は犠牲者に補償するという目的しか持っていないのではなく，当事者の私的利害を超えた公的関心に対しても対応しなければならないことを強調した[35]。1972年事故補償法の施行後，ニュージーランドの裁判所は懲罰的損害賠償を求める請求は同制定法により認められないものとなったのか否かの問題に直面した。*Donselaar v. Donselaar*事件[36]で控訴院は，事故補償法に基づく補償は何らの懲罰的要素を含んでいないので，懲罰的損害賠償の可能性を残しておくことには十分に理由がある，と判示した[37]。したがって，控訴院は，懲罰的損害賠償を与える目的は，原告の権利に対する高圧的な無視や同様な邪悪な行為を理由に被告を処罰することであることを明確にした。

1992年事故後の社会復帰および補償保険法の成立以降，同法は事故補償制度のもとで支払われていた身体傷害を理由とする一時金をなくし補償額を引き下げたので，原告は自身に対して加えられた侵害に対する賠償を得るために懲罰的損害賠償を求める請求を起こすようになった。このような背景のもとで，ネグリジェンス訴訟で

の懲罰的損害賠償の利用可能性が，*McLaren Transport Ltd. v. Somerville*事件判決[38]で，15.000ニュージーランドドルの懲罰的損害賠償を与えることで確認された。Tipping裁判官は，ニュージーランド法は被告の行為が十分に悪い場合には過失により生じた身体傷害を理由とする懲罰的損害賠償を求める請求を認める，と判示した[39]。様々な先例を注意深く検討し関連する要因をまとめた後で，Tipping裁判官は以下のように事案を処理した[40]。

> 「身体傷害を引き起こす過失を理由とする懲罰的損害賠償は，過失の程度が非常に高く，それが非難と処罰に値し，原告の安全に対する著しく正義に反し明らかな無視に相当する場合には，しかし，その場合に限り，付与されうる。」

懲罰的損害賠償の利用可能性に関するもう1つの重要な影響が，*Daniels v. Thompson*事件控訴院判決[41]により加えられた。同裁判所は，懲罰的損害賠償は申立てられている行為を処罰するものであるので，かかる行為に対してすでに有罪が確定し量刑が言渡されている場合には民事手続において懲罰的損害賠償は絶対的に禁止されるべきである，と判示した[42]。同裁判所はまた，被告に対して刑事裁判で本質的に同一の行為に関して無罪判決が下されている場合には，懲罰的損害賠償請求は手続の濫用として退けられるべきである，と判示した[43]。さらに，同裁判所は，刑事訴追が開始されているか，あるいは，開始されそうな場合は，手続の濫用を避けるために，懲罰的損害賠償を求める手続は停止されるのが適切である，と結論付けた[44]。

*Daniels*事件控訴院判決は，*W v. W*事件枢密院司法委員会判決[45]により支持された。枢密院司法委員会判決の前に，立法府によりもう1つの展開がなされた。1998年12月にニュージーランド議会は法律を成立させた。1998年事故保険法396条により，以下の場合であっても，身体傷害を生じさせた被告の行為を理由に懲罰的損害賠償を求める手続をとることができるようになった。

1）被告がすでに，懲罰的損害賠償を求める請求に関連する行為を含む犯罪で，起訴され，無罪判決を受けているか，または，有罪判決を受けている場合。

2）被告がすでに，そのような犯罪で起訴され，1985年刑事裁判法19条に基づき有罪宣告されずに免責された場合，または，同法20条に基づき有罪宣告を受けかつ免責された場合。

3）被告がすでに，そのような犯罪で起訴されているが，懲罰的損害賠償を求める請求に対し裁判所が決定を下す時点で，起訴に基づく審理が執り行われ

ていない場合。

　4）懲罰的損害賠償を求める請求に対し裁判所が決定を下す時点で,被告に対してそのような犯罪でいまだ起訴が行なわれていない場合。

　したがって,ニュージーランドでは,民事手続の被告が民事手続におけるのと同一の行為で起訴されているか,あるいは,起訴されそうな場合であっても,身体傷害を理由とする懲罰的損害賠償請求を起こすことができる。しかし,身体傷害以外の理由による懲罰的損害賠償請求は,被告が刑事手続を受ける場合には,*Daniels*事件における準則のより絶対的に禁止される。

4　日　　本

　日本では,少なくとも原則上は,民事手続において懲罰的損害賠償という考え方は採っていない。しかし,日本でも数は多くないが,懲罰的損害賠償の利用可能性を裁判所が検討した事件がある。ここでは,懲罰的損害賠償の問題に関する4つの事件を取り上げる。

　1997年に最高裁判所は,懲罰的損害賠償を認めたカリフォルニア州裁判所判決の承認および執行を拒んだ[46]。その理由は,懲罰的損害賠償はわが国法制度の基本的原則もしくは哲学に相入れないので,わが国の公序を考えると懲罰的損害賠償を認める判決は拒むべきであるというものである。

　第2の事件は,建設工事に関する争いである。原告は工事現場近くの住人であった。工事の時間や曜日に関する協定が原告と被告建設会社との間に成立した。同協定の中には,建設会社が条件に違反した場合の違約金の条項があった。建設会社はジレンマに陥った。期日までに工事を完成しなければ工事完成の遅れを理由に施主に違約金を支払わなければならなかった。建設会社は,原告に対して違約金を支払うより,工期に間に合わせて完了することがより利益が上がることを考慮に入れ,協定の条件に違反した。原告は,精神的苦痛を理由とする塡補的損害賠償とならんで懲罰的損害賠償を求め訴えを提起した。京都地方裁判所は,もし被告が意図的に協定の条件に違反したのであれば,通常の塡補的損害賠償に加えて,処罰と制裁の性格を持つ慰謝料を認める余地がある,と判示した[47]。

　第3の事件は,エレベーターのドアが閉まるとき軽傷を負った入院患者が提起した事件である。原告は,病院のエレベーターのドアが閉まる速度は通常の場所にあるエレベーターのドアが閉まる速度よりも遅くあるべきだと主張し,塡補的損害賠

償に加えて明示的に懲罰的損害賠償を求めた。東京地方裁判所は，塡補的損害賠償を認めたが，当該事実関係に基づいて懲罰的損害賠償は認めなかった[48]。同裁判所は，現在の法制度のもとで懲罰的損害賠償という概念を確立された司法判断上の規範として受け入れることはできない，と判示した。

　第4の事件は，1999年の民事訴訟の中で最も関心を集めた事件の1つであった。被告は当時の大阪府知事であり，原告は21歳の大学生であった。1999年4月，統一地方選挙が行なわれた。被告は再選を狙う知事であった。原告は被告の選挙キャンペーンに加わっていた。選挙活動中に被告はキャンペーンに使用していた車の中で原告に性的暴行を加えた。原告は，被告によるみだらな行為を理由に訴えを提起した。この訴えに対し，被告は，かかる訴えには根拠がなく，原告により提起された訴えにより自己の名誉が傷つけられたと主張し，起訴を求めた。被告は出廷せずに，審理当日に，知事として記者会見を行ない，原告の主張は真っ赤な嘘であると述べた。大阪地方裁判所は原告勝訴の判決を言渡し[49]，原告に対して，みだらの行為を理由に200万円，虚偽の訴追請求を理由に500万円，審理初日以降の嘘の発言を理由に300万円，そして，訴訟費用として100万円を認めた。裁判所は，明示的には，合計1,100万円の賠償に懲罰的要素があるとは述べていない。しかし，この損害賠償額は，類似のハラスメントの事件と比べ，かなり高いものである。このことの1つの理由は，事件のあらゆる状況の中での被告の行為を裁判所がひどく嫌ったことであったと言えよう[50]。

結　論

　確かに，コモン・ローにおいては加重的損害賠償と懲罰的損害賠償との区別ははっきりと確立している。前者は塡補的であり，後者は非塡補的であると分類されている。しかし，両者とも被告の行為に目を向ける。

　オーストラリアでは，保険がかけられている行為にも懲罰的損害賠償が利用できるので，懲罰的損害賠償が処罰として機能しない場合がありうる。Grayは，訴訟手続のもっと早い段階で加重的損害賠償を求めていたら，不法行為者の行為が犯罪に相当するほど邪悪であったので，加重的損害賠償を得たかもしれない。しかし，同事件において懲罰的損害賠償は，その目的が不法行為者を処罰することであり，不法行為者はすでに刑事手続により処罰されているので，利用できなかった。保険がかけられている場合には処罰という目的が果たされない一方で，刑事処罰の有無で，

懲罰的損害賠償が得られる原告と得られない原告が存在しうるというのは，論理的ではなく，また，公正でもない。

ニュージーランドでは，加重的損害賠償は，身体傷害を理由とする事件では与えられないが，身体傷害以外の事件では与えられうる。また，民事手続における被告が刑事で訴追される場合は，懲罰的損害賠償は身体傷害を理由とする事件においてのみ認められるが，他の事件では認められない。

日本では，裁判所は，民事事件で懲罰的損害賠償を与えることができるとは決して言わない。せいぜい，加重的損害賠償に相当する慰謝料を認めるにすぎない。しかし，上記の日本の最後の事件が示すように，何らかの懲罰的要素が塡補的損害賠償の付与のなかに見出せる。犠牲者に対する補償が不法行為上の救済手段の主要な目的ではあるけれど，塡補的損害賠償は，特にその額が高額な場合は，処罰と抑止として機能しうる。同様に，懲罰的損害賠償は，ニュージーランドにおけるように，特に補償の水準が十分でない場合には，補償として機能する。懲罰的損害賠償の機能が処罰と抑止に限られるものではないとよく言われている[51]。処罰と抑止は懲罰的損害賠償の中心的目的であり続けているが，懲罰的損害賠償の目的がそれらのみに尽きるわけではない。懲罰的損害賠償が従来の定義と目的から開放されれば，紛争解決における有効な手段となる場合がある。この意味で，イギリスの法律委員会の勧告[52]とは異なり，懲罰的損害賠償は，"punitive damages"ではなく"exemplary damages"と呼ぶべきである。

本稿では，懲罰的損害賠償が自由に敵対する武器になりうることを論じていない。また，懲罰的損害賠償を受け入れられる形で算定し，そして，満足の行く程度に制限する実際的の方法や基準も示していない。実際，懲罰的損害賠償に関しては，本稿では触れなかったアメリカにおける経験に例証される多くの問題がある。しかし，民事手続で懲罰的損害賠償を認める利点もある。もし，懲罰的損害賠償に何らの利点もないのであれば，それがたとえ確立された先例のなかで認められていたとしても，はるか以前に姿を消していたであろう。私の考えでは，オーストラリア連邦最高裁判所およびニュージーランド控訴院は，原則として，懲罰的損害賠償の利用可能性を拒絶する制限的なアプローチを採るべきではなかった。

(1) *Rookes v. Barnard* [1964] AC 1129 at 1221 per Lord Devlin.
(2) Patrick S. Atiyah, "Personal Injuries in the Twenty First Century: Thinking

the Unthinkable" in P. Birks (ed.), *Wrongs and Remedies in the Twenth-first Century* (Clarendon Press, Oxford, 1996) p. 1 at 1.
(3) (1763) Lofft 1; 98 ER 489.
(4) Ibid. at 18-19; 498-499.
(5) [1964] AC 1129.
(6) Ibid. at 1221.
(7) Ibid. at 1226.
(8) Ibid.
(9) Ibid. at 1227.
(10) Ibid.
(11) Ibid.
(12) Ibid. at 1228.
(13) Ibid. at 1230.
(14) *Broome v. Cassell & Co. Ltd.*事件でDenning記録長官が率いるイギリスの控訴院は、*Rookes v. Barnard*事件貴族院判決に公然と反抗した（[1971] 2 QB 354）。しかし、貴族院は控訴院判決を覆し、4対3の僅差の多数で*Rookes v. Barnard*事件判決を支持した（[1972] AC 1027）。
(15) オーストラリアの状況に関しては、Michael Tilbury教授、特に、同教授の*Civil Remedies* (Butterworths, Sydney, 1990) vol 1、および、"Regulating 'Criminal' Conduct by Civil Remedy: The Case of Exemplary Damages" 1 *Waseda Proceedings of Comparative Law* 80 (1999)によるところが大きい。もちろん、誤りは筆者自身のものである。
(16) (1966) 117 CLR 113 at 131.
(17) Ibid. at 137.
(18) Ibid. at 138.
(19) (1920) 29 CLR 71.
(20) Ibid. at 77.
(21) Michael Tilbury, "Regulating 'Criminal' Conduct by Civil Remedy: The Case of Exemplary Damages" 1 *Waseda Proceedings of Comparative Law* 80 at 90 (1999).
(22) (1987) 164 CLR 1.
(23) Ibid. at 9.
(24) (1998) 158 ALR 485; 73 ALJR 45. Jane Swanton and Barbara McDonald, "The High Court on Exemplary Damages" 73 *Aust. L.J.* 402 (1999)、および、James Edelman, "Exemplary Damages Revisited" 7 *Torts L.J.* 87 (1999)参照。
(25) (1998) 158 ALR 485; 73 ALJR 45.
(26) 1935年（南オーストラリア州）刑事法統合法第21条。

⑰　*R v. Bransden*, unreported, Supreme Court of South Australia, 26 Feburary 1991.

⑱　*R v. Bransden*, unreported, Supreme Court of South Australia, 14 March 1991.

⑲　委員会がBransdenに代わって被告となったのは，自動車法第125A条に従ったものであった。

⑳　(1998) 158 ALR 485 at 494; 73 ALJR 45 at 52.

㉑　(1987) 164 CLR 1.

㉒　[1973] Tas SR 16.

㉓　(1998) 158 ALR 485 at 510-511; 73 ALJR 45 at 63-64.

㉔　[1982] 1 NZLR 81.

㉕　Ibid. at 90.

㉖　[1982] 1 NZLR 97.

㉗　Ibid. at 107 per Cooke J; 116 per Somers J.

㉘　[1996] 3 NZLR 424. John Smillie, "Exemplary Damages for Personal Injury" [1997] *NZL Rev.* 140; Joanna Manning, "Professor's Smillie's 'Exemplary Damages for Personal Injury': A Comment" [1997] *NZL Rev.* 176; Goff McLay, "Negligence, ACC and Exemplary Damages....What's too Bad?" (1996) *NZLJ* 425, および, Andrew Beck, "Exemplary Damages for Negligent Conduct" (1997) *Tort L. Rev.* 90参照。

㉙　[1996] 3 NZLR 424 at 433.

㊵　Ibid. at 434.

㊶　[1998] 3 NZLR 22. Jone Smillie, "Exemplary Damages and the Criminal Law" 6 *Torts L.J.* 113 (1998), および, Joanna Manning, "*Daniels v. Thompson*: Double Punishment or Double Trouble?" [1998] *NZL Rev* 721参照。

㊷　[1998] 3NZLR 22 at 47.

㊸　Ibid. at 51.

㊹　Ibid. at 52.

㊺　[1999] 2 NZLR 1. Joanna Manning, "Exemplary Damages and Criminal Punishment in the Privy Council" 7 *Torts L.J.* 129 (1999)参照。

㊻　平成9年7月11日最高裁判所判決，平成7年（オ）1762号，民集56巻(6)2573頁。Norman T. Braslow, "The Recognition and Enforcement of Common Law Punitive Damages in a Civil Law System: Some Reflection on the Japanese Experience" 16 *Arizona Journal of International and Comparative Law* 285 (1999)参照。

㊼　平成元年2月27日京都地方裁判所判決，昭和63年（ワ）1076号，判例時報1322号125頁。

(48)　平成5年4月28日東京地方裁判所判決，平成3年(ワ)10941号，判例タイムズ848号269頁。
(49)　平成11年12月13日大阪地方裁判所判決，平成11年(ワ)8121号。
(50)　被告は，再選されたが，大阪地方裁判所判決後に辞任した。また，被告に対するその後の刑事裁判で，有罪が確定した。
(51)　Bruce Feldthusen, "The Canadian Experiment with the Civil Action for Sexual Battery" in Nicholas Mullany (ed.), *Torts in the Nineties* (LBC Information Services, Sydney 1997) 274, および, *Daniels v Thompson* [1998] 3 NZLR 22, 特に, Thomas裁判官の反対意見参照。
(52)　Law Commission of England and Wales, *Aggravated, Exemplary and Restitutionary Damages* (Law Com No 247, 1997) para 6.3 (16). イギリスの法律委員会の報告書に関する1つのオーストラリアの見解に関しては, Jane Swanton and Barbara McDonald, "Commentary on the Report of the English Law Commission on Aggravated, Restitutionary and Exemplary Damages" 7 *Torts L.J.* 184 (1999)参照。

あ と が き

田 口 守 一

　本書は，早稲田大学比較法研究所の共同研究の1つである「オセアニア法制の研究」（代表・大須賀明早稲田大学法学部教授）の一環として行われた3回の国際シンポジウムに提出された報告原稿を原資料として編集された。

　1997年に行われた第1回目のシンポジウムの報告原稿は，早稲田大学比較法研究所の英文年報第17号に登載された（"The Role of the State in the Eve of the 21st Century", The symposium held in Melbourne University, Australia in December 9 and 13, 1997 and Auckland University, New Zealand in December 14 and 16, 1997, Waseda Bulletin of Comparative Law, vol. 17 (1996) pp. 16-61.)。

　また，第2回目のシンポジウムの原稿も同研究所の資料集第1号にまとめられている（"International Symposium on Asian and Oceanian Law : Free Market and Legal Regulation", September 24-25, 1998 at Waseda University, Tokyo, Japan, Waseda Proceedings of Comparative Law, vol. 1 (1998-1999))。

　第3回目のシンポジウムは，2000年3月13日～20日にメルボルン大学で行われたが，その報告原稿は印刷に付されなかった。本書は，これら3回のシンポジウムの報告原稿とその翻訳原稿に必要最小限度の補筆訂正を加えて一書としたものである。

　この3回に及ぶシンポジウムの縦糸となったテーマは，第1回シンポのテーマから窺われるように，「国家の役割とその限界」という今日的問題であった。大須賀教授の提出されたこの問題は，3回のシンポに参加した5か国（オーストラリア，ニュージーランド，中国，韓国，日本）の様々な法分野の研究者が共通して抱くことのできる問題設定であった。各論文のテーマは多様な専門分野に及んでいるが，それらの諸論文の基底には共通して「国家の役割とその限界」という問題意識が潜んでいる。法制度や法文化の異なる5か国の，しかも法分野を異にする研究者が，それぞれの問題意識に従って報告をしながら，全体として一書にまとめることができたのは，まさにこのような共通項のゆえに他ならない。その意味で，本共同研究を推進してこられた大須賀教授の問題提起はまことに卓見であった。

　もっとも，私個人としては，国際シンポジウムにおける相互理解の難しさを実感

した。私の報告は、経済犯罪を素材とした「行政規制と刑事制裁」と題するものであったが、そのカウンター報告は、オークランド大学のブルックバンクス助教授の環境犯罪を素材とした「厳格責任・絶対責任による法人活動の規制」と題するものであった（本書収録の各論文参照）。確かに、国家規制の限界如何という問題意識は共通するものの、厳格な証明基準を充足しなくてもよい「厳格責任犯罪」という「準犯罪（quasi crime）」の観念を理解することは大変だった。シンポジウムの後のパーティで「そもそも責任とは何か」が議論になり、私があまりに「概念的」な議論をしたせいと思うが、ブルックバンクス助教授をしてついに"terrible"な議論だと言わせてしまった。しかし、ドイツ法的な頑固な議論と英米法的なプラグマティックな議論とを重ねていけば、その中間あたりにほどよい考え方も生まれるかもしれないという予感もした。おそらく国際シンポジウムの学問的重要性はその辺りにあるのであろう。東アジアも含めた法律学の国際シンポジウムの重要性・必要性を感じているところである。

　今後の法律学にとって、このような学際的かつ国際的な共同研究の必要性はますます増大するであろうが、そのためにも本書のような試みが今後の参考になれば、関係者の一人としてこれにすぐる喜びはない。それにしても、本書は、5ヶ国に及ぶ20名余の研究者の全面的なご協力によって出来上がったものである。各執筆者の真摯で学問的なご協力に深く敬意を表する次第である。なお、編集に当たっては、本書にも論文を執筆されている早稲田大学比較法研究所元助手の佐野隆氏のご協力をいただいた。また本書の出版については信山社の今井貴氏のご尽力を頂いた。あわせて、深く御礼を申し上げたい。

2001年3月

STATE LEGAL INTERVENTION and FREEDOM:

Comparative Studies on Asian-Oceanic Legal Systems

〔Authers〕

Akira OSUKA, Professor of Law, Waseda University
　　　　Emeritus Professor of Northwest University, China

Cheryl Saunders, Professor and Director, Institute for Comparative and International Law, The University of Melbourne.

Koichiro FUJIKURA, Former Professor of Law, Tokyo University, Tezukayama University

Masayuki TANAMURA, Professor of Law, Waseda University

Kazuhiro TSUCHIDA, Professor of Law, Waseda University

Michael Crommelin, Zelman Cowen Professor of Law, Dean of the Faculty of Law, The University of Melbourne.

Lisa ONO, Attorney-at-law, Debevoise&Plimpton (New York)

Lui Hainian, Member of Academic Committee of Chinese Academy of Social Sciences

Qu Tao, Associate Professor of Civil Law Research Division, Law Institute, Chinese Academy of Sosial Sciences

Yang Seung Doo, Professor of Law, Dean, College of Law, Yonsei University

Tatsuo UEMURA, Professor of Law, Waseda University

Michael Tilbury, Rowland Professor of Commercial Law and Director, Commercial Law Institute, University of Zimbabwe, Edward Jenks Professor of Law, The University of Melbourne

Yutaka SANO, Lecturer of Law, Toyo University

Warren Brookbanks, Associate Professor of Law, The University of Auckland

Mitsuo SHUMI, Professor of Law, Asahi University

Morikazu TAGUCHI, Professor of Law, Waseda University

Malcolm Smith, Professor and Director, Asian Law Centre, The University of Melbourne

Fumiyo MURAYAMA, Lecturer of Law, Department of Environmental Policy, College of Environmental Health, Azabu University

Shigeo MIYAGAWA, Professor of Law, Waseda University

CONTENTS

Preface ···Akira Osuka···*189*
Foreword ···Cheryl Saunders···*193*
Foreword ···Koichiro Fujikura···*195*

Part I : Affirmative State Interventions

1 The Theory of State Intervention under the Modern-Liberal Constitution ··Akira Osuka···*197*
2 Litigation, Administrative Relief and Political Settlement for Compensating Victims of Pollution : Minamata Mercury Poisoning after 40 years ························Koichiro Fujikura···*207*
3 Care for the Elderly Management of Their Property
 ···Masayuki Tanamura···*223*

Part II : Free Market and Legal Regulations

(i) **Market Economy and Legal Regulations**
4 Globalization and Regulatory Reforms:
 Toward A New Model of Law·····················Kazuhiro Tsuchida···*237*
5 Regulatory Framework for Privatised Industries
 ··Michael Crommelin···*249*
6 Modern Market Economy and the Rule of Law in China: The Past, the Present and the Future ························Liu Hainian···*265*
7 Administrative Deregulation in Korea: Now and Future
 ···Seung Doo Yang···*283*
8 Legal Aspects of the Financial Big Bang in Japan
 ···Tatsuo Uemura···*293*

(ii) **Various Forms of Regulations**
9 Regulatiny "Criminal" Conduct by Civil Remedy: The Case of Exemplary Damages·······························Michael Tilbury···*307*

10 Regulating Corporate Activity through Strict and Absolute Liability ··· W.J. Brookbanks···327
11 Administrative Regulations and Criminal Sanctions
 ·· Morikazu TAGUCHI···343
12 Changing Regulatory Patterns in Japan:
 An Australian Perspective ···························· Malcolm Smith···353
13 New Forms of Regulation: A Challenge to Democratic Accountability and the Rule of Law ? ········ Cheryl Saunders···371

Part III : Studies on Oceanic Legal Systems in Japan

14 The Fundamental Nature of Governing Framework in Australia ··· Akira OSUKA···387
15 The Status of International Law in Australian Law: Implications of the *Teoh* Case····························· Shigeo MIYAGAWA···397
16 Exemplary Damages, Not Punitive Damages:
 A Japanese Perspetive ································· Yutaka SANO···407

Afterword ··· Morikazu TAGUCHI···423

Preface

Akira OSUKA

Asia and Oceania about which we are engaged in lively academic exchanges, is a huge and active area. There are many characteristics in this area. Firstly, it contains various countries from developed to developing countries. In this respect, it has the potential for drastic development. Furthermore, in this area there are cultural diversities, which consist of Oriental and Western elements. For this reason, communication is not always easy among these countries. However, if we succed in mutual communication, there will be infinite possibilities for development by assimilating cultural diversities. Moreover, peace and welfare in this area where lively international exchanges occur, dircctly affect those in the whole world. For this reason, it can be said that Asia and Oceania holds the key to the peace and welfare of the world.

With the end of the Cold War, the world has entered into a new period of globalization. In many parts of the world, nations and areas are becoming increasingly inter-dependent by establishing and developing democracy and market economies. Without doubt, Asia and Oceania is one of these parts. As laws make such situations possible and have a driving force of the development, it is important to establish legal systems and exchange legal cultures.

However, Asia consists of many races, languages, religions and cultures, and each country in Asia has its own legal culture. Since borders determined in the colonial period are not always in correspondence with ethnic ranges, it is not rare that those who have common history and culture belong to different states. Therefore, several legal cultures may co-exist even within some countries. Asia has a troubled history. During the long colonial period before the Second World War, exploitation took place by colonialism, and development of constitutionalism in legal systems was hindered. Even after the Second World War, though many countries in Asia became politically independent, domestically political power in each country was reinforced for the purpose of overcoming urgent problems in devastating economic situations, and internationally authoritarian goeernment and development dictatorship took place in order to establish anti-communism regimes under the Cold War. And socialism countries hindered the establishment of rights and freedom, so that conspicuous and continuous economical growth became difficult in these countries. It was not until the 1980s that the possibility of developing real democracy occurred, with that rapid economic growth in Asia which resulted in the emergence of middle classes who demanded democracy on the one hand, and the end of the Cold War and the introduction of market economies in socialism countries on the other hand.

Against these backgrounds, constitutionalism is sought after. Most legal systems in Asian countries are modeled under tense relationships with the constitutional legal systems of Western countries. At the time of independence, the legal system in each country was inevitably deeply affected by the Western style constitution of its suzerain. In the process of globalization after the collapse of socialism, each country has to establish its own legal system equivalent to that in Western countries, so as to compete internationally under the market economy. Therefore, theoretically a question arises whether Western style constitutional systems are suitable for Asian countries whose historical, social and cultural backgrounds are different from those in Western countries. Some of those systems may be directly adopted in Asian countries. Others may have to be modified partially or arranged for peculiar conditions in each country. It is necessary to consider theoretically which parts need to be modified in which countries. And finally, it is also necessary to tackle fundamental questions of what Asian values are and whether they are of any legal importance.

In order to resolve these questions, in 1998, as a director of the Institute of Comparative Law, I held an international symposium under the title of "Free Market and Legal Regulations, in which scholars of five Asia and Oceanic countries took part. As you will see in Part II of this book, many excellent works were produced by outstanding professors from prestigeous universities. In this symposium, a key role was played by the academic exchanges that started in 1996 between the Centre for Comparative Constitutional Studies, the University of Melbourne and the Institute of Comparative Law, Waseda University. In 1997 and 2000, we visited Australia and New Zealand, and in 1998 we received delegations from overseas. On all of these three occasions, Professor Cheryl Saunders, director of the Centre for Comparative Constitutional Studies, played a crucial role.

In Japan, Professor Fujikura, former professor at the University of Tokyo (and a professor of Waseda University at that time), a great authority on common law study in Japan, played, theoretically and mentally, a leading part in materializing this project. International academic exchanges demand a huge commitment of time and effort before realizing any results. They are indeed laborious tasks. I appreciate every cooperation given by Professor Morikazu Taguchi as well as all the professors who took part in this project.

Foreword

Cheryl Saunders

The papers in this volume represent the result of a series of three symposia, principally involving legal scholars from Wasada University in Japan and the University of Melbourne Australia, but with contributions from the People's Republic of China, South Korea, and New Zealand as well. The purpose of the symposia was to further the mutual understanding of the law of the countries concerned through a process which provided both time and opportunity for detailed presentation, questions, and comments. The exercise was all the more challenging in view of the substantial differences between the countries involved, not only in the substance and procedure of law, but in legal culture.

The symposia undoubtedly were a success. Part of this lies in their obvious achievements. These include the establishment of scholarly links, which will continue to bear fruit through further dialogue; the insights into other legal systems gained by participation in the symposia; and this volume of papers itself. The papers cover a variety of fields, ranging from fiscal law, to environmental law, to administrative law. The connecting theme, however, is the changing role of law and government in Japan and Australia at the end of the 20th century, including the changing expectations and needs of the societies to which law necessarily responds.

An obvious but equally significant achievement concerns the methodology employed in the symposia. This merits elaboration as a contribution to the effectiveness of comparative law scholarship. The importance of comparative law in a globalised world increasingly is recognised. Substantial differences between legal systems and the context in which they operate complicates the methodology to a greater degree than in most other fields of law. It is trite that comparative scholars must move beyond legal rules to understand how law works in practice. Achieving the necessary level of greater understanding is a much more difficult task.

Essentially three methods were used in these symposia. In the first, Japanese scholars presented papers in Australia on current developments in Japanese law and legal thought, chosen because it was expected that comparable issues might be emerging in Australia. In each case, an Australian scholar responded to the paper, which then was discussed by a larger panel, selected for the expertise of participants in the subject matter of the paper. The second symposium took place in Japan, and comprised papers by both Japanese and international scholars, including a substantial delegation from the University of Melbourne, Australia. As far as practicable, the papers complemented each other, dealing broadly with themes of regulation and damages. The final, third symposium, took place in Australia. Three Japanese scholars presented papers on aspects of Australian law, again with Australian discussants.

Each of these methods was useful and constructive. The third, for which the others had in some respect paved the way, was the most ambitious, however. Writing about another country's legal system for an audience of scholars from that country is a difficult task. The experience on this occasion suggested that the rewards are commensurate to the difficulty. Both the papers and the discussion that followed were extraordinarily effective in identifying particular problems, where different underlying assumptions about law and legal rules impeded full comprehension of the other's legal system. The result was a level of discussion and intellectual exchange that often eludes comparative scholarship. My colleagues and I would commend this methodology to others.

On behalf of the foreign scholars who participated in these symposia and in particular the delegation from the University of Melbourne, I extend my appreciation to our colleagues at Wasada University for their insight in planning and carrying into execution this highly successful series. I look forward to further collaboration with them in the future.

Foreword

Koichiro FUJIKURA

More than a century ago when she opened the country to the western powers, Japan adopted a continental legal system, drawing heavily from the French and German models. Japan's legal system again underwent through substantive changes in the period after World War II. Japan has since been exposed to Anglo-American law and common law system. In view of Japan's contacts that have remained mainly with the United States, it is gratifying for all of us to establish our contacts with the common law countries in another hemisphere and to be able to compare our notes on common legal problems of contemporary societies.

It is Professor Akira OSUKA, former director of the Institute of Comparative Law, Waseda University, whose broad vision and foresight led to this major international and comparative discourse with Australian and New Zealand colleagues in the Pacific Rim community. I found our experience with the symposium intellectually very stimulating and enlightening. Indeed, this volume is a brainchild of Professor OSUKA, and a tribute to his leadership in the field of comparative law.

PART I : AFFIRMATIVE STATE INTERVENTIONS

1 The Theory of State Intervention under the Modern-Liberal Constitution

Akira OSUKA

Introduction
1 Change of Liberalism
2 Development of a Theory of Positive Liberty
3 Contradictions in Positive Liberty
4 Guarantee of Liberty and Positive Intervention of the State
5 Social Factors in the Rights of Positive Liberty
6 The Power Element in the Rights of Positive Liberty
7 Democratization of State

Introduction

In modern liberal states, based on the concept of the night watchman state, the role of the state was generally restricted to guaranteeing human rights although the concept of human rights has developed considerably over time. In such societies, the activities of citizens were thought to be governed by private autonomy. Therefore, the states stood back from the daily activities of society and were not permitted to intervene in the free activities of citizens. Since the very role that was allotted to states was to evict those who disturbed the peace and order of a state, a primary function of the state was to maintain the public order and to defend the land. The legal relationship between state and society resulted in the rights of freedom which were guaranteed in civil consitutions and democratic governments based on the principle of individual autonomy.

In spite of this legal relationship, states were concerned with the protection of human rights. In particular, when human rights were infringed, the judiciary worked organizationally in order to obtain justice. However, in most cases the judiciary was able to start its work only after human rights had been infringed, and had to deal with each case separately and individually. Even when remedies, such as prevention or injunctions, could be given in advance, such remedies were only applied in situations where it was difficult to reinstate the injured party to its original position once infringement of rights had occurred, and such cases were extremely rare. Therefore, commitment by the judiciary to the protection of human rights was rather passive as a whole.

However, in the case of the contemporary democratic state, it has become increasingly necessary for a state to commit to the protection of human rights. Good examples of this tendency are the restrictions on economic freedom and the provision of social rights in the contemporary democratic constitutions of the 20th century. The aim of such restrictions is, as seen in the prohibition of private monopoly, to maintain sound capitalistic economic order and ensuring free competition by restricting the freedom of those who have strong economic powers. The provision of social rights is designed to resolve harms inherent to capitalism. Its components include social security benefits and social welfare, which are intended to improve the quality of life of the poor and weak who need support. For effective enforcement of these institutions, a positive intervention by the state is essential. Such enforcement has developed against the historical background of the civil state in which a night watchman state, whose role had been restricted to passive functions, has turned into a social state, which makes a positive contribution to the protection of the social life of the people.

1 Change of Liberalism

The transformation of civil states is made on the basis of the change in the basic concept of liberalism, their founding principle. Generally speaking, individualism, on which liberalism is based, is founded on an atomic view of society. In this view, a state or society is considered to be a group of individuals, and there is no existence recognized which is above individuals. In individualism, therefore, the supreme value will be found in each individual, and at the same time, an individual person is detached from society and regarded abstractly as an atomic and an absolutely equal existence. Under such a system of individualism, ideologically the guarantee of freedom would extend to the maximum point. This form of libertarianism was the classical liberalism which was a fundamental principle in modern civil constitutions. Legal subjects under this theory were citizens who had a general and abstract characteristic, and to which Radbruch referred as "Person"[1].

However, the situation changed. When the evils of capitalism brought about an increase in the number of poor people, states had to intervene in the free activities of citizens in order to protect the poor. A justification for intervention in the free activities of citizens by the state was the recognition that individuals were in extreme poverty because of social factors. In this situation, a new legal subject is recognized in the field of law. That is, like the poor and the unemployed, a social existence developed which had the characteristics of real human beings, and to which Radbruch referred as "Mensch". In this theory, an individual is thought to have some relationship with a society, and a change is made in the theory of individualism, which regards an individual as the only unit of existence. At the same time, a collectivist idea is introduced. Therefore, while it is recognized that activities based on the free will of individuals are regarded as supreme, high value is also placed on societies or states which value the concept of society. In this new theory, societies as well as individuals are considered to have high value, and it is thought to be natural and necessary for the state to intervene in order to remedy social harms. In the end, there develops a welfare state in which positive interventions by the state are justified for their social nature.

2 Development of a Theory of Positive Liberty

A new theory of liberty developed under which the change in liberalism was digested into the theory of rights. The theory was proposed by a 19th century English philosopher, T.H. Green. In addition to the negative liberty of conventional classical liberty, he advocated positive liberty. In modern liberalism, because it was thought that there was no room for both individual freedom and the positive functions of the state, and because both freedom and functions were in conflict with each other, freedom was negatively regarded as what there was without external coercion. But in the late 19th century, there appeared in England industrial and social problems, such as unemployment. These problems made it clear that a natural harmony based on the free activities of individuals was an illusion. It was realized that harmony should be made artificially in order to secure peaceful order and to gain fundamental conditions for conducting free activities. For this reason, the idea of liberty was reconstructed in harmony with the positive functions of state. In his concept of positive liberty, "the self" would be realized while looking for the common good. Construing liberty in such a way, Green pointed out that "it becomes liberty guaranteed by positive functions of the state which is not contradictory to positive functions of the state for promoting common good"[2]. Thus, positive liberty is, "one which requires the state to positively secure conditions for realizing personification of individuals"[3].

In terms of constitutional law, social rights can be within the category of positive liberty. However, not all social rights, but only those rights which are directly related to protection of the right of liberty, fall into this category. Those rights whose aim is to secure a precondition for full enjoyment of the right of liberty, and which are only related indirectly with protection of the right of liberty, like provision of materials, are not within this category of positive liberty. Examples of positive liberty are guarantees of adequate employment conditions and working conditions, the right of organization, the right of collective bargaining and the right to strike. For, although those guarantees and rights place restrictions on freedom of contract for employers, the life of poor people and workers would be harmed without those restrictions, and therefore it is necessary for the state to remedy harms positively.

3 Contradictions in Positive Liberty

How can we reconcile the fact that positive interventions by the state, which is central to the concept of positive liberty, may contradict the traditional concept of liberty? With regard to anti-trust law, for example, there are opposing opinions as to whether the law is a law which promotes liberty or a law which restricts liberty[4]. It is true that state interventions which restrict or prohibit private monopoly formally also entail restriction on economic freedom from the state. However, such economic freedom is freedom for enterprises which may hamper free and fair economic competition by private monopolies. Furthermore, the aim of restrictions by anti-trust law is to recover real economic liberty by removing obstacles to the free competition. For these reasons, anti-trust law can be said to a law which substantially promotes liberty. This positive intervention by the state is formally in contradiction with liberalism, but substantially in harmony with liberalism.

4 Guarantee of Liberty and Positive Intervention of the State

Taking into consideration the historical background of modern constitutions and the inclination of state power to injure rights, it cannot be denied that the basic relationship between individuals and state power appears to be in opposition. But, as shown in the examples of social rights, both individuals and state power do not fully stand in opposition, and there is some room for compromise. In modern liberal states, democracy is the fundamental principle which demands realizaion of liberty and rights of the individuals. For these reasons, state power and liberty are part of the same principle. There is room for the state to do positive activities for the substantial protection of the liberty of individuals.

Given such a relationship, to what extent are state power and liberty related to each other? It is apparent from looking at the changes in guarantees of human rights under modern-liberal constitutions to those under contemporary constitutions that positive liberty is now founded on negative liberty. For this reason, state power, as a principle, cannot be allowed to intervene in matters which are the object of autonomous rights of liberty. Therefore, state power can provide a framework for realizing rights of liberty, that is, provide external conditions for those rights, when it is intended to create the protection of rights of liberty for the purpose of securing conditions for the realization of individual ability and personality. I shall describe right to claim on the state to provide external conditions for those rights of liberty as the right of positive liberty apart from the concept of positive liberty.

5 Social Factors in the Rights of Positive Liberty

The first factor is the advent of a highly informational society. In this society, because of the rapid development of media which have the means of transmitting valuable information, and because of the dominant monopoly of information by a small number of large enterprises, there appears a risk that a few might intentionally manipulate the values of a society. For the purpose of removing obstacles which hamper the free flow of information and securing a free market for thought, the right to know and the right to access have come to be claimed. These are rights of positive liberty. Whatever the political or economic system, one characteristic of the present day is technocracy, which gives priority to ideas characteristic of highly developed science and technology, and by which society can be controlled. The shortcomings of technocracy can be seen in the use of scientific and technological thinking at the expense of the dignity of human beings, the dehumanization which is brought about by giving priority to the scientific and technological efficiency, and the risk of bringing about a non-humanistic society. In order to overcome these shortcomings, secure the liberty of individuals, and recover humanity, there is no alternative but to extend the rights of positive liberty.

In addition, contemporary societies are often managed societies. Managed societies are said to be societies in which "the relationship between the managers and the managed is generalized a new form of domination and suppression"[5]. Among other things, suppressive management in the middle world of the society tends to expand.

In order to reduce such suppression, it is necessary for the strong power of the state to destroy the suppressive function of the social intermediary apparatus, and to make more room for liberty, and secure humanity.

6 The Power Element in the Rights of Positive Liberty

Because the right of positive liberty may, whether it may be a provision of external conditions, result in the positive intervention by the state, the risk of injuring liberty through its power element is much higher than any other type of positive liberty. Since the necessary conditions for the 'realization of personality' and 'free development of human abilities' might only be achieved through the exercise of state power, there is always the danger that the state may act in a way that injures the substance of liberty. Another problem that may be brought about by the right of positive liberty is the harm to liberalism which is inflicted by expansion of power through using power itself. We can find a classic example of responding to power in the United States, where a variety of interest groups have been established and sound liberalism is achieved through the system of balance of powers.

7 Democratization of State

It is necessary to democratize a state before overcoming the negative effects of liberalism or preventing them from arising. As an ideological condition, it is necessary to democratize the consciousness of civil servants as bearers of power. As executors of the formation and realization of the wills of power, civil servants must believe in individualism, liberalism, and democracy. Then, as an institutional condition, there must be a system of democratic government by which the formation and realization of state will fully reflect the will of the people of the state. Therefore, parliamentary democracy, the principle of democratic liability of administration, and the principle of local government must not only be declared expressly in constitutional documents, but also realized in real institutions and the ordinary administration of power. Regarding the expansion of power, which is brought about by ensuring the right of positive liberty, first, constitutional self-government must be guaranteed through direct participation by the citizens of the state in the formation of state will, and secondly, a democratic basis must be added to the power intervention by allowing citizens to take part in the decision making. Thus, by maintaining the balance between power and citizens, we can ensure liberalism.

Good examples of constitutional self-government[6] will be found in legislation such as the National Industrial Recovery Act and the Agricultural Adjustment Act which were driving forces in the age of the New Deal in the United States. In regard to the NIRA, a huge self-governing power was vested to the industrial bodies in making regulations for fair competition, which served the role of preventing the President, who held a large variety of powers, from inflicting harm to liberty. Therefore, constitutional self-government was guaranteed in response to the situation that powers were concentrated with the President and Federal Government in order to improve the economic order, to secure social stability and overcome the economic depression through positive intervention by the state in the social and economic process. In response to sharp restrictions on rights, constitutional self-government aims to minimize the negative effects of such relations by securing liberalism in the process.

It is also necessary to secure political freedom as a right of positive liberty. Freedom of participation in the political process is a positive freedom. For this reason, it is a freedom which directly secures the realization and embodiment of the sovereignty of the people. The more effective it is, the more the political will of the people is reflected in the process of forming the state will. This may make it possible to secure a confluence between state will and the will of the people. Generally, it is pointed out that, because of its power element, securing positive liberty brings about an expansion of power and raises the fear of turning society totalitarian. To democratize the state is of significance, because it secures the participation of the people in the political process, and thereby the state will reflects the will of the people. Democratization of a state is a strong driving force for liberalism and a brake to totalitarianism.

Notes:
(1) Gustav Radbruch, Vom individualistischen zum sozialen Recht. 1930. in Der Mensch im Recht, S. 36-7.
(2) Kiich Kusaka, "Political Thoughts of T.H. Green," in Yukiyasu & Fujiwara et al. eds., A Sutudy of T.H. Green, p. 86.

(3) Yasunobu Fujiwara, "Idealism in the U.K. and the Problem of 'Positive Freedom': Concerning the Thought of T.H. Green," Shibuya *et al.* eds., *Freedom and Order in Political Thoughts*, p. 255.

(4) Youichi Higuchi, "Intellectual Status about Freedom: From the Constitutional Point of View," *Julist* vol. 978 (May 1991).

(5) Sousuke Mita *et al.* eds., *Dictionary of Sociology*, pp. 172-3.

(6) Akira Osuka, "New Deal and Constitutional Self-government," in *Social State and Constitution*, p. 2 ff.

2 Litigation, Administrative Relief and Political Settlement for Compensating Victims of Pollution: Minamata Mercury Poisoning after 40 Years*

Koichiro FUJIKURA

1 The Minamata Story
2 Minamata Victims Sue Chisso for Damages
3 Administrative Compensation System Established
4 A Political Settlement
5 Some Lessons

1 The Minamata Story

The first incident of mercury poisoning appeared in Japan in the mid-1950s during a period of growing economic prosperity. In 1954, several people were hospitalized. They were suffering from violent shakings, narrowing field of vision, and loss of control and coordination over their body movements. The number of victims increased rapidly and they were all living in fishing villages in the vicinity of Minamata Bay, Kyushu, the southern most of the four main islands of Japan. The Minamata disease, as it became known, was feared contagious in its initial period of the outbreak and the victims and their families were discriminated against by the rest of community.

It took more than ten years before teams of scientists determined the cause of disease as methylated mercury. The Ministry of Public Health officially recognized the cause and made a public announcement in 1968. Methylated mercury was a byproduct of the production of acetaldehyde, which was manufactured at the Minamata plant of the Japan Chisso (Nitrogen Manufacturing) Company. For years the Chisso plant discharged methylated mercury in its effluent directly into the bay. Gradually the chemical had become concentrated in the tissues of fish, other marine organisms, and ultimately in the inhabitants of the Minamata fishing community. Mercury affected the central nervous system when it was taken into the human body through a food chain.

In 1965, a similar outbreak of Minamata disease was reported in Niigata City on the Japan sea side of the main island, where the Showa Denko Corporation operated a plant by employing the same production process and method as Chisso.

Although the cause of disease was not determined until later, fishermen and village people instinctively knew from the beginning that the effluent with sickening color discharged from the Chisso plant was killing fish, and also birds and cats which fed on fish. The people from villages tried repeatedly to negotiate with Chisso to stop the discharge, but Chisso was never responsive. The local residents resorted to such traditional means of dispute settlement as conciliation, mediation, and arbitration. They asked the governor of prefecture to intervene, and appealed to the central government for help. They protested, demonstrated, picketed, staged sit-ins, and even attempted at forcefully breaking into the plant. However, all their efforts produced little result. Chisso, denying any wrongdoing, continued its operation.

2 Minamata Victims Sue Chisso for Damages

The victims finally decided to take the polluters to court. The Niigata group (of 77) sued Showa Denko in 1967 and the Minamata group (of 139) sued Chisso in 1969. The only cause of civil action available to them was one for damages based on a theory of negligence under article 709 of the Civil Code. ("A person who violates intentionally or negligently the rights of another is bound to make compensation for damages arising therefrom.") In a negligence action, the plaintiff must prove the critical elements of liability, namely, breach of duty of care, foreseeability of harm and causation.

In both cases, the courts found the polluters negligent and awarded the substantial amount of damages to the plaintiffs. In applying the traditional negligence principle to the modern pollution context, the courts demonstrated an innovative approach in deciding the defendants' liability. First, the courts imposed an extensive and high degree of care on the defendants' chemical plants. Second, the courts found that the defendants could have foreseen injuries from their discharges to people living in the surrounding areas. Third, the courts created a presumption of causation in favor of the plaintiffs.

The courts stated the following reasoning as to each issue raised.

(1) Degree of Care. The defendants owed a high degree of care since the production process of the chemical industry generally utilized large quantities of dangerous substances such as raw materials and catalysts. There was an extremely high probability that unpredictably harmful substances would be in the factory's wastewater. When dangerous materials were discharged into the rivers and seas, harm to plants, animals, or people could be easily anticipated. Therefore, when a chemical plant discharged wastewater, it must always use "the best knowledge and technology" to determine whether harmful substances were present and what effect there might be on plants, animals, and humans. In addition to assuring the safety of its wastewater, if by any chance harm became apparent or there arose doubt about its safety, the factory should immediately suspend operations and adopt the necessary maximum preventive measures. Especially with regard to the life and health of area residents, the factory must exercise a high degree of care to prevent harm before it should happen.

(2) Foreseeability. The defendants contended that foreseeability was limited to the foreseeability of the production of the specific causal agent, and that they did not violate any duty since they could not possibly have foreseen this specific outcome. However, the courts found that if one were to proceed along the defendants' contention, the degree of danger could only be proven after the environment was polluted and destroyed and lives and health of people harmed. Until that point, the discharge of dangerous wastewater would have to be tolerated. The inevitable consequence would be that the encroachment on the lives and health of residents would not be stopped, and this would be tantamount to allowing the residents to be human experiments. The courts found it clearly unjust.

(3) Causation. The courts analyzed the causation in three parts: (a) the

characteristic symptoms of the disorder and its causal (etiological) agent; (b) the pathway of pollution; and (c) the discharge of the causal agent by the wrongdoer. With regard to (a) and (b), the courts held that causation might be proved by an accumulation of circumstantial evidence if the plaintiffs' explanation was consistent with the relevant scientific findings (of clinicians, pathologists, epidemiologists and other medical specialists). When the above level of proof was obtained, and the search for the source of pollution led to the very doorstep of the factory, it should be factually presumed that the factory was the source, and legal causation should be fully established.

In these cases of mercury poisoning, the courts in essence imposed strict liability on the polluters, while still using such terms of negligence under the article 709 as breach of care, probability and foreseeability of harm. The courts also created a presumption of causation in favor of the plaintiffs. Once the plaintiffs demonstrated the causal agent and the pathway implicating defendants, the burden of proof then shifted to the defendants to prove that the causal agent could not be discharged from its plant.

Other victims of air and water pollution in other parts of Japan also sued and won in all of the major litigation. The courts provided a public forum where victims could confront and expose the polluters' wrongdoing. The victims were morally outraged and their assertion of civil rights in a very basic sense was finally vindicated by the courts. The courts' holdings on those issues were adopted into and formed the foundation of a national administrative compensation system established in 1973.

3 Administrative Compensation System Established

The Diet in 1970 enacted a dozen environmental protection measures. The Law for the Compensation of Pollution-Related Health Injury was enacted in 1973, and established a national administrative compensation system. The law was supported by all major actors, namely, pollution victims, business and industry, politicians and bureaucrats. Pollution victim organizations supported it because the administrative compensation system could offer victims much needed monetary relief promptly and fairly. Business and industry people supported it because the system could provide them with some predictability and control as to the costs of compensation. They could not predict nor control the magnitude and extent of tort liability that the courts might impose on them in potential law suits against them. Politicians and bureaucrats could take credit for doing something for the victims and retain control over the national pollution crises.

The law established the administrative system to provide scheduled compensation payments for certified victims of air and water pollution. Polluted areas were designated around major industrial cities and sites. In the case of air pollution, eventually, the 41 areas were designated by using the level of SO_x concentration as an index. Seven areas of water and soil pollution caused by mercury, cadmium and arsenic were also designated. In these areas, usually a specific source of toxic pollution had been identified. People living in designated areas who developed certain prescribed symptoms were certified by doctors. Upon certification they became eligible for receiving compensation for medical expenses, lost earnings and other incidentals. A special Health Damage Certification Council of medical, legal, and other experts was set up for the purpose of reviewing certification.

The costs of compensation were imposed upon polluters. In the case of air pollution, a graduated emission charge was levied on stationary sources (factories with smoke stackes) and a tonnage tax on automobiles, respectively contributing 80% and 20% of the amount paid into the central fund each year. The emission charge was collected and pooled at the national level. Thereafter, the fund was distributed to provincial governments for payment to the victims. In the case of water-related pollution traceable to a specific substance and source, identified polluters (like Chisso in Minamata) were required to pay directly to certified victims at the local level.

In 1988, after 15 years of its operation, there were 108,489 certified victims of air pollution and 1,898 certified victims of toxic pollution who were receiving compensation under the system.

The administrative system was designed primarily for the purposes of (1) compensating pollution-related health damages and (2) making polluters pay for the costs. However, the system may also serve the following functions: (3) identifying harm caused by pollution; (4) legitimating compensation to victims; (5) providing polluters an incentive to reduce emission; (6) accounting the costs of pollution; and (7) generating information vital for environmental policy making. The functions listed (3) through (7) may not have been intended, but are interesting theoretically and significant to explore.

The system identifies and defines the extent and nature of harm of pollution. It makes people in designated areas aware of a possible link between pollution and their illness by prescribing typical symptoms caused by harmful substances. It provides an incentive for victims to come forward to be identified.

The system legitimates payments to victims by admitting officially that pollution exists and victims are entitled to receive compensation. The victims of pollution often suffered discrimination and were accused of using their personal misfortune for obtaining public assistance. The system publicly admits that pollution related health damages does exist in many parts of Japan, and that victims are indeed entitled to receive compensation for their sufferings. Once certified and legitimated, victims become a symbolic existence whose force cannot be ignored politically.

The system provides polluters with an incentive not to pollute or to reduce the amount of pollutants. In the case of air pollution, the system charges the emission sources according to the amount of SOx discharged. In addition to the direct regulations setting certain emission standards, there is an economic incentive for polluters to pollute less by adopting anti-pollution measures, if those measures cost less than emission charges imposed. The air quality in designated areas improved sufficiently that the law was amended in 1987 and all area designations as to air pollution were removed. The marked reduction of SOx was largely brought about by industrial policy to import low sulfur oil. However, the emission charges under the system may, theoretically at least, have some effect.

The system accounts the costs of pollution in terms of health damages every year. The system reports mumbers of applications for certification, by area, of certified victims, of the amount of compensation paid to them, and of the amount of charges imposed upon polluters. Theses numbers are not otherwise accounted and produced for the public to see.

The system generates general information relating to pollution and public health otherwise not available. A large scale public health survey may produce similar data, but it is costly and may be difficult to obtain funds to do the survey every year in a systematic way. This information is vital for making the public aware of pollution as well as making a long and medium range environmental policy.

The system worked well for providing compensation for victims of air pollution. Their typical symptoms were defined and the fund necessary to pay victims was generated by charging numerous emission sources. However, the system experienced many difficulties with compensating the Minamata victims. First, the number of applications for certification greatly increased once Chisso's liability was clearly established by the court decisions. Soon, the backlog of applications to be processed reached several thousands toward the end of 1970's. Second, the medical standards for certification became progressively uncertain as many applications involved not acute mercury poisoning, but milder, cumulative effects of poisoning indistinguishable from ordinary ailments. The doctors on the certification board could not agree on what typical symptoms were. The courts, reviewing several cases of appeals from persons whose applications for certification had been denied, held the board's standards too strict. The Environment Agency also proposed more flexible guidelines for certification. However, these judicial and administrative attempts could not resolve the certification problem. Third, Chisso, the sole party responsible for continuously paying compensation to the certified victims had been on the brinks of bankruptcy many times. Each time, the prefectural government rescued Chisso by issuing public bonds, a large portion of which the central government purchased, and by making the capital generated therefrom available in the form of low interests loans to Chisso. Nobody could afford to see Chisso go bankrupt

As of 1995, there were 2,950 certified victims of mercury poisoning (Chisso -related 2,260 and Showa Denko 690). Upon certification, a victim received on average a lump sum payment of US$180,000 (@100yen=1 US dollar), and annual payments $20,000. Chisso paid $27,500 per certified victim, a total of $31 million. Showa Denko paid $16,500 per certified victim, a total of $7 million. From 1973 to 1994, both companies paid a total of $1,288 million to certified victims.

Meanwhile, litigation involving other issues, civil as well as criminal, continued after the initial action against Chisso for damages. A criminal charge was brought against a plant manager of Chisso for criminal negligence in discharging the waste water, and he was convicted.

The victims sued the certification board to contest its determination denying them certification. The courts found the board's certification standards too strict and inflexible, and ordered some of the plaintiffs to be certified. The victims also sued the governments (national and local) for their failure to take necessary and prompt action. Major issues involved in this group of litigation are: (a) whether the government should have banned fishing and sale of fish caught in the Minamata bay under the food safety act (The central government said no in response to the inquiry from the local government because there was no clear evidence that all fish and shell fish in the bay were contaminated); and (b) whetehr the government should have ordered Chisso to stop its operation because it violated the water quality preservation act. (The defendant contended that there was no violation because the area was not designated for preservation under the act).

The decisions of six district courts in ruling on these issues were evenly divided, three holding the government liable and three not liable. Both parties appealed to appellate courts. Toward the end of the 1980s, a total of 2,300 plaintiffs were in those suits pending before the 11 district and appellate courts.

Meanwhile, the central government in 1992 in cooperation with the local governments initiated a health care plan for uncertified victims. By the end of

1995, about 4,600 people were receiving on average $2,900 for medical care annually.

By the mid 1990s it became apparent that the certification process for Minamata victims had broken down. Chisso had been in a chronically precarious financial situation. Litigation was in at an impasse. The only option remaining seemed to be a political resolution of the problem.

4 A Political Settlement

In April of 1994, the ruling political party, a coalition of Liberal Democrats, Socialists and one other faction, decided to make a national political settlement with the Minamata victims. The major political issue was the treatment of and remedies to be accorded to those who were claiming some effects of mercury poisoning, but still uncertified and uncared for. The government proposal contained the following features: (1) the polluters shall make a lump sum payment to those who meet certain requirements; (2) the national government and the Kumamoto prefectural government shall make a statement expressing sincere regret for their handling of the Minamata problem; (3) the parties who sign this agreement shall terminate all pending law suits; and (4) the central and prefectural governments shall continue the comprehensive health care plan, and shall provide financial measures to assist Chisso and to develop the affected areas, and reopen the application process for the health care payment.

In May, accepting and acting on the government proposal, the National Coordinating Conference of the Minamata Victims-Plaintiffs and the Plaintiffs' Lawyers (the Conference), and Chisso Corporation (Chisso) entered an agreement for the purpose of achieving the "final and comprehensive solution of all problems" concerning the Minamata disease.

The following text of the agreement recaptured in its preamble the events leading to the final settlement.

(1) On March 20, 1973, Kumamoto District Court rendered the judgment for the plaintiffs, holding Chisso liable for damages. Following the court decision, a compensation agreement was signed by patient groups and Chisso, thereby

providing compensation to the certified patients. Since the conclusion of the compensation agreement, however, the number of applications for certification had markedly increased, and so correspondingly did the number of rejected applications. Several rejected patients-applicants filed suits, contesting the determination of the certification board as well as its procedure and standards.

(2) The Fukuoka Appellate Court, on August 16, 1985, held that four of five plaintiffs deserved to be certified. The court found that those losses of skin feeling and sensation of the hands and feet, though the same might be caused by the neck bone deformation, were quite distinctive symptoms of mercury poisoning. It was reasonable to presume, the court held, that the symptom was in fact that of the Minamata disease, unless it should be proved otherwise, and that even a diagnosis of such symptom alone, when accompanied with those epidemiological conditions and cumulative symptoms observable among the family members of a particular patient, should warrant the finding of Minamata disease with high probability.

(3) Since 1980, a series of suits was brought against the central government and Kumamoto prefectural government under the government torts claims act. The plaintiffs alleged that the governments were liable for the occurrence and the spread of Minamata disease. During September to October of 1990, several courts where those suits were pending recommended the parties to settle. The plaintiffs, the Kumamoto prefectural government, and Chisso participated in settlement negotiations, but the central government refused to join in. On January 7, 1993, the Fukuoka Appellate Court drafted and proposed the terms of settlement. However, the settlement was not finally reached since Chisso did not accept the proposal. Meanwhile, several district courts found for uncertified patients, ordering Chisso to compensate them.

(4) The central government initiated a comprehensive medical care measure which provided 4,600 persons with medical care. In June, 1994, a new cabinet was formed under Prime Minister Murayama, the head of the Socialist Party, and a solution for Minamata disease was placed on a high priority list of his government's political agenda. The government agreed on a framework for a

political solution of the Minamata disease problems. Prime Minister Murayama, speaking for the government, issued the following official statement on December 15, 1995. "I expess a deeply felt condolence for those who died in the midst of sufferings and frustration and when I consider those who have been put under indescribable sufferings for many years and must have felt irreparably hurt, I am filled with the sincere feeling of regret."

In the context described above, the Conference and Chisso entered the agreement to settle the Minamata disease problems, stating that "taking into consideration, to the utmost degree, the early resolution is urgently needed."

The agreement sets forth the following terms of settlement.

(1) Chisso gravely accepts the following: that Chisso's legal responsibility for causing Minamata disease by its own discharge of methyl mercury was adjudged by the court on March 20, 1973; that Chisso's legal responsibility for four uncertified plaintiffs was affirmed by the appellate court judgment on August 16, 1985; and that a series of other district court decisions, while appealed, held Chisso liable for uncertified-patient plaintiffs. Chisso shall make apology to the plaintiffs, the residents of the affected areas and to society in general for the fact that it has taken such a long time to reach the resolution today since the beginning of the Minamata problem.

(2) Among those who were possible exposed to the above-natural level of methyl mercury in the past and were suffering from the loss of sensation in their hands and feet, the administrative compensation act has set those certified apart from the others whose cetification was denied. The diagnosis of Minamata disease has been made on the basis of exposure to methyl mercury and of a combination of symptoms of mercury poisoning. This agreement intends to provide some relief for those whose certification was denied. However, since the medical determination of the Minamata disease is dependent on a matter of degree of probability, the fact that their applications were denied does not mean that they are entirely without the effects of methyl mercury. Therefore, the agreement provides relief for those who are suffering from the loss of sensation in their hands and feet, and who consent to the termination of

their litigation.

(3) The National Conference and Chisso actively shall work with the residents of the area for reviving and redeveloping the community, by participating and coordinating in the efforts of repairing and reconstructing the community's bonds.

Under the agreement, Chisso is required to make a lump sum payment to (1) those who are currently registered and receiving health care under the comprehensive health care measure, and (2) those who are determined to be eligible in the reopened application process for the comprehensive health care measure by the prefectural governor in consultation with the review board. The amount of lump sum payment to a person eligible is $26,000 per person plus a $3,000 medical care payment per year for those who applied between January and August, 1996. The number of renewed applications was over 9,300, of which 5,885 were determined eligible (roughly 60%). In March of 1997, when the review of all applications was completed, the final number of persons eligible for receiving a lump sum payment and the continuing medical payment reached 10,350 (including about 4,400 who were determined eligible before the reopening of the application).

It is estimated that those who have been determined eligible would continue to receive medical care payment, on average, for 10 to 14 years. The total amount of medical care payments per person at the end of these years may be around $29,000 to $40,000. With the lump sum payment, the total amount one person would receive may become comparable to the average damage award ($58,000) by the courts in six cases where the plaintiffs sued the governments as well as the polluting companies.

Aside from an individual lump payment, a total of $50 million is allocated to six victims organizations involved in litigation. The eligible person if he is a member of one of those organizations may receive an additional amount determined by each organization in addition to his or her lump sum payment. This portion of payments comes from Chisso. The medical care costs are to be borne by the central and local governments as a part of the costs of the public health insurance system.

The national conference and its members agree, upon receiving the lump sum payments, to settle all disputes and pending litigation, and to refrain in the future from litigation for damages, attempting negotiations, and activities for demanding official certification under the administrative compensation system.

The group of people in Niigata who sued Showa Denko also reached a settlement with similar terms to the groups of Minamata. Showa Denko agreed to contribute $2,500,000 for the reconstruction of the community ties in addition to a lump sum payment to eligible persons.

5 Some Lessons

The magnitude and full extent of harm caused by mercury pollution in Minamata has yet to be determined. It has been reported that about 20,000 people living along the nearby coast have been affected. About 17,000 applied for official certification, and of those about 4,000 were certified. About 1,200 have died from mercury poisoning. The compounding effects of 40 years of litigation, the administrative compensation system, and the final political settlement have been very divisive within the community. People are divided between those who sued and those who did not; those who applied for certification and those who did not; and those certified and those not certified. The victims were at one time fragmented into 20 different factions.

Some people fear that the political settlement may create a false impression on the part of the general public that the Minamata story is over. The steel net which sealed the mouth of bay to prevent fish to go out was finally removed in 1997. Fish caught in the bay were tested for mercury and declared safe. Commerical fishing is now possible in and around the bay, but few fishermen still remain in the area. A large portion of the bay (about 138 acres) was landfilled and a layer of concrete covered the heavily contaminated sediments in the bottom of the bay. A memorial museum was built on the site. Other use of the acquired space remains undecided. The Chisso plant is there still operating, the sole purpose of its existence seems to be continuing to pay compensation to the certified victims of mercury poisoning.

Three different institutional approaches have been used over 40 years. The victims resorted to the court for the vindication of their rights after all traditional means of dispute settlement failed. The courts provided the victims with a forum to confront the polluters and to gain public attention. Through litigation, the local incident of mercury poisoning far away from Tokyo finally drew the attention of politicians and bureaucrats in the central government.

The courts created a presumption of causation in favor of the plaintiffs and imposed a very high degree of care on the polluting companies. The courts awarded damages to the plaintiffs in all major pollution cases in the early part of 1970s, and laid a foundation for the administrative compensation system.

The administrative compensation system served its function sufficiently in terms of providing payment to victims of air pollution. In the case of air pollution, scientific and medical standards for designating the heavily polluted areas and certifying victims were relatively clear and never in dispute. Also, a sufficient fund was created at the national level by charging numerous emission sources. The amount needed to pay certified victims each year was assessed and charged to those sources. The collection of charges was effectively made through relevant industrial associations, and the fund remained solvent all through the years of its operation. In contrast, in the case of compensating the victims of mercury poisoning, the certification process broke down under the large volume of applications and because of medical uncertainty as to certification standards. Ever since the courts found it liable for damages, Chisso has been on the verge of bankruptcy several times. Chisso has been kept afloat by infusions of public money in the form of low interest loans. If Chisso were to go under, about 2,000 certified victims currently receiving compensation directly from the company would be left uncompensated.

The political settlement came only after 40 years. It certainly extended remedies to a large number of uncertified victims. It incorporated a comprehensive health care plan which was designed to improve public health care in the affected community. The measure has provided such treatments as acupuncture and hot spring bathing to those who were not eligible for medical care payments. The political settlement also emphasized the need of healing the divided community and made some attempts to promote cooperation among the once adverse parties.

In mass torts cases, litigation leads often to a political settlement. Judges may actively be involved in formulating the terms of settlement. Possible advantages and disadvantages of setting up compensation systems of funds have been debated. Unless a society decides to adopt a comprehensive national health and welfare system, it takes all three different approaches to resolve a mass tragedy like Minamata. In hindsight, we can ask several questions yet to be answered. Why was not Chisso ordered to stop the discharge when mercury was found in the wastewater? Why was not commercial fishing in the Minamata Bay prohibited? Why did Chisso continue its operation even after an internal experiment on cats established its wastewater caused the disease? Why were only damages and not injunctions sought in all those suits? Why did regulatory agencies remain unconcerned and did not initiate actions in the critical stages? What is the most effective and efficient combination and sequence of litigation, regulatory relief and political intervention? Why has it taken forty years to reach the settlement? To find answers to these questions is certainly a step toward preventing the tragedy from happening again. The Minamata story urges all of us to do so.

* This paper was presented to two symposiums organized by the Institute of Comparative Law, Waseda University, respectively with the University of Melbourne Law School and the University of Auckland, Faculty of Law, where each symposium was successively held in December of 1997 (Footnotes omitted).

3 Care for the Elderly and Management of Their Property

Masayuki TANAMURA

1 The Present Situation of Aging and the Elderly in Japan
2 Care for the Elderly and the Burden on Their Families
3 The Management of Property of Elderly People and the Guardianship for Adults
Conclusion

1 The Present Situation of Aging and the Elderly in Japan

How does aging in Japan proceed? What are the characteristics of Japanese aged society and what is the present situation in Japan?

Characteristics of Japanese Aged Society

① **Aging in Japan with Rapid Speed**

The ratio of people whose age is over 65 in Japan was more than 7% in 1970, which figure is the touchstone of the "aged society", and more than 15% in 1996, which means that Japanese society became a matured "aged society" similar to European countries and the United States. The raito is estimated to increase to 17% in 2000, 25.8% in 2020, 27.4% in 2025 and 32.3% in 2050. According to the research by the Institute of Population Problems in the Ministry of Health and Welfare, while it took 130 years in France, 85 years in Sweden, 60 years in Italy, 50 years in the United Kingdom and 45 years in Germany, for the ratio of the elderly to increase from 7% to 14%, it took only 24 years in Japan. And while it took 95 years in France, 66 years in Sweden and 62 years in Germany, for the ratio to increase from 10% to 20%, it took only 22 years in Japan. All these figures indicate the especially rapid pace of aging in Japan.

② **Rapid Increase of the Elderly in Need of Care**

According to a report by the Ministry of Health and Welfare, in 1995 the number of the elderly who needed care was 1,410,000, the number of elderly bedridden people was 811,000 and the number of people suffering from senile dementia was approximately 1,000,000. It is estimated that in 2025 the number of elderly bedridden people will be 2,290,000 and the number of people suffering from senile dementia will be 3,320,000. The total figure of 5,620,000 is about three times as large as the present figure. The number of the household of the elderly living alone is also increasing and will reach 4,630,000 by 2010. There two types of dementia. One is Alzheimer's disease, which causes contraction of the brain. The other type is cerebral blood vessel dementia caused by a brain thrombus or brain bleeding. In the case of people aged over 65, some 7% of them are suffering from dementia. The older they are, the higher the ratio of people who are always bedridden or suffering from dementia.

③ **Decreasing Capability of Care in the Home**

In 1995 the average number of members of one household was 2.83. Of all the elderly who need care, 862,000 are in the home and 554,000 are in institutions. That means some 60% of the elderly who need care are cared for by their family members in the home. More than 50% of them have been bedridden for more than three years, and 35.7% of the care-takers are people aged over 65. This means the elderly are caring for the elderly. 85.9% of those caring for old people who are bedridden are female. The burden on female family members has been increasing.

Anxieties about Life for the Elderly

The elderly tend to have three major anxieties. One is an anxiety for health. In the case of the people aged over 65, the ratio of people who are suffering from disease is much higher than that of people under 65. The older people become, the more likely they are to be ill. Secondly, the number of elderly people living alone is on the increase, and 17.4% of elderly people were living alone in 1995. The elderly are now likely to live apart from other parts of the society. They suffer anxiety over loneliness and mental emptiness. It is advisable that the elderly should be respected and live with people from other parts of the society. Thirdly, having retired, elderly people often feel anxiety about their economic situation. The average amount of annuity for an elderly couple (including the national pension) is some ¥200,000 (approximately A$22,500, NZ$25,000) per month. Minimum expenses for an elderly couple is said to be ¥231,000, which is some ¥30,000 higher than their pension benefit.

According to a research by the Management and Coordination Agency, in Japan 52.3% of the elderly suffer anxiety over health, 31.1% for loneliness and 28.2% for their economic situation, while in the United States the numbers are 27% for health, 16.8% for loneliness and 15.3% for their economic situation. It followed that many old people experience strong anxieties for the three causes. A public opinion poll made by the Prime Minister's Office in 1995 showed that 67.2% of elderly worried that they would need care and support in the future and 72.9% of elderly people worried their family members would become in need of care, and nearly half of them were dissatisfied with the present situation of care in the home.

Development of Policy for Social Welfare in the Aged Society

Social welfare services in Japan, including care and support services for the elderly, have been dependent on the public welfare financial disbursements from taxes, on the one hand, and the public welfare measures for which beneficiaries have to pay in order to receive benefits on the other hand. In the 1980s, in response to the change of policies from the highly economic growth policy to the slow economic growth policy, it became necessary to rationalize the finance of social welfare, to make supports for self-help, to encourage a cooperation between medical and welfare services, to improve the quality of social resources, to make use of private enterprises, and to promote the function of care in the home. By the Gold Plan (10-year campaign for the promotion of health and welfare for the elderly) in 1989, and the new Gold Plan in 1995, several measures for care in the home were to be promoted by municipal corporations, and the following targets were established for each service and institution:

	1993	1999	
Home Helper	50,000	170,000	(number of people)
Day Service	4,300	1,700	(number of sites)

Short Stay	20,000	60,000 (number of beds)
Support Center for Care in the Home		10,000 (number of sites)
Elderly People's Home for Special Care	200,000	290,000 (number of beds)
Health Center for the Elderly	113,000	280,000 (number of beds)
Care House	17,000	100,000 (number of capacity)
Life & Welfare Centerfor the Elderly	160	400 (number of sites)

2 Care for the Elderly and the Burden on Their Families

Who should care for senile and bedridden people? What kind of relationship is between private support provided in the Civil Code and public aid by the state?

The Present Situation of Care for the Elderly Who Need Care

At present, the number of elderly people who need care is 1,416,000 of which 862,000 are in their home and 554,000 are in institutions (76,000 in welfare institutions for the elderly, 200,000 in nursing homes for special care, and 278,000 in hospitals). The number of elderly bedridden people is 811,000, 60% of which are cared for in their home, and 20% of which are in institutions or nursing homes. The remainder are in hospitals. This shows that the majority are treated and cared for in their home. The ratios of the old people who need care and the elderly bedridden people are 4.93% and 1.62% at the age of 65 or more, and 14.43% and 5.12% at the age of 80 or more. This shows that the older they are, the more likely they are to need care and be bedridden. More than 80% of those who care for elderly people are female, such as their sons' wives, their spouse (mostly wives) and their daughters. Moreover, 37.5% of the people who care for elderly people are more than 65 years old themselves. 53% of the elderly bedridden people are bedridden for more than three years. The ratio of elderly people 65 or over living with their children was 68% in 1980, and dropped to 54.3% in 1995. And the ratio of those living with their children and their spouses was 52.5% in 1980 and dropped to 35.5% in 1995.

Recently nationwide research was conducted at 400 Support Centers for Care in the Home. 220 Centers replied and reported that there were 209 incidents of abuse or neglect for a total of 144 persons. Typical examples are neglect by sons' wives because of their fatigue from hard work of care, and violence by sons. 70% of abuse and neglect are against females, and there is a clear tendency that the older they are, the higher the ratio of elderly abuse. According to the experts' opinion, since public care services are not sufficient and supports by the state or municipal corporations are not enough, heavy burdens are imposed on family members, and consequently ill treatments are inflicted on weak old people who need care. We should reconfirm the general principle that the elderly people have the right to live safely, free of violence, abuse, neglect and exploitation.

Family Support

The Civil Code has a provision in regard to the support by family members (s. 877). This provision imposes generally on the lineal relatives by blood and brothers and sisters a duty to support each other, and also prescribes that if there are special circumstances, the Family Court may impose a duty to support as between the relatives within the third degree. Therefore, a duty to support which civil law imposes on family members is between lineal relatives by blood such as parents-children, grandparents and grandchildren, or brothers and sisters. There are only exceptionally rare cases in which a duty to support is imposed on uncles, aunts, nephews and nieces, or in-laws such as between a father and his son's wife.

Theoretically, the duty to support is divided into two types; a duty to maintain life and a duty to assist life. The duty to maintain is said to be a heavier duty such as sharing a piece of meat, a cup of rice, or even a grain of rice, and a duty to keep the living standard at the same level as their own. Examples of this duty are maintenance between husband and wife (ss. 752 and 760 of the CC.) and maintenance by parents of their minor children (ss. 766 and 877 (1) of the CC.). On the other hand, examples of the duty to assistance are support for elderly parents by their adult children, and support by brothers or sisters. Such duties are only imposed if the children or brothers/sisters are able to support other family members after they discharge their primary duty. Some writers assert that a duty to support for old parents by their adult children should be the duty to maintain life. The dominant opinion is that the duty is the duty to assist life. Practical benefits conferred under the duty to support is determined after the needs of the person entitled to support, financial capacity of the person under the duty, and all other relevant factors are taken into consideration (s. 879 of CC.). Therefore, both parties concerned with support can negotiate as to what is needed and what can be conferred. They can also consult with a third party, and accept mediation by the third party. Only if they do not reach any agreement as to family support, they can seek an court order in Family Court (s. 878 of the CC.).

In 1996, 9,360 petitions were made as to matters of support in all Family Courts in Japan. 8,945 petitions (96%) dealt with supports for minors. Cases for adults were only 415 (4%). Mediation agreements were reached in 162 cases, 112 of which dealt with financial supports (69%), 23 cases were resulted in living together (14%), 9 cases were on in-patients or inmates (6%) while the remainder included both financial support and living together (11%) ("Judicial Statistics Annual 1996" at pp. 130-134).

Many cases of support for elderly parents are settled by negotiating between the parties, and only a few cases are decided by the Family Court. Care and support in daily life have real meaning if they are tendered with affection and trust of family members voluntarily, and they should not be provided only out of the sense of obligation or under the external pressures. Family support in the form of living together is not legally enforceable in nature, if the person entitled to the support and the person under the duty don't reach an agreement on support with living together, because it necessarily goes with living together in the same house. In particular, in cases of elderly bedridden or senile people, they may need 24-hour care. For these reasons, it is highly questionable for the Court to order reluctant children to provide support with living together, or to bear high costs of care.

Family Support and Public Assistance

There may be cases where problems concerning care for poor elderly, senile and bedridden people and their financial capacity are too serious and complex for their family member to deal with. What kind of relationship should exist between family support and public assistance as state responsibility? Among individual responsibility, family responsibility and state responsibility, a primary duty is imposed on certain family members to take a private duty to support for family members who are poor or need care. On the other hand, if a family cannot support their members, they are entitled to be supported by the state as a welfare state under the right to life which is guaranteed in the Constitution. However, the state responsibility of support is secondary and supplementary. As the Life Protection Act prescribed, the support by family members is first and public assistance is supplementary protection in principle (supplementary nature of the public assistance, s. 4(2) of the Life Protection Act).

Public Care Insurance System

The public assistance in Japan has been provided by using nursing homes for special care under the welfare scheme for the old system or by using hospitals for the elderly under the medical system. Its costs are covered by taxes and premiums from medical insurance respectively. However, with rapid aging, it becomes apparent that the present system for the public aid will collapse financially. For example, because the medical expenses for elderly people increase rapidly, the financial situation of the medical insurance has deteriorated, and although the Ministry of Health and Welfare estimates that the expenses for care services in 2000 will be ¥5 trillion (approximately A$55 billion, NZ$62 billion), it is thought to be extremely difficult to find the financial sources to cover the expenses.

For these reasons, the part of medical services which has the nature of care for elderly people is detached from the medical services for elderly people, and in addition to medical insurance, a care insurance is to be established in order to improve the financial sutuation of the medical insurance. The idea of the public care insurance is introduced in view of opposition of the people to increase taxes for care services in welfare institution for elderly people and also in view of ensuring financial resources by introduction of care insurance as a social insurance.

In June 1997, the Care Insurance Bill prepared by the Ministry of Health and Welfare did not pass in the Diet, and a slightly amended bill is being discussed in the extraordinary session of the Diet in autumn 1997. The contents of the bill are that the insurers are cities, towns, villages and special districts which are sponsored by the state and prefectures, that the insured are the medical insurance policy holders who are more than 40 and under 65, provisions in kind are made to people over 65 who need care in the home or in support institutions, and that benefits are made within the extent of provision for care under the recognition of the entitlement to care. However, there are criticisms against the care insurance scheme to the effect that the social security program should be carried on by the state, that a heavier burden will be imposed on the people by introducing private insurance, that arguments are concentrated only on financial aspects, and that the components and quality of care services which will be provided are not clear.

3 The Management of Property of Elderly People and the Guardianship for Adults

What kind of legal system should be applied for the management of property of those whose capacity of judgment has been lowered such as elderly senile people? How is such a system applied in practice? What system is the guardianship for the adult? What kind of legislation will be made in the future?

The Transaction and Management of Property by Elderly People

As people become older, their abilities cannot help decreasing both mentally and physically. As their capacity for judgment decreses, many elderly people become victims of dishonest dealings or fraudulent transactions such as the *Toyotashyoji* case, the *Wagyushoho* cases (dealing with Japanese oxen), and *Genyashoho* cases (transactions of valueless lands). There are cases in which children or other family members transact the property of elderly people without any authority or permission, or misuse the property as a security or collateral for their obligations. There are also cases in which savings and deposits of old people are withdrawn or spent by their family members or others, when they are in nursing homes or hospitals for elderly people. However, it is impossible to deny the legal capacity of elderly people to make transactions by themselves, because it amounts to a denial of self-determination, and because it is not suitable to the fact that capacity of judgment will gradually decrease. For these reasons, the question of the management of property of elderly people is extremely important in the aged society.

The Limit of the Existing System of Incompetency and Quasi-incompetency

In the present Civil Code, when a person lose completely his or her capacity of judgment, a petition for adjudication of incompetency may be made to the Family Court, and the person shall be placed under guardianship if the Court thinks it is suitable to do so (ss. 7 and 8 of the CC.). In the case of guardianship, the guardian does all transactions for the person adjudged incompetent, and the acts of that person are voidable (s. 9 of the CC.). When a person becomes feeble-minded or spendthrift, but does not completely lose capacity, that person may be adjudged quasi-incompetent and placed under curatorship (s. 11 of the CC.). In the case of quasi-incompetency, it is necessary to obtain the consent of the curator in order

232 Part I : Affirmative State Interventions

to do certain acts such as borrowing money, surety, transactions regarding real property or valuable personal property and disclaims of inheritance. Such acts are voidable if they are made without the consent of the curator.

Therefore, under the present system for the management of property of elderly people whose capacities have decreased, there is no other option other than the selection of the adjudication of incompetency with a guardian or quasi-incompetency with a curator, taking the degree of lost capacity into consideration. However, under this present system, there is no reflection that decreasing of capacities of elderly people become worse gradually, and that elderly people whose capacity of judgment decreased may sometimes make an adequate judgment. The present system also lacks flexibility, for it denies capacities of elderly people evenly and uniformly. Moreover, lots of time will be spent in the proceedings for the adjudication on the Family Court, and ¥300,000~500,000 (approximately A$3,350~5,600, NZ$3,750~6,250) will be needed for the necessary experts' opinions. Furthermore, when the adjudication is made, it will be published as an "official announcement" in the Official Gazette, and in a notice board of the Family Court, and the entry "On the 1st of December 1997, adjudication of incompetency is made, and on the same day, xxx is appointed as the guardian" is made in the family registration, so-called "koseki," which the person adjudicated and his family does not like. When a person is adjudicated incompetent or quasi-incompetent, lots of disadvantages occur to the person, because the adjudication makes it impossible for that person to take a certain job such as civil servant or some kind of expert, of which the total number of disqualification is estimated to be 140. The word "incompetent" may be discriminatory, for the meaning of the word is to prohibit from transaction of property. There is another criticism that although public prosecutors are eligible applicants for the adjudication, representatives of public interests such as the head of municipal corporations should be entitled to apply for the adjudication. For these reasons, although the number of the cases of adjudication has increased (2,242 cases of incompetency and 730 cases of quasi-incompetency in 1996), it is severely criticized that the system is hard to use. The Subcommittee of Property Law in the Civil law Division of the Legislative Council started to review the system of incompetency and quasi-incompetency in June 1995.

The System of Guardianship for Adults

Against this background, arguments are made for the legislation of the system of guardians for adults. It is argued that the present system or a newly introduced system should be given flexibility, and the scope of the system should be extended to include the intellectual disables and elderly people whose capacity of judgment becomes worse, and supplementary function to support the management of their property and personal care should be added to the system in order to protect their tights. The system is called guardianship for adults or law of guardianship of adults, for the objects of protection under the system are adults in comparison with the guardianship for minors. In European countries and U.S.A., in view of the respect for self-determination and the promotion of participation in social activities (Normalization), such systems have been established and social conditions have been improved for that purpose. Examples are the system of advocacy in Austria, the system of adult guardian in Germany, the system of public guardianship in the United States and Canada, and the system of endurable power of attorney in England. Such systems do not deny full capacity of act as the present system in Japan, but have flexibility in order to respond each case separately to the extent that it is necessary to represent or support the people under the systems. There are a variety of types such as voluntary guardianship and statutory guardianship. However, a common feature is that both management of property and care and support for daily life are done only to the necessary extent, respecting the self-determination and personal dignity in view of the protection of human rights. In Japan, it is not desirable to deny or restrict the capacity formally and evenly. The right of self-determination and the will of elderly people should be respected to the utmost extent. And a similar system, which is closely related to the care and support for daily life, should be established to support supplementarily to the necessary extent.

In April 1998, the tentative plan for revision of Civil Code regarding Adult Guardianship Law will be proposed by the Justice Ministry.

Maintenance Services of Property by Municipal Corporations and the System of Using Assets

Some municipal corporations such as Nakano Ward, Suginami Ward and Bunkyou Ward of Tokyo tender services for elderly people living alone, in which services for keeping of their passbooks, the deposits or withdrawal, the payment of charges of public utilities, the keeping in safe-deposit boxes in banks of important documents such as title deeds and negotiable instruments are included. In some municipalities such as Musashino City, a system of using assets of elderly people like reverse mortgages is established, under which with their assets as collateral the city lends money for a welfare fund to the users of the services in public non-profit corporations for welfare.

However, there are shortcomings such as the reduced value of collateral in case of the increase of total money lent when the users live longer, what kind of step should be taken in cases of the loss of mental capacity of elderly people while using the services, and the unexpected event of decrease in value of the assets.

Conclusion

In addition, there are problems about charged nursing homes which have increased in number rapidly since 1980. In 1996, there were 250 homes in Japan. It cost ¥20 million (approximately A$225,000, NZ$250,000) on average to enter such a home, and after that it also cost some ¥100,000 (approximately A$1,150, NZ$1,250) per month for living expenses. It is rather expensive for elderly people to enter such a home. Although charged nursing homes have the advantage of promoting self-help under the difficult circumstance of financial resources for the welfare budget of elderly people, some troubles have occurred. For examle, private enterprises run homes without adequate staff and training for care and treatment, elderly people in such a home dissatisfied with care services and expenses, and bankruptcies after the payment of the entire amount necessary to enter a home.

Although elderly people in Japan are willing to work and have working ability, it is very difficult for them to find a suitable job. It is true that they have considerable assets, but they mostly consist of real property as their residence. If it can be turned into cash flow, elderly people can ensure living expenses in addition to the public pension system. In Japan, it is a crucial question whether elderly people can help themselves, what type of support their family members should provide, and what the state should do for them in order for the elderly people to live a peaceful life.

PART II: FREE MARKET and LEGAL REGULATIONS
(I): MARKET ECONOMY and LEGAL REGULATIONS

4 Globalization and Regulatory Reforms
──Toward A New Model of Law──

Kazuhiro TSUCHIDA

>   Introduction
>   1 Problems of Harmonization and Neoliberal Theories
>   2 Toward A New Model of Law
>   Conclusion

Introduction

1. After the demise of socialism in the USSR and Eastern Europe, it seemed that "human rights, democracy and market economy" were increasingly becoming "global standards" of the New World Order and that many nation states experienced similar neoliberal reforms, including reorganization of administrative bodies and deregulation, even in the Western countries called "Keynsian welfare states."

It is a complex problem how one can assess "global standards" of the New World Order. Although human rights are said to be universal and cosmopolitan values that are valid in all societies and times, they are basically the products of the modern Europe and, therefore, it is not evident that they are applicable in all the Asian societies at the end of the twentieth century. In addition, there is a sensitive problem whether citizens' political rights may be restricted in order to promote economic developments in the developing countries.

As for "market economy," it is sometimes pointed out that market economy may reshape unclear relations between government and businesses in the Asian countries ("crony capitalism"), including Japan, into those of economic rationality and transparency[1]. Free trade is also said that it can contribute to the world peace through formation of economic dependence among many nations, preventing economic blockages in the world[2]. However, so-called free market or market economy as one of global standards of the New World Order, is, in reality, a new world economic-regime in which powerful multinational enterprises can freely set production facilities in, procure capital and labor from, and export to any countries all over the world. It is in this process that infringements of human rights, crises of democracy and survival of people and global environmental problems are coming into existence.

In any event, during the latter half of the 1990s, the superiority of capitalism or market economy has been becoming extremely dubious especially since monetary and economic crises in the Eastern and South Eastern Asian countries, the threat of Russia's default, long continuing depression in Japan, the crisis of American hedge-funds which were believed to be free from losses, growing support for social democracy in Europe and a "tragedy in Seattle" in 1999. But no one knows where the world is going.

2. Confronted with the global socio-economic transformation mentioned above, many nation states have still been in the midst of domestic reforms. For instance, in Japan, since the advent of Hosokawa Administration in 1993, the government has more vigorously enforced deregulation policies with reference to not only economic but also social regulations. The number of deregulatory measures, decided by the Cabinet in March 2000, amounted to 1,268 in sixteen fields[3] (telecommunication, environment, competition policy, legal affairs, banking, security & insurance, transportation, energy, distribution & agriculture, housing & land use, public works, medical care, welfare, employment & labor, education, product standards & certification and public/official qualifications).

Important principles of deregulation are as follows:
(1) economic regulations are, as a general rule, to be abolished and permitted only exceptionally; social regulations are to be decreased to the minimum

extent necessary,
(2) transparency and harmonization with global standards are to be required,
(3) prior regulations should be abolished and post-inspecting regulations ought to be preferred, and
(4) accountability for the necessity of a regulation is to be on the side of an administrative agency.

These principles have gradually been shaped since 1981 by some neo-corporative agencies, such as the Second Temporary Investigation Committee of Administration, the Administrative Reform Promotion Committee and the Administrative Reform Commission and so forth, of which members were mainly from business circles and major governmental departments, and seldom from labor unions, never from consumer groups which should be main beneficiaries from deregulation. What is worse, these principles of deregulatory measures have been decided without significant involvement of the Diet, which "shall be the highest" and the "sole law-making organ of the state" (Article 41 of the Constitution).

The main reason leading to active deregulation policy is seen in the recognition of its proponents that Japan has no choice but to abolish governmental regulations that are believed to be the main cause of "domestic high cost constitution" in the face of "world-wide fierce competition under the global market economy." They also advocated that Japan should have "simple, efficient and transparent government" which costs less to the nation.

As to reorganization of the central administrative organizations, the Administrative Reform Conference submitted its final report that recommended reorganization of the central administrative departments, reinforcement of the Cabinet capacities and outsourcing the administrative departments' functions to the private sector[4]. Moreover, the Judicial Reform Council, established in 1999, is going to publicize a report that will reform a part of Japanese judicial system.

Part II : Free Market and Legal Regulations
(i) Market Economy and Legal Regulations

This essay grasps that the nature of these national reforms, deregulation in particular, and international changes since 1989 have neoliberal and neoconservative aspects, restoring economic liberalism.

1 Problems of Harmonization and Neoliberal Theories

1. What precisely is a problem with these reforms and changes? Although there are many problems to be discussed about them, I will, here, examine "harmonization with global standards" of regulations. Admittedly, economic globalization and international market competition have been putting some regulations in the nation states into convergence. However, there are some internal contradictions as regards harmonization or, at least, formalistic harmonization of law.

A contradiction is that formalistic harmonization of nation states' laws may produce substantial disharmony of the market situations. A good example is a social regulation, such as food safety regulation. According to Section 3 of the Agreement on the Application of Sanitary and Phytosanitary Measures (SPS), which is one of Annexes to the WTO Agreement, member countries shall base their sanitary and phytosanitary measures on international standards, which are, in effect, set by the Codex Alimentarius Commission, a joint commission of FAO and WHO. For instance, the Commission sets a maximum standard of Malathion, 8 PPM, applied to unpolished rice. Because the amount of a food a consumer ingests varies depending on social and cultural factors of a nation, setting a single maximum standard of an agricultural chemical applied to a food makes its total amount consumers ingest completely different among the nations. The reason why this problem happens has something to do with the fact that agribusiness multinational enterprises have powerful influences upon the Commission through submitting position papers to it as scientific data on food safety standards[5]. Agribusiness multinational enterprises are mainly interested in export standards of food additives or agricultural chemicals and not in how much additives or agricultural chemicals consumers will take. This suggests that WTO/SPS gives priority to multinational enterprises' concerns for trade costs over people's health and safety in the world.

2. A similar problem arises as to harmonization of antimonopoly laws. For example, in a hypothetical case, an automobile manufacturer, which engages in business both in A and B countries, merges with its competitor and results in occupying a market share of 40% in A market, and merges with another car manufacturer, resulting in a market share of 30% in B market. If one, based on formalistic harmonization, assumes that a threshold market share of 35% is presumed to impede effective competition, the merger in A market will be prohibited and the merger in B market will be tolerated. Is this a right solution in all cases? If, in B market, other automobile manufacturers have little competitiveness against the merging companies, if car dealers have little bargaining power against them, and if consumers in B market have little sense of right against the automobile manufacturers, shouldn't the merger in B market be prohibited even if its market share is below the formalistic threshold of 35%? In short, in such a case, formal disharmonization of law will be necessary in order to produce substantial harmonization of market situations.

3. A word must be said about one of the most fundamental thoughts of deregulatory measures. It is often pointed out that advantages of deregulation consist in the fact that the whole gains enjoyed by firms, laborers and consumers outweigh the whole losses suffered by them[6]. Fundamentally, the same or similar way of thinking is found in neoliberal theories such as R. Posner's. He decides desirability of an act or a legal institution depending on whether it increases social whole surplus or not[7]. The social whole surplus increases in the case of "Pareto improvement," that is, when one's surplus increases without decreasing others' surplus. However, Posner doesn't take it the only case increasing the social whole surplus. It increases when producers' (sellers') surplus increases more than consumers' (buyers') surplus decreases.

He makes this "principle of wealth maximization" basic normative criterion in deciding whether an act is legal or a legal institution is desirable. Posner's theory of wealth maximization does not seem to be inconsistent with the fundamental thought of deregulation in Japan. If this is right, the basic idea of deregulation in Japan should be faced by the criticism that it is utilitarianism which give priority to the increase of the whole surplus over distributive inequality or infringements of human fundamental rights. Another model should be pursued from different viewpoints.

2 Toward A New Model of Law

1. Based on the recognition above mentioned, I will address myself to the problem of how a regulatory reform should be done in the age of economic globalization and world-wide market competition. Although developing trends toward market economy might be inevitable, trade liberalization or market competition ought to be qualified within the sphere of its grounds. Domestic systems of regulations should be designed from the standpoint of what legal structure is necessary to secure human fundamental rights and survival[8].

2. It is difficult to design in detail an ideal legal framework of a state's regulatory system at this point of time. However, only proposing a few principles of regulations, such as transparency, impartiality, minimum extent necessary and so forth[9], is not enough. Another approach is to count, as contemporarily important areas to be governed by regulations, finance, telecommunication, environment, labor, social security and so forth in addition to night watchman state's function—the police, national defense and judicial system. But what we should pursue is not in what areas we must maintain regulations, but for what purposes and of what contents regulations are essential. Here I will approach from a rather theoretical viewpoint—normative and legal theories of justice and property.

3. In *A Theory of Justice*, John Rawls states that political and social institutions of a society ought to conform to two principles of justice which are intended to be a protest against compensating infringements of minority's rights with majority's utilities. In the book, Rawls argues how free and equal persons

agree with each other, in the "original position" covered with "the veil of ignorance," to adopt two principles of justice as to major social institutions that distribute "primary social goods" and burdens of social life. Principles of justice are,

(1) the principle of equal liberty, and
(2) the principle of fair equality of opportunity and the difference principle[10].

In Part Two, he argues the relationship between the two principles and market system as follows. Market system can be sustainable, so far as it assures advantages that it is consistent with freedom of occupation, dispersion of economic powers, and efficiencies (in production, allocation of resources and distribution of goods), on the condition that it be surrounded by requisite background institutions, such as constitutional law that secures citizens' equal rights, the principle of fair equality of opportunity, and guaranteeing social minimum by family allowances, special payments for sickness and unemployment or a graded income supplement[11].

Attention should be paid to "market economy," "market system" and "free market" used by Rawls. He does not necessarily equalize these words to capitalism. "It is evident, then, that there is no essential tie between the use of free markets and private ownership of the instruments of production." Even a "socialist regime can avail itself of the advantages of this system[12]." "Which of these systems and many intermediate forms most fully answers to the requirements of justice cannot, I think, be determined in advance." It "depends in large part upon the traditions, institutions, and social forces of each country, and its particular historical circumstances[13]."

4. Moreover, in contrast to theorists arguing for 'universal commodification,' M.J. Radin admits coexistence of both market and nonmarket domains and presents an idea that it is related to human flourishing and social justice to preserve and evolutionarily foster the nonmarket aspect of provision and use of goods that deviate most from laissez-faire—human beings' home, work, food,

environment, education, communication, health, bodily integrity, sexuality, family life, and political life[14] ("evolutionary pluralism"). As a part of it, she presents an idea of preserving and fostering nonmarket aspects in market domain, for instance, judging that a relationship between a person and a "personal property[15]" is stronger in entitlement than a relationship between a person and a "fungible property[16]." According to her, legislatures and judges are already doing these things tacitly and without directly focusing on the issues.

Another strategy against universal commodification is to distinguish four kinds of inalienability[17]—status inalienability, community inalienability, prohibition inalienability, and market inalienability—and to judge whether a thing may be treated as a commodity according to non-commodification, permission of gifts (voluntary transfer) and incomplete commodification[18].

5. What do these theories mentioned above suggest as a hint for a model of law that assures an ideal situation? Whereas deregulation in Japan seems to be extremely influenced by efficiency-oriented theories, my tentative takes it important and essential to address two issues: "rights-based structuralization of market connotation" and "limitation of market boundary." While the former is based on utilitarian wealth maximization principles, the latter is a version of rights theories. The latter aims to conceptualize, as rights and non-rights, interests in a society and set a framework of priorities that a nation state ought to assure, and it attempts to restrict certain kinds of commodification.

Concretely, market connotation of a nation state can be classified from my point of view as,

(1) fundamental human rights as citizens' and laborers' rights to life, health and safety,

(2) property rights as human rights which are enjoyed by small merchants, independent businessmen, farmers, fishermen and consumers,

(3) small corporations' property rights as non-human rights and non-monopoly possessions,

(4) private monopoly possessions as institutional assurance of capitalism.

Basically, priority should be given in this ordinal order. (1) and (2) are pre-state natural human rights and therefore are given priority over (3) and (4). (3) are the rights which are assured by state laws. In order to assure the priorities, nation states ought to regulate some kinds of market participants, goods and services to deal, market processes and market consequences, by means of economic, social and antimonopoly measures.

5. It is important, as regards limitation of market boundary, that there are differences in grounds, contents and spheres among four categories of inalienability mentioned above. For example, inalienability of voting right is grounded in that it is a right and, at the same time, a kind of duty as well. On the other hand, the reason of inalienability of entitlements to social security and welfare benefits is that it rigidify possession, precluding change, signifying some strong form of inseparability from the holder. Furthermore, while neither onerous nor gratuitous transfers of voting rights are permitted, gratuitous transfer of human organs should, according to Radin, be permitted. In any event, it is essential to decide whether a thing may be treated as a commodity according to non-commodification, permission of gifts (voluntary transfer) and incomplete commodification against a background that there are asymmetric relationships of power in a real world.

Conclusion

This essay has tried to describe a "legal structure model of egalitarian market system" as of a nation state level in order to control unbridled market economy, which is linked to globalization of capitalism and world-wide competition. In this sense, it is essential for nation states to coordinate one another if they enforce law based on this model. Especially essential are coordination and solidarity among civil societies. As a first step, people can make a network of regional coordination toward controling of global capitalism.

(1) Yoshikazu Sakamoto, "An Alternative Agenda Against the World-Wide

Market Economy," *The World*, No. 652, p. 57(1998). However, Sakamoto's focus is on whether rationalization of a state and a market leads to their democratization or not.

(2) Ernst-Urlich Petersmann, Paul Krugman and Brian Barry, "The Feasibility and Desirability of Global Free Trade," in Gerain Parry, Asif Qureshi and Hillel Steiner ed., *The Legal and Moral Aspects of International Trade* 7(1998).

(3) Cabinet Decision on March 31, 2000.

(4) The Administrative Reform Conference, *The Final Report* (December 3, 1997).

(5) Michiyo Kondo, "Harmonization under the WTO Regime and the Health and Safety of the Consumers" in I. Takahashi & S. Honma ed., *The Modern Economy and Reforms of Legal Structure* 310(1997).

(6) For instance, see Akira Kawamoto, *Regulatory Reform-Competition and Coordination*-135 (1998).

(7) Richard Posner, *The Economics of Justice*, Part 4(1981).

(8) See also, Kazuhiro Tsuchida, "Deregulation──In the Age of Reform and Globalization──" Review of Law (Horitsu Jiho), Vol. 70, No 3 (1998), "Market Ideology and Modern Theories of Justice," 26 Law and Science (Ho no Kagaku) 39(1997) and "Antitrust Law of the USA and A Neoliberal Theory of Chicago School," in I. Takahashi & S. Honma ed., *The Modern Economy and Reforms of Legal Structure* 159(1997).

(9) A. Kawamoto, supra note 6, at 190.

(10) John Rawls, *A Theory Of Justice*, Part One (1973, Oxford paperback).

(11) J. Rawls, supra note 10, at 274-284.

(12) J. Rawls, supra note 10, at 271. See also, David Miller, *Market, State and Community* (1989), arguing for market socialism.

(13) J. Rawls, supra note 10, at 274. It is well known that Rawls, in *A Theory of Justice*, confined his theory to "the basic structure of society conceived for the time being as a closed system isolated from other societies." According to Charles Beitz, the reason why Rawls did not consider the justice of the law of nations is that each society was thought to be self-sufficient and believed to have little mutual interaction(Charles Beitz, *Political Theory and International Relations* 100(1979)). But this assumption is hard to maintain in the world at the end of the twentieth century. Beitz is one of theorists who tried to apply Rawls' theory to international society. I had thought, according to Beitz, that extension of Rawl's theory to international relations would have been as follows. That is, participants of the "original position" come from not only

national but also international societies. Because there is the "veil of ignorance", they neither know what kinds of natural resources lie under the ground nor where they are, although they are thought to know natural resources are distributed partially all over the world. Moreover, participants are presupposed that they don't know in what society they are to be reborn—highly industrialized society or least developed society where people's lives have to critically depend on export of a single kind of agricultural product. This is one of the most decisive reasons why international participants of the original position must agree two principles of justice, according to the maximin rule that one is to adopt the alternative the worst outcome of which is superior to the worst outcomes of the others (C. Beitz, ibid. pp. 136-161).

Although Beitz had not concretely written about an implication in terms of international extension, my presumption had been as follows. Firstly, the rights assured by the first principle of justice, such as freedom of speech and assembly, freedom of the person, the right to hold personal property and so forth, are to be given priority in international relations as well. Secondly, people in the world should be assured to have the same social and economic opportunity, free from social surrounding differences such as "caste system," so far as they have the same talents, abilities and willingness. Furthermore, they are to be secured to get rid of bad influences on their socio-economic situations caused by the partial distribution of natural resources in the world or differences of human natural talents. These are human beings' common assets that are though to have been agreed, as to the international difference principle, to share among people on earth at the "international original position" (K. Tsuchida, "Theories and Problems for Regulatory Reform," Shizuoka University Review of Law and Politics, Vol. 3, No. 3/4 (1999)).

However, Rawls showed a different way of extension in his lately published book, *The Law Of Peoples* (1999). As I haven't had preparation to examine it, I have no choice, at this point of time, but to limit my tentative to national aspects, that is, domestic regulatory reforms and theories for them.

(14) M.J. Radin, "Justice and Market Domain" in J. W. Chapman & J. R. Pennock ed., *Markets and Justice* 179 (Nomos 31, 1989).

(15) In *Reinterpreting Property* (1993), she wrote that she should have called it property that is bound up with personhood constitutive rather than personal (p. 2). An example is a wedding ring that is owned by someone who feels it has symbolic emotional significance (p. 16).

(16) A wedding ring is a fungible property when owned by a jewelry store for

resale (p. 16), as individuals are not attached to it except as to a source of money (p. 2).

(17) M.J. Radin, "Market-Inalienability," 100 Harv. L. Rev. 1849, 1852-1855 (1987). Examples of status-inalienability, community-inalienability, prohibition-inalienability, and market-inalienability are, respectively, nontransferability of entitlements to social security and welfare benefits, voting rights, heroin, and restrictions on salability of work and housing.

(18) M.J. Radin, supra note 17, at 1915-1921.

5 Regulatory Framework for Privatised Industries

Michael Crommelin

Introduction
1 Competition Policy
2 Competition Law
3 Access to Infrastructure
4 Economic Regulation
Conclusion

Introduction

Government has always played a prominent part in the Australian economy. In the nineteenth century, government assumed responsibility for provision of major components of social infrastructure: transportation, communications and power. The task was too great for the private sector. In the twentieth century, government remained dominant in those fields, and entered others such as banking and insurance. The rationale was more often pragmatic than ideological. In a small and isolated economy, the risk of monopoly was high; public monopoly was preferable to private.[1]

Government participation in the economy has taken various forms. The shortcomings of the government department were soon recognized, and boards, commissions and statutory authorities were established to perform functions which were seen to be beyond the capacity of the department. The quest for both efficiency and accountability produced a rich variety of public institutions which reflected the inherent tension between those two objectives.[2]

Australian administrative law has several instruments designed to enhance accountability for the exercise of government authority. These include rights of access to information[3], investigation of claims of maladministration by ombudsmen[4], administrative review by tribunals[5], judicial review by courts[6], and overall supervision by parliaments. These instruments, more or less, provide the regulatory framework not only for government officials and departments but also for boards, commissions and statutory authorities.

In recent years, accountability has yielded considerable ground to efficiency. This explains the process of corporatisation of government agencies. The term "corporatisation" has been coined to describe the conversion of an agency from a statutory authority structure (established by Act of Parliament) or a departmental structure (established by Cabinet) to a company structure in conformity with the Corporations Law applicable to the private sector[7], with the government as the owner of the shares in that company. One consequence of corporatisation of government agencies has been to remove most of the decisions of government corporations from the ambit of scrutiny and review pursuant to administrative law.[8]

But corporatisation may represent the beginning rather than the end. To quote Farrar and McCabe:[9]

"Corporatisation can be viewed from one perspective as the extension of the drive for efficiency within the public sector while retaining ownership within the public sector. The other perspective is that corporatisation is simply a poor man's privatisation."

Moreover:[10]

"Corporatisation is part of a policy of commercialisation which in its turn is part of a policy liberalisation or deregulation of the economy. It uses the private sector as the model of efficiency and aims to replicate as far as possible the corporate firm in the private sector. Yet the replication can go only so far: the absence of low-cost monitors and political interference means that corporatised entities are almost inevitably less efficient in agency cost terms than their counterparts in the private sector."

Privatisation releases the corporate entity from the last vestiges of scrutiny and review pursuant to administrative law. The new member of the private sector is subject to the general law applicable to its commercial activities. In some cases, that may suffice. The discipline of competitive markets may deliver the desired efficiency. In cases of market failure, however, there is no reason to expect efficiency. Consideration must be given to new forms of regulation designed to mitigate the consequences of private monopoly.

1 Competition Policy

On 11 April 1995, the Council of Australian Governments (COAG)[11] adopted a National Competition Policy, following a detailed review of the Australian economy by an Independent Committee of Inquiry chaired by Professor Fred Hilmer.[12] The National Competition Policy is based upon the philosophy that efficiency in the Australian economy will be enhanced by removal of barriers to competition. The principal components of the policy include:

- extension of the ambit of the anti-competitive provisions of Part IV of the *Trade Practices Act 1974* (Cth.);
- establishment of a national access regime providing rights of access to essential infrastructure;
- restructuring government monopolies by separating the business functions which are amenable to competition from those which are not, subjecting the former to competition law and developing new regulatory mechanisms for the latter;
- placing public and private businesses on an equal footing ("competitive neutrality"); and
- monitoring the prices of government businesses in those cases where such businesses retain a significant degree of market power.

Under this National Competition Policy, the new regulatory framework for privatised industries in Australia relies heavily on competition law, supplemented by new provisions for access to infrastructure and new instruments of economic regulation designed to deal with residual areas of "natural monopoly".

2 Competition Law

Part IV of the *Trade Practices Act 1974* (Cth.) deals with four types of restrictive trade practices. These provisions apply to privatised industries and usually to government corporations.

- Section 45 of the Act prohibits contracts, arrangements or understandings which have the purpose or effect of substantially lessening competition.

- Sections 45A, 47 and 48 prohibit a wide range of price-fixing practices, including resale price maintenance and price discrimination.
- Section 46 prohibits abuse of market power by corporations which have a substantial degree of power in a market for goods and services.
- Section 50 regulates market concentration. It prohibits the acquisition of the shares or assets of a corporation if that acquisition would allow the purchaser to dominate a market for goods or services or strengthen its existing domination of a market for goods or services in Australia.

The Act confers power on the Australian Competition and Consumer Commission (ACCC) to grant an authorisation of arrangements which lessen competition (s. 45), exclusive dealing arrangements (s. 47) and mergers and acquisitions (s. 50) where it is demonstrated that the public benefit derived from the arrangement or acquisition exceeds the public detriment attributable to it.[13] A decision of the ACCC is subject to review by the Australian Competition Tribunal.[14]

The Act does not contain any exhaustive definition of "competition"; it merely states that the term includes competition from imported goods and services.[15] The determination of any matter relating to competition requires the identification of the relevant "market". Section 41 provides that "market" means a market in Australia and includes goods and services which are substitutes for those under examination.[16] Specification of the relevant product and the geographical area of the market for that product in Australia gives rise to considerable practical difficulty.[17]

The structure of a market is also relevant to competition.[18] Two important aspects of market structure are concentration and entry. Concentration requires a consideration of the number, size, distribution and importance of market participants. The greater the concentration in a market, the more likely that any arrangement or conduct will impinge upon competition. Entry refers to the capacity for a non-participant to commence business in a market or to the capacity for participants to expand their businesses in a market. Any arrangement or practice which constitutes a barrier to entry lessens competition.

Privatised industries are frequently engaged in markets characterised by concentration and barriers to entry. Part IV of the *Trade Practices Act 1974* regulates the conduct of these industries in such markets.

3 Access to Infrastructure[19]

3.1 Essential Facilities Doctrine

Courts in the United States of America have developed an essential facilities doctrine under section 2 of the Sherman Act to deal with barriers to entry created by monopoly control of infrastructure. Where infrastructure cannot be duplicated (for economic or practical reasons) and access to that infrastructure is required for entry into a market, this doctrine provides a right of access to a potential entrant upon reasonable terms.

In Australia, the characteristics of natural monopoly which gave rise to the essential facilities doctrine in the USA are found in electricity transmission grids, natural gas pipelines, telecommunication networks, railways, ports and airports. The Hilmer Report found that competition was inhibited in a number of industries by lack of access to infrastructure. At the same time, however, the Report noted that existing competition law (in particular, section 46 of the *Trade Practices Act 1974*) may not include an essential facilities doctrine comparable to that in the USA. Accordingly, the Report recommended amendment of the *Trade Practices Act 1974* to include provision of an access regime.[19]

That recommendation was implemented by the *Competition Policy Reform Act 1995* (Cth.) which introduced Part IIIA into the *Trade Practices Act 1974*. Part IIIA includes three mechanisms for allowing access to services provided by essential facilities such as rail networks, electricity grids and natural gas pipelines. These are the access declaration, the access undertaking and the effective access regime procedure. These mechanisms are mutually exclusive; an essential facility cannot be subject to more than one of them at any time.

3. 2   *Access Declaration*

An access declaration is made by the designated Minister, usually the Commonwealth Minister but occasionally the State Premier in the case of a service provided by a State authority.[20] A person seeking access may apply to the National Competition Council (NCC) for a recommendation that a service be declared.[21] Before making any such recommendation, the NCC must be satisfied that:

- access to the service will promote competition in a market other than that for the service;
- it would be uneconomical for anyone to develop another facility to provide the service;
- the facility is of national significance having regard to its size, its importance to interstate or overseas trade and commerce or its importance to the national economy;
- access would not cause undue risk to health and safety; and
- access would not be contrary to the public interest.[22]

In the event of a recommendation for access from the NCC to the designated Minister, the Minister must also give consideration to the same matters in deciding whether to make a declaration.[23] Once a service is declared, a person may enter into negotiations for access with the owner of the facility and failing agreement may apply for binding arbitration by the ACCC.[24] The ACCC must then take the following matters into consideration in deciding the terms and conditions of access to the service:

- the legitimate business interests of the provider of the service and the investment in the facility;
- the public interest in competition;
- the interests of all persons currently entitled to use the service;
- the direct cost of providing access;
- the value to the provider of extensions where the cost of those extensions is met by a person other than the provider;
- the requirements for safe and reliable operation of the facility;
- the requirements for economically efficient operation of the facility; and
- any other factors that the ACCC thinks relevant.[25]

Decisions of the Commonwealth Minister and the ACCC are subject to review by the Australian Competition Tribunal.[26]

3.3 Access Undertaking

An access undertaking may be given in respect of an existing or proposed service.[27] Such an undertaking comes into operation only if accepted by the ACCC, which is required to have regard to the following matters:

- the legitimate business interests of the provider of the service;
- the public interest in competition;
- the interests of persons who might want access to the service; and
- any other factors that the ACCC thinks relevant.[28]

3.4 Effective Access Regime

The effective access regime procedure is designed to provide recognition of an existing access regime for a service. The procedure involves a recommendation by the NCC and a decision by the designated Minister.[29] Both the NCC and the Minister must apply the relevant principles set out in clause 6 of the Competition Principles Agreement concluded in 1995 by the Commonwealth, the States and the Territories. These include:

- whether it would be economically feasible to duplicate the facility;
- whether access to the service is necessary in order to permit effective competition in another market;
- whether the facility is of national significance having regard to its size, its importance to interstate or overseas trade and commerce or its importance to the national economy;
- whether safe access is possible;
- whether the facility has influence beyond a State or Territory boundary;
- whether substantial difficulties could arise from the location of the facility in more than one jurisdiction.

A decision by the designated Minister that a State access regime is not an effective access regime for the purposes of Part IIIA of the *Trade Practices Act 1974* is subject to review by the Australian Competition Tribunal.[30]

3.5 *National Third Party Access Code for Natural Gas*

On 7 November 1997, the Commonwealth, States and Territories concluded the Natural Gas Pipelines Access Agreement providing for the establishment of a National Third Party Access Code for Natural Gas Pipeline Systems (the Code). Pursuant to that Agreement, the South Australian Parliament enacted the *Gas Pipelines Access (South Australia) Act 1997* to provide the legislative foundation for the Code and the Commonwealth Parliament enacted the *Gas Pipelines Access (Commonwealth) Act 1998* to give effect to the scheme.

The Code sets out the access principles to apply under a uniform framework for natural gas transmission and distribution pipelines. The owner or operator of a pipeline that is subject to the Code must lodge an access arrangement with the relevant regulator, which in the case of transmission pipelines is the ACCC. An access arrangement is similar to an access undertaking Part IIIA of the *Trade Practices Act 1974* and sets out the terms and conditions upon which access will be made available to gas transmission and distribution services. Those terms and conditions must include a description of the services offered by the owner or operator of the pipeline, reference tariffs for services determined through a competitive tender process or set in accordance with principles contained in section 8 of the Code, the terms and conditions applicable to services, and the policies governing management of pipeline capacity, trading of pipeline capacity and priority of access to pipeline capacity. An access arrangement for a transmission pipeline must be approved by the ACCC, which is empowered to do so only if satisfied that the access arrangement satisfies the minimum requirements prescribed by the Code. Decisions of the ACCC are subject to review by the Australian Competition Tribunal.

3.6 *The Victorian Draft Determination*

The significance of the natural gas access regime is demonstrated by a draft determination issued in May 1998 by the ACCC in respect of access to the transmission services provided by Transmission Pipelines Australia Pty. Ltd. This company is owned by the Victorian Government. In turn, it owns and maintains the existing high pressure transmission pipelines in Victoria. Prior to this draft determination, the Victorian Government had announced its intention to sell the company as part of the process of privatisation of the gas industry in Victoria. The draft determination proposed a fair rate of return of 7% before tax on an asset base of 100% of the depreciated optimised replacement cost. This was significantly below the rate of 10.16% advocated by the Victorian Government. The draft determination, if adopted, would result in a reduction of about 17% in projected revenue of Transmission Pipelines Australia Pty. Ltd., with a consequential reduction of some $800 million in sale price of the company. The Victorian Government has suspended the privatisation of the company pending resolution of this matter.

4 Economic Regulation

The Victorian electricity industry provides a useful case study of the privatisation of a government monopoly and the establishment of a new regulatory framework applicable to the private participants in that industry.

Part II: Free Market and Legal Regulations
(i) Market Economy and Legal Regulations

Until 1995, the electricity industry was conducted as a government monopoly by the State Electricity Commission of Victoria (SECV), which was responsible for the generation, transmission, distribution and sale of electricity plus the regulation of technical and safety matters.

The *Electricity Industry Act 1993* (Vic) gave effect to the State Government's objectives with respect to the structure and regulation of the industry consequent upon privatisation. The structural changes were designed to separate national monopoly elements of the industry from potentially competitive elements. The SECV was replaced by the following bodies:[31]

- Generation Victoria, comprising 5 separate business divisions engaged in generation of electricity;
- PowerNet Victoria, a transmission grid entity established to own, maintain and manage the high voltage grid;
- Victorian Power Exchange, an independent entity to monitor and control the wholesale electricity market and ensure the security of electricity supply;
- Five regionally-based private distribution companies formed under the Corporations Law comprising former distribution assets of the SECV and the eleven municipal electricity undertakings; and
- State Electricity Commission of Victoria to discharge existing contractual commitments on a limited basis.

Part 12 of the *Electricity Industry Act 1993* deals with regulation of the industry by providing that the electricity industry is a regulated industry under the *Office of the Regulator-General Act 1994* (Vic). In addition, Part 12 establishes a licensing system for electricity generation, transmission, distribution, supply and sale, administered by the Regulator-General.

The declared purpose of the *Office of the Regulator-General Act 1994* is:

"the creation of an economic regulatory framework for regulated industries which promotes and safeguards competition and fair and efficient market conduct or, in the absence of a competitive market, which promotes the stimulation of competitive market conduct and the prevention of the misuse of monopoly power."

The objectives of the Office of the Regulator-General under the *Electricity Industry Act 1993* are:[32]

- to promote competition in the generation, supply and sale of electricity;
- to ensure the maintenance of an efficient and economic system for the generation, transmission, distribution, supply and sale of electricity;
- to protect the interests of consumers with respect to electricity prices and the safety, reliability and quality of electricity supply; and
- to facilitate the maintenance of a financially viable electricity supply industry.

In other words, the regulatory framework for the electricity industry encourages industry participants and their customers to negotiate commercial outcomes, with intervention by the Office of the Regulator-General only where it is necessary to correct abuse of market power in the interests of competition or customers.[33]

Section 11 of the *Office of the Regulator-General Act 1994* provides that the Office is not subject to the direction or control of the Minister in the performance of its functions except as provided in any Act of the Victorian Parliament.

The main powers of the Office of the Regulator-General in relation to the electricity industry relate to standards and conditions of service and supply of electricity, licensing and market conduct.[34] The Office may conduct inquiries into such matters and may publish reports.[35] It has extensive powers to enforce its determinations and licence conditions.[36] Both the Government and the Office of the Regulator-General have powers to regulate tariffs, charges and

Part II: Free Market and Legal Regulations
(i) Market Economy and Legal Regulations

prices with respect to electricity.[37] On 20 June 1995 the Government exercised its powers by way of an Order in Council known as the Tariff Order, thereby excluding the Office from this function for the time being.

The behaviour of participants in Victoria's wholesale electricity market (VicPool) is regulated by pool rules developed by the electricity industry and approved by the Office of the Regulator-General. The rules cover areas including the application and admission of participants, prudential requirements, dispute resolution, bidding into the pool, generator scheduling, determination of payments to generators, customer charges and pool fees.[38]

The Office of the Regulator-General has also approved a series of codes developed by the industry, including the System Code (dealing with the safe and secure operation of the power system), Wholesale Metering Code (ensuring measurement of electricity transferred between pool participants), Distribution Code (designed to ensure safe, efficient and reliable operation of the distribution system), Supply and Sale Code (setting conditions of sale of electricity to franchise customers) and Retail Tariff Metering Code (regulating the installation of new metering equipment).[39]

An additional layer of regulation will apply to the Victorian electricity industry when the National Electricity Market is established by 1 July 1999. The National Competition Policy endorsed by Commonwealth, State and territory governments at the COAG meeting in April 1995 included electricity arrangements to be implemented through the National Grid Management Council. Subsequently, in May 1996 the governments of New South Wales, Victoria, Queensland, South Australia and the Australian Capital Territory entered into the National Electricity Market Legislation Agreement. Pursuant to that Agreement, South Australia enacted the *National Electricity (South Australia) Act 1996* and each of the participating States and the ACT has subsequently adopted that statute in its jurisdiction. This legislation gives effect to the National Electricity Code, and establishes the National Electricity

Tribunal to deal with allegations that a Code participant has breached a provision of the Code.

Conclusion

Privatisation of government monopolies in Australia has not been accompanied by deregulation. Instead, new regulatory regimes have been devised to meet new challenges. These regimes are based upon concepts of competition, market and price. Although sometimes described as "light-handed", these regimes are far from simple in their nature and effect. Complexity is as much a feature of the new regimes as it was of the old. It is too early to judge their effectiveness. What is clear, however, is that these new approaches reflect a fundamental shift in attitude towards government in Australia. They are constructed on the premise that government has failed to perform adequately in industries hitherto entrusted to government monopoly. They acknowledge the problems inherent in natural monopoly, but prefer the solution of regulated private monopoly to that of government monopoly. Above all, they mark the ascendancy of efficiency over accountability in Australian public policy.

(1) See, for example, Crommelin, M and Hunter, R, "Monopoly and Competition in Energy Supply: Australia" *Journal of Energy and Natural Resources Law* (December 1989 Supplement) 135.

(2) Wettenhall, "Corporations and Corporatisation: An Administrative History Perspective" (1995) 6 *Public Law Review* 7.

(3) *Freedom of Information Act 1982* (Cth).

(4) *Ombudsman Act 1976* (Cth).

(5) *Administrative Appeals Tribunal Act 1975* (Cth).

(6) *Administrative Decisions (Judicial Review) Act 1977* (Cth).

(7) Michael Howard, Statement before the Industrial Relations Commission of NSW (IRC No 789 of 1993) quoted in Wettenhall, R, "Corporations and Corporatisation: An Administrative History Perspective" (1995) 6 *Public Law Review* 7, 11.

(8) Allars, M, "Private Law But Public Power: Removing Administrative Law Review from Government Business Enterprises" (1995) 6 *Public Law Review* 44.

(9) Farrar, J and McCabe, B, "Corporatisation, Corporate Governance and the Deregulation of the Public Sector Economy" (1995) 6 *Public Law Review* 24, 30.
(10) Ibid., 42.
(11) The Council of Australian Governments (COAG) comprises the heads of Commonwealth, State and Territory governments.
(12) Independent Committee of Inquiry (Hilmer Committee), *National Competition Policy Review*, AGPS, Canberra, 1993.
(13) Section 88.
(14) Section 101; see, for example, *Re AGL Cooper Basin Natural Gas Supply Arrangements* (1997) ATPR 41-593, in which the Australian Competition Tribunal revoked the determination of the ACCC terminating an authorisation for joint marketing of natural gas from the Cooper Basin field.
(15) Section 4 (1).
(16) Cross elasticity of demand is a relevant factor in determining substitutability of goods and services.
(17) See, for example, *Queensland Wire Industries Pty Ltd v The Broken Hill Proprietary Company Limited* (1989) 167 CLR 177.
(18) Rose, "Resources Joint Ventures and the Trade Practices Act 1974" (1991) 9 *Journal of Energy and Natural Resources Law* 95, 100-1.
(19) This section draws upon McDonald "Access to Gas Trunk Pipelines in Queensland" (1998) 17 *Australian Mining and Petroleum Law Journal* 138.
(20) *Trade Practices Act 1974* (Cth.), s. 44H.
(21) Ibid., s. 44F.
(22) Ibid., s. 44G.
(23) Ibid., s. 44H.
(24) Ibid., s. 44V.
(25) Ibid., s. 44X.
(26) Ibid., ss. 44K, 44L, 442P.
(27) Ibid., s. 4422A.
(28) Ibid.
(29) Ibid., s. 44M.
(30) Ibid., s. 44O.
(31) Order made under s. 10 of the *Office of the Regulator-General Act 1994*, Statement of Government Policy, 29 September 1994.
(32) Office of the Regulator-General, Electricity Industry Regulatory Statement, 1 September 1995; see also *Electricity Industry Act 1993* s. 157.
(33) Ibid.

(34) *Office of the Regulator-General Act 1994*, s. 26.
(35) Ibid., ss. 28, 33.
(36) Ibid., ss. 35, 36.
(37) *Electricity Industry Act 1993*, ss. 158, 158A.
(38) Office of the Regulator-General, Electricity Industry Regulatory Statement, 1 September 1995.
(39) Ibid.

6 Modern Market Economy and the Rule of Law in China: The Past, the Present and the Future

Liu Hainian

1 General Theories and Experience
2 Historical Development in China
3 Goals, Opportunities and Challenges

The modern market economy and the rule of law are indispensable component parts of the modern civilization, both of them have gradually taken form and established during the development of human society. They are the indicators of the levels of the people's understanding of the law of natural and social developments, of the people's ability to master their own fate in the process of transforming the objective and the subjective worlds, and of the level of development of human civilization. Today, how to properly understand the basic conditions of, and the laws governing, the formation and the establishment of the market economy and of the rule of law, as well as the relationship between them and how to summarize and evaluate the problems encountered and the experiences accumulated by different countries in the process of establishing the market economy and the rule of law remains a very challenging academic questions.

1 General Theories and Experience

Looking from the angle of the development process, the economy and the law are inseparable. On the one hand, the economy is the basis for the formation and the development of the law, on the other hand, the law reacts upon the economy. "In each historical time, the economic production and the social structure resulting from it are the basis of the political and spiritual development of that time."[1] The politics, the law and other spiritual products that are developed on the economic basis are called superstructure. Once come into being, they will react upon, and serve the need of, their economic basis.

Up to now, there exist three types of economy, namely the natural economy, the product economy and the market economy. Natural economy is a closed, self-sufficient economy based on agriculture; product economy, also called planned economy, is an economy in which the production and the distribution of products are directed by the state plan. Under the product economy, the level of industrial and agricultural developments are higher than those under the natural economy, although the general level of development is still relatively low; the market economy takes two forms: free capital market economy and modern market economy. Under free capital market economy, the allocation of the capital, the labor, and other resources and the distribution of products are entirely regulated by the market, whereas under the modern market economy the state plays a certain role in regulating and directing the market. Although the state plan, as a means of macro-control, still plays certain role, it no long has a dominant position in the economy.

Along with the above mentioned three different types of economy, there exist three different types of legal system. In the natural economy, the family, the plantation and the village are the units of social production. The people are both producers and the consumers of their own products. The levels of division of labor and the level of specialization are very low, the links between economic organizations are weak. The people live in a narrow, closed society. As a result, the norms regulating the social relations are mainly the patriarchal clan system based on blood ties and the laws developed on the basis of this system. It is characterized by the arbitrary, hierarchical and cruel methods of punishment, which are used to maintain the dependency of producers to the economically dominant classed. Product economy emerged in the former Soviet Union, the eastern European socialist countries and China during a period in which the market economy was beginning to take form in western European countries and its shortcomings became more and more apparent. These countries hoped to get rid of the natural economy by way of revolution but their level of economic development was still very low. They designed a highly planned economic system to avoid the problems encountered by the western countries in the process of development, such as the blindness of production, the cruel competition, the polarity between rich and poor, and economic and political monopoly. This system is based on the collectivization of agriculture, the nationalization of private industrial and commercial enterprises, the development of state-owned economy and the commercial enterprises, the development of state-owned economy and the implementation of highly centralized system of production and distribution. The original intention of the designers of this system was good. In practice, however, they had ignored the objective conditions for development. As a result, "the politics and the economy were mixed together and the economy became a handmaid of the politics".[2] Under such economic conditions, the private law, which regulates horizontal eonumic relations among the people, was negated and administrative orders, regulations and instructions, designed for the implementation of the from-top-to-bottom economic plan and distribution sysytem highly developed. Under these conditions, not only was it impossible to develop a system of "the rule of law", but even a simple "legal system" was considered as a hindrance. As a result, a situation of outright "rule of man" had emerged in these countries.

It is generally agreed the modern market economy is the "midwife" of the rule of law. However, people have different opinion as to why and how the market economy becomes the midwife of the rule of law. To some extent, these differences reflected the different understandings of the rule of law and the preference for different modes of the rule of law. For example, Marx Weber believes that the reason why the market economy can create a society under the rule of law is that the market activities require predictability and calculability. In my opinion, it is mainly because that the modern market economy has created far great demand of laws, both in terms of quality and in terms of quantity, than the natural economy or the product economy does.

1. Modern market economy is a kind of exchange economy. Those who enter

into the market must be able to freely sell their products or labor. This demands that the people should have more personal and other freedoms than they do under the natural economy or product economy. Under the natural economy, this kind of freedom is impossible for the majority of the people; under the product economy, although the constitution and the law have provided for such freedom, since most people are, to a great extent, tied to a certain area (in the case of peasants), a certain enterprise (in the case of workers or employees) or a certain system (in the case of state personnel), their freedom has been greatly restricted. Modern market economy demands that people have independent personality, and their freedom be truly guaranteed and realized.

2. Those who enter into the marked should not only have the freedom to exchange with other people, but also have something to exchange with other people. That is to say, they must have the ownership and the right to dispose of their products. They must have clearly defined property right and enjoy the legal status as the subjects of the market.

3. The realization of exchange and the health operation of market economy depend on good contract relationship and credit relationship. These relations must be guaranteed by a complete set of laws of obligations.

4. Modern market economy takes benefit as its main consideration. Any investor has to be concerned with the economic results of the operation of his capital and with the application of new scientific and technological development. This will inevitably result in the fierce competition in the whole economic operation. In a time of high technological development with complicated social conditions, relevant laws are necessary to ensure that the competitions in various fields are fair and free from the influences of blood ties and nepotism and to avoid the economic collapse caused by the monopoly of power and economy.

5. While competition promotes development and enhances efficiency, it also means that only the fittest will be able to survive. In order to ensure sustainable social development and to create a favorable and stable environment for

development, a complete social security law is necessary to provide the losers of competition and various vulnerable groups of the society with an effective social security system.

6. In the process of fierce competition and pursuit of maximum benefit, various actors in the modern market not only engage in struggle against each other, but also will not hesitate to jeopardize the interests of the state and of the society. This will inevitably result in various conflicts of interests. In order to keep these conflicts within bounds and prevent them from intensifying, the state must regulate the conducts of the subjects of the market fair judgments on the claims of various parties of the conflicts, and gradually establish a legal order suitable for the development of modern market economy.

7. Replacing the planned economy with modern market economy does not mean that we do not need any planning. "Planning and the market are both economic methods".[3] In order to avoid the negative effects by the blindness of the free competition of the market economy and in order to avoid the huge waste of social labor and resources as well as the social instability resulting from such negative effects, the state must conduct macro-economic control and carry out necessary planned intervention. Therefore, it must adopt laws for the macro-control of the market.

8. The development of market economy requires not only civil, economic and administrative laws that directly regulate the market, but also laws that safeguard the fundamental rights of the citizens, regulate the conduct of the government, maintain social order, and protect the environment and the natural resources. These laws are necessary in order to create favorable external conditions and social environment for the operation of the modern market economy and to ensure the stable and sustainable economic development.

The development of the market economy in any country of the world will inevitably be based on the concrete conditions of that country. It will strengthen the ties between the domstic market and the international market and gradually achieve the unification and globalization of the world economy. This not only demands that all countries must abide by common rules in the international economic relations, but also demands that their law in the political and cultural fields should also be compatible with international standard. This is the external condition for the establishment of market economy as well as the driving force for the social development in each country.

2 Historical Development in China

Natural economy based on small-scale farming by individual owners had been the dominant form of economy in China's history. Although China has had glorious times in its long history, during the past 200 years its economic development had always been lagged behind that of the western capitalist countries. After the 1949 revolution, China experienced a short of economic recovery and then began to build a product economic system. Although this system had brought some vitality to the economy and was a great progress from the natural economy, due to the ignorance of the objective law of economic development and the foolhardy production method of high investment and low output during a certain period of time, a huge amount of resources and man power were wasted and the system finally landed itself in a predicament. After the end of the "Cultural Revolution" especially after 1978, the Chinese Government conducted deep-going self-examination, restored things to order and established the guiding principle of seeking truth from facts. While implementing the fundamental policy of taking economic construction as the central task, China is also gradually developing a modern legal system. The development in the past 20 years can be divided into three stages.

1. From 1978 to 1992. The 3rd Plenary Session of the 11th Party Central Committee in 1978 put to an end the erroneous line of "taking class struggle as the guiding principle" and decided to put the focal point of work on the economic cnstruction. It abolished the rigid planned economic system and

first carried out reform in the rural areas by implementing a contract responsibility system with remuneration linked to output. After its initial success in rural areas, the reform was also carried out in the urban areas. From its experience of reform, China realized that the development of commodity economy is a precondition for the realization of modernization. In response, Chinese economists had put forward, successively, three different theories, namely the theories of "taking the planned economy as the leading force in the national economy and the market economy as a necessary complement to planned economy", of "combining planned economy with market economy", and of "taking market economy as the leading force in the national economy and the planned economy as supplement to market economy". The above theories were confirmed by the state policies and China is making progress in its economic development through experimentation. To be compatible with the economic development, China also began the construction of its legal system. At the beginning, the Chinese people, the horrible scenes of gross violation of human rights during the "Cultural Revolution" still fresh in their mind, demanded that a legal system be established to safeguard their rights and freedoms or, at least, to restore as soon as possible the social order they enjoyed in the 1950s. In 1978, Deng Xiaoping put forward the "Sixteen-Character Guiding Principle" of "There must be laws to go by, the laws must be observed, the enforcement of the law must be strict, and the lawbreakers must be prosecuted".[4] This guiding principle was very important and had a profound impact on the legal construction in China. However, the formulation "there must be laws to go by", as the guiding principle, was too general. As a result, the legal provisions made at the beginning were "imperfect and need to be improved gradually in the future".[5] Although during this period China had revised the Constitution, adopted the Criminal Law, the Criminal Procedure Law, and some laws that directly regulated the economic relations, such as the General Principle of Civil Law, Law on Economic Contract and Law on Economic Contract Concerning Foreign Interests, and although the lawmakers had tried their best to make these laws compatible with the needs of economic development, due to various influences from the planned economy, some laws were found contradictory to the needs of reform and of social development shortly after their adoption or implementation.

2. From 1992 to the convening of the 15th National Congress of the Chinese Communist Party in 1997. In 1992, for the first time, China formally adopted the policy of building a socialist market economy system. With regards to the debate concerning whether the reform and the development of socialist market economy in China were compatible with the socialist principles, the 14th National Congress of the Chinese Communist Party confirmed the basic criteria put forward by Deng Xiaoping, namely "This should mainly depend on whether it is conducive to the development of socialist production force, to the strengthening of the comprehensive national power of the socialist state, and to the raising of the people's living standards".[6] This had further strengthened and clarified the goals of reform, opening to the outside world and development of socialist market economy. In order to suit the needs of the development of socialist market economy, the Standing Committee of the 8th National People's Congress had set the task of establishing a legal system of socialist market economy and made legislative plan in accordance with this task. During the terms of the 8th National People's Congress, 85 laws and 33 decisions on legal questions had been adopted by the National People's Congress and its Standing Committee.[7] During this period, with the establishment of the goal building socialist market economy and with the increase of the consciousness of serving this goal, the quality of legislation had markedly improved and greater achievement had been made in the construction of the legal system. China had accepted many principles of rule of law, not only in its economic, political, administrative and criminal legislation, but also in its law enforcement and judicial systems. However, the formulation "the legal system of socialist market economy" as a guiding principle for legislation, although was more specific and clear than the formulation of "there must be laws to go by" and provided some guidance to the legislative organs, was apparently not comprehensive enough. Moreover, there were

different views among the legal scholars and the legal workers concerning the scope of "the legal system of socialist marked economy", which had inevitably affected the people's general understanding as well as the practice of legal construction.

3. In 1997, the 15th National Congress of the Chinese Communist Party put forward the basic lines and guiding principles concerning the economic, political and cultural development at the primary stage of socialism. It has more clearly emphasized the need to develop market economy in China under socialist conditions and the need "to further increase the level of democracy, to improve the socialist legal system, to administer the state affairs in accordance with the law, and to build a socialist state under the rule of law". It also put forward the tasks of "strengthening the legislative work, improving the quality of legislation, and establishing a socialist legal system with Chinese characteristics by the year 2010."[8] It had further clarified the aim of the legal construction as "to build a socialist legal system with Chinese characteristics", not merely a "legal system of the socialist market economy". This legal system will be a component part of the socialist state under the rule of law, and must comply with a series of principles of rule of law. Currently, China's legal construction is at the beginning of the third stage of development.

Generally speaking, the economic reform aimed at establishing a modern market economy and the development of rule of law in China have been well coordinated during the past 20 years. The long period of rapid and sustainable economic development in China was inseparable from the attention paid to the coordination between the economic reform and the legal system. Such coordination, based on the recognition that China is still at the primary stage of socialism, has ensured the economic development as well as social stability, and avoided the economic decline, social unrest and political instability experience by some countries in the process of reform. Of course, everything has its negative side. Because the Chinese Government has attached too much importance to the maintenance of social stability, it has not made enough effort to use the law as the tool to promote the political reform and the transition from the rule of man to the rule of law is a bit too slow. The phenomenon of corruption, which currently is receiving much attention from the public, is one of the consequences. The Chinese Government should deepen its understanding, strengthen its self-consciousness and adopt decisive measures so as to avoid the serious consequences which no of us would like to see.

3 Goals, Opportunities and Challenges

On the basis of the past achievements, the 4th Session of the 8th National People's Congress in 1996 and the 15th National Congress of the Chinese Communist Party in 1997 had set the grand goals for the development for the coming new century. In the process of realizing these goals, China is faced with both good opportunities and serious challenges. To grasp the opportunities, meet the challenges and achieve the fixed goals are the glorious historical tasks of the Chinese people for the next 5 to 50 years.

1. In 1996, the 4th Session of the 8th National People's Congress approved the "Ninth Five-year Plan" for the National Economic and Social development in China and the Long-range Development Program for the year 2010. The program provides that: during the "Ninth Five-year" period, China will complete second stage of the strategic plan of modernization. Namely, but the year 2002, while China's population will increase by 300 million from that of 1980, the *per capita* GNP will quadruple that of 1980; the phenomenon of proverty will be basically eliminated and people will be able to live a relatively comfortable life; the establishment of modern enterprise management system will be speeded up and a socialist market economic system will be basically established. By the year 2010, the GNP will double that of the year 2000, the people will be able to live a more comfortable life, the socialist market economic system will be further perfected, and a sound foundation will be laid for the realization of the modernization by the middle of 21

Century.⁽⁹⁾ To achieve this goal, China "should uphold and further improve the basic economic system of mutual development of different types of economies based on different types of ownership with the economy of socialist public ownership as its main body, uphold and further improve the socialist market economic system and, under the macro-control of the stage, give fully play to basic role of the market in the allocation of resources; uphold and further improve different modes of distribution with the system of distribution according to labor as its main body, allow some areas or some people to become rich first so as to help and bring along the poor areas and to gradually achieve mutual prosperity; uphold and further improve the policy of opening to the outside world and actively participate in international cooperation and competition".⁽¹⁰⁾ The document have not only prescribed the task of economic reform and economic development, but also set the goals of political reform and construction, namely "to further expand democracy, improve socialist legal system, administer the state affairs in accordance with the law, and build up a socialist state under the rule of law"; "to ensure that the people have the power to administer the state affairs, to implement the system of democratic election, democratic decision-making, democratic administration and democratic supervision, to ensure that people enjoy extensive right and freedoms under the law and to respect and protect human rights".⁽¹¹⁾ The achievement of the above political and economic goals will play an important role in accomplishing the historical task of building China into a prosperous, democratic and civilized socialist state as provided for by the Constitution.

2. To achieve the above-mentioned goals, China must reform and improve its various systems and further perfect the laws that are the means for the controls of these systems and for the implement the rule of law. Therefore, in setting the goals of economic and political development, China has also put forward the tasks of "strengthening the legislative work, improving the quality of legislation and establishing a socialist legal system with Chinese characteristics". To accomplishing these tasks, all government organs must administer the state affairs in accordance with the law, the government

functions must be changed according to the needs of the market economy, the organization, the size and the work procedures of the state organs must be legalized so as to enhance its abiity to serve the people and safeguard the citizens' rights; judicial reforms must be carried out to improve the quality of judicial personnel and to ensure, at the institutional level, that the judicial organs exercise their adjudicative and procuratorial powers impartially, independently and in accordance with the law; step must be taken to enhance the legal consciousness and the sense of legal system among the whole people, especially among the leadership at various levels and to promote their ability to perform their functions in accordance with the law; to further improve the system of democratic supervision, to establish and perfect the mechanisms for ensuring lawful exercise of power, uphold the principle of equality, fairness, and openness, strengthen the supervision of the implementation of the Constitution and the law, and uphold the uniformity of the state legal system.

3. There are sound basis and good opportunity for China to achieve the above goals.

1) Administering state affairs in accordance with the law and constructing a socialist state under the rule of law have been established as the basic state policies of China and have profound ideologically basis among the Chinese people. In China, slogans such as "to administer provincial affairs according to the law", to "administer municipal affairs according to the law"; "to administer county affairs according to the law", "to administer township affairs according to the law", "to manage the enterprise according to the law", "to regulate rivers according to the law", and "to transform mountains according to the law" can be seen throughout the country and have receive wide support from the people.

2) With the popularizatin of the law and the development of market economy, the citizen's right consciousness has been geatly enhanced. The people demand that laws should be adopted to protect their economic, political, cultural, social, and personal rights and freedoms.

3) Hong Kong was turned over to China in 1997, Macao will also to be returned to China in December 1999, and the peaceful unification of Taiwan and the mainland is an inevitable trend of historical development. Although the above three regions have laws, which are different from those of the mainland both in nature and in form (the laws of Hong Kong belong to the common law system), they are basically modern societies under the rule of law. After the return of Hong Kong and Macao to China and the unification of Taiwan with the mainland, the increasingly close ties between these regions and the Central Government and various inland provinces and cities will certainly promote the rule of law in the whole country.

4) With the development of the market economy in China, the Chinese market will be increasingly linked to, and achieve a certain degree of integration with, the international market. As one of the permanent members of the UN Security Council, China always actively participates in international affairs and upholds justice. Up to now, it has already ratified a series of international conventions, including 17 human rights conventions. In 1997, China signed the International Convenant on Economic Social and Cultural Rights, and recently, both Vice-Premier Qian Qicheng and President Jiang Zemin had declared that China would also sign the International Covenant on Civil and Political Right. The signing of or accession to any international convention implies that the state will accept certain international obligations. Closer ties with the international market in the economic field and the undertaking of more international obligations in the political field will inevitably demand that China modify the provisions of many domestic laws so as to make them compatible with the international standards and learn from the legislative experience of the major countries in the world. Which will result in a trend towards uniformity between the Chinese law and the laws of these countries. This uniformity is reflected not only in the field of private law but also in the field of public law. The safeguarding of human rights will become an important content of the rule of law in China.

5) Today, after 20 years' continued efforts, China has established a basic legal framework with the Constitution as its core and the basic administrative, civil, economic, criminal and social security laws as its mainstays. Most of these laws are compatible with the economic, political and cultural developments as the primary stage of socialism, although some of them need to be revised, supplemented or even redrafted. Compared with the situation of 20 years ago when there was no law to go by or that of 10 years ago when the laws were very incomplete, this is a great improvement. Today we have laws and regulations to go by in basically every field of social life and through the making and implementation of the law, we have acquired much new information, and accumulated rich experience, concerning the rule of law.

6) After many years' efforts, China has trained a large number of legislative, law enforcement, and judicial personnel as well as lawyers and legal research and teaching personnel. In the next century, they will become the backbone elements in the construction of modern legal system in China.

4. Despite the above-mentioned favorable conditions and opportunities, China is still faced with many challenges in its effort to build a legal system compatible with modern market economy.

1) In China, the natural economy based on small-scale farming by individual owners had been the dominant economic mode for a very long period of time. After 1840, when China was reduced to a semi-feudal and semi-colonial society, the national capitalism developed slowly and bureaucratic capitalism, which had a strong dependent nature, had emerged. Semi-natural economy became the dominant economic mode of the society. After the success of the communist revolution in 1949, China implemented a system of product economy in which the state played a dominant role in both production and distribution. Therefore, the development of modern market economy in China is based not so much as on the existence of the necessary conditions as on the deepening of understanding of the laws of

economic development. It is a development both from top to bottom and from bottom to top. It must be a gradual process and that relevant laws must be adopted to create favorable conditions for the development of this economic system. Therefore, the state must attach great importance to the improvement of the household contract responsibility system and the villagers' self-management in rural areas, to the safeguarding of the rights of the self-employed industrial and commercial households in urban areas, and to the separation of the ownership and the managerial authority in state-owned enterprises, all of which are the basic conditions for the establishment and development of market economy.

2) China is a country with more than 2,000 years' history of feudal autocracy and "the rule of man " had prevailed throughout that long history. The laws in the past were merely the tools in the hands of the rulers, which emphasized only government control and obligations and totally ignored rights. The feudal kings and emperors often acted arbitrarily, their words were taken as laws, and throughout the country, the state laws were combined with the clan rules. After 1949, although great changes had taken place, due to the influence of the product economic system, formulation and implementation of economic plan were still an important content of state activities. As far as the law was concerned, the problem of putting too much emphasis on state control and obligations still existed. Even today, this influence is still reflected in some of the current law. The questions of how to democratize the legislative process, how to make the rights the basic content of law and organically combine rights and obligations, and how to make law the code of conduct applicable not only to the ordinary people, but also to the state leaders and government of officials are yet to be answered in the future.

3) China is a huge country with 1.3 billion population, 56 ethnic groups, and a vast territory with different levels of economic, political, cultural development in different areas. In order to develop modern market economy and to construct a modern state under the rule of law, it is necessary for the

cadres and the masses from different nationalities, different areas and different systems to make concerted efforts and it is necessary to give full play to the initiatives of both the central and the local governments. The questions of how to correctly handle the relations between the central and local governments and between various systems and departments, how to prevent some department and regions from using the legislative, law enforcement and judicial processes as tools for extending or protecting their own powers, and how to ensure the effectiveness of the law and the establishment of a unified market are also still to be answered in the future.

4) With the deepening of the economic reform and gradually progress of the political reform, many social relations are also undergoing transformation. Law and systems require stability so as to uphold their authority whereas reform will inevitably lead to changes which are necessary for the promotion of economic and political developments. How to properly handle the relation between stability and change and strike a balance between these two factors is also a question that needs to be carefully studied.

5) The reform in China is carried out from top to bottom and under the unified leadership of the Chinese Government. We must continuously strengthen the Chinese leadership so as to ensure the ultimate success of this great reform. However, the current leadership system is established under the strong influence of the product economic system. Therefore, in order to strengthen the role of the leadership in the reform, we must also carry out reforms on the current leadership system itself. Its functions must be changed so as to serve the needs of the development of market economy. Since the decisive factor in the social distribution under the product economic system was a person's position in the whole system and, even today, how high a position a person holds in the public organ of power is still an important criterion for deciding how much he should get in social distribution, the reform on the leadership system will inevitably affect the interests of some reformers. How to deal with this kind of problems and how to reduce the resistance to the reform are also questions that should be

carefully studied and solved in the process of reform.

6) The road towards integration of the Chinese and the international markets is by no means a smooth and rosy one. On that road we will encounter opportunities as well as risks and pitfalls. This is not only because we have no familiarize ourselves with the various relations in the international market, but also because some foreign countries will easily allow other countries to enter their traditional market and some major international profiteering groups are doing their best to prevent the developing countries, including China, from achieving their goal of modernization.

The reform carried out for the establishment of the modern market economy and the rule of law in China is unprecedented and is unfolding on a magnificent scale. Although in the process of achieving this goal, we will inevitably encounter many difficulties and challenges, the direction of the reform has already been determined and the road to success opened up. I am confident that, through the concerted efforts by the people of various nationalities, China will be able to accomplish this histrical task.

(1) Selected Works of Marx and Engles, Vol. 1, (Chinese Edition), p. 232.
(2) Zhang Wenxian, Studies on the Basic Scope of Law Science, Publishing House of China University of Political Science and Law, March 1993, p. 309.
(3) Selected Works of Deng Xiaoping, vol. 3, p. 737.
(4) Selected Works of Deng Xiaoping (1975-1982), p. 136.
(5) Selected Works of Deng Xiaoping (1975-1982), p. 137.
(6) Selected Works of Deng Xiaoping (1975-1982), p. 372.
(7) Tian Jiyun, Working Report of the Standing Committee of the National People's Congress, in: the People's Daily, March 25, 1998.
(8) Compilation of the Documents of the Fifteenth National Congress of the Communist Party, People's Publishing House, September 1997, pp. 33-34.
(9) Report on the Ninth Five-year Plan for National Economic and Social Development and Long-range Development Program for the Year 2010, Separate Edition, People's Publishing House, March 1996, p. 19.
(10) Compilation of the Documents of the Fifteenth National Congress of the Chinese Communist Party, People's Publishing House, September 1997, p. 19.

Part II : Free Market and Legal Regulations
(i) Market Economy and Legal Regulations

(11) Compilation of the Documents of the Fifteenth National Congress of the Chinese Communist Party, People's Publishing House, September 1997, pp. 31-32.

7 Administrative Deregulation in Korea: Now and Future

Seung Doo Yang

Introduction
1 The Effort toward Deregulation in Korea: Now
2 Future

Introduction

During the 4 years of Korean War, the Korean peninsula was devastated completely, and so was industrial infra-structures. The per capita income of the Korean people during the 1960s was merely US$80, and Korea was one of the poorest countries of the world.

General Park Chong Hee usurped the political power by a coup d'etat, and his justification of toppling a freely elected, democratic government down and seizing political power by a coup d'etat was that the incumbent government headed by Prime Minister Chang Myon was totally incapable of defending the country against the communist infiltration from North and so politically unstable to initiate any economic development to free the Korean people from the "absolute poverty". Naturally, the primary goal set by Park Chong Hee's government was to industrialize and modernize his country.

Under the strong leadership of President Park Chong Hee, the government, staffed by loyal, well educated and trained bureaucrats, embarked the hard to achieve project of industrializing and modernizing Korea. The Korean government, firstly, started to seek the capital, which seemed to be a vital factor for the Korean economy, by concluding the treaty with Japan normalizing her relation with Japan and successfully secured approximately 600 Million US dollars of hard currency. Secondly, the government undertook to formulate ambitious economic development policies and plans. Thirdly, the legislature, the substantial majority of law-makers were under the control of the President

Park, produced a large numer of statutes which would be vehicles to achieve the goal of economic development.

By virtue of successful achievement of consecutive 5 year economic development plans under the strong development oriented dictatorship of Presidents Park Chong Hee, Chon Doo Whan and Ro Tae Woo (all of them were professional soldiers before seizing the political power), Korea began to win praises and acclamations of many political leaders of developing countries for her successful economic development, albeit they could not escape from the unfortunate criticism of being undemocratic by their friends and foes alike. The per capita income of Korean people in mid-1990s was raised to nearly US$10,000 and Korea was said to be one of the "four dragons" which achieved the successful economic development.

During the course of economic development and modernizing the social structures of Korea under the so-called development oriented dictatorship, fairly large number of administrative and economic regulations to control not only the economic activities but also virtually every and all aspects of social activities of the people, were introduced. The principle of "open market and fair competition" was ignored conveniently, and fairly large industrial conglomerates were emerged threatening the very existence of many small and medium size industrial entities. The economic efficacy and efficiency fell sharply.

With the economic growth, emerging middle class began to voice to uphold the democratic principles. And industries started to whisper to abide by the principle of "open market and fair competition."

With the advent of the so-called "civilian government"[1] of President Kim Young Sam, their voices grew so loud enough as the government could not ignore the voice. And during the first part of 1980s, the prevailing trend in the developped countries was "deregulation", and the popular *cliche* was "the smaller government is the better government."

1 The Effort toward Deregulation in Korea: Now

(1) A brief history of deregulation efforts by the government

The "civilian government" of President Kim Young Sam realized that the excessive regulation over the activites of industries would work as a major factor deteriorating competitiveness of Korean industries in the international market. And in order to avoid frequent international trade conflicts, President Kim's government was cornered to adopt the globalization policy and to open the domestic market to foreign businesses.

In this context, the civilian government enacted several statutes related to regulations, to name a few, "The Act on Special Measures for Renovation of Regulations over Activities of Industries" (1993)[2], "The Basic Act on Administrative Regulations and Administrative Procedures over Licensing" (1994)[3], etc., to lay the legal basis for deregulation, and, established a few administrative committees to carry the business of deregulation, such committees as The Committee on Administrative Renovation[4], The Committee on Renovation of Adminitrative Regulations over Economy[5], The Committee on Deliberation of Regulations over Activities of Industries[6], and others.

However, the efforts to repeal, renovate or mitigate various regulations by these committees were carried out seperately and independently, thus lacking comprehensiveness and coherency. Therefore, the government decided to establish a single, powerful, central committee under the Office of President.

(2) The Basic Act on Administrative Regulation

Hence, "The Basic Act on Administrative Regulation"[7] was enacted and promulgated on August 22nd, 1997 by President Kim Young Sam's government, and "the Committee on the Renovatin of Administrative Regulation" was organized.

The necessity of accelarating efforts to deregulate was doubled when the Republic confronted a new economic crisis in 1997[8], which pushed the nation on the very verge of national default

The newly elected President Kim Dae Jung in 1998 declared that the deregulation would be the primary target to be achieved by his "people's government"[9], and that his government should renovate or repeal the existing administrative regulations by 50% by the end of 1998. The Presidential Decree for the Execution of the Basic Act on Administrative Regulation was promulgated to make the law in force. And the Committee on the Renovation of Administrative Regulations was reshuffled.

(3) Principles declared by the Basic Act

The Basic Act on Administrative Regulations declares a few basic principles: the principles that the state and local government shall guaranttee the freedom of the people and shall honor the creativeness of people, and shall not violate intrinsic nature of the right and the freedom of the people, and, the objects and the scope of the regulation shall be the minimum to achieve objectives of imposing the regulations, and at the same time, the means to achieve the objectives shall be fair, transparent, efficient and effective, even when regulations are required; that the regulations to protect the life, the health of the people and the environment shall be such that fully achieve the goal; and that the regulations shall be automatically repealed by the lapse of 5 years since the first imposition of the regulations (the principle of "sun-set").

Another very important guide-line the Basic Act on Administrative Regulations stipulates is that each and every regulation shall be imposed by the law, that is, the regulation can not be imposed without the legal authority given by provisions of statutes, presidential decrees or ministerial decrees enacted in accordance with the specific delegation by statutes, or by municipal ordinances and rules issued by hands of local governments with the specific delegation by statutes or by resolutions of an assembly of autonomous bodies.

(4) The Committee on the Renovation of Administrative Regulations

The newly reshuffled Committee on the Renovation of Administrative Regulations would be chaired by two persons, the Prime Minister and a private citizen, and would be composed of 15 to 20 members, of which majority would be private citizen. Presently, 7 members are from the government, namely, the Prime Minister who serves as a co-chairman, the Minister of Finance and

Economy, the Minister of Administration and Local Autonomy, the Minister of Industry and Resource, the Director of the Office of Coordination of State Affairs, the Chairman of the Fair Trade Commission, and the Minister of Legislation. And 13 members of the Committee are from the private sector. The co-chairman of the Committee is a president of a university, 3 members are university professors, and remaining members represent various private sectors, such as, mass media, industry, private research institute on economy.

(5) Definition of Regulation

The Basic Act stipulates that regulations are acts imposed under the legal authority of a statute, a presidential decree, a ministrial decree, or a directive made by the delegation of a statute, or a presidential decree, etc. by the State or the local government for the purpose to achieve administrative objectives limiting the right and imposing the duty. However, the Basic Act provides that the Act shall not be applied to those dispositions imposed by the National Assembly, the Courts, the Constitutional Court, The Central Election Management Committee, the Office of Audit, and to those administrative acts related to criminal, military, tax administration.

(6) Registration of Regulations

Ministers and heads of central administrative organizations must register administrative regulations and their legal grounds within their jurisdiction to the Committee on the Renovation of Administrative Regulations, and the Committee must make the list of the regulations thus registered, and must publish by means of public announcement using either official government gazette or computer communication. When the Committe, by its own investigation, finds any regulation not registered to the Committee by ministers and heads of central administrative organizations, the Committee shall make a request to ministers and heads of central administrative organizations to register or to repeal those regulations.

(7) Review of New Regulation

When a central administrative organization introduces a new regulation or makes any existing regulation more stringent one, it has to undergo the following procedures. Firstly, the public hearing should be conducted and the prior public notice should be made in accordance with provisions of the Administrative Procedure Act. Secondly, the analysis the effect of the new regulation or the regulation made more stringent should be made by the administrative organization. Thirdly, the head of the organization shall review the legitimacy of the new regulation by examining the object, the scope and the method of the regulation based upon the report on the analysis of the effect of the new regulation. And, finally, the head of central administrative organization shall apply to the Committee for the examination of the proposed regulation. The application to the committee shall be made by submitting the report on the analysis of the effect of the proposed regulation, the results of the review made by the administrative organization and the opinions expressed by related administrative organizations and interested parties. As a regulation should have its legal ground upon a statutory provision, the application shall be made prior to the administrative organization submits its application to the Ministry of Legislation for the enactment of the related provisions installing the said regulation.

The Committee on the Renovation of Administrative Regulations examines the necessity and the legitimacy of introducing a new regulation. A subsection of the Committee will preliminarily examine the proposed regulation. When the proposed regulation has an important effect upon the daily life of the common people, or has a grave effect upon the socio-economic activities of the people[10], the examination shall be referred to the plenary session of the Committee. When the Committee finds that the proposed regulation is legitimate, the regulation will be affirmed. If not, the Committee advises to withdraw or to renovate the proposed regulation. When the head is so advised, he or she shall follow the advice of the Committee.

(8) Examination of Existing Regulations

As to the already existing regulations, the Basic Act on the Administrative Regulation stipulates four channels for their repeal or renovation.

Anyone, a Korean or a foreigner, residing in the Republic may submit proposals for repealing or renovating regulations to any administrative organization, local government or business association (such as the Korean Trade Association, the Korean Federation of Industries, etc.). The proposals, then, will be referred to the Committee on the Renovation of Administrative Regulations, and, the Committee will examine the proposal. When the Committee finds the proposal has legitimate grounds, it advises to the concerned administrative organization to repeal or to renovate the related regulation.

Heads of central administrative, organizations may initiate the repeal or the renovation of existing regulation, and report to the Committee the result of deregulation. Presently, the number of the existing regulations registered to the Committee on the Renovation of Administrative Regulations is approximately well over 11,000, and, as mentioned earlier, President Kim Dae Jung made public announcement that his government will either repeal or renovate approximately one half of the existing regulations. In accordance with the guide-line set by the President, central administrative organizations established special task force to review the existing regulations, and worked out lists of regulations to be repealed or renovated. The lists prepared by central administrative organizations have already been submitted to the Committee for the approval, and the Committee will conclude the examination of the lists by the end of October of this year. It is estimated that the number of existing regulations will be repealed or renovated by 50 to 60% through this initiative of administrative organizations.

(9) Comprehensive Deregulation Plan

At the same time, the Committee on the Renovation of Administrative Regulations is required by the Basic Act to make a comprehensive plan for the repeal and renovation of regulations, and to make a public announcement when and how the plan would be carried out. Presently, the Committee recruited several groups of experts, and asked them to study about one hundred deregulation projects. When the study will be completed, the Commmitte, after the deliberation of the results of studies, will formulate concrete and specific recommendations for the repeal and renovation of regulations and send them to each and every central administrative organizations to repeal and renovate regulations in accordance with recommendation suggested by the Committe.

2 Future

Presently, the strong proponent groups for the deregulation are those in businesses and industries. Consequently, the stress is given mainly to the elimination of regulations which would cause inconveniences to their business activities, and the main target of deregulation, namely, "the promotion of market competition" is, more or less, neglected.

Primary regulations, which work against free market competition in Korea, are those imposed over the finance system (such as banking systems, insurance systems, securities, foreign exchange, etc.), utilization of land (control of population migration into the metropolitan area), and those regulations related to labor force. The reality is that the venture of deregulation has been just started over these areas.

It is true that substantial efforts toward the deregulation in Korea is just started, and it has yet to produce an excellent and satisfactory results. Once the mechanism formulated by the Basic Act gains the momentum, and when civil servants fully understand and support the principle of free market and fair competition, our efforts would surely bear an excellent fruit.

(1) Against the so-called "military governments" of Presidents Park Chong Hee, Chon Doo Whan and Ro Tae Woo.
(2) 企業活動規制緩和에관한特別措置法
(3) 行政規制및民願事務基本法
(4) 行政刷新委員會

(5) 經濟行政規制改革委員會
(6) 企業活動規制審議委員會
(7) 行政規制基本法
(8) Caused by the shortage of hard currency to pay back the international debt.
(9) President Kim Dae Jung claims his government is "people's government" as he was elected by the people who chose the opposition political leader as their president for the first time in nearly 50 years since the birth of the Republic.
(10) The preliminary examination by a sub-committee will begin by investigating whether the proposed regulation is an important regulation. When the regulation affects the daily life of the common people seriously or has a grave effect upon the socio-economic activities of the people, it is regarded to be important. The criteria set by the by-law of the Committee for the important regulation are whether the proposed regulation causes 10 billion Won or more of expense annually, affects upon a million or more of persons, has clearly a nature curtailing the competition, or whether the degree of intensity the proposed regulation is exceeding compared with that of international standards (such as laid down by WTO, OECD), or clearly unreasonable. When the effect of the proposed regulation does not fall in any of the afore-said category, the sub-committee may make a final decision after the examination of the proposed regulation.

8 Legal Aspects of the Financial Big Bang in Japan

Tatsuo UEMURA

1 Collapse of the "Bubble" Economy in Japan and Defects of Legal Viewpoints
2 The Third Modernizaion—Barriers of the Legal System
3 The Financial "Big Bang" and Conversion of Regulation Ideology
4 Trends in the Reformation of the Financial System
5 Arrangement of Financial Legislation and the Reinforcement of Comprehensive Legal Power
In Conclusion

1 Collapse of the "Bubble" Economy in Japan and Defects of Legal Viewpoints

In Japan, a huge expansion, or "bubble" in the securities market collapsed at the beginning of 1990 and Japan is still suffering from the effects of the large aftermath. The frightening aspect of the bubble was not in the fact that it collapsed, causing great losses, but rather that the excessive economic structure upon which the bubble peaked was not founded on facts. When the bubble collapses, economic activities within, such as excessive economic structure, will fail. Collapse caused by this excessive econimic structure that is not bases on facts causes many unfortunate results: company failures, unemployment, downward slide into recession, crime, etc. Trying to find sulutions to this problem overseas could even lead to war. The happiness and fortune created during the expansion of the economic bubble is incomparably temporary and small when compared to the troubles caused at the time of the collapse of the bubble. Moreover, experiencing the excesses of the expanding economic bubble spoils the human spirit. There is a tendency to always dream of reviving the bubble.

So then, what caused the birth of the giant bubble? In Japan there is a strong tendency to see it as exclusively the problem of financial policy and/or of economic policy. However, this case has not been persuasively explained or prescribed from the standpoint of economics. Rather it is largely the voice of those who distrust Economics. In my opinion the problem was caused by the fact that, without having a system of legal checks and balances, Japan promoted economic growth from the point of zero following World War II. It can be said that the original strong guidance from the top by bureaucrats and executives like absolute monarchs led to the rapid development of the Japanese economy after the war. Japan needed to set up a reasonable legal framework for the stage of economic development that would nip such expansive bubbles in the bud. Howerver, we have to acknowledge that we did not do that.

There was a time in which Japan was regarded as an engine of the world's economy, but now there is a strong perception that the engine pulls for nothing more than the benefit of local rule. At present, international distrust heightens for the whole body of Japan's financial and business system. At present nothing is left of the explanation that theorizes that Japan's successful economy is due to the excellence of the nation's culture, management, natural features and characteristics of its people. Far from that, just mentioning "Japan's Financial Organization" undoes the "Japanese premium". Recognition has grown that Japanese legal resistance is weak against financial and business impropriety. Trust in information disclosure and financial statements has dropped through the floor. Further, the certified audits of the auditor corporations are not trusted at all. And it has become clear that major Japanese corporations have not cut off their relations to gangsters (the "econmic Mafia").

2 The Third Modernizaion—Barriers of the Legal System

As stated previously, the present condition of Japan shows the misfortune caused by continuously stepping on the accelerator without having the business, securities and financial systems set up on a proper base—that is in having strong brakes to maintain legal terms and conditions. Japan appears to have business, securities and financial systems similar to other countries. However, Japan has not had an instinctive sense of danger or fearfulness which does seem to be present in other countries' systems. Japan has only been pursuing successful economic results without having enough wariness. In European countries and the USA, the systems seem similar and historically have suffered repetitions of failure and collapse. And every time a serious failure was repeatedly experienced. Many devices to protect the systems were put into place as standard maintenance. These protection devices are the legal capital system, dividend regulation, information disclosure systems, auditing systems, regulations prohibiting severe market improprieties, the establishment of market watchdog organizations, strict self regulation, etc. However, Japan, without knowing the value these devices have, has simply repeated the failures of other countries, as one would expect.

Additionally, Japan did not pay attention to the fact that it is a great danger for stock to be possessed, or mutually possessed by corporations or financial organizations. Japanese financial organizations are constituted so that their management is influenced by the price of stock, as they added the hidden profit of stock to the calculation of the self-capital ratio of BIS (45% of the hidden profit—the economic world insisted on 90% at that time, but this matter was forgotten entirely). So they were reduced to organizations that took the lead in worsening the economic situation of Japan. Also, they could not grasp the reason why the possession of stock by financial organizations is prohibited in the USA. Although Japan has huge economic power, it is now in the situation of not having the proper systems and management know-how to satisfactorily handle it.

Japan was opened to foreign trade and diplomatic relations 130 years ago, but the purpose was to stay abreast of worldwide competitors by reinforcing the military and economic powers as shown in the national purpose statements issued at that time, entitled "The Policy for National Prosperity and Military Strength" and "Increase in Production and Promotion of Industry." An opportunity was presented when the war was lost 53 years ago, but the state concentrated on solely reinforcing economic power. It was calld "National Prosperity and Enhancement of Fortune." The purpose seems to have been attained, but a third major hurdle remains before the non-western country of Japan is to be considered a truly modern nation. That is legal discipline, or "rule of law," or "National Prosperity and Enhancement of Law." Naturally, it cannot be said the all fields throughout Japanese society should be solved with a Western approach. There are fields in which cultural theories are effective. But the financial, securities, and industrial fields are governed by global standards and therefore: Firstly, equal business development is not possible without commonalites in the legal systems. Secondly, in order to conduct business development with various foreign countries, our nation must have strong authority to resist illegalities and improper acts by them. However, we cannot set up rules for that purpose which are applicable to foreign companies only. The rules must apply to domestic companies as well. Under present circumstances, Japanese companies are required to pay penalties, legal fees, and damages but cannot receive the same. (Because of illegal transactions of copper at the LME (London Metal Exchange), Sumitomo Shoji Co., Ltd. had to pay ¥13 billion to CFTC in Ametica.) Thirdly, the special legislation needed to establish rules which apply to the ever-changing living organism that is the financial market, and to conduct motivational legal management is an area for which Japan has little experience. However, we must accomplish it quickly. Fourthly, there is the more basic question as to whether Japan has a strong enough juducial system to develop laws in this field. Japan has never been creative in solving things by administration of justice.

3 The Financial "Big Bang" and Conversion of Regulation Ideology

After World War II, when Japan was in a stage of economic reconstruction, finance was under strong control. In short, the basis of the policy was to provide the nation with low interest rates, low dividends and provide priority funds for industry. The government asked the people to be patient as it attempted to make "Major Players" in various industrial fields very quickly in order to compete on the world stage. If the "Major Players" were successful, the people would share in the profit of the riches obtained overseas. This succeeded to a certain degree, but the rules and system set up for this "Major Player" plan have not changed at all.

In 1948, a securities law was enacted under the influence of GHQ. The law itself was based on the American rule adopted after the Great Depression, and was a legislation assuming a securities market participated in by the general public. But, as in Japan the securities market was starting from zero, there was a great difference in the beginning between the law and reality. At first it was necessary to protect the general public, who were unfamiliar with the securities market, from over-policing. Initially the ideology of the regulation was to police the industry. The leading actor in industiral finance was bank financing. Banks governed all companies through financing and created a "Main Bank" in each company. The second stage of securities regulations was a policy oriented to promoting protection of securities companies, the securities market and investors. The flow of the financial channel was being diversified from centering on bank financing to include the securities market as well. In Japan, this administration centered method, which includes the banking field, is calles the "Convoy Fleet of Ships Method" with the Ministry of Finance as the lead vessel. But this was the ideology of the Japanese finance and securities regulations just before the economic bubble collapsed. At the peak of the bubble in 1989, the total price of listed stock was 630 trillion yen, with a one year increase of 130 trillion yen, the same as Italy's annual GNP. The wave of skyrocketing prices (total land value in Japan increased to 4 times that of the total land value of the U.S. and the land cost of Tokyo alone was enought to purchase all of the United States) came crashing down and the bubble had completely collapsed by the end of 1990. Together with the securities scandal revealed at that time, this caused great criticism from nation toward the administration of the Ministry of Finance. In spite of the fact that the Japanese securities market had become gigantic, the Ministry continued to conduct administration promoting protection. This led to illegal concealment of problem securities companies by the Ministry, just like a parent conceals the juvenile delinquency of its child. It was revealed in one case after another that conspiratorial relationships had been formed.

Thus the Ministry of Finance had no alternative but to clearly recognize the need to change the ideology of securities and financial regulations to be market-centered. The aim of "market-centered" regulations is to enhance the market's ability to move autonomously to the maximum degree possible. In order to use the market mechanisms that are in place to their highest level, existing terms and conditions are arranged, an eye is kept on the management status of the market, and defects in the market are removed. Regulations making this their puropose are what is called "market centered regulations". Here the leading actor is not administration, rather it is the market mechanism itself; administration is only given a supporting role. And this administration must take a form that government cannot directly intervene in—an independent administrative committee system is required. In Japan, the Securities Exchange Observation Committee was established in 1992 as an extra-ministerial bureau; also in May of this year, the Finance Management Bureau was started as an independent administration commission. Here bank regulations, insurance company rules and securities rules are unified, and the previous Securities Exchange Observation Committee became a part of the Finance Management Bureau. Regulations based on administrative intervention gave way to rules-based regulations. In a mere 50 years, Japan has experienced all three stages of securities regulation.

In November 1996, then-Prime Minister Ryutaro Hashimoto announced a plan entitled, "Reformation of Our Country's Financial System," and declared that the realization of a large scale reform of the financial system was targeted for the year 2001. The guiding ideology of the plan was to build up a free, fair, and global financial market that works on an international scale. It was the start of what has become to be called, the financial "Big Bang."

4 Trends in the Reformation of the Financial System

So all at once discussion began about reforming systems related to all areas of the financial world. Written reports from various policy deliberation committees of related authorities have been announced publicly one after another. A concrete schedule, specifying when each item will begin to be enforced, has been made for the Big Bang financial reforms. In my opinion, the financial Big Bang consists of four stages of systematic reformation. The first stage relates to the reformation of the financial system which had already been under discussion before the securities scandal occurred, as well as correspondence that must be conducted after a scandal occurs. The Amendment of Securities Exchange Law of 1993 that makes compensation to clients for losses illegal[*], as well as the amendment of related laws concerning the establishment of the Securities Exchange Observation Committee are related to the latter—action taken after a scandal. It was a major reform including the item that it is now possible for banks, through their subsidiary companies, to conduct business in securities. The reformation of securities exchange laws, bank laws, etc., in 1994 are an example of the former—action taken to prevent a scandal from occurring. A large part of System Reformation arguments that were taking place before the financial scandal were based on the optimistic ideology that insists that the liberalization of finance would be only a wonderful thing; this perspective is reflected in the 1994 actions taken to prevent scandal from occurring. But this can certainly also be seen to refer to the situation that existed even before the above actions were taken. The second stage is to try to attain to international standards as quickly as possible and in the areas that change is possible, without working on present legal system itself. They are clearly targeting the financial Big Bang, and the laws which were established on June 5th of this year relating to the financial system is part of this. This was a general call for a great many reform laws, including a major reform of

Part II: Free Market and Legal Regulations
(i) Market Economy and Legal Regulations

securities exchange laws, banks laws, securities investment trust law, insurance business laws, and so on. Just looking at the securities exchange laws, the contents cover a wide range of issues—the concept of expansion in the securities exchange market (in the past only the exchange market was treated as the securities market; legally the over-the-counter market was nothing but the traditional way things were done), recognition of over-the-counter derivative dealings, registration systems for securities companies (in the past it was a licensing system), permission for a system of private transactions, mitigation for a specialty system for securities companies (the general rule was that only securities companies could be engaged in securities exchange, though there were many exceptions to this), clearly delineated custody obligations for customers' properties, reinforcement of equity capital ratio regulations for security companies, the establishment of an investor protection fund system as a counter-measure against the bankruptcy of securities companies, the liberalization of buying and selling consignment commission, the reinforcement of regulations regarding unjustifiable dealings (the prohibition of market price manipulation between the markets, the prohibition of front running, etc.), the relief of general rules regarding market concentration, etc.

Along with such laws relating to the reform of the financial system, first there is the SPC law which provides legal grounds for special purpose companies (SPC) which are conduit companies for the finance securitization plan. In addition, the "Credit Assignment Exception Law" gives the requirements to make simple opposition to an assignment to a collective credit group for the purpose of securitization. A special law has also been enacted to determine the legality of a mass liquidation of a "swap" exchange in cases of the bankruptcy of a financial organization. Even just one part of these major legal reformations would be significant in Japan, but they have all already been realized in Western countries.

Thus, the reforms of the second stage are large-scale, but the necessary reformation was conducted, searching for common legal principles as much as possible, while making the present system of legislation a priority. Using bank laws, security exchange laws, insurance business laws and commodity exchange laws (each coming under a separate government ministry). The third stage is to enact breakthrough laws that relate to the legal framework of financial services. The "Round Table Conference Relating to a New Monetary Financial Flow" which was set up by the Ministry of Finance and consisted of varied experts and many representatives of ministries and government offices, was held on June 17th of this year, dealing with the theme of "Organizing Ideology." They made a proposal to enact crosscutting and comprehensive financial legislation that imitates British financial service law. Although nothing has been firmly set as of yet, quick realization of these proposals is hoped for.

The fourth stage is my own viewpoint and hasn't been completely firmed up yet. However, my thought is to completely reconsider all the individual concepts themselves, taking the securities exchange laws and banking laws as a matter of course, and to see how Japan's system interacts with the rest of the world. When England enacted its financial service laws, they did away with each of their individual concepts, and made new financial service laws by carefully thinking things through over time. Japan also needs to take time to search out a proper Japanese model. To start, what can be done right away are reflected in the third stage's financial service laws. However, since it will take time to make up a theoretical model that backdates to the roots of the concepts, it seems to me that it is better for us to begin thinking about the theories of the fourth stage.

The problem is whether or not such work has promise; from my point of view, it has great promise. Without a doubt, Japan's financial reform has just begun. It also appears that Japan has no alternative but to follow Western models. However, humbly studying Western regulations does not mean the same thing as limiting your choices to only the Western theoretical models. America's regulation standards are very high. But in America, corporate law exists only on the state level, creating a rare condition of a nation that has no federal corpoate law. This is a special circumstance in which various kinds of securities laws have had to be used in substitute for corporate laws, in order to make federal corporate policies. This makes it difficult to totally refine the securities related laws as market regulation law. Also, England, due to historical reasons, entrusted market laws to the rules of their securities exchanges, entrusted anti-embezzling, prospectus regulations and inside trader regulations to corporate laws and entrusted many trader regulations to voluntary restraint. The first time comprehensive trader laws were enacted was with the financial service law of 1986.

I cannot go into details here, but Japan has an example of a valuable, comprehensively positioned regulation, under the security exchange law, that has a single purpose which combines market and activity regulations and trading regulations. These various laws combine the universal concepts of enhancing market function and securing the formation of fair prices in the market. Under this unified purpose I do not think it unreasonable that by the systemization of capital market legislation a model of universal theory which can stand the test of time in the market mechanism can be presented for world wide discussion. If we compare the financial system to a gingantic dam, small cracks must not be ignored, but mended as they occur, always keeping an eye on the status of the system, it is important for Japan to set up a legal framework to enforce laws using various steps. This is a work that has broad, all-encompassing meaning. At the very least, with an aggressive spirit, it is necessary to hammer out a new plan for Japan's model.

5 Arrangement of Financial Legislation and the Reinforcement of Comprehensive Legal Power

(1) Although it is impossible here to fully detail the concrete content of a new comprehensive capital market legislation plan that aims at the security of the market mechanism, some of the items included are the speed up of the develop-

ment and the listing of financial products used in transactions, the establishment and managemet of a variety of markets, and acting regulations such as the regulation of mediators who are supporters of market regulations, regulations of the voluntary restraint organizations which undertake indirect regulations, information disclosure legislation, illegal exchange regulations, and security and financial administration by independent administrative management agencies which are not affected by politics. Here, not only a highly systematic market, but also a relative exchange market are both treated as jointly owning the purpose of market regulation in pursuit of realizing a fair price.

Under such a system, crimes of finance and securities are positioned as an abstract critical crime against the market mechanism, which is public property, and therefore it is recognized as serious crime. On the other hand, actions that interfere with the market are different from outright crimes in which the act is punished and therefore in doing so criticize that act as wrong. Rather, in market interference, it is not enough that the perpetrator be punished once; countermeasures are needed to remove the improper influence on the market, as well as preventative steps against such problems, and preventing repetition of the problems. To fulfill this purpose, it is necessary to prepare a variety of regulations that cover such things as diversity of administrative disposition (discharge of profit, removal steps, etc.), civil trials and surcharges. In this situation, market regulations are meaningless if we are unable to respond to illegal acts and the market is adversely affected. For that reason, the rules of the law must be specified in as much detail as possible, but in order to correspond to the market's flexibility, it is necessary to establish a lasting, usable system that uses comprehensive regulations for the operation of setting rules and corresponding with prior enquiry (no-action letter in the U.S.). In market regulation, stability, reliability, and transparency in the practical application of laws are attained, not by explaining all the necessary matters in advance, but by establishing flexible, practical application of laws over the long run.

Also, in order to support financial legislation, it is indispensable for us to heighten the reliability of accounting and auditing systems, but to accomplish that the theory for the accounting and auditing system itself must support the recognition of the public good and face it squarely.

(2) Generally, if we speak of the reformation of legal systems in conjunction the financial "Big Bang" people think only in terms of the reformation of finance and securities legislation. However, the thing that is most important to our country is to have this new finance and security legislation exist along with the perfection of general private law. This would include civil law, commercial law and procedural law (court law). There are two meanings to this. One is the problem that for the reformed finance and security legislation to work, the general private law must be reformed. The other is the problem that the general private laws will be there to eagerly await you shoud you find loopholes and ways around the finance and securities legislation! In the first instance, for example, in order for the system of compensation for loss according to the security exchange law to function, recognition of the difficult-to-prove property damage amounts for illegal acts and causal relations in the market must be overcome. Flexible theories appropriate for the market place must exist. The second instance is a point to which Japan must specially pay attention. Originally, both the concepts particular to finance and securities law and the concepts of general private law were gradually made to conform to market dealings. The manipulation of market prices began with illegal acts and fraud and gradually took shape as crime in the secondary market. Insider trading is also based in the concept of fraud. Therefore, in the case of America, even if securities law does not apply, an attempt to circumvent general private law, which was established with these concepts, is not possible. On the other hand, in Japan such a vast system of general private law based on these principles, that covers financial legislation as well, does not exist. If an action falls outside of the sphere covered by financial and securities legislation, people feel they have entered an area where "anything goes."

(3) Financial organizations and security companies are listed companies, and even more basically they are corporations. For any financial and security legislation to be formed, it must be based on the premise that it is right for a corporation, and next that it is right for a general listed company. For instance, when the Bank of Japan examines a financial organization or the Ministry of Finance inspects a securities company, these activities should be base on the corporate law and accepted certified public accounting audit to at least the same degree as required for a general company. However, in Japan even this level of reliability is absent. Japan must again take a fundamental look at "corporate governance" and must return to basics, establishing a practical, effective management supervisory system.

Additionally, there are many problems such as the discovery system, induction of class action system, strength of the no-justice procedure for arbitration, etc. In the judiciary itself, reformation of the justice system is crucial in the areas of excessively long court cases, an excess in the number and regional areas of judiciary officers. In short, fundamental perfection of finacial legislation has to be supported by enhancing Japan's comprehensive legal power.

In Conclusion

Japan is now in the middle of a financial crisis centering on non-performing loans that has caused an extreme downturn in business. Reformation of the financial system must be steadily pursued along with a parallel response to emergencies as they arise. Clear navigation through these, difficult waters is increasingly necessary. I myself am pessimistic as to whether or not meaningful work can be pursued while at the same time conducting the current emergency countermeasures. However, it must be recognized that fundamental and extreme counter-cyclical measures are exactly what must be undertaken to raise international trust in Japan. If this is not done, it will be a long time before Japanese companies will be able to step on the accelerator of business with confidence.

Part II : Free Market and Legal Regulations
(i) Market Economy and Legal Regulations

(*)Security companies reimbursed large investors for losses on securities transactions. The amounts announced by only large security companies as having been reimbursed exceede ¥200 billion. I am still convinced that this practice of guaranteeting prior losses was an illegal act even before this occurred, but the matter was disposed of as not being illegal because there was no specified rules concerning compensating loss discovered after the fact. This was ratified by the court.

(ii) VARIOUS FORMS of REGULATIONS

9 Regulating "Criminal" Conduct by Civil Remedy: The Case of Exemplary Damages

Michael Tilbury

1 The Background
2 Definition and Terminology of Exemplary Damages
3 Deregulation, the Criminal Law and Exemplary Damages
4 The Major Obstacle: Due Process
5 Limitations on the Award of Exemplary Damages
6 Making Exemplary Damages More Generally Available
  Conclusion

1 The Background

Speaking very generally, the criminal law exists because society at a particular point of time finds that given conduct is so anti-social and unacceptable that it wishes to denounce, deter and punish it.[1] In modern times it does so through the regulatory framework of the State. This has not always been the case. We know that, in earliest times, the punishment of conduct which was unacceptable was a matter of group vengeance.[2] That vengeance was exacted by the group (whether an extended family unit, clan or tribe) either against a member of the group whose behaviour failed to live up to the standards of the group, or against another group which, collectively or through one of its members, had failed to live up to the customary and acceptable norms which governed relations between the groups in question. In both cases, the failure to take group action ran the risk of unregulated violence. As groups welded together to form ethnic, and later national, entities, the task of regulating behaviour fell naturally on the new group entity, now manifested in the national State. However, at least in common law systems of law, it has only been within the last 200 years or so that the responsibility of regulating behaviour which we call "criminal" has come to be seen as the exclusive domain of the State.⁽³⁾ This has occurred by reason of the development of modern bureaucracies, especially of police forces capable of detecting crimes and bringing their perpetrators before the Courts. In that process, the role of the victim of the crime and of those who form part of his or her immediate social structure, is small, limited, traditionally, to drawing the crime to the attention of the relevant authorities.

The distinction between behaviour which is classified as "criminal" and that which is not is notoriously difficult to draw. This is hardly surprising since, at base, the distinction represents a societal consensus on the classification of conduct which is to be publicly punished and that which is not. That consensus is forged in a crucible of conflicting views of religion, morality, philosophy, social perception and economics. It is difficult enough to draw in a stable mono-cultural society; even more, in a modern democratic and pluralist society. It is probably just as well, therefore, that the essentials of the consensus were drawn in societies which, from today's perspective, were relatively homogeneous. They have left us with a core of behaviour which we classify as criminal and without which it is difficult to believe that there would be much agreement on the topic in our society.

Much of our understanding of what is criminal is, indeed, determined historically.⁽⁴⁾ Suppose, for example, the question arises whether or not it is appropriate to deter some interference with land ("trespass to land") by subjecting it to criminal sanctions. This answer depends, in principle, on the value which society places on the "victim's" relationship with the land and the part which land plays in the overall wealth of that society. Land, and the power which comes from its ownership, can even today be a valuable political, economic and social asset. The more so historically. When those great administrators, the Norman Kings, took control of England after the Conquest of 1066 and began to weld England into a nation by concentrating power in their hands at the expense of the local lords and barons, they were faced with this question: on what basis were legal cases to be allocated between the new national system of law (which eventually became the "common law") and the existing courts controlled by local potentates. They found the answer in "cases which threatened a breach of the peace", that is, "the King's peace". For it was now the function of the monarch to guarantee his subjects the minimum social standards associated with a peaceable life which would, at least, avoid resort to mob or individual violence. A first encounter with the "breach of the peace" concept implies serious offences against public order and contains the hint that the King's courts should concern themselves with "criminal conduct". Indeed, they did so, but no distinction was drawn between crime and tort (delict). Interference with interests in land of their nature threatened a breach of the peace so, not surprisingly, they became subject to the jurisdiction of the King's courts, where the liability which they attracted came to be both criminal and civil.[5]

Thus the inherent difficulty of defining criminal conduct combines with historical considerations to ensure that much conduct in our law is both a civil wrong[6] and a crime.[7] This provides the first reason for asking the question whether such conduct ought to be the subject of both the criminal and civil law or is more appropriately dealt with by only one of these.

There is also another reason for asking the question. I have suggested that the inherent difficulty of obtaining agreement on what conduct should qualify as criminal is exacerbated in a pluralist democracy. Suppose that the courts, in the course of civil proceedings, witness conduct which they consider ought to be classified as criminal but it is not. An example may be a novel manifestation of "fraud" in the context of a transaction involving computer technology which does not quite come within any of the existing fraudulent offences since, in respect of each possible offence, it is lacking some relevant element. Ought the court to be able to "punish" such conduct in the course of civil proceedings the first time it comes across it? What if it begins to come before the courts with regularity but Parliament has not yet acted to create a new offence covering the conduct?

This paper addresses these two problems by raising the issue of whether or not it is appropriate for a court in civil proceedings to grant exemplary damages. I also suggest how this issue could be relevant to the debate about deregulation. I leave the resolution of this issue to another day.[8]

2 Definition and Terminology of Exemplary Damages

Exemplary damages, commonly known as punitive damages in the United States, are damages whose object is to punish the defendant and to deter the defendant and others from similar conduct in the future.[9] Exemplary damages are a feature of common law systems and are unknown in civilian systems of law,[10] although they have had some influence in mixed systems of law,[11] sometimes through statutory introduction.[12]

Even though the distinction is often difficult to draw, exemplary damages must be distinguished from aggravated damages.[13] Aggravated damages are compensatory.[14] They are given in cases involving injury to the plaintiff's "dignatory interests"[15] where it can be assumed that the plaintiff's loss is increased by the outrageousness of the defendant's conduct.[16] They are, therefore, similar to exemplary damages because it is the defendant's behaviour which provides the occasion for their award. Defamation is an example of a tort which attracts aggravated damages.[17] The conduct of the defendant which may call into play the award of aggravated damages includes: the defendant's failure to apologize for the defamatory allegation when, in all the circumstances of the case, an apology ought to be made;[18] or, sometimes, the defendant's conduct of the litigation (for example, the persistence in a false plea of truth).[19]

Four practical points ought to be noted about the way in which exemplary damages operate in Australia. First, exemplary damages are not, in practice, awarded in as many cases as in the United States. Secondly, until recently, exemplary damages tended to be restricted in practice to cases involving intentional injury to the plaintiff, but they are now coming to be awarded in cases of negligence where the defendant's conduct is particularly egregious[20]-for example where a defendant employer has recklessly or negligently exposed employees to health risks over a number of years.[21]

Thirdly, when exemplary damages are awarded, their assessment tends to be modest and, in Australia, we simply do not have the massive awards of punitive damages which are common in the United States.[22] One of the reasons for this is that, apart from Victoria, there are very few jury trials in civil case in Australia. Fourthly, in New South Wales, which is where most defamation litigation takes place in Australia,[23] statute outlaws the award of exemplary damages.[24] This means that aggravated damages are very important in defamation cases in that State.

3 Deregulation, the Criminal Law and Exemplary Damages

Politically, "deregulation" is in fashion. It is fuelled by a philosophy which, in its essentials, believes that the greater good is achieved through the promotion of self-interest which, in turn, generates economic efficiency and suggests small government. A State monopoly on criminal law is at odds with the philosophy of deregulation. A priori, it is at least arguable that deregulation of the criminal law by dismantling State monopoly should take place because of the greater efficiencies which it would generate. The creation of private prisons shows that this argument has already met with some success. From a political point of view, private prisons have great attraction. Not only do they reduce one costly item in government budgets,[25] but they enable politicians to point to the fact that prisoners are not being maintained at taxpayers' expense. Instead, the prisons are being run as commercial enterprises. It is, however, far too early to tell whether or not private prisons, by utilizing the time and labour of prisoners and operating independently of an invasive State control, can achieve a net social benefit through efficiencies which have proved elusive in State prisons. "Net social benefit" is, of course, not simply an economic one, whether viewed through a Pareto[26] or Kaldor-Hicks[27] lense.[28]

Now, if prisons can be made more efficient by privatising them, what about other aspects of the criminal justice system? For example, where conduct is both civil and criminal, could we not argue, at least in some cases, that it is more efficient that the costs of punishment should be transferred to civil proceedings? After all, taking the State out of the picture has immediate economic benefits, which can range from eliminating the expense of deciding whether or not to prosecute, of gathering evidence, of the criminal trial and of administering criminal sanctions. These arguments are met immediately by two major obstacles: first, due process concerns; and, secondly, the limited availability of appropriate (that is, criminal-type) sanctions in civil cases. For our purposes, this means the limited availability of exemplary damages.

4 The Major Obstacle: Due Process

Civil and criminal proceedings are quite distinct. Criminal proceedings enforce the social policy of the community. The State enforces that social policy by exacting a penalty from those who have been found in breach of it. The State's object in doing so is variously expressed: to punish those found guilty; to act as a warning to them not to offend again; to deter others from committing offences; to vindicate the policy of the law by denouncing those in breach of it; to exact retribution on behalf of those who have been injured by the breach so as to prevent them from taking the law into their own hands; and to rehabilitate those who have offended.[29] By contrast, the object of civil proceedings is to enable the plaintiff to obtain compensation, restitution or some form of coercive relief against a defendant who has wronged him or her.[30] The overwhelming emphasis on compensation in civil proceedings stresses their essence: to heal a situation created by the defendant's conduct by requiring the defendant to put the plaintiff in the position in which the plaintiff would have been if the defendant had not engaged in the conduct in question. Although both criminal and civil proceedings involve, in the final analysis, sanctions against particular types of conduct, those of the criminal law are, typically, more severe than those of the civil law. The sanctions of the civil law, particularly compensation, are justified, simply, in terms of corrective justice. But those of the criminal law go well beyond this. The serious consequences which they entail include, in particular, the deprivation of personal liberty through imprisonment.

For this reason, it is not surprising that criminal proceedings are subject to strict controls in terms of "due process", using that expression in the widest possible sense. These include:

- the clear definition by the State of the offences which can result in punishment following criminal proceedings;
- the institution, management and control of criminal prosecutions by the State itself;
- the protection of the accused at all stages of that prosecution, especially, the presumption of innocence, the right to silence and the requirement that the State prove the accused's guilt beyond reasonable doubt;
- the legislative prescription of maximum penalties for offences;
- the enforcement by the State of criminal sanctions, or at least the State's accountability for their enforcement.

It can be seen that the State is involved at all stages of criminal proceedings. Traditionally, this has been an exclusive involvement. But this needs the following qualifications:

- Where the State takes a decision not to prosecute a criminal breach of the law, persons with an interest in enforcing that area of the law may be able to bring a relator action in the name of the Attorney General in order to do so,[31] but they will need the Attorney's consent.[32]
- Victims of crimes may be able to intervene at various stages of the criminal process. In particular, they are now widely accorded the right to make a "victim impact statement" at the point of sentencing.[33] Under some systems of law, they may be allowed a voice in the decision whether or not to prosecute.
- Victims of crimes may also have rights of compensation enforceable directly against the person found guilty of committing the crime, or, more generally, against the State. These rights are enforceable in separate proceedings.[34]

Notwithstanding these qualifications, it remains the case that the State is the principal actor in criminal prosecutions. This may, in fact, provide little or no protection for the accused where State officials act incompetently or corruptly. And it must be remembered that the State has a wide field of discretion in criminal cases, particularly in the decision whether or not to institute proceedings.[35]

5 Limitations on the Award of Exemplary Damages

The objectives of punishment and deterrence are common to exemplary damages and criminal proceedings. The result is that the potential overlap between exemplary damages and the criminal law is great. In practice, however, the extent of overlap depends on how widely exemplary damages are available in civil cases.

The common law has, for some centuries, awarded damages in civil actions which are variously described as exemplary, punitive, retributory or vindictive.[36] The function of such damages, as well as the circumstances in which they were available, were not clearly articulated until 1964, when the English House of Lords decided *Rookes v. Barnard*.[37] In that case, Lord Devlin held, in a great speech, that exemplary damages were anomalous since they confused the function of the criminal and civil laws and that, in future, they were only to be awarded in three clearly defined circumstances:

- those in which servants of the government had engaged in oppressive, arbitrary or unconstitutional conduct;
- those where the defendant had calculated that his conduct would result in a profit which would exceed any compensation which may be payable to the plaintiff; and
- those in which exemplary damages were authorised by statute.[38]

These categories represented a compromise between principle, policy and precedent. The principle and policy was that exemplary damages, designed to punish and deter, ought not to be recoverable at all in civil cases since they confound the purposes of the civil and criminal laws; in short they are anomalous.⁽³⁹⁾ On the other hand, there clearly existed a "chaotic" body of authority⁽⁴⁰⁾ which established that damages aimed at punishment and deterrence were recoverable. To the extent that the compromise requires that exemplary damages only be awardable in certain types of actions, it is, in this as in other respects, illogical⁽⁴¹⁾ since it does not address the defendant's conduct which, in principle, should alone determine the circumstances in which exemplary damages are recoverable.⁽⁴²⁾

For these reasons, Lord Devlin's restatement of the law was not followed in Australia,⁽⁴³⁾ New Zealand⁽⁴⁴⁾ or Canada.⁽⁴⁵⁾ This left the law in those jurisdictions in the "choatic" state that it was before 1964. However, as I have argued elsewhere,⁽⁴⁶⁾ there are, in fact, four factors which are, or have been, relevant to the question of whether or not exemplary damages ought to be awarded. They are:

- the nature of the defendant's conduct;
- the nature of the plaintiff's cause of action;
- the fact that the plaintiff needs to be the victim of the defendant's conduct; and
- the capacity of exemplary damages to fulfil their purpose in all the circumstances of the case.

The defendant's conduct

The conduct of the wrongdoer is central to the decision whether or not to award exemplary damages.⁽⁴⁷⁾ In Australian law, that conduct must amount to "conscious wrongdoing in contumelious disregard of the plaintiff's rights".⁽⁴⁸⁾ The expression originates in the writings of Sir John Salmond, the great torts lawyer and writer on jurisprudence.⁽⁴⁹⁾

Two points should be borne in mind about this description. First the mens rea, or mental element of the conduct, is expressed in terms which accord with the criminal law. The defendant must be at least be a conscious actor, and the defendant's motive for acting may be taken into account.⁽⁵⁰⁾ For example, the fact that the defendant acted with the best of motives and in what were thought to be the plaintiff's best interests may prevent an award of exemplary damages.[51] But, secondly, the actus reus, or objective description of the conduct, is extraordinarily vague. The conduct must be "contumelious". Yet, most native English speakers would not have heard the word. If they had, they almost certainly would not know what it means, except to gather from its context that it must be very bad! The courts tell us that the conduct must be such as to warrant more than the mere disapproval of the court.[52] But the cases are no more than individual illustrations of what factual situations do, and what do not, merit the censure of the court in exemplary damages.

The plaintiff's cause of action

One of the factors relevant to the award of exemplary damages when the law existed in its "chaotic" state before *Rookes v. Barnard* was the plaintiff's cause of action. The reason was that English law developed as a formulary system through a variety of specific causes of action, so that it is not surprising that the plaintiff's cause of action provided a basis to determine when exemplary damages would (and would not) be available. This continues to be the case in England where it is established that exemplary damages are only available in the same cases as they were before *Rookes v. Barnard*.[53] The English Law Commission has, rightly, recommended that this should be changed so that exemplary damages will, in principle, be available in response to most wrongs.[54] Put shortly, once *Rookes v. Barnard* had identified the nature and purpose of exemplary damages, there was no longer any need to tie it to the plaintiff's cause of action. This is now the position in Australian[55] and Canadian law.[56] As Clement JA said in the Alberta Court of Appeals in *Paragon Properties Ltd v. Magna Envestments Ltd*:[57]

> "It is the reprehensible conduct of the wrongdoer which attracts the principle, not the legal category of the wrong out of which compensatory damages arise and in relation to which the conduct occurred. To place arbitrary limitations upon its application is to evade the underlying principle and replace it with an

uncertain and debatable jurisdiction".

Plaintiff the victim

In *Rookes v. Barnard*[58] Lord Devlin said that the plaintiff can only recover exemplary damages where he or she is the victim of punishable behaviour, so that exemplary damages will not be given to a plaintiff who, for some reason or another (for example, because of a thick skin), is unaffected by the defendant's egregious conduct.

In Australia there is some support for the proposition that what this consideration really means is that exemplary damages are only available where a plaintiff has a claim to compensatory damages, or, as it is put, exemplary damages are "parasitic" on compensatory damages.[59] But New Zealand case law has shown that this is too narrow.[60] Where, as in personal injury cases in New Zealand, statute abolishes common law claims for damages, there seems no reason why the statute should not be read to allow an independent claim for exemplary damages (that is, to read "damages" as limited to compensatory damages).[61]

Capacity to fulfil its purposes

It may seem obvious that exemplary damages will not be available where they do not have the capacity to fulfil their purpose, namely, to punish and deter. But it is easier to state the proposition than to apply it. Take, for example, the situation where the defendant's conduct is covered by insurance. Can exemplary damages really fulfil their purpose in such a situation? Quite clearly, they will not punish the defendant, since the defendant will not feel their "sting". Nevertheless, it is arguable that they still have the capacity to deter others. For this reason and one other, the High Court of Australia held in *Lamb v. Cotogno*,[62] which it subsequently confirmed in *Gray v. Motor Accident Commission*,[63] that exemplary damages were available against a defendant whose outrageous behaviour in the use of his motor vehicle had caused personal injury to the plaintiff even though the defendant was covered by compulsory third-party motor insurance. Professor Luntz has called the decision "absurd".[64] I agree with him. It simply stretches the imagination too far to say that other motorists (also covered by compulsory third party insurance) would be deterred from the sort of conduct in which the defendant engaged, even if the rather fanciful assumption is made that such motorists knew of the risk of an award of exemplary damages and its potential effect on their premium levels. The other reason given by the Court was that the award of exemplary damages assuaged the plaintiff's urge for revenge.[65] But, while the plaintiff's urge for revenge should, no doubt, be assuaged by the punishment and deterrence which the award of exemplary damages holds out, it must, surely, still be appropriate to deter and punish the defendant in the first place.

It does not follow that exemplary damages should be excluded in all cases where the defendant is insured. For example, exemplary damages have recently been awarded in England in a number of cases in which the police have violated plaintiffs' rights.[66] Such damages would seem to be justified as achieving deterrence. Following a number of such awards, pressure would be brought to bear on the police to cease offending activities because their insurance premiums were rising out of control and they ran the risk of being uninsured. But this normative argument makes assumptions about the factors which determine insurance premiums which may or may not be justifiable – for example, the increased risk may simply be borne by insurers through effective reinsurance arrangements.

Apart from the situation where the defendant is covered by insurance, there are two other circumstances in which exemplary damages may have no purpose. First, where the plaintiff's compensatory award is so high that it is, in itself, a sufficient punishment and deterrent.[67] Secondly, where the defendant has already been punished.[68] In *Gray v. Motor Accident Commission*[69] Gleeson CJ, McHugh, Gummow and Hayne JJ said:

> "Where ... the criminal law has been brought to bear upon the wrongdoer and substantial punishment inflicted, we consider that exemplary damages

may not be awarded. We say may not because we consider that the infliction of substantial punishment for what is substantially the same conduct as the conduct which is the subject of the civil proceedings is a bar to the award: the decision is not one that is reached as a matter of discretion dependent on the facts and circumstances in each particular case."

The principles underlying this rule of law are, first, the consideration that the reasons for awarding exemplary damages have been met wholly met where the criminal law has meted out substantial punishment;[70] and, secondly, the desire to avoid double punishment.[71] While the principles underlying this rule of law are clear, its statement by the High Court leaves many issues unanswered, as the Court itself acknowledged.[72] These include the difficulties of determining: whether or not the criminal punishment is "substantial"; when "substantial identity" exists between the criminal and civil proceedings; the effect on civil proceedings for exemplary damages of an acquittal in the related criminal proceedings; and, the implication for the civil proceedings of the existence or likelihood of criminal proceedings.[73] In Australia, these difficulties remain to be worked out in subsequent case law.[74] Meanwhile, the New Zealand Court of Appeal has avoided many of the difficulties by stating a wider rule. In *Daniels v. Thompson*,[75] the Court of Appeal decided that a claim for exemplary damages cannot be brought where the defendant's conduct has been, *or is likely to be*, the subject of a criminal prosecution.

Both the course chartered in *Gray v. Motor Accident Commission* and (a fortiori) that adopted in New Zealand, reinforce the primary role of the criminal law, and hence the State, in the exacting of punishment. In *Daniels v. Thompson* the majority of the New Zealand Court of Appeal (Richardson P, Gault, Henry and Keith JJ) said:[76]

"The role of the State in dealing with criminal conduct will take priority, and the intervention of private interests postponed until that role has been concluded ... It would also ensure that the infliction of punishment for the criminal offence lies, as it should, primarily with the criminal law".

The practical effect of all this is to limit the availability of exemplary damages perhaps even more than if Australia and New Zealand had adopted the approach in *Rookes v. Barnard*. For the defendant's conduct potentially attracts the criminal law and its sanctions in most cases in which exemplary damages are available. This may mean that, in practice, exemplary damages will only be important in those cases in which the court wishes to censure conduct which is not, or not yet, defined as criminal.

6 Making Exemplary Damages More Generally Available

Ought exemplary damages to be more generally available and the costs of prosecution and punishment transferred from criminal to civil litigation? Apart from purely economic considerations, the arguments in favour seem to me to be that the plaintiff benefits in these distinct ways:

- The plaintiff has control over the issue of whether or not to "prosecute" and on the management of the case. This could be important where there is a pre-existing relationship between the plaintiff and defendant —— such as a family relationship in a sexual abuse case.
- If the New Zealand approach towards the relationship between criminal and civil proceedings is followed, the court is given some, admittedly small, control over prosecutorial discretion in those cases in which the prosecutor is delaying or avoiding the decision whether or not to prosecute. This is because the court will put pressure on the prosecutor's inertia by requiring him or her to exercise the discretion.
- The plaintiff obtains the "fine" rather than the State. Traditionally, this has been regarded as a "windfall" to the plaintiff. The use of "windfall" implies that the plaintiff really ought not to be receiving the money. But this argument assumes a State monopoly on punishment.[77]

Against these arguments are the due process concerns which have been mentioned above. There are three in particular which, I submit, are of primary importance:

- The first is the burden of proof. If the defendant is to be punished, proof must go beyond the civil standard. The solution may be that, in view of the serious consequences of a award of exemplary damages, there must be clear and convincing evidence. In Australia, this is possible in civil cases under the *Briginshaw* test.[78]
- The second is more difficult. We have seen that the description of conduct which justifies an award of exemplary damages is indeterminate, so much so that Lord Reid once remarked that it is expressed in "terms too vague to be admitted to any criminal code worthy of the name".[79] This is even more pronounced where the conduct in question does not, in fact, already attract the censure of the criminal law. Without determinacy in the nature of the conduct attracting exemplary damages, the award of exemplary damages can be seen as breaching the principle of legality which underlines modern civilian criminal codes —— that is that there should be no crime and no punishment without a prior penal provision.[80] For the moment, I do not see how the current indeterminacy in the definition of conduct attracting exemplary damages can be overcome.
- Thirdly, legislation or the development of principles of common law will be needed to place control on, and obtain some consistency in, the amount of damages which can be awarded as punishment. This cannot be left to the complete discretion of a judge or, a fortiori, a jury. In this respect, current exhortation to moderation may not be enough.[81]

Conclusion

Even if convincing arguments can be made for the breakdown of the State monopoly on criminal prosecution in favour of greater reliance on exemplary damages, the points raised in the last paragraph will need to be seriously addressed. To leave them unanswered in the context of deregulating the criminal justice system would be to place too much power in the hands of judges and plaintiffs. Indeed, we perhaps ought not to be entertaining the idea of deregulation at all until we are really satisfied that exemplary damages have a justifiable role in civil law. Like Professor Burrows, I am simply not convinced that they do.[82]

For the moment at least, exemplary damages must retain their anomalous status as an exceptional remedy[83] in the scheme of civil remedies.

(1) See J. Smith and B. Hogan, *Criminal Law* (8th ed., Butterworths, London, 1996) Ch 1.

(2) A.S. Diamond, *Primitive Law Past and Present* (Methuen, London, 1971) p. 18, Ch. 18. For examples from extant communal societies, see further E. Adamson Hoebel, *The Law of Primitive Man: A Study in Comparative Legal Dynamics* (Harvard U.P., Cambridge, 1961).

(3) See especially A H Manchester, *A Modern Legal History of England and Wales 1750-1950* (Butterworths, London, 1980) pp. 226-230.

(4) For a brief history of the development of English criminal law, see J.H. Baker, *An Introduction to English Legal History* (2nd ed., Butterworths, London, 1979) Ch. 24.

(5) See T.F.T. Plucknett, *A Concise History of the Common Law* (Butterworth & Co. (Publishers) Ltd., London, 1956) pp. 463-482.

(6) Usually a tort or delict, but a breach of contract may also be a crime.

(7) See *Uren v. John Fairfax & Sons Pty Ltd*. (1966) 117 CLR 118 at 149 per Windeyer J (roots of tort and crime greatly intermingled). See also *Gray v. Motor Accident Commission* (1998) 158 ALR 485 at 489 per Gleeson, C.J, McHugh, Gummow and Hayne JJ.

(8) For an economic analysis of exemplary damages, see A Ogus, "Exemplary Damages and Economic Analysis" in K Hawkins (ed), *The Human Face of Law: Essays in Honour of Donald Harris* (Clarendon Press, Oxford, 1997) Ch. 4.

(9) *Whitfeld v. De Lauret & Co Ltd* (1920) 29 CLR 71 at 81; *Uren v. John Fairfax & Sons Pty Ltd* (1966) 117 *CLR* 118 *at* 149; *Australian Consolidated Press Ltd v. Uren* (1967) 117 CLR 221; *Lamb v. Cotogno* (1987) 164 CLR 1 at 9.

(10) See R Zimmermann, *The Law of Obligations: Roman Foundations of the Civilian Tradition* (Juta & Co. Ltd., Cape Town, 1990) p. 909 n. 54.

(11) See, eg, P.J. Visser and J M Potgieter, *Law of Damages* (Cape Town, Juta & Co Ltd, 1993) pp. 156-157 (Roman-Dutch law of South Africa).

(12) See D Gardner, "Reflexions sur les Dommages Punitifs et Exemplaires" (1998) 77 *Canadian Bar Rev*. 198 (damages for breach of copyright in Quebec).
(13) See M Tilbury, "Factors Inflating Damages Awards" in P.D. Finn (ed.), *Essays on Damages* (Law Book Co. Ltd., Sydney, 1992) at 92-96.
(14) *Uren v. John Fairfax & Sons Pty Ltd* (1966) 117 CLR 118 at 149 per Windeyer J.
(15) *BHP Ltd. v. Fisher* (1984) 38 SASR 50 at 66.
(16) See M J Tilbury, *Civil Remedies* (Butterworths, Sydney, 1990) vol. 1 para. 3208 ("The justification of assigning a special label to increased damage in the case of injury to feelings is that such loss is *implied* by reference to the defendant's conduct of which the court disapproves").
(17) For a full analysis see M J Tilbury, *Civil Remedies* (Butterworths, Sydney, 1993) vol. 2 paras. 11012-11023.
(18) Ibid., para. 11019.
(19) Ibid., para. 11015.
(20) Eg *Backwell v. A* [1997] 1 VR 182, discussed by M. Tilbury, "Exemplary Damages in Medical Negligence" (1996) 4 *Tort L. Rev*. 167.
(21) See *Trend Management Ltd v. Borg* (1996) 40 NSWLR 500, discussed by M Tilbury, "Exemplary Damages in Negligence Claims" (1997) 5 *Tort L. Rev*. 85.
(22) See M. Tilbury and H. Luntz, "Punitive Damages in Australian Law", 17 *Loyola of Los Angeles Int'l and Comp L.J*. 769 at 791-792 (1995).
(23) Sydney has been called the defamation capital of the world: see R. Pullan, *Guilty Secrets: Free Speech and Defamation in Australia* (Pascal Press, Glebe, 1994) at 3. This description is not sustained by available empirical evidence: see New South Wales Law Reform Commission, *Defamation* (LRC 75, 1995), para. 3.25. London is more properly so regarded: see E. Barendt, L. Lustgarten, K. Norrie and H Stephenson, *Libel and the Media: The Chilling Effect* (Clarendon Press, Oxford, 1997), p 16.
(24) *Defamation Act 1974* (NSW) s. 46(3)(a).
(25) For the cost of imprisonment in New South Wales, see New South Wales Law Reform Commission, *Sentencing* (LRC 79, 1996), paras. 1.18-1.21.
(26) Put very simply: no one must be worse off by what has happened.
(27) Put very simply: what has happened must allow those who are better off to compensate those who worse off.
(28) See, generally, R. Posner, *Economic Analysis of Law* (4th ed., Little Brown & Co, Boston, 1992) Ch. 1.

(29) See New South Wales Law Reform Commission, *Sentencing* (DP 33, 1996) paras. 3.2-3.24.
(30) See Tilbury, op cit., n. 16, paras. 1028-1029.
(31) A celebrated example is *Gouriet v. Union of Post Office Workers* [1978] AC 435.
(32) See M Aronson and B Dyer, *Judicial Review of Administrative Action* (3rd ed, LBC Information Services, Sydney, 1996) pp. 917-920; C Lewis, *Judicial Remedies in Public Law* (Sweet & Maxwell, London, 1992) pp 21-22.
(33) See New South Wales Law Reform Commission, op. cit., n. 29, Ch. 11.
(34) Ibid., Ch. 10.
(35) See J. Fionda, *Public Prosecutors and Discretion: A Comparative Study* (Clarendon Press, Oxford, 1995).
(36) See especially H McGregor, *Mayne & McGregor on Damages* (12th ed, Sweet & Maxwell, London, 1961), para. 207.
(37) [1964] AC 1129.
(38) Ibid. at 1226.
(39) See especially *Broome v. Cassell & Co. Ltd*. [1972] AC 1027 at 1086-87 per Lord Reid.
(40) *Broome v. Cassell & Co. Ltd*. [1972] AC 1027 at 1070 per Lord Hailsham of St Marylebone.
(41) Ibid. at 1087 per Lord Reid.
(42) Consider *Gray v. Motor Accident Commission* (1998) 158 ALR 485 at 493.
(43) *Uren v. John Fairfax & Sons Pty Ltd*. (1966) 117 CLR 118; *Australian Consolidated Press v. Uren* (1967) 117 CLR 221.
(44) *Taylor v. Beere* [1982] 1 NZLR 81; *Donselaar v. Donselaar* [1982] 1 NZLR 97.
(45) *Vorvis v. Insurance Corporation of British Columbia* [1989] 1 SCR 1085.
(46) Tilbury, op. cit., n. 16, Ch 5.
(47) *Gray v. Motor Accident Commission* (1998) 158 ALR 485 at 493.
(48) *Whitfeld v. De Lauret & Co Ltd* (1920) 29 CLR 71 at 77 per Knox CJ. See also *Gray v. Motor Accident Commission* (1998) 158 ALR 485 at 489 per Gleeson CJ, McHugh, Gummow and Hayne JJ.
(49) See J Salmond, *A Treatise on the Law of Torts* (5th ed., Sweet & Maxwell, London) p. 129.
(50) See Tilbury, op. cit., n. 16, paras. 5005-5007.
(51) Eg *Proprietary Schools of Western Australia Ltd v. Crown* (1943) 46 WALR 37.

(52) See *Uren v. John Farifax & Sons Pty Ltd.* (1966) 117 CLR 118 at 153 per Windeyer J.
(53) *AB v. South West Water Services Ltd* [1993] QB 507.
(54) Law Commission of England and Wales, *Aggravated, Exemplary and Restitutionary Damages* (Law Com. No. 247, 1997), paras. 5.49-5.77.
(55) Especially *Lamb v. Cotogno* (1987) 164 CLR 1 at 8.
(56) *Vorvis v. Insurance Corporation of British Columbia* [1989] 1 SCR 1085.
(57) (1972) 24 DLR (3d) 156 at 167.
(58) [1964] AC 1129 at 1227.
(59) *XL Petroleum (NSW) Pty Ltd. v. Caltex Oil (Australia) Pty Ltd.* (1985) 155 CLR 448.
(60) See especially *Donselaar v. Donselaar* [1982] 1 NZLR 97.
(61) This provided the opportunity to the courts unjustifiably to pass off compensatory awards as exemplary ones: see J Smillie, "Exemplary Damages for Personal Injury" [1997] *NZ L. Rev.* 140.
(62) (1987) 164 CLR 1.
(63) (1998) 158 ALR 485 at 493 per Gleeson C.J., McHugh, Gummow and Hayne JJ.; but compare at 505 per Kirby J.
(64) H. Luntz, *Assessment of Damages for Personal Injury and Death* (3rd ed., Butterworths, Sydney, 1990) para. 1.7.6. The absurdity is diminished where the insurer has a right of recovery against the insured: see *Gray v. Motor Accident Commission* (1998) 158 ALR 485 at 494.
(65) *Lamb v. Cotogno* (1987) 164 CLR 1 at 9.
(66) See especially *Thompson v. Commissioner of Police* [1997] 2 All ER 762 (CA).
(67) Eg *Backwell v. A* [1997] 1 VR 182.
(68) See *Gray v. Motor Accident Commission* (1998) 158 ALR 485; *Watts v. Leitch* [1973] Tas SR 16.
(69) (1998) 158 ALR 485 at 494.
(70) *Gray v. Motor Accident Commission* (1998) 158 ALR 485 at 495.
(71) Ibid.
(72) Ibid. at 495-496.
(73) Id.
(74) Eg *McDonald v. State of New South Wales* [1999] NSWSC 350 (20 April 1999) (non-custodial sentence may amount to substantial punishment).
(75) [1998] 3 NZLR 22. For a full discussion, see J. Smillie, "Exemplary Damages and the Criminal Law" (1998) 6 *Torts LJ. 113*.
(76) *Daniels v. Thompson* [1998] 3 NZLR 22 at 53.

(77) For further criticism, see N J McBride, "Punitive Damages" in P Birks (ed), *Wrongs and Remedies in the Twenty-First Century* (Clarendon Press, Oxford, 1996) p. 196.

(78) See *Briginshaw v. Briginshaw* (1938) 60 CLR 336 especially at 362-363 per Dixon J. And see *Backwell v. A* [1997] 1 VR 182.

(79) *Broome v. Cassell & Co Ltd* [1972] AC 1027 at 1087.

(80) *Nulla crimen nulla poena sine praevia lege poenali*.

(81) See, eg, *XL Petroleum (NSW) Pty Ltd v. Caltex Oil (Australia) Pty Ltd* (1985) 155 CLR 448 at 463. Compare *Thompson v. Commissioner of Police* [1997] 2 All ER 762 (CA).

(82) A Burrows, "Reforming Exemplary Damages: Expansion or Abolition?" in P Birks (ed), *Wrongs and Remedies in the Twenty-First Century* (Clarendon Press, Oxford, 1996) Ch. 7.

(83) *Gray v. Motor Accident Commission* (1998) 158 ALR 485 at 490-491 per Gleeson C.J., McHugh, Gummow and Hayne JJ.

10 Regulating Corporate Activity through Strict and Absolute Liability

W. J. Brookbanks

Introduction
1 Classification of Offences in New Zealand
2 The Scope of Strict Liability in New Zealand
3 Strict Liability and Environmental Offences
4 Sentencing Policy
5 Liability of the Principal for the Acts of Agents
Conclusion

Introduction

The complexities of modern society and the pressure these create on our social and natural environments, have dictated the need for regulatory measures that are strong and restrictive. One aim of such regulation is to balance the need to protect the environments in which people live against the need to encourage economic and commercial growth in order to achieve a prosperous economy.

As part of this regulatory approach many Western countries, including New Zealand, have adopted the strategy of employing the machinery of the criminal law to enforce a new class of offences, called generally offences of strict liability, which are not criminal in a real sense and to which the traditional principles of criminal law may have only limited application. Indeed, it might be better to regard these offences as a branch of administrative law, enforced by criminal sanctions for reasons of economy and efficiency. For the most part the defendants in such proceedings are corporations, often performing their normal activities but in a manner which constitutes a breach of a specific regulation or statute.

The proliferation of these offences has begun to impact a broad range of social activities including road transport regulation, food and drug administration, industrial safety and environmental management. The emphasis of regulation is upon forcing high standards of personal or corporate performance without the necessity of overcoming rigorous standards of criminal proof in order to achieve conviction. A broad issue of concern, however, is whether the criminal law is being incrementally expanded while traditional protections of the criminal law are being gradually eroded.

The purpose of this paper will be to examine the scope of the concepts of "strict" and "absolute" liability with particular reference to offences in breach of environmental legislation. I will endeavour to show that while traditional justifications for strict liability have emphasised the lack of stigma associated with such offences and the relatively minor penalties imposed, in reality in many instances the penalties available are severe and the consequences of prosecution for the offender, whether an individual or a corporation, are serious. What is not so clear is whether these strong measures of enforcement are in fact deterring offending by corporations, particularly in the environmental area. That is an area in which further research is clearly needed.

1 Classification of Offences in New Zealand

Current New Zealand law recognises three broad categories of offences for the purposes of criminal classification. They may be broadly characterised as "true" crimes, "strict" liability and "absolute" liability. As between the first category and the remaining two, there is a significant conceptual division in that the two broad bands of offence categories arguably serve quite different purposes in the regulation of criminal conduct.

The category of so-called "true" crimes concerns the standard category of offences requiring proof of mens rea, usually in the form of intention or recklessness. These are typically those offences contained in the Crimes Act 1961 and related Summary Offences legislation. In New Zealand "true" crimes are also to be found in legislation like the Transport Act 1969 and the Misuse of Drugs Act 1975.

The purpose of true crimes is to punish individual wrongdoing and by the imposition of appropriate sanctions, to protect the public from future offending. They are typically *offender-facing* sanctions which provide an outlet for the expression of the community's disapproval through such formal sentencing goals as retribution, deterrence and incapacitation. Of particular significance with this category of offences is the fact that traditional protections regarding the burden and standard of proof continue to apply so that in each case the prosecution has the full probative burden to prove all the elements of the offence, including mens rea, beyond a reasonable doubt according to general common law principles.

Offences of "strict" and "absolute" liability, on the other hand, do not depend on the sort of public condemnation that is implicit in a conviction for, say, homicide or robbery. They are, typically, *conduct-facing* offences. In particular, whereas great public stigma attaches to a conviction for a true crime, because of the "disgrace of criminality", strict and absolute liability offences are said to involve little or no stigma. For this reason it would seem that these "quasi crimes" are becoming increasingly attractive to lawmakers in many Western countries as a means of regulating the activity of corpotations where some sanctioning of unlawful activity is required in the interests of public health and safety but where it is deemed inappropriate to apply the full condemnation inherent in a conviction for a "true" crime.

In New Zealand it is increasingly common for the legislature to define offences of "strict liability" to regulate new forms of conduct proscribed by a growing body of 'regulatory' legislation. As noted earlier, this typically deals with such things as road transport licensing and environmental management and has also extended to industrial machinery, liquor licensing and immigration. The essence of these 'regulatory' offences (sometimes called *public welfare regulatory offences*) is that they do not have a true mens rea element to prove and therefore tend to favour the prosecution.

The down side, however, at least from the perspective of a principled approach to the criminal law, is that they challenge fundamental and hallowed precepts concerning burden of proof and the right of a defendant to fully defend a criminal charge. An effect of 'strict' liability offences is that traditional defences based on lack of mens rea are eliminated where the offence, by its nature, does not require proof of a mental element, although a defendant may avoid liability by proving that she was "totally without fault". By contrast where the offence is characterised as 'absolute' liability, there is no requirement to prove mens rea, nor can the defendant claim an absence of fault in his own defence.

Because of the increasing popularity of this form of penalisation, there are important implications for corporations which, in the conduct of their lawful activities, may breach the requirements of legislation governing particular forms of activity. Because liability may attach without fault on the part of the management of companies, there may be a perception that this form of criminal liability is "draconian" and liable to create unnecessary hardship for corporations and other public bodies whose activities contribute to the economic strength of the community.

In some areas, like environmental management, New Zealand courts have addressed this issue by formulating principles relevant to sentencing in such cases. These will be considered later in the paper.

2 The Scope of Strict Liability in New Zealand

Before considering the way in which strict liability has developed in New Zealand, I should make some preliminary observations about terminology. The concept of "strict" liability derives from English common law. In that jurisdiction the terms "strict" liability and "absolute liability" are used almost interchangeably, which can cause confusion. In fact, this confusion has affected the development of the doctrine of strict liability in New Zealand where the courts have drawn a clear distinction between the concepts of strict and absolute liability.[1] Regrettably, however, the distinction is not so clearly drawn by the legislature.[2]

Offences of strict and absolute liability developed during the nineteenth century in Britain as a convenient means of dealing with the rapidly changing social and industrial practices that follwed the Industrial Revolution. Typically they involved the regulation of conduct that was considered to be injurious to public health or safety, such things as the sale of adulterated tobacco[3] and unsound meat[4] or the sale of intoxicating liquor to persons who were either underage or drunk.[5] This new type of statutory offence reflected the perception that the need to protect the public might on occasion justify convicting people of offences even where they were not necessarily at fault. Often, though not invariably, offences of strict and absolute liability are aimed at regulating the harm resulting from specialised activities which could be controlled by regulatory rather than "truly criminal" prohibitions.[6] Enforcement is often undertaken, not by the police, but by specialist agencies created to monitor and control the effects of particular types of activity such as pollution and industrial safety.

What then is the actual distinction between strict and absolute liability offences and what particular social purposes does each category fulfil? Is the distinction between them one of substance or merely one of form? Some guidance can be gleaned from developments in Canadian criminal jurisprudence.

Canadian Developments

English law has traditionally only recognised two categories of offences. Regulatory offences are always absolute unless the offence is "truly criminal" in which case mens rea will be required. *Strict* liability in this context always means *absolute* liability. There is no intermediate type of category. In the 1978 case of *R v. The City of Sault Ste Marie*[7] the Canadian Supreme Court paved the way for recognising the existence of a new category of offence falling between the extremes of offences requiring full mens rea on the one hand and absolute liability on the other. The charge was one alleging pollution by the illegal discharge of contaminating substances into a river. The Supreme Court decided that although mens rea need not be an essential ingredient of an offence, an alternative to absolute liability was possible. This was done by conceiving a wholly new category of offence, which would come to be known as *public welfare regulatory offences*, where the defendant might avoid liability by pleading that she was "totally without fault", the onus of proving which would lie on the defendant. This new third category of offences, also known as *strict* libility, was characterised by the Court in the following terms:

"..the doing of the prohibited act *prima facie* imports the offence, leaving it open to the accused to avoid liability by proving that he took all reasonable care. This involves consideration of what a reasonable man would have done in the circumstances. The defence will be available if the accused reasonably believed in a mistaken set of facts which, if true, would render the act or omission innocent, or if he took all reasonable steps to avoid the particular event. "[8]

The Court noted that *public welfare* offences exist for the purpose of maintaining high standards of public health and safety through effective enforcement. They are a judicial creation founded on expediency. Offences of absolute liability are justified on the basis that they protect social interests by requiring a high standard of care and attention on the part of people who follow certain pursuits and who are more likely to be encouraged to maintain those standards if they know that ignorance or mistake will not excuse them.[9]

Rationale for Strict Liability

As was noted above, one of the reasons commonly given for abandoning a full mens rea requirement is that the protection of the public sometimes requires a high standard of care on the part of those who undertake risk-creating activities. Proper care needs to be taken by such persons, and without liability for negligence the careless will be able to transfer the great cost of their negligence to the rest of society in the absence of any serious incentive to reduce or eliminate those risks.[10] It is supposed that the threat of criminal liability will provide a motive for persons in highly risky activities to be more cautious in preventing or eliminating errors.

In New Zealand strict (and absolute) liability is a partial subsitute for tortious liability for personal injury, which has been displaced by accident compensation legislation. It is not possible to sue for personal injury in an accident in New Zealand. This fact may encourage carelessness amongst some commercial operators who, because the threat of civil liability is absent, otherwise lack the usual economic incentive to avoid negligent accidents. For this reason strict liability is seen as being particularly appropriate where the offence is directed towards controlling the activity of corporations. The reasons for this are threefold:

First, corporate convictions do not normally involve the same level of stigma as do those attaching to individuals.

Secondly, corporate activity is typically on a larger scale than that of individuals, and so creates a greater level of social threat.

Thirdly, and most importantly, the proof of mens rea presents special difficulties in relation to corporations, because there is usually no one person who can be identified as the agent when a corporation acts. On the other hand the standard of negligence contained in strict liability is appropriate to companies because it is measured by reference to *conduct* rather than mental state.

Absolute Liability

In contrast to "strict" liability which, by its nature, permits a general defence of absence of fault to apply where the breach of a "regulatory" offence is alleged, "absolute" liability makes no such concession. Liability is truly absolute. This means that liability may exist even where the alleged offender is completely without fault. Absolute liability, in this sense, is by its nature aberrant and should be found to exist rarely. The approach of the New Zealand courts is to say that with the emergence of the new category of *public welfare regulatory offences*, with the onus on the defendant of establishing the defence of total absence of fault, it is likely that there will be a diminishment in the number of statutory offences which the courts feel compelled to hold to be absolute.[11] Nevertheless, it seems to be an increasingly common practice for the New Zealand legislature to identify statutory offences as imposing "strict" liability but to structure them in such a way that they effectively impose "absolute" liability. This is achieved by defining an offence in absolute terms then declaring in the statute itself the (limited) extent to which defences claiming lack of fault are available to the defendant. If the accused is unable to bring himself within the narrow terms of the statutory defence (which typically are expressed in *conjunctive* terms requiring proof, for example, of necessity and/or act of God *and* reasonable conduct by the defendant *and* mitigation of the effects of conduct) then liability is absolute and conviction invariably follows. This is a model which is commonly used in environmental legislation in New Zealand.[12] It has been held that such statutory defences represent the extent to which the legislature has adopted and codified the general defence of total absence of fault in the particular statutory context.[13] In effect this means that there is no room for the defence of total absence of fault in such cases because the statutory codification may be taken to have excluded any similar defence.

I would like now to examine these broad propositions with reference to a number of New Zealand court decisions involving environmental offences to illustrate how strict and absolute liability are employed to regulate corporate activity. I will also comment on sentencing policy in this area.

3 Strict Liability and Environmental Offences

The principal legislation concerned with the regulation of environmental matters in New Zealand is the Resource Management Act 1991 (the "RMA"). The RMA establishes a structured hierarchy of penalties reflecting the differing severity of breaches of duties of obligations or duties under the Act.[14] The most serious offences are punishable by imprisonment for up to 2 years and fines of up to NZ$200,000 and NZ$10,000 a day for continuing offences. At the other end of the scale of penalties fines of up to NZ$1500 are available for the lowest level offences, which include wilfully obstructing any person in the execution of powers conferred under the RMA.

Traditionally the courts have regarded contraventions of environmental legislation more as "misdemeanours" rather than as true crimes.[15] That was certainly the case in New Zealand under earlier environmental legislation. In the case of *Hastings City v. Simons*[16] Cooke J. (now Lord Cooke of Thorndon) observed that the relevant offence under the former Water and Soil Conservation Act 1967 was "squarely within the public welfare regulatory category..."[17] and as such appropriately categorised as not criminal in any real sense but better regarded as a branch of administrative law to which traditional principles of criminal law have limited application.[18]

However, under the RMA the very high available fines and the possibility of imprisonment for the most serious offences, suggests an intention on the part of the legislature towards criminalising actions which seriously damage the environment or which are contrary to principles of sustainable management. But where the offences attract only financial penalties without the possibility of imprisonment, it is suggested that such offences are more in the realm of simple regulatory offences and not "criminal" in the true sense.[19]

As was noted earlier in this paper, it is increasingly the practice in New Zealand for the legislature to expressly designate certain statutory offences as "strict" liability, typically where the legislation concerned is aimed at the regulation of activities that are or might be injurious to public health or safety. Environmental offences are perceived as falling within this general category.

An example of such an offence occurs in s 341 of the RMA, which establishes a form of statutory strict liability for breach of the duties and responsibilities set out in Part III of the Act. The prosecution need not prove *mens rea* to establish liability. However, the statute provides that the accused can escape liability for the actus reus by himself proving on the balance of probabilities, that the action was "necessary" or that the offence was due to the occurrence of events beyond the defendant's control. In addition the defendant must prove in respect of both defences that the conduct was "reasonable" and that the effects of the action or event were adequately mitigated.

Generally, offences of strict liability in New Zealand are common law or judge made offences which means, as discussed above, that they are amenable to the general defence of total absence of fault. However, offences under s 341 RMA represent a deliberate attempt by the legislature to limit the scope of the absence of fault defence, or at least a codification of the extent to which general principles governing absence of fault are applicable in the context of environmental offences.[20] It has been suggested that s 341 is exclusive and, at least in relation to the most serious offences under the Act, effectively imposes "absolute" liability save for the narrow statutory exceptions granted.[21] The effect of this determination is that even though the terms of imprisonment available for the most serious offences are substantial, mens rea, whether recklessness or negligence, is irrelevant.

The difficulty with this development, is that increasingly, it seems, formal and traditional principles of criminal law are being eroded in favour of a pragmatic model which is not dependent upon a finding of criminal culpability as such but simply whether or not the offender "caused" the prohibited event. From an official point of view this has the advantage that the costs of prosecution are reduced while the ostensible advantages of penalisation are enhanced. However, from the point of view of an offender it is arguable that the conditions of penalisation are much less certain. An offender may be so labelled on the basis of alleged conduct for which he/she lacked relevant knowledge and for the consequences of which were neither intended nor foreseen.

4 Sentencing Policy

The RMA has heralded a wholly new sentencing regime for environmental offences. Yet the Act itself is silent on matters which may be taken into account on sentencing. To a large extent these must be inferred from a consideration of the broad legislative objectives.

It has been held that the Act's emphasis on the avoidance of adverse effects on the environment is exhibited in a more stringent approach to penalties. These include the power to imprison and separate criminal liability for company directors and managers, subject to proof of lack of due diligence. These factors have been interpreted by New Zealand courts as indicating a legislative direction to the courts that penalties under earlier legislation are irrelevant to the RMA and that a flexible, innovative approach should be taken to sentencing, not only for purposes of punishment, but also to achieve economic and educative goals.[22]

In *Machinery Movers v. ARC*,[23] which involved the prosecution of a company which had allowed toxic wastes stored in liquid storage tanks to escape into a stream, the High Court addressed the economic implications of environmental pollution, in terms of where the "external" costs of pollution should lie. The Court held that the economic reason why society may not, in the absence of regulation, strike a proper balance between economic output and environmental quality is that the costs of pollution are not borne by polluters but by somebody else. Consequently, these "external" costs will not, in general, be taken into account by those who cause pollution. To the extent that pollution costs are not borne by those actually causing pollution, or by those who purchase their products, some part of the total benefits resulting from economic activity in the community is wrongly redistributed away from the victims of pollution to other groups in society. The Court held that in order to correct this market failure, the government must intervene to impose financial costs or penalties which bring the external costs back to the polluter. In endorsing this principle the Court quoted with approval Principle 16 of *The Rio Declaration on Environment and Development* adopted at the United Nations conference on Environment and Development, Rio de Janerio 3-14 June 1992, 31 1LM 874 (1992) 879. Principle 16 states:

> "National authorities should endeavour to promote the internalisation of environmental costs and the use of economic instruments, taking into account the approach that the polluter should, in principle, bear the cost of pollution with due regard to the public interest and without distorting international trade and investment"

In determining the principles relevant to environmental offences the Court in *Machinery Movers v. ARC* approved the principles identified by the Ontario Court (Provincial Division) in *R v. Bata Industries Ltd*[24]. The Court differentiated between *general considerations* applicable to environmental offences and those *relevant to corporations* convicted of environmental offences. The factors relevant in the first category include:

A. The nature of the environment affected;
B. The extent of the damage inflicted;
C. The deliberateness of the offence;
D. The attitude of the accused.

In relation to the second category the relevant considerations were:

A. The size, wealth, nature of operations and power of the corporation;
B. The extent of attempts to comply;
C. Remorse;
D. Profits realized by the offence;
E. Criminal record or other evidence of good character.

The New Zealand Court agreed with the approach in *Bata Industries* that *general deterrence* best achieves the protection of the public, not in the usual negative sense of achieving compliance by the threat of punishment, but rather by emphasizing community disapproval and publicly branding an act as reprehensible. It also agreed with the proposition that the notion of deterrence should also contain an element of "encouragement", in the sense that the penalty imposed should not be so high as to deter other companies in like situations from co-operating with the abatement of the environmental damage. That is to say, the penalty should not "over-deter".

Up until the present time, most prosecutions under the RMA have been for the unlawful discharge of contaminants or destruction of protected flora and habitat. Fines imposed have ranged from NZ $5,000-$80,000.[25] These fine levels are not insignificant and are, on the whole, much higher than would normally be imposed for a serious "true" crime. They demonstrate that the mere naming of offences as "strict" or "absolute" liability does not eliminate the possibility that they may produce severe penal consequences for the convicted offender, whether an individual or a corporation.

5 Liability of the Principal for the Acts of Agents

The RMA allows for the prosecution of principals for the acts of their agents "as if [they] had personally committed the offence."[26] In such cases, however, the statute provides a defence to the principal if he is able to prove that he did not know or could not reasonably be expected to know the offence was being committed or that he took all reasonable steps to prevent the commission of the offence. Similarly, if the offender is a body corporate, there will be a defence for the company to prove that neither the directors nor any person "involved in the management of the body corporate" knew that the offence was being committed and that the company took all reasonable steps to prevent the commission of the offence.[27]

It has been noted that although the meaning of "management" in this context has not been judicially considered, it could include mortgagees and other secured financiers given a broad interpretation of the provision.[28] An important effect of the provision is that liability can be visited on a corporate official even if he or she does not have actual knowledge of the offence if the prosecution is able to prove that he/she should have known in the circumstances.[29]

Conclusion

The use of strict and absolute liability as a means of enforcement, is becoming more common in many Western jurisdictions. The principal advantage of these forms of liability is that they eliminate the obligation upon the prosecution to prove fault in order to secure a conviction and, therefore, maximize the prospect of successful outcomes for prosecutors. It is not known, however, whether these conceptual devices actually produce benefits for the community in terms of more efficient business operations, less damage to the environment and better protection in the workplace. It is hoped this is so since without such gains, strict and absolute liability exact a high price in terms of the compromise of established principles of criminal liability.

In particular, these forms of liability heavily target corporations since the conduct they typically prohibit often, by its nature, involves the actions of corporate bodies and their human agents.

While strict liability is consistent with broad policy objectives which properly favour the protection and minimal diminution of the environment, such enforcement should not be sought at any cost, least those affected lose respect for the rule of law. It is necessary to maintain a balance between traditional methods of enforcement of criminal sanctions and other methods, like strict and absolute liability, which may in limited circumstances provide the most effective means of regulating a particular type of conduct.

(1) See *Civil Aviation Dept v. MacKenzie* [1983] NZLR 78.
(2) A common practice in drafting modern statutory offences of strict liability is to include a marginal reference to "strict liability" offences. However, upon closer examination it is clear that the legislature is defining an offence of absolute liability, using the expression "strict liability" in a generic sense.

(3) See *R v. Woodrow* (1846) 15 M & W 404.
(4) *Hobbs v. Winchester Corporation* [1910] 2 KB 471, CA.
(5) *Cundy v. Le Coq* (1884) 13 QBD 207.
(6) Simester, A & Brookbanks, W J, *Principles of Criminal Law* (Brookers', Wellington, 1998) 124.
(7) (1978) 85 DLR (3d) 161.
(8) *R v. City of Sault Ste Marie* (1978) 85 DLR (3d) 161, 181.
(9) Ibid., 170.
(10) Simester & Brookbanks, supra. 128.
(11) *Civil Aviation Department v. MacKenzie* [1983] NZLR 78, 85 per Richardson, J.
(12) See *Mc Knight v. NZ Biogas Industries Ltd* [1994] 2 NZLR 664 and see *Canterbury Regional Council v. Doug Hood Ltd* 30/6/98, Judge Skelton, DC Christchurch, CRN 7076006424.
(13) Ibid., 669.
(14) See D. Grinlinton, "Liability for Environmental Harm in New Zealand" [1997] Env. Liability 106, 108.
(15) Ibid., 109.
(16) [1984] 2 NZLR 502.
(17) Ibid., 506.
(18) *Civil Aviation Department v. MacKenzie* [1983] NZLR 78, 84 per Richardson, J.
(19) Grinlinton, supra. 109.
(20) *Mc Knight v. NZ Biogas Ltd* [1994] 2 NZLR 664, 669.
(21) Crinlinton, supra. 110.
(22) *Machinery Movers v. ARC* [1994] 1 NZLR 492, 500-01.
(23) Ibid.
(24) (1992) 9 OR (3d) 329.
(25) Grinlinton, supra. 110.
(26) Resource Management Act 1991, s. 340 (1).
(27) RMA s. 340 (2).
(28) Grinlinton, supra. 111.
(29) Ibid.

11 Administrative Regulations and Criminal Sanctions

Morikazu TAGUCHI

Introduction
1 Administrative Sanction Against Economic Crimes
2 Criminal Sanction Against Economic Crime
3 Procedural Problems
Conclusion

Introduction

(1) Deregulation in Economic Activities and Control of Economic Crimes

An "economic crime" is a crime that infringes economic order and/or economic profit. The size (the number of persons attending the criminal activity) and complicity of those crimes have grown dramatically in the past few years. Economic crimes range from the smaller crimes such as fraud, embezzlement, or breach of trust, to the larger crimes such as violation of the Anti-Monopoly Law and the Securities and Exchange Law. Not only individuals but also enterprises commit those economic crimes.

To fight against such economic crimes, both pre-crime control (prevention) and post-crime control (sanction) are necessary. While voluntary restraint by enterprises and administrative regulations are helpful in preventing economic crimes, criminal and other sanctions are used in the context of post-crime control.

So-called "deregulation" diminishes the significance of administrative regulations, making voluntary restraint by enterprises and post-crime control more and more important. Today, I would like to introduce the sanctional system in Japan.

(2) Sanctional System in Japan

First of all, there are two types of sanctions against economic crimes. Voluntary sanctions and legal (coercive) sanctions. Voluntary sanctions include "*kataikin* (fine for default)" provided in the Securities and Exchange Law, expulsion from the industry groups, publication of the name of the enterprise, or dismissal, demotion, personnel change, salary cut by the enterprise. Because those voluntary sanctions, if imposed properly, will diminish the number of crimes effectively, the enterprise must take notice of its social responsibility of providing/imposing voluntary sanctions in the struggle against economic crimes. We must also mention social sanctions such as impeachment by the mass media and boycott of goods by citizens. Such informal sanctions, too, could be of big influence in controlling crimes. However, it should be noted that too much expectations in the power of informal sanctions could cause a setback in the development of legal sanction system.

Secondly, there are three types of legal sanctions. Civil sanction, administrative sanction, and criminal sanction. A typical civil sanction is damages. But damages and other civil sanctions have problems such as the heavy burden of proof of the plaintiff, and the expensive costs of justice that deny civil sanction to be the sole method of controlling economic crimes.

1 Administrative Sanction Against Economic Crimes

(1) Types of Administrative Sanctions Generally

Administrative sanctions (in the narrow sense) and penalties are imposed when economic regulations are violated. The former sanctions consist of money sanctions and other administrative dispositions.

Money sanctions consist of "*hansokukin* (pecuniary penalty)", "*karyo* (non-penal fine)", and "*kachokin* (surcharge)". *Hansokukin* is a sanction that replaces criminal punishment. When the administrative agency notifies the actor of a certain amount of *hansokukin* to be paid to the agency, and he pays this amount, he will not be prosecuted. *Karyo* is inflicted on persons that violate administrative duty. Unlike the criminal transaction, the violating act itself does not offend the society or an individual. *Karyo* is imposed to maintain order of the administration. Anti-Monopoly Law orders the payment of *kachokin*. The sum of *kachokin* is calculated through multiplying a certain rate by the amount of proceeds gained in the period during which he had violated the law (Art. 7 para. 2, Art. 2). *Kachokin* prevents future violations by stripping the undertaker of his illegally gained profit.

Other administrative dispositions are as follows : ① The order of "suspension of business", or "cancellation of business license" will be issued occasionally, and ② when the company does not observe these orders, the administrative agency makes that fact public.

(2) Administrative Sanctions Against Violation of the Anti-Monopoly Law and the Securities and Exchange Law

Violations of the Anti-Monopoly Law include undue restriction of business activities, such as cartel, collusion, etc. The penalty imposed on these violations is "imprisonment with forced labor for not more than 3 years, or a fine of not more than 5 million yen" (Art. 89). The Fair Trade Commission officially announced in 1990 "the policy of criminal accusation against violations of the Anti-Monopoly Law" and promised an active use of its right to prosecution. However, from 1991 to 1997, the right was exercised only four times. On the other hand, from 1990 to 1995, the number of administrative dispositions against cartels and collusions was 107. Those dispositions consisted of recommendations, warnings, cautions and so on. The revision of the law in 1977 introduced the *kachokin* system and *kachokin* was imposed to the important cases such as those involving cartels. From 1985 to 1994, the number of cases in which *kachokin* was imposed was 109, and the number of persons that paid *kachokin* was 1592, and the total amount of *kachokin* paid was 28.5 billion yen.

The sum of *kachokin* is designed to equal the total amount of illegally gained profit, and does not contain money sanction. Therefore, it is theoretically possible to impose fine in addition to *kachokin*. However, in general, it is unnecessary to do so, because *kachokin* is considered to have the deterrent effect as well. The principle of punishment as "ultima ratio" supports this outcome. Criminal accusations should be limited to those cases in which the violation is especially vicious.

Violations of the Securities and Exchange Law include market manipulation

(Art. 197), insider trading (Arts. 166, 167), etc. Penal provision of insider trading was introduced in 1988 under the influence of so-called Japan-U.S. Trade Friction. In 1992, Securities and Exchange Surveillance Committee was established and the number of accusations was expected to increase significantly. However, until 1997, the number of criminal accusations by the Committee had been only six. The prescribed penalty was "imprisonment with forced labor for not more than 3 years or fine of not more than 3 million yen" (Art. 198 no. 15), and "a fine of not more than 500 million yen" for the corporation (Art. 207 para. no. 2). The actual sentence averaged from 200,000 to 500,000 yen in fine, and there was only one case in which imprisonment (though with the order to suspend its execution) was imposed. It may be said that the deterrent effect of imposing penalties in those cases were equal to (or close to) nothing.

Sanctions against insider trading other than criminal sanctions are the following. Administrative dispositions such as ① cancellation of security company license, suspension of business (Securities and Exchange Law, Art. 35), ② prohibition order or suspension order issued by the court, on request of the Minister of Finance (Art. 192), ③ compensation for damages, the suit for which is to be brought up by private citizens whose damage was caused by the registration of false securities and/or market manipulation (Arts. 21, 160), and ④ *kataikin* of not more than 500 million yen imposed by Japan Securities Exchange and Securities Dealers' Association, and also ⑤ suspension, expulsion of business group membership, which method is taken voluntarily by business groups. Among these, suspension orders issued by the court on request of citizens and the private suit for damages have never been utilized because of the difficulty in proving the case. The cancelling of business license and suspension of business have never been imposed because they have too much influence when imposed. The maximum amount of fine for a corporation was raised to 500 million yen through the revision of the Securities and Exchange Law in 1997. At the same time, the maximum of *kataikin* was raised to 500 million yen as well. As a result of all this, *kataikin* became the most common sanction against the violation of the Securities and Exchange Law. The sum of *kataikin* imposed, however, has been undoubtedly much smaller than the entire amount of illicitly gained profit. In light of this fact, there is a strong opinion that the *kachokin* system provided in Anti Monopoly Law should be introduced to the Securities and Exchange Law as well.

2 Criminal Sanction Against Economic Crime

(1) Use of Criminal Sanction as *"Ultima Ratio"* and the Principle of Culpability

When we consider the meaning of criminal sanction, it is necessary to take two things into consideration. The character of criminal penalty as *"ultima ratio* (the final means)"*,* and the principle of culpability. It is said that "the criminal law is the final means to protect human life". It means that "criminal penalty should be imposed only when other social controls such as civil/administrative sanction do not suffice", because "criminal penalty strips a citizen of his liberty and property, and carries many evil effects". The meaning of the culpability principle in substantive criminal law derived from this notion.

As to the civil responsibility, especially in the field of public nuisance, the responsibility of torts seems to become more and more strict (as in "strict liability"). It is becoming more and more "objective". On the other hand, criminal responsibility is still understood as a more "subjective" responsibility. The main rationale for punishment is still thought to be the legal blame against the previously committed illegal act. This means that the punishment presupposes the existence of an alternative (legal) act, and *mens rea* (intent or negligence) on the part of the actor. The theory that the actor can not be punished unless he had *mens rea* is called the principle of culpability (*Schuldprinzip*). It is a fundamental principle of our criminal law. This culpability principle is a principle that replaces the principle of result liability (*Erfolgshaftung*) or strict liability.

(2) Rationale for Imposing Punishment Against a Corporation

When an economic crime takes place, a corporation is often punished (fined) in addition to the acting individual. Why can a corporation be punished ? The theory of strict liability had been the answer to this question, as strict liability also meant responsibility deriving from the negligent act of another person. However, "criminal" fine is different from "civil" damages and its substantial meaning is a legal blame against an illegal act committed by someone with *mens rea*. Thus, the theory of strict liability is inconsistent with the principle of culpability.

The prevailing view among scholars and judicial decisions today use a "negligence" liability rationale. According to this view, a violation of supervisory duty of the corporation is presumed, and the corporation is to be punished for its own negligent act, unless the corporation proves that the violation by its employee had been committed by *"force majeure"* (that the violation had been inevitable).

Under this view, the basis of corporation's negligence is different from that of an individual. The duty must be specified, because there must be causation (cause and effect) between the violation by its employee and the negligence of the corporation. The duty should be the duty of management, or the duty of supervision. Supervisory duty is considered to have existed if the violation was abstractly foreseeable through the nature of the business concerned. Foreseeability of the concrete violation is unnecessary. In other words, the negligence of the corporation has a less rigid character than that of an individual, which requires concrete foreseeability of his conduct. The principle of culpability is somewhat modified in this area.

(3) Reform in the System of Fine

The penalty imposed upon a corporation is a fine. When the sum of fine is low, it has a less deterrent effect on the commission of crime. Also because fine is almost always imposed through summary (judgment) procedure, it is less effective to deter criminal transactions.

One way to strengthen the power to control crime by imposing fine is to raise its maximum. In the Securities and Exchange Law, for example, maximum was raised from 3 million yen to 5 million yen in 1997. The traditional idea, that the fine for a corporation must be the same amount of fine provided for an individual was corrected, and a more expensive fine for the corporation was enacted. In the revision of 1992, the Securities and Exchange Law raised the maximum of fine for a corporation from 3 million yen to 300 million yen, and in 1997, to 500 million yen. The Anti Monopoly Law sets the maximum of fine for a corporation at 100 million yen (Art. 95 no. 1), the Law on Disposal and Cleaning of Wastes at 100 million yen (Art. 30 no. 1), the Trademark Law at 150 million yen (Art. 82 no. 1), and the Banking Law at 300 million yen (Art. 64 para. no. 1) and so on.

The theoretical grounds for imposing such expensive fine on the corporation are ① the corporation has acted negligently ② corporations generally have more financial resources, ③ imprisonment can not be imposed on a corporation.

3 Procedural Problems

(1) Difficulties in Investigating Economic Crime

Now, let's consider some procedural problems. An economic crime is often committed in form of legitimate business, and business activities are performed under complicated economic rules. It is difficult to detect a crime that lurks behind legal activity. This could cause inefficiency in the enforcement of criminal justice. One way to overcome such difficulty may be to give more power to the investigatory organizations. Giving such strong investigatory power to those organizations, however, may result in depriving a citizen of his human rights, or diminishing the freedom of business.

(2) Administrative Examination and Criminal Investigation

As for the investigation of large scale economic crimes, the 2-step system is used in Japan. Initially, an administrative agency carries out an examination and makes accusation to the public prosecutor if necessary. Then (and only then) the criminal organization begins the investigation. For example, Anti-Monopoly Law authorizes the Fair Trade Commission to examine the case first. The Commission is under control of the Prime Minister but it has a quasi-judicial function as well. It enjoys autonomy in this area and can never be interfered by other administrative powers. The Commission sometimes makes non-judicial dispositions such as recommendations, warnings, admonitions, or motions of suspension orders. When the Commission finds a major (vicious) violation, it must make an accusation to the Public Prosecutor General (Art. 73 para. 1). Without the accusation from the Commission, the prosecutor can not make a prosecution (Art. 96 para. 1). In my opinion, the parties concerned should also be permitted to make an accusation in the near future. Not only fair trade but also the interest of consumers and involving enterprises should be protected by Anti-Monopoly Law.

Insider trading is one of the violations of the Securities and Exchange Law. The detection of this type of crime is difficult, because it is always carried out secretly. The Securities and Exchange Surveillance Commission was established in the Ministry of Finance in 1992 to be the organization responsible for controlling insider trading. The Commission has the right of compulsory examination and criminal accusation (Arts. 210, 226). The police and the prosecutor can also begin their investigation apart from the examination of the Commission, but because of the difficulty in detecting the crime, in most of the cases, investigation relies on the outcome of the examination carried out by the Commission. Up to this day, the number of accusations from the Commission is rather small. As I mentioned earlier, in order to detect insider trading more thoroughly, the party concerned must be allowed (or encouraged) to cooperate in the investigation.

Conclusion

(1) Administrative Sanction and Criminal Sanction

Deregulation means the liberalization of business. It will undoubtedly increase types and numbers of economic crimes. Therefore, the post-crime control over economic crimes will be required. What kind of post-crime control should be the main method to control those crimes in the future ? There are various answers to that question. ① The use of the criminal sanction should be reinforced, ② the administrative dispositions should be mainly utilized, ③ the effort of the corporation, for example, rationalization of management, and consolidation of crisis management, should be encouraged. Utilization of "corporate justice" is expected as well.

In my opinion, self-control (voluntary-restraint) by the enterprise should be encouraged in the first place. Secondly, utilization of administrative sanctions is to be expected. Criminal sanction should be imposed against truly vicious violations, only after those non-criminal sanctions had been fully considered. I did not describe closely the system of deprivation of illegally gained profit, and the system of civil sanction, but they must be taken into consideration as well.

(2) "Total Consideration" Approach

To prevent economic crimes effectively, it is important that self-control by enterprises, administrative sanctions, and criminal sanctions be considered as a whole. Formerly, there was a fixed idea that the sanction against a crime should always be the criminal punishment. Actually, however, the use of criminal punishment had been strictly limited because of its character as *"ultima ratio"*. This so-called "humbleness" of criminal law has interfered with the development of criminal sanctions. The proper role of criminal sanctions must be sought under the total ("as a whole") consideration of these various types of sanctions.

 * I am grateful to Jun Kojima, Research Assistant of Waseda University, for having helped me with my English.

12 Changing Regulatory Patterns in Japan
——An Australian Perspective[1]——

Malcolm Smith

  1 The Elements of a US Administrative Model
  2 Key Steps on the Road to a US Model
  3 What Do Japanese Regulators Regulate?
  4 Some Notable Trends in Administrative Powers vis a vis the Other Arms of Government in Australia
     Conclusion

When I began my research on Japanese Law in 1969, almost 30 years ago, my first topic was "Joint Ventures with Japan"[2]. This necessarily involved an examination of the then system for regulating foreign investment into Japan, as well as an introductory study of corporations and securities regulation and anti monopoly laws. All of these areas involved administrative regulation. My second major research project was on administrative discretions in international trade regulation in Australia, Japan and the United States, for Harvard Law School[3], so I had to expand my knowledge of Japanese administrative law. My interest has continued until today, though my focus has moved to regulation of capital and financial markets. I want to share with you some impressions about your system from an Australian perspective, to introduce some interesting features of the Australian system, and, I hope, provoke both discussion today and interest in the future for joint research on administrative regulation in our two countries.

In 1969, a superficial examination of the Japanese system by an Australian offered a lot of scope for comparative work. Australia at that time was very much influenced by English concepts, and this was also true of administration and administrative law. We boasted a career civil service at both state and national levels on the English model, which we contrasted to the US system. Our administrative laws were adopted directly from England. We assumed we were close to the English model and used the USA or the European systems for comparisons.

Only five years before I began my research, in 1964, the English House of Lords had delivered its famous judgment in *Ridge v. Baldwin*[4], establishing principles of natural justice for administrative decision making. My undergraduate course focused on judicial control of administrators thorough ancient English writs, or forms of procedure. These procedures were highly technical, and generally my teachers focused on these technicalities and disguised the simplicity of the overall sceme of the writs (of which more later). We also looked at controls on judicial bias and the power of parliaments to remove issues from the courts by what we called privative clauses[5]. There was no concept of review on the merits, as few administrative rulings reached the courts. Our concept of prior controls on administrative rule making was implemented through the process of new regulations lying on the table of the relevant parliament for possible challenge by legislators. There was little or no legislative countrol through the specification of criteria to govern delegations of authority by parliaments to administrators. Freedom of Information was unknown. We were a very English system, with little or no reference to US processes.

By contrast, in 1969 the small amount of material in English on Japanese administrative law said that it was based on German law, with an important overlay of US principles derived from the Occupation period. Most of the literature then, and regrettably still, focused on the phenomena of "administrative guidance" or *gyosei shido*, not the detail of the legal system for administration[6]. It was clear that evaluations of administrative guidance were either written by, or for, US lawyers. In fact, Australia in the 1950s and 1960s could point to a similar structure of regulation to that described in Japan. The late 1960s literature on Japan stressed the difficulty of obtaining review of administrative decisions by courts and the extent of uncontrolled exercises of discretion by bureaucrats. The situation was similar in Australia.

Looking back in 1998, I think it is possible to assert that both our systems have evolved dramatically towards a US model since the 1960s, in terms of the essential elements of the process, not the technical details. However, I would assert that the process of evolution in our two countries has been significantly different. In Australia the evolution has been in response to internal choice driven by reform of our economic laws along US lines (e.g. Securities and Trade Practices Laws). The evolution has been supported by a significant exposure of Australian lawyers to US legal training since the 1950s. Australia has also experienced over 15 years of economic deregulation and privatization, a policy common to, and energetically pursued by, our two major political parties. Administrative law reform has been a necessary part of this process. In Japan, administrative reform seems to me to be more closely tied to foreign pressure (*gaiatsu*) from the United States, linked to trade and investment disputes. To the observer from Australia, administrative reform in Japan seems reactive rather than proactive, grudging rather than willing.

1 The Elements of a US Administrative Model

If we step back from the detailed rules and try to identify key elements of the US administrative model, it seems to me that the following elements are crucial in the late 1990s.

- All government activity should be subject to the rule of law
- The Constitution is the apex of the legal system and sets up key principles to define institutional interactions and the relationship between the people and the government
- The separation of powers doctrine allows that the administration be subject to parliamentary direction in the definition of allowable authority by specifying criteria for action in legislation, and judicial oversight in the exercise of delegated decision making powers
- The rule of law requires that all administrative activities be transparent, in the sense that applicable rules and processes are public and known in

advance

- Any administrative rule making authority must be circumscribed by clear criteria in enabling legislation and public scrutiny during the process of developing the rules
- All administrative decisions must be referable to clear criteria which can form the basis of a review
- All administrative decisions must be arrived at through a proper process which protects individual rights
- Individuals are entitled to access to material in government files which is relevant to their rights
- Independent agencies are key regulatory instruments

2 Key Steps on the Road to a US Model

I think it is clear that the essentials of the basic principles set out above have been replicated in Australia and Japan over the last 50 years. Both countries entered the 20th century professing to adhere to the rule of law. Both countries have strengthened that commitment in fact as the century has progressed. Both countries have adopted the US model of judicial review of the constitutionality of legislation and administrative activity. Both countries have constitutions which set out the limits of administrative authority, although the Japanese constitution is much clearer on this point. In Australia, judicial decisions have been required in order to set the limits clearly, Japan has the added element of Chapter 3 of its Constitution, which sets out the Rights and Duties of the People. Australia has no Bill of Rights, so, again, analogous restraints on administrators have been mandated by legislation, or tentatively imposed by the courts, based on specific provisions in the Constitution.

The striking developments in the last 50 years have been in the following areas:

- Establishment of administrative review processes
- Changing legislative models of delegation to include clear criteria for

delegated rules
- Administrative Procedure Laws addressing the rule making process
- Freedom of Information systems
- Establishment of economic regulatory agencies

Let me deal briefly with each in turn, and spell out their importance to the overall theme of the Conference.

- Establishment of administrative review processes

The Occupation reforms introduced the first basic US style administrative review processes in 1948 in Japan. They were expanded in the early 1960s in the Administrative Complaint Law and the Administrative Litigation Law. The weakness in these laws then, and now, remains the problem of independent review within the administrative structure and the ease with which a challenge in the courts can be subverted. This is because the law allows the administrative activity complained of to continue unless a collateral injunction style action is successfully argued in court by the complainants. Either the injunction is successful, in which case it can be overridden by a direct action of the Cabinet, or it fails, and by the time the principal action reaches trial, usually years later, the complainant is met by a finding that the administrative activity has been completed and the complainant can show no damage.

The approach in Australia has been based on establishing a new administrative tribunal structure since 1975 to expedite administrative reviews. Article 76(3) of the Japanese Constitution may well make such a development difficult in Japan. The success of these developments in Australia can probably be best measured by recent attempts by governments to remove certain matters like refugee claims from the general system and place them under special tribunals.

The relationship between administrative intervention in markets and the ease of challenging administrative conduct has been clear in all my work researching the regulation of foreign investment, foreign trade and more recently capital markets. Abuse of regulatory powers cannot flourish if challenges to administrative abuses can be launched expeditiously, cheaply, and with a reasonable chance of an effective remedy. Often the success of any challenge depends on the next point, the limits on delegated powers.

- Changing legislative models of delegation to include clear criteria for delegated rules

In 1969 Japan and Australia shared one clear legislative characteristic: both were in the habit of making open-ended delegations of rule making power to administrative authorities. If the delegations contained no criteria, and did not demand that any subsequent administrative rules themselves contain clear criteria, the stage was set for courts to excuse themselves from intervening in what appeared to be bona fide decisions. The importance of this point did not come home to me until I researched in detail US forms of legislative delegation in the same areas.

The impact of these delegations was marked in the area of economic regulation, especially foreign trade. My favorite comparisons were in the import and export control areas, both vital areas of market regulation. In both Australia and Japan the delegations were completely open-ended. In the Australian case the original Customs Act 1900 (Cth) simply said "The Governor-General in Council may make regulations to prohibit [imports or exports]"[7]. The Act provided no criteria at all to restrain the administrators in framing decisions based on the delegation. The Japanese provisions in the Foreign Exchange and Foreign Trade Control Law were similar, but article 1 seemed to impose some criteria, which attracted the attention of the District Court in the famous Cocom Case[8]. However, a finding in favour of the complainant, one of the few successful judicial challenges to the exercise of foreign trade powers in almost half a century, did not lead to a change in practice, and the law was ultimately amended in 1987 to meet the problem[9]. The US, on the other hand, had so many legislative constraints on administrative authority in the same area that it appeared to engage in trade disputes at the time with one hand tied behind its back.

The Kerr Committee, which led to the most important administrative reforms this century in Australia, apparently felt that there was no need to limit discretions if a proper review process was established. I sense that Japanese officials would agree with this view. However, I have always favoured the view of another leading Australian expert, Henry Bland, who had chaired the old Tariff Board. His report on discretions argued that:

"The greater the detail in which are stated the circumstances in which a decision may be made, the more certain the citizen will be of his rights and the less demand there will be for processes of review of decisions taken under administrative discretions."[10]

- Administrative Procedure Laws addressing the rule making process

My interest in the way discretions are set out in rules led me to take an interest in the rule making aspects of US Administrative Procedure Laws. The changes introduced in Japan in its new APA in 1994[11], and their debt to the US model, is a rich field for future research. The importance of the APA for future reform of administrative activities in Japan is probably best evaluated by a consideration of the many areas of activity specifically excluded from its application[12]. Put simply, I think the key to Japanese administrative activity has always been the power of the administrators to define their own areas of operation under blanket and sweeping delegations. No real reform will occur until both rule making powers and decision making activities are subjected to proper oversight.

- Freedom of Information systems.

This is the most recent of the reforms which have changed the balance between administrator/regulators and the regulated in Australia in the past 15 years. In Australia, FOI laws[13] have been a favorite policy of opposition parties, and a favorite weapon used by opposition parties to gather useful information to use against governments. The success of these laws in Australia can be measured by the extent of attempts by governments to limit their application.

On the one hand, while s 3(1)(a) of the FOI Acts states its object in very broad terms 'to extend as far as possible the right of the Australian community to access to information in the possession of the Government of the Commonwealth', section 3(1)(b) then places a limit on this general right of access through a range of exemptions. These exemptions exist for the protection of essential public interests and the private and business affairs of persons in respect of whom information is collected and held by departments and public authorities. However, the courts of Australia have given s 3(1)(b) a broad interpretation, in favour of disclosure[14]. While FOI laws have been in place at national and state levels in Australia since the mid 1980s, and locally in Japan for some time, a national law is only now on the horizon in Japan[15]. The impact of the new law in Japan will be another rich area for comparative research in the years to come, but I would argue these laws are essential in the design of a new concept of regulation.

- Economic regulatory agencies

This a major topic, so I will only point out that both Japan and Australia have adopted US style regulatory agencies in the economic area. Japan was bequeathed the Fair Trade Commission and a Securities and Exchange Commission by the Occupation. The JFTC has continued to function uninterrupted. The Securities Commission was abolished during the 1950s only to be resurrected in the early 1990s, in response to a series of scandals. The Australian bodies were set up in their present form after a major High Court decision upheld the constitutionality of the Trade Practices structure in the late 1960s. A national corporations and securities body followed in the 1970s. The Australian Competition and Consumer Commission (ACCC) arguably is now our most powerful economic regulator. The corporations body has developed into the Australian Securities and Investment Commission (ASIC), with extensive regulatory powers over the securities markets and corporations.

3 What Do Japanese Regulators Regulate?

The second crucial issue in examining the Japanese administrative process over the last 30 years is the sort of activities that have been regulated. When Japan talks of administrative reform, as in the Maekawa Report, it is referring both to the "way" in which administrators behave and the "what" they regulate. Australians are more likely to refer to the later aspect of the topic as "deregulation". My research into first foreign investment regulation, then foreign trade regulation, and more recently capital market regulation suggests that Japanese administrators have been heavily involved in interventions in micro-economic activity. They have been telling business what they can do and how to do it. Is this the proper role of regulation?

If you gather the standard works on capital market deregulation in Japan, it is hard to avoid the lists, often running to up to 20 pages, of individual decisions which have been deregulated[16]. Too often the decisions which were deregulated went to business decisions, either as to the nature of a transaction, or the size of a transaction, and not to the framework within which decisions are made.

It seems to me that the modern concept of regulation involves setting general frameworks for a fair market in which participants cannot abuse their market power. These frameworks include:

- anti monopoly laws
- fair trading laws
- consumer protection laws

In specific sectors, like the financial markets, the focus has moved from intervention in individual transactions, or proscribing particular types of transactions, to a more general focus on maintaining the stability and integrity of the system through ensuring the solvency of those who work within it and ensuring the rapid withdrawal of those who cannot meet the solvency tests.

This issue has been brought into sharp relief in the ongoing problems of dealing with the current banking crisis in Japan. In telling the banks how to make a whole lot of business decisions in the last fifty years, like fixing interest rates or limiting the development of commercial paper products, the regulators failed to address their real task: to ensure that there were adequate processes in place to ensure the banks were solvent. Commentators are in agreement that the regulators failed to properly supervise the prudential requirements of the system in Japan, or the external operations of Japanese financial institutions.

It seems to have been assumed that the system itself was beyond threat and so the regulators should and could busy themselves in intervening in the day to day operations of the businesses they dealt with. This was compounded by their administrative method: administrative guidance, or "window" guidance, which was not referable to clearly enunciated and public principles. Unfortunately, the system was capable of being destabilized and the few bureaucrats actually in charge of protecting the public from prudential abuse were amenable to corruption, so the oversight system itself was ineffective.

Most importantly, the key principle of the postwar approach to regulation of the financial sector by the government, namely that the public purse should be seen to back any major player in the system, delivered the opposite result. Instead of ensuring the integrity of the system, it lead to the ultimate in moral hazard in the system. In addition to failing to enforce the few prudential rules that did exist, the government allowed the boards of banks to evade their duties to adequately assess the risks of transactions they approved, it allowed bank officials to approve loans on grounds other than risk assessment, it allowed depositors to evade their duty to assess the soundness of the institutions to which they gave their funds, and it allowed the shareholders to avoid their duty to call directors to account. In other words, the bureaucrats negated all normal market control mechanisms by seeming to guarantee solvency, and then failed to ask the right questions to ensure that the banks were in fact solvent.

Against this background it is very noticeable that the proposed banking reforms have been hailed by commentators as introducing clear rules to govern any bureaucratic intervention, and limiting bureaucratic intervention in the business of banking[17]. Administrative reform must also be seen as part of a parallel strengthening of laws which reinforce market mechanisms of accountability. Prudential rules on capital adequacy ratios, maximum exposures to sectors such as real estate, loans to related companies, etc., must be supported by adequate corporate disclosure of accounts, and laws which facilitate actions by shareholders or creditors against directors who breach their duties. The development of these legal structures for the future will be as important as solving the immediate problem of the existing bad debts of the major Japanese financial institutions.

4 Some Notable Trends in Administrative Powers vis a vis the Other Arms of Government in Australia

In this final section I will outline three trends in Australian regulation which may be of interest for future comparative research.

• The power of an administrative agency effectively to change legislation

When I was studying in Japan in 1973, the Australian government introduced the first national corporations and securities draft law. One feature that attracted a lot of attention in Australia and Japan was the power granted to the proposed national regulatory commission to make its own rules in a way that can vary the legislation itself. That feature has been part of the national corporations and securities structure ever since, and a current example is found in Part 7.12 of the *Corporations Law* which sets down guidelines and rules for companies when they are offering securities for subscription or purchase. The law empowers the Australian Securities and Investment Commission to 'exempt persons from compliance with all or any of the provisions'[18] of the law. This has resulted in the Commission amending the law through discretionary exemptions on an ad hoc basis, rendering it difficult for those regulated to find the actual law in this area.

Could a law in Japan do the same thing consistently with the Constitutional requirement in article 41 that the Diet be the "sole law-making organ of the State"?

• Excluding or circumscribing Judicial Review[19]

The immigration portfolio in Australia recently has been made subject to a special regime to the exclusion of normal administrative law principles.

The 1992 Amendments to the *Migration Act 1958* which came into effect in 1994, aimed to end the 'uncertainty about what is required to make a fair decision on a visa application' (Explanatory Memorandum to the 1992 Bill). However, in displacing entirely the rules of natural justice from the procedures involved in visa applications (see Part 2, Division 3, subdivision AB of the Act), the legislation reflects the Federal Government's belief that responsibility for migration decision-making should rest with the executive and not with the judiciary. These reforms increase government and administrative control over applicants rather than improving the system of merits review itself.

Section 476, the key feature of the reforms, has been analyzed by the Federal Court in several decisions[20]. The unanimous opinion is that s 420 obliges the RRT in reviewing a decision to comply with the rules of natural justice, and s 476(1) empowers the Federal Court to undertake judicial review. However, s 476(2) and (3) drastically limit the reach of the review grounds. Section 476(2) (a) 'explicitly denies an applicant for refugee status any entitlement to challenge an RRT decision rejecting his/her application on the ground that a breach of the rules of natural justice has occurred in connection with the making of the decision'[21]. Further, s. 476(2)(b) denies an application challenging a decision based on an exercise of power "that is so unreasonable that no reasonable person could have so exercised the power."

Section 476(3) narrowly defines an improper exercise of a power to three grounds, but expressly excludes
- not considering relevant considerations, or
- taking into account irrelevant considerations, or
- acting in bad faith.

It is also interesting to note that several Federal Court decisions have concluded that whatever the content of s 420, it does not prescribe a procedure to be followed by the tribunal which permits the court to review the decision on the merits[22].

Furthermore, this section also limits review which would otherwise be available under the Administrative Decisions Judicial Review (ADJR) Act 1977 (Cth) and the Judiciary Act 1903 (Cth). Therefore, the situation is one where the law imposes an obligation on the RRT to comply with natural justice, but the applicants are denied any remedy in circumstances where a breach of these rules has occurred.

Another example of administrative discretion afforded by the law in this area is s. 417, whereby decisions made under it are also exempt from judicial review by virtue of s. 485[23]. Section 417 allows the Minister to substitute a Tribunal decision with another decision, being one that is more favourable to the applicant. The Full Court in *Minister for Immigration & Ethnic Affairs v. Ozamanian*[24] held that despite s 485 limiting the rights of review, it should not be characterized as abrogating or curtailing fundamental rights, freedoms or immunities.

Again, I believe this sort of limitation on judicial review would be difficult in Japan in the light of article 76(2) of the Constitution which reposes final judicial power in the courts.

- Merging judicial and administrative review in a single Tribunal

The relationship between the regulators and those regulated may again be affected by recent government reforms. In March 1997, the Commonwealth Attorney-General announced that Cabinet had agreed in principle to amalgamate the five leading merits review tribunals at the federal level: the AAT, the Social Security Appeals Tribunal, the Veterans' Review Tribunal and the RRT. There will now be a single tribunal, the Administrative Review Tribunal (ART)[25].

The Victorian State government in August 1998 restructured the system for its review tribunals and combined civil and administrative review processes with judicial review in the same structure. There are three judicial members of the new Tribunal who can hear reviews on points of law from the administrative panels in the Tribunal in their judicial capacity, as if appeals were being taken to their courts. The President of the Tribunal is a Supreme Court judge and the two Deputy Presidents are County Court judges.

The Victorian Attorney General has described the new structure in the following terms:

'VCAT will be the most comprehensive reform in Australia in this area to date'[26].

Conclusion

While I have argued that there has been a clear convergence between the Australian and Japanese administrative law systems over the past 30 years, both influenced by US models, nevertheless there are important differences Anglo-American observers are largely ignorant of the German theory that underlies much of the basic administrative law in Japan. Again, the Japanese Constitution has explicit procedural rights which are not present in the Australian Constitution. The Japanese Constitution also sets out a more explicit government structure, based on the separation of powers, which would make the legislative restrictions on judicial review developed in Australia more difficult to achieve. The prohibition of special courts in article 76(2), designed to outlaw the old prewar Administrative court would also make the most recent Victorian experiment a problem to copy. Finally, there is a rich field of comparative research in the operations of the economic regulators in each of our countries, as we mould US models to our own long established practices.

(1) My thanks to Kerry Liu BA (Hons), 4th year law student, my Research Assistant, for her assistance with this paper.
(2) LL.M. thesis Law School, University of Melbourne, 1971.
(3) "Administrative Discretion in Foreign Trade Regulation: United States, Australia and Japan", SJD dissertation, Harvard Law School, 1976
(4) [1964] AC 40
(5) In other words, legislation expressly limits judicial review in defined situations.
(6) English translations of Japanese administrative law theory, such as Professor Endo's "Administrative Law Theory During the Thirty Years after the War" (1981) 14 Law in Japan: An Annual 82 or Professor Shiono's "Public and Private Law" (1986) 19 Law in Japan: An Annual 15, did not appear until the 1980s. See also Vol. 19 of Law in Japan, a special issue devoted to administrative law issues.
(7) Section 50.
(8) See generally, Matsushita, M., International Trade and Competition Law in Japan, (Oxford 1993) 218-241.
(9) Ibid, 221-223.
(10) Committee on Administrative Discretions, Final Report, October, 1973, para 191.
(11) Law No. 88 of 1993 (Management and Coordination Agency translation by Professor K. Uga).
(12) see Boling, D., "Administrative Procedure Law Makes Inroads on Bureaucracy but Leaves Web Largely Intact", (1994) East Asian Executive Reports, 7.
(13) Freedom of Information Act 1982 (Cth); equivalent laws exist in each State and Territory of Australia.
(14) For example see Accident Compensation Commission v. Croom [1991] 2 VR

32, per Young CJ; *Sobh v. Police Force of Victoria* [1994] 1 VR 41,per Ashley J. This approach appears to be consistent with that taken by the Supreme Court of the United States.

(15) Repeta, L. and Chafce, J., "Japanese government Information: New Rules for Access", Japan Information Access Project Special Report; June 1988, www.nmjc.org/jiap/specrpts/joho.html

(16) e.g., Kaufman (ed.) Banking Structure in Major Countries (Kluwer, 1992) Appendix: Chronology of Major Changes in the Japanese Financial and Monetary Environment, 1975-1990. Khoury, The Deregulation of the World's Financial Markets (Pinter, 1990), 114, Exhibit 4.6 Chronology of Money and Credit Market Deregulation in Japan 1984-89.

(17) Shikano, Y., "Prospects for Financial Reforms in Japan" The 21st Century Policy Institute Symposium, March 5, 1998, New York, cited, http://www.keidanren.or.jp/21ppi/english/symposium/19980305/shikano.htm

(18) Section 1084(2).

(19) This section was largely contributed by Kerry Liu.

(20) For example see *Thanh Phat Ma v. Billings* (1996) 142ALR 158, per Drummond J; *Zheng v. Minister for Immigration & Ethnic Affairs* [1996] ACL Rep 77 FC 8; *Yao v. Minister for Immigration & Ethnic Affairs* [1997] ACL Rep 77 FC 45; *Eshetu v. Minister for Immigration & Ethnic Affairs* [1997] 142 ALR 474, per Hill J.

(21) Drummond J, *Thanh Phat Ma v. Billings* (1996) 142 ALR 158, 163.

(22) *Velmurugu v. Minister for Immigration & Ethnic Affairs* (Fed Ct, 23 May 1996, unreported), per Olney J.; *Zakinov v. Gibson* (Fed Ct, 26 July 1996, unreported), per North J.

(23) Except to the extent that the original jurisdiction of the High Court extends to review these decisions.

(24) (1996) 141 ALR 322, Jenkinson, Sackville & Kiefee JJ.

(25) J. Barnes, "From the AAT to the Federal Court: Treading the Path of Reform" (1998) 26 *Aust Bus LR* 205, 211.

(26) Hon. Jan Wade, MLA (A-G), 2nd Reading Speech, VCAT Bill, Victorian Hansard, 9 April 1998, p. 975.

Appendix: Some extracts from legislation

Victorian Civil and Administrative Tribunal Act 1998
98. General procedure

(1) The Tribunal--
  (a) is bound by the rules of natural justice;
  (b) is not bound by the rules of evidence or any practices or procedures applicable to courts of record, except to the extent that it adopts those rules, practices or procedures;
  (c) may inform itself on any matter as it sees fit;
  (d) must conduct each proceeding with as little formality and technicality, and determine each proceeding with as much speed, as the requirements of this Act and the enabling enactment and a proper consideration of the matters before it permit.

(2) Without limiting sub-section (1)(b), the Tribunal may admit into evidence the contents of any document despite the non-compliance with any time limit or other requirement specified in the rules in relation to that document or service of it.

(3) Subject to this Act, the regulations and the rules, the Tribunal may regulate its own procedure.

(4) Sub-section (1)(a) does not apply to the extent that this Act or an enabling enactment authorizes, whether expressly or by implication, a departure from the rules of natural justice.

FREEDOM OF INFORMATION ACT 1982
PART 8

29. Statement of reasons for decision

A decision-maker complies with section 46 in relation to a request for a statement of reasons for a decision made under the Freedom of Information Act 1982 if the decision-maker gives, or has given, the person who made the request a notice that complies with section 27 of that Act.

30. Tribunal file in FOI proceeding not open for inspection

Despite anything to the contrary in section 146, the file kept by the principal registrar under that section in a proceeding under the Freedom of Information Act 1982 is not open for inspection or copying by any person.

13 New Forms of Regulation: A Challenge to Democratic Accountability and the Rule of Law?

Cheryl Saunders

Introduction
1 Traditional Institutions and Principles
2 Changing Times
3 Judicial and Other Forms of External Review
4 Democratic Accountability
Conclusion

Introduction

This paper concerns the impact on the Australian legal and constitutional system of new mechanisms used by Australian governments, as well as by governments elsewhere, to deliver services, implement policies and raise public monies. The mechanisms include the corporatisation and privatisation of government agencies, delivery of government services through the private sector under contract, and imposition of user charges and fees of other kinds, in lieu of taxation. In an extreme manifestation, they raise a question about the need for government itself, at least at the local level.

The use of these mechanisms has been driven by a number of factors. One is loss of faith in the efficiency and responsiveness of the public sector, based partly on ideology and partly on experience. Another, which is related, is the need to be more competitive and to maximise limited resources in an increasingly competitive world, ostensibly committed to the free flow of trade.

My argument in this paper is that traditional procedures for democratic and legal accountability have not yet adjusted to these changes, in either theory or practice. A process of adjustment is going on through the courts, within the limits of the Australian constitutional and statutory framework. Adjustment of the democratic process may be more difficult, however, without fundamental changes to the nature of representation itself.

1 Traditional Institutions and Principles

The Australian constitutional system draws upon both Britain and the United States. Those aspects of it which are particularly relevant for present purposes, however, are modelled largely on British arrangements.

In particular, Australia uses the Westminster or parliamentary system of government, at both Commonwealth and State levels. Government is conducted almost entirely through elected representatives.[1] The Burkeian rejection of Members of Parliament as delegates of their constituents prevails. The "clearest conviction of... judgement and conscience" which Burke argued that a Member should bring to the Parliament now is taken to the party room, whose decision now is operative.[2] Both political culture and the design of the electoral system ensure a dominance of Parliament by two principal political groupings and a highly adversarial style of politics. The executive government is drawn from the Parliament and is responsible to it for its policies and their administration. This relationship is underpinned by well-settled constitutional principles that only Parliament can make or authorise the making of new law or can alter existing law; only Parliament can impose taxation; only Parliament can authorise the expenditure of public funds. Historically, independent public service departments have no independent legal existence of their own but advise Ministers who can properly be held accountable for their actions.

A parallel set of principles applies for Australia a version of the rule of law that is broadly similar to that articulated by A. V. Dicey one hundred years ago.[3] A government must act subject to law. Government and the private sector alike are subject to the same law and in the ordinary courts. There is little by way of constitutional prescription of the content of this law but some complacency that the principles of the common law, combined with the natural virtue or instinct for self-preservation of a democratically-elected Parliament will respect individual liberty.

Since Dicey's day, these principles have been embellished through the growth of a distinct administrative law, which Dicey himself derided, but which in fact is broadly consistent with his thesis. The lawfulness of government decisions is determined by courts. The grounds on which the courts rely for this purpose originally derived or inferred the intention of Parliament about the scope of the power or the need for procedural fairness from the statute by which the authority to make the decision was conferred. In Australia, judicial review now is supplemented by other mechanisms as well, including procedures for tribunal review of decisions "on the merits"[4]; for investigation of complaints of maladministration by an Ombudsman; for the compulsory release of government information[5] or reasons for decisions[6]; for the protection of privacy[7].

Both the principles of responsible government and those associated with the rule of law assume that new policies will be implemented through legislation and decisions affecting individuals taken under legislation; that monies will be raised through taxation; that laws will be administered by agencies responsible to a Minister who also is responsible to the Parliament. At the same time, however, the common law accepts that some activities may be undertaken by the executive alone, without reference to Parliament. Inherent executive powers include the capacities possessed by all legal persons, to form corporations, to make contracts, to charge for services, to spend money. They also include functions more closely associated with the exercise of sovereignty and sometimes described as "prerogative" in nature. The most important of these include signature and ratification of treaties, declarations of war, making peace. The rationale for characterising these functions as executive rather than legislative rests partly on analogy with the position of other legal persons, and partly is functional or historical. There has been no significant change to the boundaries between legislative and executive power since the Bill of Rights 1689 brought an end to the main phase of the struggle between Parliament and the Crown. Parliament can override the exercise of executive power but the dynamics of responsible government make it unlikely to do so.

2 Changing Times

Australian jurisdictions have always made more extensive use of quasi-independent statutory authorities, supplementing the functions of public service departments. Otherwise, however, the assumptions about the structure of the executive and the centrality of legislation in the process of government, on which the principles of responsible government and the rule of law are based, have broadly applied. This has begun to change in recent years, however. The nature of these changes and the challenges which they present are described below. The remaining parts of the paper deal with the responses to them, by governments, legislatures and courts.

(a) Statutory Authorities

It is convenient to begin with the role of independent statutory authorities, as an historic exception to the traditional model of responsible government in Australia. The assumption that administration is carried out by an independent public service advising a minister who in turn is responsible to Parliament has never been entirely correct. The public service has and always has had an important role. But there also has been a long tradition of performance of government functions through statutory authorities especially constituted for the purpose, with varying degrees of independence from executive government[8]. And for almost as long, there has been debate and dissension about the operation of the principles of responsible government in relation to bodies of this kind. Legally, the power of Ministers over such authorities is limited, in varying degrees, by their constituent statutes. Practically and politically, however, the Minister may wield extensive influence, through power to appoint senior managers, or to withhold funds, or to initiate amending legislation or in the other more subtle ways. In a recent contribution to this debate, Justice Finn, of the Federal Court of Australia, described "the constitutional status and standing in our system of government of statutory corporations that by statute are subject to prescribed (hence, presumably, correspondingly limited) powers of ministerial direction" as one of "two rather significant fissures in Australian jurisprudence."[9]

The problem has continued and if anything been compounded by more recent tendencies to require authorities to operate on commercial principles. Increasingly, this has been sought to be achieved by reconstituting authorities to mirror their counterparts in the private sector. This may be done in a variety of ways[10]. In its most extreme form, however, the authority is established under the general Corporations law, with a Board of Directors drawn from the public sector and government as shareholder.

A host of questions is raised by this structure for the application of constitutional principles and procedures. Corporations law will regulate the decisions taken respectively by the Board and general meeting of such a company subject to any general or specific legislation structuring the operation of government business enterprises. Superficially, at least, judicial review has no application at all. Even if Ministers are the nominal holder of the government shares, it is far from clear how far, if at all, they can be held accountable to Parliament for the actions taken in the exercise of shareholder rights and responsibilities. The difficulties are greater still where the body is partly privatised through the sale of a minority or even a majority of shares to the public sector. If the government is a minority shareholder, albeit still a substantial one, even the mechanisms for scrutiny of the use of public funds may no longer apply.

(b) Contracting Out-Outsourcing

Increasingly Australian governments, like governments elsewhere, are outsourcing their functions, through contracts with the private sector. In recent years this has affected, for example, the administration of prisons, the provision of ambulance services and the generation and sale of electricity.

Where outsourcing coincides with the transfer of an industry formerly owned by the public sector to private ownership, or privatisation, government may seek to retain a measure of control through the imposition of a regulatory framework. This is the subject of the paper by my colleague, Professor Crommelin. In such a case, questions of democratic accountability depend on the transparency of the regulatory mechanisms and links between the regulator and the Minister and the Minister and Parliament. Questions of external review, by courts or other agencies, may be raised as well, particularly where an effective review regime has been in operation while the industry was in public hands. This was the case, for example, with the telecommunications industry which, before corporatisation and part-privatisation, generated a large number of complaints to the Commonwealth Ombudsman.

The outsourcing of government services raises other issues as well, for democratic accountability and review. In a sense, these are not new, except in degree. Governments have always entered into contracts, in the exercise of executive power. By their very nature government contracts are difficult for Parliaments to scrutinise and have been largely immune from review by courts. But the scale of outsourcing in recent times has highlighted the magnitude of the challenge to traditional constitutional practices, partly because of the implication of the private delivery of public services for people and partly because of the potential of the contracting mechanism for de facto regulation.

The impact on people takes at least two forms. The first concerns the relationship between government and contractors. The size and relative wealth of government makes its business valuable to a point which can determine the viability of some contractors. How can fair treatment be assured in the contracting process, undue preference and accountability preserved? The answer generally is assumed to lie in elaborate tendering processes. Unless these also are efficient, transparent and fair, however, they compound, instead of resolving the problem, because of the time and resources which necessarily are devoted to preparing substantial tender applications.[11]

The other group affected are those to whom services ultimately are provided, by private sector providers using public funds. If these services were provided by the public sector, the recipients would have rights of review of decisions by courts and tribunals or the ombudsman, and access to information about how decisions which affected them were made. Theoretically, at least, there also would be some measure of democratic accountability for the provision of such services as well, through individual Members of Parliament or Parliament itself. Under these new arrangements, should review mechanisms be introduced to replicate those offered through the public sector or are the mechanisms of the market sufficient? What stand should Members of Parliament take on complaints about the provision of services by the private sector agencies? How should governments be expected to respond?[12]

A third, as yet relatively unexplored issue, concerns the potential of contracts for de facto regulation by government. Daintith drew attention to this phenomenon in 1989, in his analysis of the growing use of "dominium" rather than "imperium" to secure compliance with policy.[13] If contracts are used to impose service standards, encourage the development of social or economic norms, establish priorities as between, for example, the rehabilitation of prisoners and prison security, questions arise as to whether and how governments should be held accountable for such choices.

(c) User Pays

A different aspect of greater reliance on commercial practice by governments or, in Daintith's terms, the use of dominium rather than imperium is the funding of public services through user charges rather than taxation. Again this is not a new phenomenon. Its novelty lies in its extent and the greater exposure of underlying issues of principle.

The Australian Constitution itself excludes fees for licences or fees for services from the definition of taxation.[14] The definition has been elaborated by the courts, which have held that a tax is a compulsory exaction of money by a public authority for public purposes, enforceable by law, and... "not a payment for services rendered."[15] The courts have tended to scrutinise carefully imposts which masquerade as a fee for a privilege or a service but which in fact are general, compulsory levies.[16] The distinction is significant. The authority of Parliament is required to impose a tax but not for at least some fees of other kinds. This was graphically illustrated some years ago, when a requirement to pay a fee for review of certain government decisions was imposed through administrative practice, after delegated legislation to impose the fee was disallowed by the Senate. The question whether an impost is a tax also is relevant to the respective powers of the two Houses of Parliament under the Australian Constitution.[17]

The broader constitutional issue remains unresolved, however. The proceeds of many taxes are dedicated or "hypothecated" to particular purposes. For example, road taxes may be hypothecated to road-maintenance. Tobacco taxes may be hypothecated to health care arising from tobacco-related diseases, or to advertising campaigns to discourage smoking. It may be difficult to distinguish some of these taxes from user fees for those or other services. The issue presses the limits of the definition of a tax. If charges are imposed for the use of a facility which provides a general community service, such as a road or hospital or school, should these be characterised as taxes either because of the generality of their application or because the users effectively have no choice and the levy is compulsory in practice? And if the answer to that is yes, when the facility is in public ownership, what different does it make if the facility is privately owned but made available under government authority?

(d) Governance Without Government

The final illustration of the issues to which current trends give rise is drawn from recent experience of the redevelopment of the old Melbourne Docklands. The economic opportunity in the Docklands is one which has been compared with the Osaka waterfront development although on a smaller scale. Geographically, the area is within the jurisdiction of the local government of the municipality of Melbourne. So far, however, planning and development has been handled by a statutory authority, under the auspices of the State Government, with no council involvement at all. While this is controversial in some quarters, it has broadly been accepted as necessary for the efficient handling of the initial stage of a major and complex redevelopment and on the grounds that, until the area is settled, democratic representation is not realistic in any event.

The arrangements for future governance are less obvious, however, and are likely to cause greater dissension. The plans for the area envisage approximately 15,000 residents as well as office space, a stadium, an entertainment precinct and a theme park. Each precinct will be developed as a whole by a single tenderer, who will be responsible for providing all amenities in the area. The infrastructure for the whole of the redeveloped Docklands, including the road network, will be provided under tender as well. At this stage it is not clear, because the contracts remain confidential, whether the infrastructure ultimately will revert to public ownership and, if so, when.

The City of Melbourne was anxious to resume governance of the area as soon as possible. It argued its case partly by reference to the need for a range of social, economic and environmental services to be provided by a body with democratic legitimacy, funded by local taxes which are levied by elected representatives on local communities to whom they can be held accountable. The outcome of their claim is not known and it is possible it will succeed. It may be resisted until the development is complete, however, and this may take as long as thirty years. And even then, there may be a question whether local representation will be countenanced by the State Government or even demanded by what is expected to be an atypical, young professional residential population of the area. The alternative scenario is that the area will continue to be serviced by private corporations in a contractual relationship with the residents imposing fees for the use of communal facilities which in fact are privately owned.

3 Judicial and Other Forms of External Review

Since the trend of commercialisation, corporatisation and outsourcing became clear, numerous enquiries have been held into the extent to which the traditional mechanisms of judicial review and other more recent procedures to provide redress of grievances or transparency of decisions should be adapted or extended. These include reviews by the Administrative Review Council of government business enterprises[18]; freedom of information law[19]; intergovernmental service delivery programs[20] and contracting out.[21]

In varying degrees, these reports reveal the tensions between the competing approaches of public and private law and uncertainty about how either is likely to operate in this new context. A central question is whether private sector remedies, including corporations law, trade practices or competition law and contract law, coupled with market forces and, perhaps voluntary codes of conduct[22], provide adequate accountability for the provision of commercial services by a public sector agency or the provision of public services by a private contractor. But there are underlying issues as well, which produce their own tensions. One is a degree of hostility towards public law procedures and remedies in some quarters even in their application to the public sector. For those of this persuasion, the new private face of government offers an opportunity to check or to wind back administrative law. Ranged against this is the view, held equally strongly in other quarters, that governments should provide a model for others to follow. Adherents of this view are divided over whether the precept is absolute, or whether it may properly be varied where a government service is in competition with the private sector.

The policy reaction to these issues by government has been limited and, generally, piecemeal. To the extent that existing procedures cover corporatised bodies and privatised services by and large they have been left in place. Otherwise, however, the public and legal accountability of services and agencies have been tackled pragmatically, in a way which has not enabled underlying and coherent principles to emerge. There is a clear government preference, at least in rhetoric, for regulation through the market, including self-regulation rather than the extension of the principles and institutions of public law. In rare instances, specialist dispute resolution mechanisms have been established to deal with complaints against both public or private agencies in simple, discrete industry.

By contrast, the scope of judicial review gradually has begun to expand into this new field. It has been inhibited by historic assumptions, doctrine and, to a degree by statute. Traditionally, courts have been prepared to define the scope of the prerogative or inherent executive power[23] but wary of scrutinising its exercise. It has been made difficult to do so in any event by the fact that the grounds for review, procedural fairness or ultra vires, have been developed in connection with the review of decisions made under authority conferred by statute and justified by reference to the intention of Parliament. Partly for these reasons, the legislation by which judicial review has been made more accessible in recent decades also has defined the jurisdiction of courts by reference to statute. Thus the principal avenue for review of Commonwealth decisions, the Administrative Decisions (Judicial Review) Act 1977, confers jurisdiction on the Federal Court to review decisions of an administrative character "taken under an enactment."[24]

The pattern is now breaking down. Although there still are some dissenting views, courts are prepared to review the decisions taken in the exercise of inherent executive power. Procedural fairness at least will apply, and also, depending on the circumstances, some ultra vires grounds[25]. The Federal Court of Australia recently has held that a public body has an obligation to conduct a tender fairly, partly as a term of the contract, but partly also because it has an obligation to be a "moral exemplar."[26] English courts have even gone so far as to apply public sector remedies to at least one private body performing self-regulating functions.[27] In Australia, such a development would not be possible, at least at the Commonwealth level, in view of the manner in which jurisdiction is conferred on the courts.[28]

4 Democratic Accountability

The impact of changing government practices on the accountability of the executive to Parliament and through Parliament to the electors has been equally profound. It is also significant. The executive legislative relationship is a fundamental element of the Australian constitutional system, despite cynicism about its effectiveness in practice.

The parliamentary system assumes that major new government policies will be based in legislation. One characteristic of all new approaches to governance is that they require increasingly less legislation. Existing laws may need to be altered to convert government agencies to corporate status. Beyond that, framework legislation is often provided[29], but is not essential, unless the body is to be given a legal regulatory function or a privilege. A body established by incorporation under the general law may not need additional legislative support at all.

The same is true of other techniques used by governments in the age of corporatisation and privatisation. Outsourcing classically relies on contract. In many cases there is no legislative framework at all. The status of user fees is ambivalent but there is no doubt that some, at least, may be imposed without the authority of Parliament.

Even in the absence of legislation, constitutional theory assumes that Parliament will monitor government activity. The difficulty is that its tools for doing so are limited. There is a requirement for most government bodies to submit annual reports to Parliament, and this provides one avenue for intervention. The requirement for Parliament to approve expenditure through the appropriation process provides a context in which particular contracts, or contracts generally might be raised. Parliament's effectiveness for this purpose is assisted by the independent office of Auditor-General and by parliamentary committees charged with the responsibility of monitoring public accounts. In this regard, the increasing conflict in recent years between governments and auditors-general, threatening the independence and scope of authority of the latter, is worthy of note. Significantly also, important details of contracts of this kind can be withheld from Parliaments on the ground that they are commercial in confidence.

For Parliaments to meet this challenge, new procedures must be designed which recognised the different ways in which governance now is undertaken. The Administrative Review Council, for example, has examined one such procedure.[30] The Council invited comment on the desirability of a general Contracting Out Act to impose minimum requirements for monitoring contracts and evaluating contractors' performance and requiring contracting agencies to provide details of contracts in their annual report. The Council also suggested that such an Act could be useful in providing remedies for service recipients and others affected by the actions of a contractor. The reactions to the proposal from government were not entirely favourable and the Council did not proceed with this recommendation in its final report.

This relatively novel suggestion for a Contracting Out Act has a parallel with a different procedure recently put in place at the Commonwealth level to involve Parliament in decisions to enter into treaties.[31] Treaty-making and ratification also is an executive power in the Australian system whose status increasingly is under question. The present procedure, which has no statutory base, requires treaties to be tabled in the Parliament and establishes a parliamentary committee to invite public comments on them. Undoubtedly the procedure has brought greater transparency to the treaty-making process although the role of Parliament is a limited one and there are grounds on which the procedure can be waived altogether in the case of urgent or confidential treaties.

The difficulty in opening executive processes to greater parliamentary involvement lies in features of the Parliament itself. Parliament is slow and cumbersome. Ironically this is likely to increase if, in consequence of a diminished legislative program, Parliament meets less often. And it is highly adversarial. Arguably, this is appropriate for consideration of proposed new laws which involve a contest between government and opposition, however stylised. The adversarial mode is less acceptable, however, for instruments which involve third parties or other governments and which deserve careful and sometimes confidential consideration on the merits.

Conclusion

It has become commonplace that in late-twentieth century western states citizens are being transformed into consumers and the relationship between people and government increasingly is one of business and client. This phenomenon often is reflected in government rhetoric, describing those with whom agencies deal as customers. The motivation may originally have been to encourage a service culture in impersonal bureaucracies. If so, it is a sad reflection on the concept of citizenship and the relations of citizens to the state that it has been necessary to invoke the market to place people centre-stage. As it happens, however, the analogy with the market is becoming increasingly apt as the mechanism through which governments make and implement policy and deliver services change.

This is in many ways a revolution which calls for a comparable response in constitutional and legal terms. So far, the response has been piecemeal, and developed on a case by case basis. Some interesting ideas are beginning to emerge, but they have no underlying coherent philosophy. Unless and until this occurs, the slow drift towards the consumer state will continue, fostered by weakening citizenship ties and the growing disrepute of representative institutions.

One project for constitutional scholars in the twenty-first century is to accept the reality of the new governance but to develop institutions and principles for its exercise, reconceiving, if necessary, some of the fundamentals of a democratic polity itself. Comparative study will be essential. I look forward to further exchanges on these issues with scholars in Japan.

(1) The approval of the voters themselves is required to change the national Constitution. Constitution section 128.

(2) Edmund Burke, speech to the electors at Bristol, in Jack Lively and Adam Lively (eds) *Democracy in Britain*, Blackwells, 1994, 62-63.
(3) A.V. Dicey, *The Law of the Constitution*, extracted in Lively and Lively op cit, 178-180.
(4) Eg, Administrative Appeals Tribunal Act 1975.
(5) Freedom of Information Act 1982.
(6) Administrative Decisions (Judicial Review) Act 1977 Section. 13.
(7) Privacy Act 1988.
(8) R. Wettenhall, *Corporations and Corporatisation: An Administrative History Perspective* (1995) 6 PLR 7.
(9) *Hughes Aircraft Systems International v. Air Services Australia* (1997) 146 ALR 1, 24.
(10) Dominic McGann, "Corporatisation, Privatisation and Other Strategies – Common Legal Issues" in Bryan Horrigan (ed.) *Government Law and Policy: Commercial Aspects* (Federation Press, 1998) 55.
(11) Dan Young, "Current Issues in Government Tendering and Contracting Practice" in Horrigan, *op. cit.*, 69, 74-5.
(12) These questions, and others, were the subject of inquiry by the principal advisory body to the Australian governments or administrative law matters, the Administrative Review Council: *The Contracting Out of Government Services*, Issues Paper, February 1997.
(13) Terence Daintith, "The Executive Power Today: Bargaining and Economic Control" in Jeffrey Jowell and Dawn Oliver (eds.) *The Changing Constitution*, Clarendon Press, Oxford (2nd edition 1989), 193.
(14) Section 53.
(15) *Air Caledonie International v. The Commonwealth* (1988) 165 CLR 462, 467.
(16) Thus, in *Air Caledonie* itself, an "immigration clearance fee" payable by all passengers on arrival in Australia, was held to be a tax.
(17) Section 53. Bills which impose taxation must not originate in the Upper House, the Senate. See also section 55.
(18) *Government Business Enterprises and Administrative Law*, Report no. 38.
(19) *Open Government: A Review of the Federal Freedom of Information Act 1982*, with the Australian Law Reform Commission, Report No. 40.
(20) *Administrative Review and Funding Programs*, Report No. 37.
(21) *op. cit.*
(22) Increasingly, these take the form of "Charters", apparently inspired by the use of "Citizen's Charter" in the United Kingdom: Administrative Review

Council, *The Contracting Out of Government Services*, op. cit., 41-43; Robin Creyke, "Sunset for the Administrative Law Industry?" in John McMillan (ed) *Administrative law Under the Coalition Government* (1997) 20, 57.

(23) *Barton v. Commonwealth* (1974) 131 CLR 477.

(24) Section 3.

(25) *Council of Civil Service Unions v. Minister for the Civil Service.* [1985] AC 374.

(26) *Hughes Aircraft Systems International v. Air Services Australia* (1997) 146 ALR 1, 41.

(27) *R v. Panel on Take-overs and Mergers; ex parte Datafin p.lc* [1987] 1 QB 815.

(28) The body would not be acting under statute, for the purpose of the AD (JR) Act 1977. Nor would it be an "officer of the Commonwealth" for the purposes of the jurisdiction conferred on the High Court by section 75 (v) of the Constitution and on the Federal Court by section 398 of the Judiciary Act 1903.

(29) For example, Commonwealth Authorities and Companies Act 1997.

(30) *The Contracting Out of Government Services*, op. cit.

(31) Daryl Williams "Treaties and the Parliamentary Process" (1996) 7 *Public Law Review* 199.

Part III: STUDIES ON OCEANIC LEGAL SYSTEMS IN JAPAN

14 The Fundamental Nature of the Governing Framework in Australia

Akira Osuka

Introduction
1 Monarchical Elements in the Australian Constitution
2 Republican Elements in the Australian Constitution
3 The Fundamental Framework of the Governing System in Australia in Comparison with Those in Other Western Countries

Introduction

The reason I started to study this issue is that I would like to know whether the basic framework of the Commonwealth of Australia is monarchical or republican, how the Constitution provides the basic framework, and how it actually works. This paper aims to answer these questions, and present a fundamental analysis of the Australian system of government. This paper is the first step toward reaching these goals.

Unfortunately, there is not much literature in Japan on the legal system of Australia. There have been few studies on Oceanic law in the Japanese Anglo-American law academy.

However, fortunately, I have been able to make many personal contacts with Australian legal scholars through cooperative studies and Waseda University's academic exchange program with the Law School of the University of Melbourne, the most prestigious in Australia. This has promoted me to begin this project with the aim of explaining the Australian legal system to my Japanese colleagues.

1 Monarchical Elements in the Australian Constitution

The Australian Constitution is delineated in section 9 of the Commonwealth of Australia Constitution Act of the British Parliament. The preamble and the first eight sections of the Act, which are usually referred to as the "covering clauses", are distinguished from the sections which make up the Constitution.

Looking at the Constitution as a whole, there are several monarchical elements in it.

For example, the preamble says, the people of Australia have agreed "to unite in one indissoluble Federal Commonwealth under the Crown of the United Kingdom of Great Britain and Ireland". And, covering clause 3 authorised the Queen to bring the Commonwealth of Australia into effect and appoint the first Governor-General. Section 1 of part 1 (General) of Chapter 1 (The Parliament) of the Constitution vests legislative power of the Commonwealth in a Federal Parliament. The Federal Parliament consists of the Queen, a senate and the Parliament.

Section 2 provides that, "A Governor-General appointed by the Queen shall be Her Majesty's representative in the Commonwealth, and shall have and may exercise in the Commonwealth during the Queen's pleasure… such powers and functions of the Queen as Her Majesty may be pleased to assign to him." Section 4 gives the Queen the power to appoint an administrator if the Governor-General is unable to act for some reason, and also under section 126, the Queen may authorise the Governor-General to appoint a deputy[1].

2 Republican Elements in the Australian Constitution

I have pointed out the direct construction of clauses provided by the Commonwealth of Australian Constitution Act 1900. During the hundred years of the 20th century, however, great changes emerged in the governing framework in Australia. These changes were brought about by new legislation, it's interpretation and administration as well as judicial decisions. In particular, the independence of the Commonwealth of Australia, even within the framework of the (British) Commonwealth has progressed along with changes in the nature of the Crown and the Governor-General and in the way in which the Governor-General is appointed.

It may be clear that covering clause 3 has only historical meaning, judged from its provision. As for the provision that "the Queen is considered to be part of the Parliament," historical development shows that real power has been transferred from the Crown to Parliament in Australia as well as in Britain. This does not mean that the Crown has been totally excluded from the Power. It is said that the role the Crown now plays as part of the Parliament is limited to giving assent to bills that have gone through the rest of the legislative process[2]. It is unclear whether this assent means an act of recognition, which gives real legal authority to a bill that has gone through the rest of the legislative process, or whether it means an attestation, which is only ritual, to a bill that already has substantive legal authority through the rest of the legislative process. If the first construction is the right answer, it can be said that the Queen has real power and that the basic framework of government tends to the monarchy. If the second construction is the right answer, then the principle of government tends to be republican.

Judging from the whole of the Constitutional framework, it seems to me that the right answer is the second. If it is, substantive meaning of covering clause has been totally lost.

By an Act of 1973, the Queen was specifically appointed the Queen of Australia. It is pointed out that the legal effect of this change is that the Queen may act concernig issues in Australia on the advice of Australian ministers, not British ministers[3]. In comparison with the position at the time of the enactment of the Commonwealth, monarchical elements in Australian government have largely reduced, and the degree of independence of Australia has grown.

Section 2 of the Constitution provides that the Governor-General shall be Her Majesty's representative in the Commonwealth. It is true that at the time of the enactment of the Constitution, the Queen was the Head of State and the

Governor-General was her representative. At that time, Australia was a colony of the British Empire, although its position was special, because Australia was regarded as a Dominion. In the early stages, all Govenor-Generals were from Britain, appointed by the Head of State on the advice of the British Prime Minister. The Australian Government had no legal right to influence the appointment of the Governor-General. In 1930, however, the Australian Government, for the first time, recommended an Australian candidate (who was born and living in Australia) for the Governor-Generalship, and the Crown reluctantly appointed him. It is said that since that time the Australian Government has had the right to recommend candidates for the Governor-Generalship.

By the mid-60's, the practice of appointing an Australian citizen as Governor-General had been established[4]. From a legal point of view, the Governor-General is only responsible to the Australian Government, not to foreign powers. That means that Governor-General is not responsible to the Queen.

By convention, the only role the Queen now plays in relation to Australia is to appoint (and, if required, to dismiss) the Governor-General. Even these powers are exercised on the advice of the Australian Prime Minister. Furthermore, under section 2, the term of office of the Governor-General is described as being "during the Queen's pleasure," but, in practice, appointment is usually for five years. Moreover, the Governor-General has all necessary executive power under section 61 of the Constitution[5]. Today, all the important functions of the Head of State are exercised by the Governor-General, not by the Queen at all.

As stated, the power of appointment by the Queen under section 4 is exercised on the advice of the Australian Prime Minister. Under the Australian Act 1986, the Government of the United Kingdom abandoned to the States every power concerning State matters, and Parliament in the United Kingdom delegated all legislative powers to the Commonwealth, States and Territories of Australia. Furthermore, the Queen appoints the Governor-General on the advice of the state Prime Ministers. As Goverer-Generals are always Australians, it can be said that the powers that the Queen once had over them has now been abandoned.

According to definitions in law dictionaries published in Japan, a republic is "a system of government by elected representatives"[6] or "a form of state in which the administration of politics is carried through the will of the people. Where administration is performed, not by a monarch, but by a group of aristocrats or the people, the form of state is called republic"[7].

In contrast, the elements which a monarch is conventionally said to have are: a) sole authority and hereditary succession, b) authority to exercise important functions of government, or power to coordinate the governing process, c) a power to represent the State in foreign relations, and d) a symbol of the State[8]. Under the Constitution of Japan, the Emperor does not have element b) because article 4 of the Constitution provides, "The Emperor⋯shall not have powers related to government," and because he can only perform ritual or nominal acts with the advice and approval of the Cabinet.

As the Cabinet has a power to conclude treaties and manage foreign affaires under the Constitution, the Emperor does not even play a nominal role in these respects. What he can do is to attest the full powers and credentials of Ambassadors and Minsters, and ratification and other diplomatic documents. For these reasons, he does not have element c) at all. This is why the Emperor cannot be called a monarch in the conventional sense of the word. Furthermore, as we adopt the system of separation of powers under the sovereignty of the people, and govern under the parliamentary system of government, it is clear that our governing system under the Constitution is republican.

As I have already shown, in Australia, all the important functions of the Head of State have been transferred from the Queen to the Governor-General, and the Governor-General and the Government and the Parliament exercise the power to represent the Commonwealth in foreign relations. For these reasons, it is clear that the Queen of Australia, lacking of elements b) and c), is not a monarch in the conventional sense of the word.

It can be said that the fundamental framework of the governing system in Australia is clearly republican, because the Governor-General is appointed on the recommendation by the Australian Government, and because, as decisions of the High Court of Australia have held, administration is carried under the parliamentary system of government with the separation of powers[9].

In many monarchical states, monarchs have changed from absolute to constitutional and then to parliamentary monarch. In accordance with this change, the powers to be exercised by monarchs has tended to decrease.

A parliamentary monarch reigns under the sovereignty of the people[10]. Monarchs in this system qualify as a representative of the people and has some political powers under the constitutional law, in particular, administative powers. Under the constitutional law of the United Kingdom or the Kingdom of Belgium, the monarch has a certain power in legislative process. Of course, even in these states, the powers of the monarch have become nominal with the development of the parliamentary system of government. Therefore, the concept of monarchy has changed today. For this reason, it is difficult to distinguish a monarchy from a republic. Against this background, there are more and more academic opinions which support the view that a monarchy is only such if the monarch has elements a) and d), because the concept of monarch itself is elusive.

No doubt, the Japanese Emperor satisfies element a). As article 1 of the Japanese Constitution provides "The Emperor shall be the symbol of the State and the unity of the people, deriving his position from the will of the people with whom resides sovereign power," he satisfies element d). In these respects, the Emperor is clearly a monarch.

However, in this theory, because there is a monarch, it does not follow that the crucial point is whether the governing system is republican or a monarchy. What matters is that, assuming that the governing system is republican, what powers and how this restricted monarch can exercise without doing harm to the republican system and the tension that this creates within the system.

In Japan, the fundamental framework of governing system is republican with the Emperor as a symbol. Constitutionally, the Emperor is expected to make a symbolic contribution to Japan and the unity of the people.

In Australia, the Queen of Australia satisfies element a). In addition, in this symposium, professor Michael Smith argues that the Queen of Australia is a symbol, which has three implications as follows: links to Australia's British heritage, links to British Commonwealth countries, and symbol of an established, stable system of government with no need for change. So it is clear that she satisfies element d). Australia, then, like Japan, is basically republican state, though it has a symbolic monarchy.

3 The Fundamental Framework of the Governing System in Australia in Comparison with Those in Other Western Countries

P.H. Lane, on Australian law, says the following:

"The monarch is only a shadow over a de facto republic. The Governor-General is a de facto President appointed by an elected Prime Minister, and answerable to this Prime Minister, almost invariably action on his advice (that is, the Governor-General may see himself, in most exceptional circumstances, to the nation). The same kind of remarks can be made about a State Governor and State Premier"[11].

Even though the Governor-General is comparable to a President, he is not similar to the American President, who is elected, if indirectly, by the people, and has the strong and concentrated political power as head of the executive branch of government. The Governor-General does have important power over the Australian Parliament. For example, as section 5 provides, he or she has the power to decide the times during which the Parliament will meet, to dissolve the House of Representatives, and to prologue the Parliament. Those powers are exercised on the advice of the Prime Minister[12]. Section 61 gives executive power of the Australian Commonwealth to the Queen, but makes this power exercisable by the Governor-General, as her representative. As a matter of law, the Governor-General exercises these powers on Australian government advice[13]. The powers of the Governor-General are therefore important and broad. In reality, however, other government branches, such as the Prime Minister of the government, have the power to decide almost all of those matters. The Governor-General seems to be nominal.

Moreover, the fact that he is appointed practically by the Prime Minister, who is an elected member of the Parliament, makes him more similar to Presidents in some European countries. However, it is plain that this analogy does not apply to the position of the French Presidency, who is elected directly by the electorate, and has the strong political powers[14]. The Governor-General is not similar to the Italian President, who is not as strong as French President, but is not a nominal Head of State, because of his or her important powers in the government. He or she has power concerning the military, e.g., to command, to preside over the Supreme National Defense Council, and to declare the war, and the power to dissolve both Houses[15]. The Governor-General, if anything, seems to be similar to the German President. He or she has little power but is expected to compensate for this lack of power with his or her personal authority. His or her power is limited fo formal acts, like the conclusion of treaties, recommending candidates for the Chancellorship, appointments of ministers of the Federal Government on the advice of the Chancellor, and attestation and promulgation of statutes[16].

Next, I would like to examine the governing systems of European countries in terms of the roles and functions of the Head of State (King or President) and the Prime Minister. First of all, it is to be noticed that in countries where a President is the Head of State, except in France for the cohabitation period (when the presidency and Parliament are controlled by different political parties), parliamentary systems of government are employed to a lesser or greater extent. That is to say, the framework of the government requires the confidence of the legislature representing the people. Second, in countries that employ Constitutional monarchies, the power of the Morarch is formal and nominal, and the Prime Minister exercises the power of the Head of State. Again, the Prime Minister must act with the confidence of the legislature.

Australia seems similar to European countries in that it employs a parliamentary system of government. However, it is most similar to her suzerain state, the United Kingdom, where the governing system employs a parliamentary system in which the Prime Minister exercises strong power under the authority of the Queen, who is still the Head of State, but has became nominal. Though the powers and functions of the Queen went to Governor-General in Australia.

Notes

(1) *The Australian Constitution*, at 25.
(2) *Id.* at 23.
(3) Zelman Cowen, "The Legal Implications of Australia's Becoming a Republic," *The Constitutional Law Journal*, vol. 68, at 589.
(4) *Id.* at 590.
(5) *The Australian Constitution*, at 24.
(6) Hideo Tanaka, ed., *Dictionary of Anglo-American Law*, at 722.
(7) Hiroshi Suekawa, ed., *Dictionary of Law*, at 966.
(8) Youichi Higuchi, *Constitutional Law* (vol. 1), at 128.
(9) *The Australian Constitution*, at 23.
(10) Isao Sato, *A Study of Monarchy*, at 40-1.
(11) P.H. Lane, *An Introduction to the Australian Constitutions*, at 263.
(12) *The Australian Constitution*, at 26.
(13) *Id.* at 69-70.
(14) Motonari Imasaki, "Bacic Framework of the Fifth French Republic," Okushima *et al.* eds., *Politics of the French Republic*, at 35 ff.
(15) Fumio Iguchi, "The Constitution of Italian Republic," Baba *et al.*, eds., *Politics of Italian Republic*, at 43.
(16) Shigenori Watanabe, "Formation and Development of the German Basic Law and Agencies of the Federal Republic of Germany," Watanabe ed., *Handbook of the Federal Republic of Germany*, at 65-6.

15 The Status of International Law in Australian Law: Implications of the *Teoh* Case*

Shigeo MIYAGAWA

    Introduction
1. *Minister of State for Immigration and Ethnic Affairs v. Ah Hin Teoh*
2. The Implication of the "Legitimate Expectation" in the Transformation Doctrine
3. Reasons to Adopt the Transformation Doctrine in Australia
4. A Broader Implication of the *Teoh* Decision

Introduction

I would like to inquire as to the status of international law in the Australian legal system. I am particularly interested in the implications of the *Teoh* decision by the High Court of Australia in 1995. The full title of the decision is *Minister of State for Immigration and Ethnic Affairs v. Ah Hin Teoh*.[1]

There were some indications that Parliament might enact a law to deny the implications of the *Teoh* decision, but such legislative attempts have failed a few times.[2] What Parliament purported to do was to overrule one line of the holding in the *Teoh* decision that seemed to impose an obligation on the executive government to comply with unincorporated treaties in Australia. Even though such a law is enacted, I think the importance of the *Teoh* decision will not be denied in the theoretical consideration of the status of international law in the domestic legal system.

I think the *Teoh* decision may suggest a step beyond the transformation doctrine on which the Australian legal system is based. It is, in a sense, a shift from the transformation doctrine to a legal system which gives treaties the status as the "Law of the Land"[3] like the United States. The *Teoh* decision suggests the undeniable influence of international human rights law on Australia law. This may sound disturbing to Australian ears, but I hope you would find some merit in my argument.

The main point of my argument is as follows: In the Australian legal system, treaties, even though ratified by the Australian Government, do not have legal effect unless enacted by the Parliament. In the *Teoh* decision, however, the High Court stated that the ratification of the Convention on the Rights of the Child[4] created a "legitimate expectation"[5] of procedural fairness in governmental actions. That is to say, the executive government and the administrative agencies must give due regard to the treaty in conformity with the terms of the Convention. This seems to be comparable to the requirement imposed on the American government to comply with the terms of non-self-executing treaties, though non-self-executing treaties are said to have no "legal effect" without implementing legislation in the United States.

I think the *Teoh* decision indicates an important influence of international human rights law on Australian law. The *Teoh* decision came at a time when the distinction between international law and domestic law does not carry as much relevance as it used to. The idea that distinguishes domestic law and international law had some relevance, when there was a clear dividing line between domestic matters and international matters. In our age of globalization, however, matters of transnational concern such as human rights carry more direct bearings upon citizens.

1 *Minister of State for Immigration and Ethnic Affairs v. Ah Hin Teoh*

To begin with, let me review the *Teoh* decision, though I understand it would be redundant and needless for Australian professors to be told about the gist of the *Teoh* decision. I would like to summarize the *Teoh* decision in order to make my points clear.

The facts of the case are as follows: The respondent in this case, Mr. Teoh, a Malaysian citizen, staying in Australia on a temporary entry permit, married an Australian woman in 1988. Three children were born to them in addition to four children born to Mrs. Teoh from a previous marriage. The respondent applied for a permanent entry permit. While his application was still pending, the respondent committed a narcotic crime and was sentenced to six years' imprisonment. His application for a permanent entry permit was denied, and an order of deportation was entered against him. The respondent applied to the Federal Court to have these two decisions reviewed. The court of first instance dismissed the application for review, but the Full Federal Court on appeal ordered that the refusal to grant a permanent entry permit be set aside, and that the order of deportation be stayed until the application for permanent entry permit was reconsidered.

The Minister of State for Immigration and Ethnic Affairs appealed to the High Court, and the Court dismissed the appeal by a four-to-one decision. The majority consists of the joint judgment by Chief Justice Mason and Justice Deane and two separate judgments by Justices Toohey and Gaudron. A dissent was written by Justice McHugh.

The majority holding by Chief Justice Mason and Justices Deane and Toohey can be summarized in five points[6]: First, ratification of a treaty is a positive statement by the executive government to the world and the Australian people that the executive government and its agencies will act in accordance with the treaty. This positive statement is "an adequate foundation for a legitimate expectation, absent statutory or executive indications to the contrary, that administrative decision-makers will act in conformity with the [treaty]."[7] Second, what the legitimate expectation produces is a requirement that, under notions of procedural fairness, the person affected be given notice of any governmental intention not to adhere to the terms of the treaty and an adequate opportunity to argue against such a course of action. Third, the treaty provision in question in this case is Article 3 paragraph 1 of the Convention on the Rights of the Child which provides that "in all actions concerning children ... the best interests of the child shall be a primary consideration." Fourth, the Immigration Review Panel and the Immigration Minister carried out a balancing exercise of the seriousness of Mr. Teoh's crime and the hardship to Mrs. Teoh and the children once Mr. Teoh is deported, and the government decided the former outweighed the latter. However, it is not shown that the government regarded the best interests of the children as a "primary consideration" as required by the Convention. Fifth, the government, in acting not in conformity with the Convention, did not give notice and an adequate opportunity of presenting a case against the taking of such a course. Therefore, there was a want of natural justice or procedural fairness.

Justice Gaudron's judgment, though part of the majority, has the characteristic of emphasizing the fact that children involved in this case are Australian citizens. He argues that the Convention is only of subsidiary significance, and that citizenship carries with it a common law right on the part of children and their parents to have a child's best interests taken into account as a primary consideration in all discretionary decisions by the Government.[8] He views the significance of the Convention as expressing a fundamental human right which is taken for granted by Australian society as in other civilized countries. With the significance of the Convention so confined, he finds it "reasonable to speak of an expectation that the Convention would be given effect."[9]

The majority judgment by the High Court makes a very careful statement with regard to the legal status of the Convention in Australia. For example, the joint judgment by Chief Justice Mason and Justice Deane states that the "existence of a legitimate expectation does not necessarily compel [a decision-maker] to act in [a particular] way," and that "[it] is the difference between a legitimate expectation and a binding rule of law." The judgment goes on to say:

> To regard a legitimate expectation as requiring the decision-maker to act in a particular way is tantamount to treating it as a rule of law. It incorporates the provisions of the unincorporated convention into our municipal law by the back door.[10]

To be sure, the majority's position is cautious enough not to step outside the boundary of the transformation doctrine. As a matter of the disposition of the case, however, there is no difference between giving a binding power to the "legitimate expectation" and treating it as an option to take. The High Court holds that the best interests of children were not given a primary consideration, though the Government did take the best interests of children into some consideration to find that the seriousness of Mr. Teoh's crime outweighed the hardship to his children. The decisive point of the High Court's holding is only a matter of what makes a consideration "primary." The High Court does not seem to give a reason why the consideration by the Government in this case is not qualified as "primary." Furthermore, the High Court treats the "legitimate expectation" as one option but sets aside as unsatisfactory the governmental action which the executive believed it took in pursuance of the "legitimate expectation." You cannot, however, expect the procedural protection to have been offered that is required for the other option of not carrying out the "legitimate expectation," because the executive acted in the belief of its compliance with the "legitimate expectation." It is something like asking for an unobtainable.

2 The Implication of the "Legitimate Expectation" in the Transformation Doctrine

Next, I would like to talk about one important implication of the *Teoh* decision. I think we can see a modification of the transformation doctrine in the holding of the "legitimate expectation." The orthodox doctrine of transformation casts double-folded constraints on treaties. First, with regard to the binding power of treaties, the orthodox doctrine denies any legal effect for international treaties in the domestic legal system. Second, with regard to the means with which treaties can be incorporated to the domestic legal system, a genuine legislative organ like the British or Australian Parliament, must enact laws to implement the terms of treaties. It is an anomaly in the transformation doctrine to impose an obligation on the executive government to comply with the terms of treaties, because treaties are supposed to have no legal effect at all in the domestic legal system. It is also a deviation from the theory to allow treaties to constrain actions by the executive government and administrative agencies without any implementing legislation.

If the transformation doctrine allows a treaty to operate of itself in the sense that it can impose the duty on the executive government or administrative agencies to act in conformity with the terms of the treaty, this doctrine seems to develop a new component comparable to the doctrine concerning a non-self-executing treaty.

Under the doctrine that distinguishes self-executing and non-self-executing treaties, a non-self-executing treaty is supposed to have no "legal effect" in the domestic legal system. It is supposed to need the implementing legislation in the domestic legal system. Professor Henkin, a prominent American scholar of international law, points out, however, that it is common mistake to think that a non-self-executing treaty is not law for the executive and legislative branches as well as the judiciary. A non-self-executing treaty cannot be directly applied by courts, but it is the law according to which the executive government and administrative agencies should carry out their duties. It is also the substantive guideline to which Congress should pay due regard in its legislative activities.[11]

In the United States where the doctrine of direct incorporation is practiced, a non-self-executing treaty cannot be directly applied in courts, but can serve as law for the executive and legislative branches. In Australia where the doctrine of transformation is practiced, the High Court in the *Teoh* case held that the Convention, not yet incorporated by the Parliament, creates the legitimate expectation for the government to comply with the terms of the Convention. This seems to be a fusion or approximation of the two doctrines. This is what I called Australia's shift to a legal system similar to the United States in the beginning of this paper.

3 Reasons to Adopt the Transformation Doctrine in Australia

Next, I would like to make a brief inquiry with regard to reasons to adopt the transformation doctrine in Australia.

Australia is said to succeed English law. Under English law, the reason to practice the doctrine of transformation is explained in the context of the strong historical heritage of the Parliamentary sovereignty. In contrast to the English heritage, the Australian practice of the transformation doctrine seems to have two uniquely Australian roots. One is the Parliamentary authority to legislate on matters of external affairs enumerated in section 51 sub-section (xxix) of the Australian Constitution. When the Australian Constitution came into force in 1901, the power to enter into treaties with other countries was entertained as one of the Royal prerogatives. As the independence of Australia gradually came to mature, an epoch-making event of which is the Statute of Westminster, 1931,[12] this Royal prerogative subsumed under the general executive power of the Commonwealth Government in section 61 of the Constitution. This section does not specifically refer to treaties, but the High Court interpreted the Constitution to mean that Parliament may legislate, under section 51 subsection (xxix), to implement in domestic law a treaty which has been entered into by the executive government pursuant to its power under section 61 of the Constitution.[13]

The other reason to practice the transformation doctrine is rooted in the basic principle of the separation of legislative and executive powers. Parliament has not firmly established the advice and consent power to check on the treaty making power of the executive government.[14] Therefore, the requirement of the implementing legislation serves to prevent the erosion of the legislative power by the treaty making power of the executive government. There is another consideration over the separation of powers. That is, the distribution of powers between the Commonwealth Government and the states governments. By denying domestic legal effect to treaties, the states governments can avoid the erosion of states powers by the treaty making power of the Commonwealth Government.

4 A Broader Implication of the *Teoh* Decision

As far as the Australian framework of law is concerned, the *Teoh* decision indicates a shift in Australia's practice of the transformation doctrine. It means the approximation of the transformation doctrine and the direct incorporation doctrine. This can be said to be a judicial response to the legislative inaction to incorporate human rights treaties in Australia, though the High Court in the *Teoh* decision takes a very cautious approach to the Convention on the Rights of the Child not to step outside the transformation doctrine. This self-restrained approach to treaties shows the prudence of the High Court not to disturb the separation of powers among the three branches in the Commonwealth Government and also the distribution of powers in the federal system of Australia.

Lastly, I would like to mention a broader implication of the *Teoh* decision. I think the *Teoh* decision indicates an important influence of international human rights law on Australian law. The reach of international law goes beyond the sphere of international affairs and permeates into the domestic arena. The domestic legal system cannot remain detached from the development of international human rights law. The *Teoh* decision reflects a qualitative change in the matters that are dealt with by international law. Those matters of transnational concern have a more direct bearing upon individuals. Once international law begins to deal with human rights matters, it necessarily means the perforation of national boundaries. The distinction between international law and domestic law becomes blurred. When there was a clear dividing line between domestic matters and international matters, treaties were mainly bilateral and they dealt with the rights and duties of party states. In our age of globalization, more and more treaties are entered into in the multilateral format. Moreover, matters of transnational concern are not limited to the protection of human rights. For example, the preservation of the environmental quality of our globe is an area of law in which concerted actions by national and transnational entities are well under way. The regulation of genetically modified organisms such as agricultural products is also a burgeoning area in which a transnational legal framework needs to be established. The *Teoh* decision is decided in our age of globalization. For this reason, it is an important case not only in the framework of Australian law but also for the new development of international law.

* This is a revised version of the paper presented at the academic exchange conference held jointly by the Melbourne University Centre for Comparative Constitutional Studies and the Waseda University Institute of Comparative Law at the University of Melbourne on March 17, 2000.

(1) (1995) 183 CLR 273, *reprinted in* 69 AUSTL. L.J. 423 (1995).

(2) Since the High Court's decision, both the Labor and Coalition Governments have made statements denying the implications of the *Teoh* case, but legislative bills to the same effect have not passed in the Parliament. *See*, GEORGE WILLIAMS, HUMAN RIGHTS UNDER THE AUSTRALIAN CONSTITUTION 20-21 (1999); Gillian Triggs, *Australia's Indigenous Peoples and International Law: Validity of the Native Title Amendment Act 1998 (CTH)*, 23 MELB. U.L. REV. 372, 396 (1999).

(3) U.S. CONST. art. VI, cl. 2.

(4) The Convention on the Rights of the Child was ratified by the Commonwealth Executive on 17 December 1990 and entered into force for Australia on 16 January 1991.

(5) *Teoh*, 69 AUSTL. L.J. 423, 432 (1995).

(6) For an analysis of the *Teoh* case, *see*, Masanao Murakami, *The Influence of the Human Rights Conventions upon the Australian Legal System: Practice of the Australian Courts and Its Implication* (in Japanese), 98 KOKUSAIHO GAIKO ZASSI 194, 206-10 (1999).

(7) *Teoh*, 69 AUSTL. L.J. 423, 432 (1995) (Mason CJ and Deane J).

(8) All Justices, including Mason CJ, in the *Teoh*'s majority accept that human rights treaties influence the development of the common law. Kristen Walker & Penelope Mathew, Case Note, Minister for Immigration v. Ah Hin Teoh, 20 MELB. U.L. REV. 236, 244 (1995).

(9) *Teoh*, 69 AUSTL. L.J. 423, 440 (1995) (Gaudron J).

(10) *Id.* at 432-33 (Mason CJ and Deane J).

(11) LOUIS HENKIN, FOREIGN AFFAIRS AND THE UNITED STATES CONSTITUTION 203-04 (2d ed. 1996).

(12) The *Statute of Westminster 1931* (UK) was adopted by Australia in 1942 by the *Statute of Westminster Adoption Act 1942* (Cth), and given retrospective effect to 3 September 1939.

(13) Senate—Legal and Constitutional References Committee, *Commonwealth Power to Make and Implement Treaties—Report*, paras. 4.6-4.22, *at* http://www.austlii.edu.au/au/other/dfat/tort4.html.

(14) *Id.* paras. 7.1-7.2, *at* http://www.austlii.edu.au/au/other/dfat/tort7.html.

16 Exemplary Damages, Not Punitive Damages
——A Japanese Perspective——

Yutaka SANO

    Introduction
1 The Background
2 Australia
3 New Zealand
4 Japan
    Conclusion

Introduction

There are great differences in legal systems between the common law countries and the civil law countries. Needless to say, Australia and New Zealand belong to the former, and Japan the latter. One of these differences is said to be the availability of exemplary damages in civil proceedings. For historical reasons, common law countries have enjoyed the availability of exemplary damages, although they are considered to be an "anomaly"[1]. On the other hand, Japan as well as other civil law countries have no idea of exemplary damages or punitive damages in civil proceedings.

In this paper I will first describe exemplary damages, especially focusing on recent developments in Australia and New Zealand. I will then turn to the Japanese situation. And finally, I will show you a tentative conclusion which incorporates some proposals and remaining questions.

It is true that differences in legal systems between Australia and New Zealand on the one hand and Japan on the other hand are so great that it may be useless and futile or even harmful to make a comparison between these legal systems. However, as Professor Patrick Atiyah pointed out, "it is one of the functions of the academic lawyer from time to time to think the unthinkable"[2], I will consider the role of the courts in settling disputes by examining the availability of exemplary damages in civil proceedings.

1 The Background

When tort law was less principled, it was not considered unusual to punish a wrongdoer as well as compensate a victim. In the famous case of *Wilkes v. Wood*[3], Pratt CJ directed the jury that[4];

"Damages are designed not only as a satisfaction to the injured person, but likewise as a punishment to the guilty, to deter from any such proceeding for the future, and as a proof of the detestation of the jury to the action itself."

In modern times, however, the primary object of tort remedies has been considered to be compensation to a victim. The availability of exemplary damages was extensively examined by the House of Lords in *Rookes v. Barnard*[5], in which Lord Devlin said that[6];

"Exemplary damages are essentially different from ordinary damages. The object of damages in the usual sense of the term is to compensate. The object of exemplary damages is to punish and deter. It may well be thought that this confuses the civil and criminal functions of the law, and indeed, so far as I know, the idea of exemplary damages is peculiar to English law."

After examining the authorities in order to see how far and in what sort of cases the exemplary principle was recognised, Lord Devlin listed three famous categories in which exemplary damages may be allowed. Those categories are: 1) cases of oppressive, arbitrary or unconstitutional action by the servants of the government[7], 2) cases in which the defendant's conduct has been calculated by him to make a profit for himself which may well exceed the compensation payable to the plaintiff[8], and 3) cases in which exemplary damages are expressly authorised by statute[9].

Lord Devlin in *Rookes v. Barnard* also expressed three considerations which he thought should always be borne in mind when awards of exemplary damages are being considered. Firstly, the plaintiff cannot recover exemplary damages unless he is the victim of punishable behaviour[10]. Secondly, the power to award exemplary damages constitutes a weapon that, while it can be used in defence of liberty, can also be used against liberty[11]. Thirdly, the means of the parties, irrelevant in the assessment of compensation, are material in the assessment of exemplary damages. Everything which aggravates or mitigates the defendant's conduct is relevent[12]. Examining these considerations and reviewing authorities referred to by the appellant, Lord Devlin concluded that a source of confusion between aggravated and exemplary damages could be removed from the law[13].

After *Rookes v. Barnard* exemplary damages are strictly limited to these three categories in England[14]. It does not mean that other common law countries follow the English approach.

2 Australia[15]

In 1966 the High Court of Australia refused to follow the decision of the House of Lords in *Rookes v. Barnard*. Taylor J in *Uren v. John Fairfax & Sons Pty Ltd*. held that[16];

"I agree that there was, perhaps, some room for a more precise definition of the circumstances in which exemplary damages might be awarded. But with great respect, I do not feel as Lord Devlin did, that such a far-reaching reform as he proposed, and in which the other Lords of Appeal engaged in the case agreed, was justified by asserting that punishment was a matter for the criminal law. No doubt the criminal law prescribes penalties for wrongs which are also crimes but it prescribes no penalty for wrongs which are not at one and the same time crimes, and in both types of cases the courts of this country, and I venture to suggest the courts of England, had admitted the principle of exemplary damages as, in effect, a penalty for a wrong committed in such circumstances or in such manner as warrant the court's signal disapproval of the defendant's conduct."

After considering the authorities which were reviewed by Lord Devlin in *Rookes v. Barnard*, Taylor J went on to say that[17];

"To my mind——and I say this with the greatest respect——the attempt, expressly made in *Rookes v. Barnard* "to remove an anomaly from the law" did not achieve this result. Nor, in my view, was such an attempt justified by the assertion that it was not the function of the civil law to permit the award of damages by way of penalty."

He continued[18];

"...the measure of research disclosed by the observations in *Rookes v. Barnard* takes no account of the development of the law in this country where frequently this Court has recognized that an award of exemplary damages may be made in a much wider category of cases than that case postulates."

Eventually, the High Court of Australia did not follow the House of Lords and maintained the position established by the decision in *Whitfeld v. De Lauret & Co., Ltd*[19]. In this case, Knox CJ held[20];

"Damages may be either compensatory or exemplary. Compensatory damages are awarded as compensation for and are measured by the material loss suffered by the plaintiffs. Exemplary damages are given only in cases of conscious wrongdoing in contumelious disregard of another's rights."

As these cases indicate, it can be said that exemplary damages are awarded in Australia in a less restricted way than in England. However, there are factors which are relevant to the question of whether or not exemplary damages ought to be awarded. One of these factors is said to be the capacity of exemplary damages to fulfil their purpose in all the circumstances of the case[21]. There are at least three occasions where exemplary damages seem not to have their capacity to fulfil their purpose of punishment and deterrence. These occasions are: 1) cases where the defendant's conduct is covered by insurance, 2) cases where the plaintiff's compensatory award is so high that it is, in itself, a sufficient punishment and deterrence, and 3) cases where the defendant has already been punished.

As to the first occasion, an earlier authority in Australia was *Lamb v. Cotogno*[22]. In this case, the High Court of Australia held that exemplary damages were available against a defendant whose outrageous conduct causing personal injury to the plaintiff was covered by compulsory third party motor insurance. It is clear that exemplary damages in such a case do not punish the defendant. But it may be said that they will deter others from similar conduct in the future. Another reason for allowing exemplary damages in *Lamb* is that their award assuaged the plaintiff's urge for revenge[23]. The decision in *Lamb v. Cotogno* is now upheld by the High Court of Australia in *Gray v. Motor Accident Commission*[24]. The decision in *Gray* not only upholds the decision in *Lamb*, but also extends the availability of exemplary damages in one respect. For the defendant in *Gray* is not the wrongdoer who caused personal injury to the plaintiff, but the compulsory third party insurer. The tortfeasor in *Gray* stepped out of the proceedings, because of statutory provisions. I will return to this case shortly after. As to the second occasion, what I would like to say is that normal compensatory remedy of tort law may work as punishment and deterrence in a certain case, even when exemplary damages are not awarded, because of a huge award of compensatory damages.

As to the third occasion, it can be said that the most important decision is the decision of the High Court of Australia in *Gray v. Motor Accident Commission*[25]. Mr. Gray (plaintiff, appellant in this case) was injured when struck by a motor vehicle driven by Mr. Bransden. Mr. Bransden drove directly at a group of Aboriginal youths, including the appellant, doing so with the intention of running the appellant down and seriously hurting him. The motor vehicle was insured under the compulsory third party provisions of the Motor Vehicles Act (SA). Mr. Bransden was charged with the criminal offence of intentionally causing grievous bodily harm to the appellant[26]. He was convicted of this offence by a jury[27] and sentenced to seven years imprisonment[28].

The appellant brought proceedings in the District Court of South Australia, initially against Mr. Bransden, claiming damages against him for negligence. At trial, liability for negligence was not disputed. Amongst the damages claimed was a specific claim for exemplary damages. In 1995 the proceedings were amended to substitute State Government Insurance Commission as the defendant[29]. The judgment at first instance was entered in favour of the plaintiff. On the claim for exemplary damages, however, the primary judge concluded that no award of exemplary damages should be made, because he took into account the fact that Mr. Bransden had already been punished by being sentenced to a substantial period of imprisonment in respect of the same conduct for which exemplary damages were claimed. The plaintiff, complaining that exemplary damages should be awarded and that the amount of compensatory damages was too low, appealed to the Supreme Court of South Australia. The Full Court of the Supreme Court of South Australia denied both claims. Then, Mr. Gray appealed to the High Court of Australia.

Although the High Court accepted the appellant's submission on compensatory damages that they were too low, the Court rejected his submission on exemplary damages. The Court held that[30];

"Where, as here, the criminal law has been brought to bear upon the wrongdoer and substantial punishment inflicted, we consider that exemplay damages may not be awarded. We say 'may not' because we consider that the infliction of substantial punishment for what is substantially the same conduct as the conduct which is the subject of the civil proceeding is a bar to the award; the decision is not one that is reached as a matter of discretion dependent upon the facts and circumstances in each particular case."

In addition to these points, there are some important opinions expressed in the *Gray* case. First, as I have already shown, the Court upheld the decision in *Lamb v. Cotogno*[31], and held that exemplary damages may be available in a suitable case for conducts covered by insurance, even if the wrongdoer is not the party in the proceedings. Secondly, the Court expressed the possibility of awarding exemplary damages in cases for negligence by saying that there can be cases, framed in negligence, in which the defendant can be shown to have acted consciously in contumelious disregard of the rights of the plaintiff or persons in the position of the plaintiff. Thirdly, the Court upheld the decision of the Supreme Court of Tasmania in *Watts v. Leitch*[32]. Kirby J said that[33];

"...the component of exemplary damages was not a right but an element of the damages which the jury could elect to provide or to withhold. In *Broome v. Cassell & Co* Lord Hailsham described an award of punitive damages as 'discretionary'. There are similar descriptions in Canadian and Australian authority. Indeed, the existence of a discretion has been described as a 'safety valve' permitting the tribunal of fact to decline the award of exemplary damages if some factor makes it proper to refuse them."

3 New Zealand

As is well known, the law of tort in New Zealand is quite unique, because of the abolition of a right of action for personal injury under the accident compensation scheme since 1974.

In New Zealand exemplary damages were awarded in cases of malicious prosecution and defamation before the English decision in *Rookes v. Barnard*. The effect of that case was examined by the Court of Appeal in *Taylor v. Beere*[34]. The Court unanimously refused to follow the restrictive approach to exemplary damages. Richardson J. stressed that tort law does not have the sole aim of compensating victims, but must make provision for public interest concerns which go beyond the private interests of the parties[35].

After the Accident Compensation Act 1972 came into force, the courts in New Zealand confronted the question of whether a claim for exemplary damages had been ruled out by the statute. In *Donselaar v. Donselaar*[36], the Court of Appeal held that because compensation under the statute had no punitive element, there was good reason to retain the possibility of exemplary damages[37]. Accordingly, the Court of Appeal made it clear that the purpose of such awards is to punish the defendant for high-handed disregard of the plaintiff's rights or similar outrageous conduct.

After the passing of the Accident Rehabilitation and Compensation Insurance Act 1992, plaintiffs began to bring claims for exemplary damages in order to obtain some satisfaction for the injury done to them, because the Act removed lump sum compensation and reduced the availability of compensation for personal injury under the accident compensation scheme. Against these backgrounds, the availability of exemplary damages in negligence claims was confirmed by the award of $15,000 in *McLaren Transport Ltd v. Somerville*[38]. Tipping J. held that the law of New Zealand allows a claim for exemplary damages for personal injury caused by negligence if the defendant's conduct is bad enough[39]. After carefully reviewing the various authorities and seeking to bring together the relevant factors, Tipping J. approached the matter as follows[40];

> "Exemplary damages for negligence causing personal injury may be awarded if, but only if, the level of negligence is so high that it amounts to an outrageous and flagrant disregard for the plaintiffs safety, meriting condemnation and punishment."

Another important impact on the availability of exemplary damages came from the decision of the Court of Appeal in *Daniels v. Thompson*[41]. The Court held that because exemplary damages were designed to punish the acts complained of, there should be an absolute bar on exemplary damages in civil proceedings, where there had already been a conviction and sentence for those acts[42]. The Court also held that a claim for exemplary damages should be struck out as an abuse of process where the defendant had been acquitted of essentially the same acts in the criminal jurisdiction[43]. Furthermore, the Court concluded that where a criminal prosecution had been commenced or was likely, it would be appropriate to stay proceedings for exemplary damages to prevent an abuse of process[44].

The decision of the Court of Appeal in *Daniels v. Thompson* was upheld by the Privy Council in *W v. W*[45]. A twist was made prior to the decision of the Privy Council by the legislature, which made a provision in December 1998. Under s 396 of the Accident Insurance Act 1998, any person can bring proceedings for exemplary damages for conduct by the defendant which resulted in personal injury, even though (a) the defendant has been charged with, and acquitted or convicted of, an offence involving the conduct concerned in the claim for exemplary damages, (b) the defendant has been charged with such an offence, and has been discharged without conviction under s 19 of the Criminal Justice Act 1985 or convicted and discharged under s 20 of that Act, (c) the defendant has been charged with such an offence and, at the time at which the court is making its decision on the claim for exemplary damages, the charge has not been dealt with, or (d) the defendant has not, at the time at which the court is making its decision on the claim for exemplary damages, been charged with such an offence.

Accordingly, a claim for exemplary damages for personal injury can be brought in New Zealand, even if a defendant in civil proceedings is likely to be, or has been, prosecuted for the same conduct as in the civil proceedings, but a claim for exemplary damages for other than personal injury is absolutely barred under the rule of the *Daniels* case, where the defendant is criminally charged.

4 Japan

At least in principle, we have no idea of exemplary damages in civil proceedings. There are, however, some, not many, cases in Japan, in which courts examined the availability of exemplary damages. I will show you four cases concerning the issue of exemplary damages.

In 1997, the Supreme Court, which is the highest court in Japan, denied the recognition and enforcement of a decision by a State Court of California, in which exemplary damages had been awarded[46]. The reason for this is that because exemplary damages are contrary to the fundamental principle or fundamental philosophy of our legal system, public policy in Japan should deny decisions in which exemplary damages are awarded.

The second case I will show you concerned a dispute arising out of construction work. The plaintiffs were people living near a construction site. A compromise about the work schedule such as time and date was once made between the plaintiffs and the construction company. There was a penalty clause in the compromise, if the construction company breached terms and conditions. The company was faced with a dilemma. If they did not finish the work by a fixed date, they had to pay a penalty to their employer, because of the delay of completion of the work. The company did breach a condition of the compromise, taking it into consideration that it would be more profitable to breach the condition and finish the work by the due date than to pay a penalty to the plaintiffs. The plaintiffs brought an action for exemplary damages as well as compensatory damages for mental distress. The Kyoto District Court held that if the defendant intentionally breaches the condition of the compromise, there may be room for awarding solatium which has the nature of punishment or sanction, in addition to normal compensatory damages[47].

The third case is a claim for personal injury to an inpatient who suffered a minor injury when a door of an elevator closed. The plaintiff submitted that the speed at which doors of elevators in hospitals close should be slower than those of elevators in ordinary places, and explicitly claimed exemplary damages as well as compensatory damages. The Tokyo District Court allowed compensatory damages but denied exemplary damages on its facts[48]. The Court held that it was hard to accept the concept of exemplary damages as an established justiciable norm under the present legal system.

The fourth case is one of the most sensational civil proceedings in 1999. The defendant was the then Governor of Osaka Prefecture. The plaintiff was a girl of 21, a university student. In April 1999, local elections were held nationwide in Japan. The defendant was the Governor who stood for reelection. The plaintiff engaged in this election campaign for the defendant. In the course of the campaign, the defendant sexually assaulted the plaintiff in a vehicle which was used for the campaign. The plaintiff brought an action for indecent conduct by the defendant. In response to this action, the defendant demanded a prosecution, complaining that the action brought by the plaintiff was groundless, and that his reputation was defamed by the action brought by the plaintiff. The defendant did not appear before the court. Instead, he held an interview as Governor with journalists on the first day of trial, and said that the submission by the plaintiff was an outright lie. The Osaka District Court handed down a judgment in favour of the plaintiff[49]. The Court awarded the plaintiff the sum of 2,000,000yen for indecent conduct, the sum of 5,000,000yen for false prosecution, the sum of 3,000,000yen for defamatory remarks after the first day of trial, and the sum of 1,000,000yen for legal costs. The Court did not explicitly say that there was a punitive element in the award of the total sum of 11,000,000yen. But, this amount of damages is considerably higher than that awarded in similar harassment cases. One reason for this can be a detestation by the Court of the defendant's conduct in all the circumstances of the case[50].

Conclusion

It is true that the distinction has been clearly established in common law countries between aggravated damages and exemplary damages. Aggravated damages are categorised as compensatory, while exemplary damages are categorised as non-compensatory. Both damages pay attention to the defendant's conduct.

In Australia, as exemplary damages are available for conduct which is covered by insurance, there may be cases where they do not work as punishment. Mr Gray might have succeeded in recovering aggravated damages, if he had claimed them at an earlier stage of the proceedings, because the conduct by the tortfeasor was so outrageous that it amounted to a crime. But exemplary damages were unavailable in that case, because the purpose of awarding them is to punish a wrongdoer and the wrongdoer had already been punished through criminal proceedings. It is quite illogical and unfair that while the purpose of punishment does not work in case of insurance, some plaintiffs can recover exemplary damages and others cannot.

In New Zealand, while aggravated damages cannot be awarded in cases for personal injury, they can be awarded in cases other than personal injury. And where a defendant in civil proceedings is criminally charged, exemplary damages can be now awarded only in cases for personal injury, not others.

In Japan, courts have never held that exemplary or punitive damages can be awarded in civil proceedings. All that they can say is that solatium, that is equivalent to aggravated damages, can be awarded in civil proceedings. But as the last of the four Japanese cases indicates, some punitive element can be found in the award of compensatory damages.

Although compensation to a victim is a primary object of tort remedy, compensatory damages may work as punishment and deterrence, especially when the amount of compensatory damages is high. Likewise, exemplary damages work as compensation, especially when the level of compensatory damages is not enough, as in New Zealand. It is often said that the function of exemplary damages is not limited to punishment and deterrence[51]. Punishment and deterrence have been the main purpose of exemplary damages, but they are not the exclusive purpose. If exemplary damages are freed from their conventional definition and purpose, they may be used as an effective means in settling disputes. In this sense, unlike the recommendation made by the English Law Commission[52], exemplary damages should be called exemplary damages, not punitive damages.

I did not examine in this paper that exemplary damages may be used as a weapon against liberty. I am not able to suggest a practicable approach or test by which exemplary damages are measured in an acceptable manner and restricted to a satisfactory extent. Indeed, there are many more problems concurring with exemplary damages, as exemplified by the experience in the United States which I did not mention in this paper. However, there are merits in awarding exemplary damages in civil proceedings. If there were no merit at all in exemplary damages, they would have disappeared much earlier, even if they were awarded in established authorities. In my opinion, both the High Court of Australia and the Court of Appeal of New Zealand should not take such a restrictive approach as to bar the availability of exemplary damages in principle.

(1) *Rookes v. Barnard* [1964] AC 1129 at 1221 per Lord Devlin.
(2) Patrick S. Atiyah, "Personal Injuries in the Twenty First Century: Thinking the Unthinkable" in P. Birks (ed), *Wrongs and Remedies in the Twenty-first Century* (Clarendon Press, Oxford, 1996) p. 1 at 1.
(3) (1763) Lofft 1; 98 ER 489.
(4) Ibid. at 18-19; 498-499.
(5) [1964] AC 1129.
(6) Ibid. at 1221.
(7) Ibid. at 1226.
(8) Ibid.

(9) Ibid. at 1227.
(10) Ibid.
(11) Ibid.
(12) Ibid. at 1228.
(13) Ibid. at 1230.
(14) In *Broome v. Cassell & Co. Ltd.*, the English Court of Appeal led by Lord Denning MR defied the decision of the House of Lords in *Rookes v. Barnard* ([1971] 2 QB 354). But the House of Lords reversed the decision of the Court of Appeal and supported the decision in *Rookes v. Barnard* by a mere majority of four to three ([1972] AC 1027).
(15) I greatly owe my understanding of the Australian position to Professor Michael Tilbury, especially his works, *Civil Remedies* (Butterworths, Sydney, 1990) vol. 1 and "Regulating 'Criminal' Conduct by Civil Remedy: The Case of Exemplary Damages" 1 *Waseda Proceedings of Comparative Law* 80 (1999). Of course any misunderstandings and errors are mine.
(16) (1966) 117 CLR 113 at 131.
(17) Ibid. at 137.
(18) Ibid. at 138.
(19) (1920) 29 CLR 71.
(20) Ibid. at 77.
(21) Michael Tilbury, "Regulating 'Criminal' Conduct by Civil Remedy: The Case of Exemplary Damages" 1 *Waseda Proceedings of Comparative Law* 80 at 91 (1999).
(22) (1987) 164 CLR 1.
(23) Ibid. at 9.
(24) (1998) 158 ALR 485; 73 ALJR 45. See Jane Swanton and Barbara McDonald, "The High Court on Exemplary Damages" 73 *Aust L J* 402 (1999), and James Edelman, "Exemplary Damages Revisited" 7 *Torts L J* 87 (1999).
(25) (1998) 158 ALR 485; 73 ALJR 45.
(26) S 21 of the Criminal Law Consolidation Act 1935 (SA).
(27) *R v. Bransden*, unreported, Supreme Court of South Australia, 26 February 1991.
(28) *R v. Bransden*, unreported, Supreme Court of South Australia, 14 March 1991.
(29) The substitution of the Commission for Mr Bransden was effected pursuant to s. 125A of the Motor Vehicle Act.
(30) (1998) 158 ALR 485 at 494; 73 ALJR 45 at 52.

(31) (1987) 164 CLR 1.
(32) [1973] Tas SR 16.
(33) (1998) 158 ALR 485 at 510-511; 73 ALJR 45 at 63-64.
(34) [1982] 1 NZLR 81.
(35) Ibid. at 90.
(36) [1982] 1 NZLR 97.
(37) Ibid. at 107 per Cooke J.; 116 per Somers J.
(38) [1996] 3 NZLR 424. See John Smillie, "Exemplary Damages for Personal Injury" [1997] *NZL Rev*. 140, Joanna Manning, "Professor Smillie's 'Exemplary Damages for Personal Injury': A Comment" [1997] *NZL Rev*. 176: Goff McLay, Negligence, ACC and Exemplary Damages... What's too Bad?" (1996) *NZLJ* 425; and Andrew Beck, "Exemplary Damages for Negligent Conduct" (1997) *Tort L. Rev*. 90.
(39) [1996] 3 NZLR 424 at 433.
(40) Ibid. at 434.
(41) [1998] 3 NZLR 22. See John Smillie, "Exemplary Damages and the Criminal Law" 6 *Torts L.J*. 113 (1998); and Joanna Manning, "*Daniels v. Thompson*: Double Punishment or Double Trouble?" [1998] *NZL Rev*. 721.
(42) [1998] 3 NZLR 22 at 47.
(43) Ibid. at 51.
(44) Ibid. at 52.
(45) [1999] 2 NZLR 1. See Joanna Manning, "Exemplary Damages and Criminal Punishment in the Privy Council" 7 *Torts L.J*. 129 (1999).
(46) Case No (*o*) 1762 of 1995, decided on 11 July 1997, 51 (6) *Minshu* 2573. See Norman T. Braslow, "The Recognition and Enforcement of Common Law Punitive Damages in a Civil Law System: Some Reflections on the Japanese Experience" 16 *Arizona Journal of International and Comparative Law* 285 (1999).
(47) Case No. (*wa*) 1076 of 1988, decided on 27 February 1989, 1322 *Hanrei Jiho* 125.
(48) Case No. (*wa*) 10941 of 1991, decided on 28 April 1993, 848 *Hanrei Taimuzu* 269.
(49) Case No. (*wa*) 8121 of 1999, decided on 13 December 1999.
(50) The defendant was reelected, but resigned after the decision of the Osaka District Court. The defendant was criminally charged and convicted.
(51) See Bruce Feldthusen, "The Canadian Experiment with the Civil Action for Sexual Battery" in Nicholas J. Mullany (ed), *Torts in the Nineties* (LBC

Information Services, Sydney 1997) 274, and *Daniels v. Thompson* [1998] 3 NZLR 22, especially dissenting decision per Thomas J.

(52) Law Commission of England and Wales, *Aggravated, Exemplary and Restitutionary Damages* (Law Com No. 247, 1997) para 6.3 (16). For an Australian perspective on the Report of the English Law Commission, see Jane Swanton and Barbara McDonald, "Commentary on the Report of the English Law Commission on Aggravated, Restitutionary and Exemplary Damages" 7 *Torts L.J.* 184 (1999).

Afterword

Morikazu TAGUCHI

This book contains the reports given in the three international symposia related to the "Studies on the Legal System of Oceanic Countries" (a research program led by Professor Akira Osuka, Waseda University, Faculty of Law). Although the reports from the first two symposia had already been printed (in 17 Waseda Bulletin of Comparative Law 16 (1997), and in 1 Waseda Proceedings of Comparative Law 1 (1998-1999)), the reports from the third symposium have not. This book consists of the reports from all three symposia and the corresponding translations, with a few minor changes in expression provided.

The theme that ran through each and every report given in the three symposia was "The Role of the State and Its Limits (Boundaries)", a theme fairly up to date. The theme was also common among the reporters from five different countries (Australia, New Zealand, China, Korea, and Japan). Of course, the actual theme of each of the reports reflected various interests among various legal fields. The theme *underlying* all of those reports, however, was the common theme, "The Role of the State and Its Limits (Boundaries)". This was the reason why we could put together, in one book, all of the reports from various legal fields, given by reporters from five countries of different legal systems and cultures. Obviously, Professor Osuka had been very clear-sighted in providing the reporters with this common theme.

Nevertheless, speaking from my personal experience, I must admit that I found difficulties in understanding the other reports and also in making my report understood. I reported on the "Administrative Regulations and Criminal Sanctions" focusing on the regulation of economic crime. Associate Professor Brookbanks gave a counter (corresponding) report on "Regulating Corporate Activity through Strict and Absolute Liability" focusing on the regulation of environmental crime. It is true that these reports (see pages 327 through 351 for details) both argued about the limits of regulation by the state. However, it was very difficult for me to understand the notion of "quasi crime" (a "strict liability crime" that did not require a strict standard of proof to be met). When Associate Professor Brookbanks and I discussed about the original meaning of "liability (culpability)" after the symposium, he had to say that my argument (which was mainly "dogmatic") was a "terrible" one. This experience, however, gave me an impression that we could come up with a decent (appropriate) suggestion that lies somewhere between the German-type stubborn argument and the Anglo-American-type pragmatic argument, by properly combining the two. The academic importance of the international symposia, perhaps, lies in this context. I felt that the international symposia in the field of jurisprudence (extending to East Asian countries as well) were becoming more and more important and necessary.

Probably, for the future of jurisprudence, a necessity of interdisciplinary, and international collective research such as this symposia will increase. If such an attempt will be useful for the future, I, as one of participants, feel it great pleasure. This publication had never been possible without the serious cooperation of over twenty scholars from five countries. I am enormously grateful to their sincere academic contributions. In editing this book, Yutaka SANO, a former assistant of the Institute of Comparative Law, Waseda University, one of contributors as well, had paid great efforts. I would like to thank him for his strenuous work. I must also thank Takashi Imai, the president of Shinzan-sha publishing company, for his enthusiastic support throughout this publication.

(translated by Research Assistant, Jun Kojima)

STATE LEGAL INTERVENTION AND FREEDOM:
Comparative Studies on Asian Oceanic Legal Systems

早稲田大学比較法研究所
叢書 28 巻

国家の法的関与と自由
——アジア・オセアニア法制の比較研究——

2001年3月31日　第1版第1刷発行　3031-0101

編集者　　　大 須 賀　　明
発行者　　　早稲田大学比較法研究所
　　　　所長　野　村　　稔
発行所　　　早稲田大学比較法研究所
〒169-8050　東京都新宿区西早稲田1-6-1
電　話　03（3208）8610
制作・販売　株式会社　信　山　社
〒113-0033　東京都文京区本郷6-2-9-102
T 03-3818-1019　F 03-3818-0344
henshu@shinzansha.co.jp

©2001 大須賀明　印刷・製本／勝美印刷・大三製本
ISBN4-7972-3031-2 C3332
3031-0101：013-0W35-W05-S20
NDC分類 323.801

早稲田大学比較法研究所叢書 既刊ご案内

巻数	書名	著者・訳者	発行年	本体
1	比較法	ガッタリッジ 著 水田義雄 訳	1964年	1,200円
2	イギリス船舶保険契約論	葛城照三 著	1962年	1,500円
3	二条陣屋の研究・公事宿の研究	滝川政次郎 著	1962年	600円
4	法治国における統治行為	ルンプ 著 有吉・竹内 共訳	1964年	1,000円
5	イギリス行政訴訟法の研究	佐藤立夫 著	1968年	1,500円
6	小野梓『国憲論網　羅瑪律要』	福島正夫他 編	1974年	4,500円
7	LEX XII TABULARUM 12表法 原文・邦訳および解説	佐藤篤士 著	1969年	1,500円
8	発展途上国における国有化	入江啓四郎 著	1974年	2,300円
9	社会主義比較法学	チッレ 著 直川誠蔵 訳	1979年	2,700円
10	西ドイツ現代刑事訴訟・刑法・行刑論文集	ペーテルス 著 内田一郎 編訳	1980年	3,600円
11	現代ドイツ公法学を築いた碩学たち	佐藤立夫 著	1982年	4,000円
12	中国における法の継承性論争	西村幸次郎 編訳	1983年	3,700円
13	比較法社会学研究	黒木三郎 著	1984年	8,500円
14	刑法審査修正関係諸案	杉山晴康他 著	1984年	3,000円
15	西ドイツの新用益賃貸借法制	田山輝明 編・監訳	1986年	3,000円
16	アメリカ合衆国の連邦最高裁判所 DUE PROCESS OF LAWの保障	ウィルバー 著 内田一郎 編訳	1986年	3,000円
17	英米不法行為判例研究	矢頭敏也 著	1988年	4,500円
18	刑法改正審査委員会決議録刑法草案	杉山晴康他 編	1989年	3,000円
19	Intellectual Property Protection and Management	土井輝生 著	1992年	10,000円
20	イギリス法と欧州共同体法	矢頭敏也 訳編	1992年	5,000円
21	改訂 LEX XII TABULARUM 12表法 原文・邦訳および解説	佐藤篤士 著	1993年	5,000円
22	ドイツ憲法	エクハルト・シュタイン 著 浦田賢治他 訳	1993年	8,000円
23	知的・精神的障害者とその権利—研修と実務の手引—	フォルカー・ヤコビ 著 田山輝明 監訳	1996年	3,500円
24	International Business Transactions: Contract and Dispute Resolution	土井輝生 著	1996年	8,000円
25	中国の経済発展と法	小口彦太 編	1998年	7,000円
26	ヨーロッパおける民事訴訟法理論の諸相	早稲田大学外国民事訴訟法研究会 編	1999年	5,000円
27	核兵器使用の違法性 —国際司法裁判所の勧告的意見—			未定
28	国家の法的関与と自由 —アジア・オセアニア法制の比較研究— State Legal Intervention and Freedom : Comparative Studies on Asian Oceanic Legal Systems	大須賀明 編	2001年	9,800円

＊ 若干在庫があります。早稲田大学比較法研究所 (Tel 03-3208-8610) または
　信山社 (Tel 03-3818-1019　Fax 03-3818-0344) までお問合せ下さい。